Dōgen and Sōtō Zen

DŌGEN AND SŌTŌ ZEN

Edited by

STEVEN HEINE

OXFORD
UNIVERSITY PRESS

OXFORD
UNIVERSITY PRESS

Oxford University Press is a department of the University of
Oxford. It furthers the University's objective of excellence in research,
scholarship, and education by publishing worldwide.

Oxford   New York
Auckland   Cape Town   Dar es Salaam   Hong Kong   Karachi
Kuala Lumpur   Madrid   Melbourne   Mexico City   Nairobi
New Delhi   Shanghai   Taipei   Toronto

With offices in
Argentina   Austria   Brazil   Chile   Czech Republic   France   Greece
Guatemala   Hungary   Italy   Japan   Poland   Portugal   Singapore
South Korea   Switzerland   Thailand   Turkey   Ukraine   Vietnam

Oxford is a registered trademark of Oxford University Press
in the UK and certain other countries.

Published in the United States of America by
Oxford University Press
198 Madison Avenue, New York, NY 10016

Library of Congress Cataloging-in-Publication Data
Dōgen and Sōtō Zen / edited by Steven Heine.
pages cm
Includes index.
ISBN 978-0-19-932485-9 (hardcover : alk. paper)—ISBN 978-0-19-932486-6 (pbk. : alk.
paper)—ISBN 978-0-19-932487-3 (ebook)   1. Dogen, 1200–1253.   2. Sotoshu.
3. Zen Buddhism.   I. Heine, Steven, 1950- editor.
BQ9449.D657D598 2012
294.3'927092—dc23
2014017357

1 3 5 7 9 8 6 4 2
Printed in the United States of America
on acid-free paper

Contents

Acknowledgments   vii

Contributors   ix

Abbreviations   xi

Introduction: Two for the Price of One—STEVEN HEINE   1

PART I: *Studies of Dōgen*

1. Dōgen's Use of Rujing's "Just Sit" (*shikan taza*) and
   Other Kōans—T. GRIFFITH FOULK   23

2. "Raihaitokuzui" and Dōgen's Views of Gender and Women:
   A Reconsideration—MIRIAM L. LEVERING   46

3. Dōgen, a Medieval Japanese Monk Well-Versed in Chinese Poetry:
   What He Did and Did Not Compose—STEVEN HEINE   74

4. Negotiating the Divide of Death in Japanese Buddhism:
   Dōgen's Difference—JOHN C. MARALDO   109

5. "When All Dharmas Are the Buddha-Dharma": Dōgen as
   Comparative Philosopher—GEREON KOPF   138

PART II: *Studies of Sōtō Zen*

6. Keizan's *Denkōroku*: A Textual and Contextual
   Overview —WILLIAM M. BODIFORD   167

7. Are Sōtō Zen Precepts for Ethical Guidance or Ceremonial Transformation? Menzan's Attempted Reforms and Contemporary Practices—DAVID E. RIGGS 188

8. Vocalizing the Remembrance of Dōgen: A Study of the *Shinpen Hōon Kōshiki*—MICHAELA MROSS 210

9. Interpreting the Material Heritage of the "Elephant Trunk Robe" in Sōtō Zen—DIANE RIGGS 235

10. Embodying Sōtō Zen: Institutional Identity and Ideal Body Image at Daihonzan Eiheiji—PAMELA D. WINFIELD 260

Sino-Japanese Glossary 287

Index 315

Acknowledgments

THE EDITOR AND the contributors express the deepest gratitude and appreciation for the life work and gracious friendship and mentorship of the late Professor Yoshizu Yoshihide (1944–2014). The research conducted by a number of these authors would not have been possible without the support and assistance of Professor Yoshizu and his colleagues at Komazawa University. The editor would also like to thank María Sol Echarren, Kristina Loveman, Ian Verhine, and Kimberly Zwez for their assistance with editing the text and developing the visuals.

Contributors

William M. Bodiford is a professor of Asian languages and cultures at the University of California at Los Angeles. Bodiford is the author of *Sōtō Zen in Medieval Japan*, the editor of *Going Forth: Visions of Buddhist Vinaya*, and the associate editor of *Encyclopedia of Buddhism*. He has authored many essays, articles, and translations concerning Zen Buddhism in particular and Japanese religions more generally.

T. Griffith Foulk is a professor of religion at Sarah Lawrence College and is the coeditor in chief of the Sōtō Zen Translation Project, established in Tokyo. Foulk has trained in both Rinzai and Sōtō Zen monasteries in Japan and has published extensively in numerous journals and collections on the institutional and intellectual history of Chan/Zen Buddhism, including ritual and doctrinal writings of Dōgen and the Sōtō sect.

Steven Heine is a professor and the director of Asian studies at Florida International University. Heine has published numerous books and articles dealing with the life and thought of Dōgen and the history and philosophy of Zen Buddhism, including *Dōgen and the Kōan Tradition: A Tale of Two Shōbōgenzō Texts, The Zen Poetry of Dōgen: Verses from the Mountain of Eternal Peace, Zen Skin, Zen Marrow: Will the Real Zen Buddhism Please Stand Up?*, and *Dōgen: Textual and Historical Studies*.

Gereon Kopf is an associate professor of Asian and comparative religion at Luther College and has taught at the Centre of Buddhist Studies at the University of Hong Kong. Kopf is the author of *Beyond Personal Identity*, the coeditor of *Merleau-Ponty and Buddhism*, and the editor of the forthcoming *Dao Companion to Japanese Buddhist Philosophy* as well as the editor of the *Journal of Buddhist Philosophy*.

Miriam L. Levering ,a former professor of religious studies at the University of Tennessee in Knoxville, has served as an international consultant at the Rissho

Kosei-kai in Tokyo. Levering has published numerous books and articles on Chan Buddhist writings and thought in Song dynasty China, as well as on the role of women in medieval and modern Buddhist texts and institutions, including Dōgen's approach.

John C. Maraldo is the distinguished professor emeritus of philosophy at the University of North Florida. Maraldo has published a translation of Heidegger, *The Piety of Thinking* (with James G. Hart), *Buddhism in the Modern World* (coedited with Heinrich Dumoulin), and *Rude Awakenings: Zen, the Kyoto School, and the Question of Nationalism* (coedited with James W. Heisig), and he is a coeditor (with James W. Heisig and T. P. Kasulis) of *Japanese Philosophy: A Sourcebook.*

Michaela Mross received a doctorate from Ludwig-Maximilians University in Munich largely based on research conducted as an exchange student in Buddhist studies at Komazawa University under the Japanese Government Scholarship program. She has also served as a visiting instructor of religion at Goettingen University.

David E. Riggs is an independent scholar based in Los Angeles who specializes in the history of the reinvention of the Sōtō Zen tradition in early modern Japan, especially the works of Menzan Zuihō. He previously taught at the University of Hawaii, Oberlin College, and other schools, and has published numerous articles on the life and teachings of Menzan.

Diane Riggs has been a visiting assistant professor of Asian studies at Pepperdine University and completed her dissertation at UCLA, titled "The Cultural and Religious Significance of Japanese Buddhist Vestments." She has published the results of her fieldwork in Japan with Sōtō Zen Buddhist robe-sewing groups in the *Japanese Journal of Religious Studies.*

Pamela D. Winfield is an assistant professor of religious studies and the coordinator of the Asian Studies Program at Elon University. Winfield is the author of *Icons and Iconoclasm in Japanese Buddhism: Kūkai and Dōgen on the Art of Enlightenment* and has been active as an organizer of various groups of the American Academy of Religion.

Abbreviations

DZZ-1   *Dōgen Zenji Zenshū*, 2 vols. Ed. Ōkubo Dōshū. Tokyo: Chikuma
         shobō, 1969–70.

DZZ-2   *Dōgen Zenji Zenshū*, 7 vols. Ed. Kawamura Kōdō et. al.
         Tokyo: Shunjūsha, 1988–93.

SZ   *Sōtōshū Zensho*, 18 vols. Ed. Sōtōshū Zensho Kankōkai. Revised and
         enlarged. Tokyo: Sōtōshū shūmuchō, 1970–73.

T   *Taishō Shinshū Daizōkyō*. Ed. Takakusu Junjirō et al., 85 vols.
         Tokyo: Taishō issaikyō kankōkai, 1924–35.

X   *Xu Zangjing*, 150 vols. Taipei: Shin wen fang, n.d. Reprinted in *Dai
         Nihon zoku zōkyō*.

ZS   *Zoku Sōtōshū Zensho*, 10 vols. Ed. Zoku Sōtōshū Zensho Kankōkai.
         Tokyo: Sōtōshū shūmuchō, 1974–77.

ZSSZ   *Zoku Sōtōshū Zensho Kankōkai*, 10 vols. Ed. Zoku Sōtōshū zensho.
         Tokyo: Sōtōshū shūmuchō, 1974–77.

Dōgen and Sōtō Zen

Introduction

TWO FOR THE PRICE OF ONE

Steven Heine

Scope and Approach

This volume is a follow-up to the recent collection published in 2012 by Oxford University Press, *Dōgen: Textual and Historical Studies.*[1] It features some of the same outstanding authors as well as new expert contributors in exploring diverse aspects of the life and teachings of Zen master Dōgen (1200–1253), the founder of the Sōtō Zen sect (or Sōtōshū) in early Kamakura-era Japan. In addition chapters examine the ritual and institutional history of the Sōtō school, such as the role of Eiheiji monastery, established by Dōgen, as well as various kinds of rites and precepts performed there and at other temples during various periods of history.

All of the participating scholars have studied at or maintain strong scholarly connections with Komazawa University, known as the Sōtōshū Daigaku until the name was officially changed in 1925. Koma-dai, as it is referred to affectionately by those in the field, houses the largest faculty of Buddhist studies in Japan that focuses its research on both the thought and the institutional development of Dōgen and Sōtō Zen, along with numerous additional topics in the history of Buddhist studies. This book represents a novel approach that enhances many of the strengths of the previous collection yet provides innovative directions about the foundation of the sect and its ongoing relations, whether consistent or strained, with the legacy of the founder, whose presence probably looms larger today than at many phases of past centuries.

Dōgen and Sōtō Zen builds upon and further refines a continuing wave of enthusiastic interest and useful scholarly developments in regard to two interrelated areas of inquiry in Western academic and popular appropriations of Zen. With its origins in the 1970s, in an era following D. T. Suzuki's nearly exclusive focus on Japanese Rinzai Zen in the preceding phase, research in English and European languages on Dōgen and Sōtō Zen has been abetted in the past couple of decades by an increasing awareness on both sides of the Pacific of the important influences exerted by the founder on the religious movement created in his honor, although he disdained sectarian labels. The school was transmitted throughout the medieval and early modern periods of Japanese history, and it is still spreading and reshaping itself during the current global age.

In addition to Dōgen, key figures in the history of the sect have recently been examined, especially the medieval popularizer Keizan Jōkin (1268–1325) and the leading reformer in the Tokugawa era, Menzan Zuihō (1683–1769). However, there are not nearly as many studies available for Sōtō Zen as for Dōgen, and generally the subfields have been divided in terms of textual-historical versus institutional-ritual methodologies. This volume exemplifies one of the first attempts to bridge and bring these interconnected areas of inquiry in the ever expanding field of Zen studies into a cohesive vision reflecting a unified method, while also allowing room for diversity and difference based on genres of texts, functions of rituals, and styles of classic and contemporary interpretations.

The chapters cover a wide variety of topics. Those dealing primarily with Dōgen's writings and their diverse implications for the medieval and modern periods include the following:

- Griffith Foulk's analysis of the role of meditation and the notion of just-sitting in relation to use of kōans in Dōgen's writings.
- Miriam Levering's examination of women and gender roles during Dōgen's era by carefully reading his writings on the topic.
- Steven Heine's discussion of the significance of Dōgen's Chinese poetry collection and its connections with his prose works in both vernacular and *kanbun* styles.
- John Maraldo's creative interpretation of Dōgen's views on death and dying in light of various aspects of Japanese Buddhist and comparative philosophy.
- Gereon Kopf's study of contemporary philosophical appropriations, east and west, of Dōgen's thought on time and ethics.

Additional chapters focus more extensively on the Sōtō Zen institution and its approach to ritualism, especially dealing with the crucial juncture in the eighteenth century when the sect was compelled by the shogun's authority to define and justify its status as a religious institution in ways that would enable it to continue to grow and spread in the early modern period:

- William Bodiford's discussion of the origins and significance of Keizan's text on transmission, the *Denkōroku*, not discovered until the nineteenth century.
- David Riggs's examination of the attempted revisions to the precepts developed through Menzan's Edo-period sectarian reforms and the impact of then-current rituals.
- Michaela Mross's investigation of early modern liturgies of gratitude for Dōgen formed by Menzan and practiced at Eiheiji.
- Diane Riggs's analysis of eighteenth-century ritual reforms involving the production and uses of the Buddhist robe in the context of Sōtō doctrinal debates.
- Pamela Winfield's historical study of the buildings constructed at Eiheiji temple and their various ritual functions based on analogies with the body.

Recent Research Developments

The year 2000 marked the 800th anniversary of the birth of Dōgen at the dawn of the Kamakura era, a historical period when the main forms of Buddhism still practiced today were emerging through the efforts of charismatic and thought-provoking leaders, such as Hōnen (Pure Land), Shinran (True Pure Land), and Nichiren, largely in response to significant changes taking place in the structure and fabric of postclassical Japanese society. As the Heian era ended, and with it the hegemony of the Tendai school, the new sects quickly began to emerge, each with a focus on a particular leader and style of training.

Just a few years later, in 2003, the 750th anniversary of Dōgen's death was observed as an even more auspicious occasion of collective remembrance for the Sōtō sect, and for cultural history in Japan more generally, since Buddhist tradition has long marked fifty-year memorials of its ancestors' deaths. Both of these occasions featured a number of celebratory commemorations, including local and international conferences discussing Dōgen's life and thought; publications, such as new editions and collections of works by and about the founder; media or cultural productions, ranging from Kabuki theater to TV shows, movie releases, and manga books; and additional memorials, such as the stele shown in Figure 0.1.

FIGURE O.I   Stele in Kamakura inscribed "Shikan taza." Photograph by Steven Heine.

In 2003 this monument was installed in the town of Kamakura across from Kenchōji temple, where Dōgen was apparently invited for a six-month visit by Hōjō Tokiyori in 1247–48 but turned down the shogun's offer to head the new temple (constructed a few years later, in 1253). Dōgen retreated to his mountain temple at Eiheiji, where he apologized for his absence to the monks in training, who feared he may have taught a different message to the secular head of state. It is interesting to note that this memorial was subsidized by a small group of Sōtō temples in the local Kanagawa Prefecture and not by the nationwide Sōtō Shūmūchō office, a fact that highlights some of the complexity of dealing with multiple levels of the religious institution in relation to the first ancestor. Furthermore this stele is inscribed with the motto "Shikan taza" or "Just Sitting." Foulk's chapter shows that, despite its prominence as a catchphrase for the kind of meditative practice long associated with Dōgen's approach to Zen, this saying probably is, on close investigation, more important as a notion created and fostered by the sect than as an actual doctrine proffered by the founder or supported by his writings.

In addition to the events in Japan at the time of the back-to-back memorials, a number of developments sponsored by or affiliated with the Sōtō sect took place in America in conjunction with the birth and death anniversaries, including a major international conference held at Stanford University in October 1999 and the launching of the Sōtō Zen Translation Project,[2] also housed at the Buddhist Studies Center of Stanford, which aims for state-of-the-art annotated renderings of works by Dōgen plus other texts that are key to sectarian practice. Figure 0.2 shows that international outreach and education are important components of the modern sectarian mission. These developments and several others, such as conferences convened at Emory University and the Zen Mountain

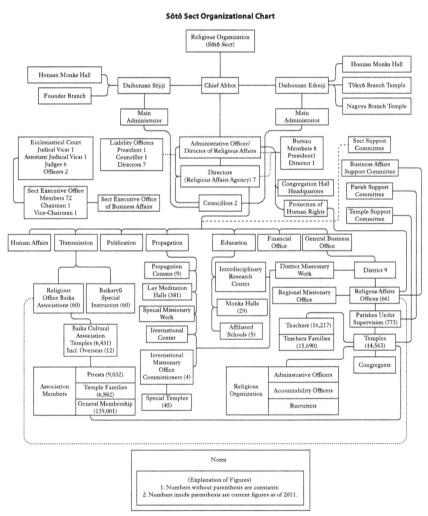

Sōtō Sect Organizational Chart

FIGURE 0.2 Figure 0.2 is a flow chart of the current Sōtō Zen institutional structure involving temples, education, outreach, and internationalization as adapted from information provided by the sect's office for business and management (Sōtōshū Shūmūchō).

Monastery in New York, helped to spawn additional interest in cultivating and disseminating advanced research ventures related to studies of Dōgen and the Sōtō sect.

In part instigated or inspired by the memorial occurrences, dramatic improvements in Western studies of both Dōgen and the Sōtō Zen sect have occurred in the past decade and a half. One notable feature is the level of accessibility currently available for multiple versions of Dōgen's writings both in print and in digitized renditions. In addition to the first-rate translations the Stanford Project is accomplishing, there are now at least three complete translations of Dōgen's major writing, the *Shōbōgenzō*, by Hubert Nearman, Gudo Nishijima and Chodo Cross, and Kazuaki Tanahashi with a long list of collaborators, as well as several versions in European languages (although there is still considerable work to be done before there is a definitive complete English edition of the *Shōbōgenzō*).[3] There are also two renderings of the kōan collection, *Mana Shōbōgenzō*, by John Daido Loori with Kazuaki Tanahashi and by Gudo Nishijima, and a complete annotated translation of the *Eihei Kōroku* by Taigen Dan Leighton and Shohaku Okumura, as well as a version by Yokoi Yūhō.[4] These texts join several others that are accessible in translation, including the *Eihei Shingi* collection of monastic rules, the *Hōkyōki* record of Dōgen's conversations in China with his mentor Rujing, the *Sanshōdōei* collection of Japanese poetry (*waka*), and the *Shōbōgenzō Zuimonki* record of evening sermons collected by Dōgen's main disciple, Ejō, in the mid-1230s.

Supplementing the new translations, and in addition to numerous journal articles on diverse topics, during the past decade important monographs have been published covering Dōgen's history, thought, and writings. These include Steven Heine's *Did Dōgen Go to China? What He Wrote and When He Wrote It*, Hee-Jin Kim's *Dōgen on Meditation and Thinking: A Reflection on His View of Zen*, Gereon Kopf's *Beyond Personal Identity: Dōgen, Nishida, and a Phenomenology of No-Self*, and Taigen Dan Leighton's *Visions of Awakening Space and Time: Dōgen and the Lotus Sutra*.[5] Also there is now a translation by Steve Bein of the seminal early twentieth-century monograph *Purifying Zen: Watsuji Tetsurō's Shamon Dōgen*,[6] perhaps the first main nonsectarian or secular analysis written in the 1920s that seeks to liberate Dōgen from being perceived primarily as the founder of a sect rather than as a world-class thinker. The Sōtō scholar Etō Sokuō challenged the view of Watsuji Tetsurō based on "Shamon Dōgen" in the 1940s in *Dōgen as Founder of a Religious Sect* (*Shūso toshite no Dōgen*). The contrast between the non- and pro-sectarian standpoints is striking and worthy of study as a field in itself.

Meanwhile studies of Sōtō Zen have also grown significantly in the West through recent works, such as Paula Arai's *Women Living Zen: Japanese Sōtō*

Buddhist Nuns, on the role of female clerics at the time of Dōgen and during subsequent periods; Duncan Williams's *The Other Side of Zen: A Social History of Sōtō Zen Buddhism in Tokugawa Japan*, which examines the role of popular religiosity as an integral part of the Sōtō sect in the context of early modern Japanese society; and Richard Jaffe's *Neither Monk nor Layman: Clerical Marriage in Modern Japanese Buddhism*, dealing with significant shifts in monastic life in relation to lay practice in modern Japan.[7]

Furthermore key writings by the sect's fourth ancestor, Keizan, known since the time of Manzan Dōhaku (1635–1715) as the Great Founder (*taiso*) to distinguish his role from that of Dōgen as the Eminent Founder (*kōso*), are available in English, such as the *Denkōroku*, *Keizan Shingi*, and *Zazenyōjinki*. There is also a book-length study of Keizan's religiosity in Bernard Faure's *Visions of Power: Imagining Medieval Japanese Buddhism*.[8] Additional topics in the textual history of Sōtō Zen have been treated, including the function of medieval *kirigami* (paper strip) commentarial literature; the innovations of Menzan Zuihō (1683–1769) as the Tokugawa-era scholastic who revived and edited many of Dōgen's writings, along with other leaders, such as Tenkei Denson (1548–1736) and Manzan; and the formation, accompanied by several translations, of the *Shushōgi*, a short liturgical text created by Meiji-era monks and laymen in the early 1890s by selecting passages from a variety of *Shōbōgenzō* fascicles.

For the most part, however, the two subfields have tended to grow apart, or at least they seem to have been developing in separate ways, with Dōgen studies having a more theoretical focus and Sōtō Zen studies putting a greater emphasis on ritualism and institution. The methodological disconnect tends to be exacerbated by the basic fact that Dōgen's relation to the sect that venerates him is tentative in that, although he is referred to as the founder, this designation occurred subsequent to his death, whereas Dōgen himself tended to deny any and all sectarian identity by considering his teachings an expression of the essence of Buddhism. For various reasons, modern critics such as Watsuji Tetsurō might go so far as to say that what the sect propagates in the name of Dōgen is nearly unrecognizable in relation to his teachings.

On the other hand, some key modern studies have sought out linkages in terms of early historical developments involving doctrines and rituals. Numerous issues were explored in a collection produced in Japan in 1985, *Dōgen*,[9] edited by Ishikawa Rikizan and Kawamura Kōdō, featuring the most current scholarship of the time by leading scholars at Komazawa University. In the West there has been William Bodiford's comprehensive study, *Sōtō Zen in Medieval Japan*, and Bernard Faure's groundbreaking article in *Monumenta Nipponica*, "The Daruma-shū, Dōgen, and Sōtō Zen."[10]

One of the main themes that points at once to areas of overlap and to an ideological gap involves recent social criticism fostered within the sect by scholars associated with a reform methodology known as Critical Buddhism (Hihan Bukkyō). This movement has examined the relation, or lack thereof, between the doctrines preached by Dōgen that are generally open and egalitarian and some of the practices of the sect regarding, for example, the acquisition of posthumous ordination names (kaimyō), which have been seen as discriminatory of the outcast community. These issues, explored in a collection produced at Komazawa University in the early 1990s, *Budda kara Dōgen e*,[11] have been discussed in several prominent outlets in English, most notably *Pruning the Bodhi Tree: The Storm over Critical Buddhism*,[12] edited by Jamie Hubbard and Paul Swanson.

It seems that several ways of viewing the complex doctrinal and institutional relations between Dōgen and Sōtō Zen have emerged in recent years. These perspectives include the orthodox sectarian position of highlighting the founder and the sect as representing complementary and consistent religious forces, yet with some areas of change and modification more or less acknowledged; the outlook of much of contemporary Western research that sees these as distinct areas of study requiring different methodological foci; and an emphasis on discontinuity or even conflict between the ideals of the founder and the observances of the sect. Despite the variety of approaches, which reflect vigorous scholarly activities but may lead to a sense of there being a cacophony of voices, it must be understood that Dōgen and Sōtō Zen are invariably interrelated on some level and cannot be disengaged or set apart, as are traditional and modern perspectives both from within and outside of sectarian scholarship.

Given the strides made in recent scholarship, but with an eye toward covering the lacunae and neglected topics that remain to be studied, *Dōgen and Sōtō Zen* provides an opportunity to develop scholarship in two directions simultaneously: one way is to continue to view the subfields as somewhat separable phenomenon by dividing the book into two parts, with the first half on the founding ancestor and the second half on the sect; the other outlook is to juxtapose and explain Dōgen and Sōtō Zen in tandem instead of as disconnected developments, which is exactly what several of these chapters accomplish by linking Dōgen's view of texts and rites to sectarian reforms.

The approach of this volume at once advances each subfield and moves forward with ways of associating and connecting some of the dots, so to speak, in order to explore and determine to what extent Sōtō Zen represents faithfully or may misrepresent, and complements or may depart from, Dōgen's thought in terms of such issues as meditation and monasticism, literature and philosophy, or gender and cultural memory. One caveat is that I would have liked to include additional contributions dealing more extensively with contemporary developments of the Sōtō sect in Japan as well as its worldwide network in the United States, Europe, and Brazil, but the richness of the history of the Tokugawa period as examined in several chapters, along with space limitations for the volume, prohibited this.

Overview of Chapters

Designed to help correct the current state of scholarship on Dōgen and Sōtō Zen that has generally resulted in frequently separated areas and methods of study for what are essentially interrelated themes, the book is divided into two main parts. The first part covers Dōgen's approach by using distinctive methods for clarifying the meaning of his writings and clearing up some common misimpressions about their significance, some of which are connected with sectarian conceptions and appropriations, while others derive from outsiders' views. This part contains careful consideration of the practice of meditation and Dōgen's use of kōans; his views on the role of women in monastic and lay training; his compositions of poetry in relation to prose works; his views of death and notions of temporality; and the role of Dōgen as a philosopher seen from modern perspectives.

The second part examines various aspects of the Sōtō Zen institutional history that reflect back on Dōgen's life and thought, including Keizan's *Denkōroku*, which is a main source for the teachings of the founder; Menzan's attempt at reforming the precepts and the contemporary applications of this process; rituals of gratitude toward Dōgen promulgated in the Edo and modern periods; new rites involving the production and use of ceremonial robes in the eighteenth century; and the ongoing rebuilding and redefining of Eiheiji, Dōgen's temple originally constructed in the 1240s in the remote Echizen Mountains, based in part on Buddhist symbolism as developed in China and Japan.

Part I: Studies of Dōgen

The opening chapter of part I, by the renowned historian of Zen T. Griffith Foulk, is "Dōgen's Use of Rujing's 'Just Sit' (*shikan taza*) and Other Kōans," which is a sequel to the chapter that appears in *Dōgen: Textual and Historical Studies* titled " 'Just Sitting?' Dōgen's Take on Zazen, Sutra Reading, and Other Conventional Buddhist Practices." There Foulk analyzed every occurrence of the expression "just sit" in Dōgen's writings and showed that it is, in all cases, a quotation of his teacher Rujing, and it cannot be taken literally as a rejection of conventional Buddhist practices, such as burning incense, reading sutras, or reciting the *nembutsu*. Building on the evidence adduced in the previous work, Foulk further argues in the current chapter that when Dōgen cites his teacher Rujing's admonition to just sit, he is actually holding it up as a kōan for his students to contemplate. Foulk then compares Dōgen's general use of kōans, including Rujing's "just sit," with the method of "contemplating phrases" (Ch. *kanhua chan*, Jp. *kanna zen*) attributed to Dahui Zonggao (Jp. Daie Sōkō), while pointing out both similarities and differences between the respective approaches.

A central thesis of this chapter is that Dōgen does not actually teach (or even conceive of) the mode of zazen practice—now generally referred to as *shikan taza*—that is attributed to him by modern Sōtō school scholars as well as Zen teachers. The instructions Dōgen does give for the practice of zazen, which Foulk analyzes in considerable detail, do not employ this term, nor do they recommend an approach that is consistent with what contemporary researchers say about just sitting. A good part of the chapter is dedicated to tracing the historical process through which so-called *shikan taza* came to be held up as the signature practice of the Sōtō school by explaining how its attribution to Dōgen largely depends on a misreading of his writings.

The second chapter, "'Raihaitokuzui' and Dōgen's Views of Gender and Women: A Reconsideration," by Miriam Levering, who has published extensively on gender roles in Zen texts, suggests important new perspectives for understanding Dōgen's statements about women in his early and later writings. A variety of interpretations of Dōgen's apparently contradictory statements about the suitability of women and female gender to Buddhist awakening have emerged in Japanese and English scholarship during the past thirty years. One approach stresses the gender inclusivity of Dōgen's early essay "Raihaitokuzui," a fascicle of the *Shōbōgenzō*, and sees Dōgen's apparently antifeminist remarks in later texts such as "Shukke Kudoku" as not being his own words. Another approach views "Raihaitokuzui" as not necessarily affirming women's Zen practice, since the text ironically compares women to wild foxes in their capacity to teach and considers the misogynist comments from later works as authentic and consistent with the teachings on practice in Dōgen's last decade.

Levering's approach is to supply a context for his statements in both periods of his career that will make Dōgen's early position understandable in relation to his later comments, while still leaving the door open to ruminations on a possible inconsistency. She considers three main aspects: (1) Dōgen as a student, including what he might have learned about women in Chan and the role of the "bloodline" (*ketsumyaku*) during his trip to China; (2) the state and status of women within Japanese Buddhism during the medieval period, when they were primarily patrons rather than practitioners of Buddhist rituals and practices, including orthodox views as well as slurs against women; and (3) understanding the context of Dōgen's nondualism and egalitarian teaching in "Raihaitokuzui" in connection to other references to women in the *Shōbōgenzō* and the *Eihei Kōroku*. When viewed from a contemporary standpoint, the portrait of Dōgen that emerges from this contextual evidence is neither as inclusive as one might wish nor as misogynist as some have feared, so that Dōgen is neither heroic nor villainous in his views.

Chapter 3, "Dōgen, a Japanese Monk Well-Versed in Chinese Poetry: What He Did and Did Not Compose," is by Steven Heine, who has published translations of Dōgen's Japanese *waka* poetry. In this chapter Heine provides an examination of Dōgen's considerable production of Chinese poems (*kanshi*) primarily contained in the last two fascicles of the ten-volume *Eihei Kōroku*, which is a compendium of his *kanbun* writings in prose and verse. According to an oft-cited passage in one of his sermons, Dōgen returned from China "with empty hands" (*kūshu genkyō*), but this does not suggest that he was empty-headed, although he had a head "full of emptiness." Dōgen came back to his native country with an immense knowledge of and appreciation for the Chinese literary tradition and its multifarious expressions through various forms of Chan writings, including poetry, which he both emulated and transformed via engagement and integration with rhetorical styles of Japanese Buddhist literature and discourse. This chapter shows Dōgen's profound understanding of Chinese Chan sources as well as his ability to cite them extensively and with great facility to recall the details of particular passages while also challenging and changing their implications to suit his own conceptual needs. This facility is probably the main key to explaining the greatness of his two major writings, the vernacular *Shōbōgenzō* and the *Eihei Kōroku* in Sino-Japanese.

Heine explains that the contents of the Chinese poetry collection cover four main categories. The first, with the largest number of verses, is contained in volume 10 of the *Eihei Kōroku*, which includes 150 poems written throughout the various stages of his career, such as the only known writings (fifty poems) from his stay in China, and encompasses twenty-five verses on the enlightenment experience of the Chan patriarchs (*shinsan*) and of Dōgen himself (*jisan*), in addition to 125 poems in a variety of styles under the general heading of *geju*; these are primarily on lyrical and naturalistic topics but also include communications with lay followers (this is true only of the poems composed in China), monastic rituals, and some of Dōgen's personal experiences and evocative self-reflections. The second largest group, in volume 9, includes 102 four-line verses, or *juko*, on ninety of the spiritual riddles or kōan cases that were the hallmark of Chan literature and practice (some of the kōans have two or three verse commentaries); all of these were composed in 1236, around the same time Dōgen was also working on the compilation of three hundred kōan cases in the *Mana Shōbōgenzō*, composed a year before. Third is verse comments that Dōgen integrated with his formal and informal *kanbun* sermons in the first eight volumes of the *Eihei Kōroku*, and the fourth group has a few additional Chinese verses that appear elsewhere in Dōgen's collected works.

The fourth chapter is "Negotiating the Divide of Death in Japanese Buddhism: Dōgen's Difference" by John C. Maraldo, a noted thinker and scholar of Japanese philosophy who presents a reading of passages in the *Shōbōgenzō* that take up the problem of living and dying. The guiding question is this: What understanding does Dōgen bring to the problem of personal death? *Personal death* refers to dying seen from a first-person point of view, in contrast to third-person, biographical, and sociological perspectives on death, as well as second-person perspectives that address the death of someone one knows. Maraldo first explains these three points of view, with examples of each, and then employs them to argue that there is a major divide concerning the sense and significance of death within Japanese Buddhism. On the one hand, "philosophical Japanese Buddhism deals with the 'great matter' of birth-and-death (samsara) and focuses on [some sense of] liberation." The relatively few Buddhist figures who treat this great matter teach practices devoted to personal liberation. "The Buddhism of the populace, on the other hand, concerns itself with a death that divides the departed from the living and focuses on the care of the corpse and of the spirit of the departed, who often is thought to care for or to curse the survivors." This popular form of Buddhism, addressing death from a second-person point of view, "recognizes the fear and pain of death and offers rites" that provide a sense of mourning over the passing of loved ones.

Maraldo then deals specifically with what Dōgen has to say about the great matter from a first-person standpoint. According to this analysis, death in a second-person or third-person perspective appears not to be of much concern for Dōgen; instead his writings seem to be aimed at undermining conventional first-person senses of death, or of what one's own death means. Maraldo offers interpretations of the relevant passages in various fascicles of the *Shōbōgenzō* to suggest that, rather than explicating the notion of liberation per se, Dōgen teaches liberation *from* first-person perspectives altogether, which stands in contrast to an elucidation of what one's own death can be taken to signify. Dōgen's philosophy shows that death, more clearly than any factor of existence, makes present the element of time in human experience.

Understanding Dōgen's philosophy from modern perspectives is further considered by Gereon Kopf, known for his research on Japanese and comparative thought, in " 'When All Dharmas Are the Buddha-Dharma': Dōgen as Comparative Philosopher." Until the beginning of the twentieth century Dōgen was barely known outside the sectarian literature and rhetoric of Sōtō Zen. However, once he was introduced to the world of academia by Watsuji Tetsurō and Kimura Uno in the early Shōwa period, his work became an object of discussion and inspiration, first, by the philosophers of the so-called Kyoto School and, later, by comparative philosophers in general. In the past thirty years Dōgen has been put in dialogue with philosophers such as Sankara, Martin Heidegger, and Jacques Derrida and, at times, even called upon to serve as the representative of Zen Buddhist metaphysics and ethics by philosophers with an interest but without training in the academic study of Zen Buddhism. Today his philosophical writings, as collected in the *Shōbōgenzō*, have been included in the discourse of and textbooks on comparative and global philosophy. These developments have contributed to the impression that Dōgen scholarship can be divided into two or more categories, in particular the textual or historical study of Dōgen's life and work, and philosophical reflection that seems to decontextualize and apply his work to comparative thought.

Kopf explores the inclusion of Dōgen's work in global philosophical discourse from the first discussions of him as a philosopher by Watsuji and Kimura, as well as the pioneering work of philosophers such as Nishitani Keiji, Masao Abe, and Thomas P. Kasulis, to more recent works in comparative and global philosophy, such as Rein Raud's essay on Dōgen's use of language. Kopf reflects critically on the methodological issues arising from the treatment of Dōgen by investigating the perils and benefits of identifying him as a philosopher. Throughout this discussion he makes a case for a method of inquiry that draws from the disciplines of history, philology, and philosophy, as it has been envisioned by the work of Heine. The benefits of this investigation are twofold: first, showing what it means to approach Dōgen's writings some eight centuries after their creation with a methodology alien to his context; second, providing a heuristic tool based on "Genjōkōan" and other writings for those inspired and seeking ways of applying Dōgen's work to some central contemporary issues, be they moral, environmental, or existential.

Part II: Studies of Sōtō Zen

The second part of the volume, focusing on Sōtō Zen, begins with "Keizan's *Denkōroku*: A Textual and Contextual Overview," in which William M. Bodiford, a specialist in medieval Japanese Buddhism, highlights an example of how Chinese elements transplanted to Japan gave birth to a new Zen culture that is neither completely the same nor completely different from its ancestors. As Bodiford shows, in 1857 a Sōtō Zen priest named Busshū Sen'ei edited and published a previously unknown text, which he titled *Keizan Oshō Denkōroku* (2 volumes). This text, which is commonly referred to simply as the *Denkōroku*, has been designated by the Sōtō Headquarters (Sōtōshū Shūmuchō) as one of the denomination's main scriptures. In spite of its exalted status, however, the *Denkōroku* has been little studied. A brief overview of the text can serve to illuminate some of the characteristics and questions presented to modern scholarship by early Japanese Zen literature.

One of the distinctive features of the *Denkōroku*, attributed to Keizan, is that its format or structure does not correspond to any particular genre of Chinese Chan literature but combines elements from several of them. The Chinese composed by Japanese Zen monks in medieval Japan (the so-called literature of the Five Mountains, or *gozan bungaku*) consists not just of poetry but of every possible manner of prose, including monastery records, legal documents, and ritual pronouncements. The *Denkōroku*, which cannot be identified with any of these standard Chinese forms of Zen literature, narrates the history of the Sōtō Zen lineage consisting of one Buddha (Sakyamuni) and fifty-two ancestors. At first glance this narrative structure corresponds most closely to the Zen genre known as flame (or lamp) histories (*tōroku*), which consist of the large hagiographic collections produced by Chinese Chan monks during the Song dynasty. Rather than the static, unchanging nature of truth, the *Denkōroku* emphasizes the dynamic, dramatic, and ultimately unique process by which one must encounter that truth. Instead of linking the generations together with dharma verses, the *Denkōroku* links them through *kōan* (pivotal events or words) that depict the crucial moment in each generation when the truth was fully authenticated (*shō*). The actual text was not written by Keizan but is a record of what he said. Thus it represents a precursor to the "lecture transcription" (*kikigaki*) genre of Zen literature that developed in medieval Japan.

Following Bodiford's discussion of early developments in the Sōtō sect affected by current appropriations is "Are Sōtō Zen Precepts for Ethical Guidance or Ceremonial Transformation? Menzan's Attempted Reforms and Contemporary Practices" by David Riggs, an authority on Menzan's career and writings. As eighteenth-century Sōtō Zen struggled to craft its sense of identity, the sect recognized that precepts and the assemblies to confer them were an essential way to wrest power from the new Ōbaku Zen teachers who had recently come from China and quickly gained popularity. Having decided that Dōgen should be the standard, to their dismay the Sōtō reformers found that it was not clear which precepts based on Dōgen should be followed. Nor was it apparent how those precepts should be used: Were they moral and aspirational maxims to be carried out in following the path, as suggested by the founder's writings, or were they an esoteric initiation that represented the completion of the path, as per medieval practices?

Menzan held the former view in arguing that precepts, along with meditation and wisdom, were one of the three primary supports for Buddhist practice. Menzan's position was closer to the mainstream thinking of Ōbaku monks about the centrality of actual practice of the precepts, but when it came to deciding which precepts to administer, Menzan argued for following a simple set of sixteen precepts, based on his reading of Dōgen, not the much more complex set used in Ōbaku, and indeed in Chinese Buddhism generally. In addition to exploring the ceremonial aspects and describing Dōgen's list, Menzan stressed the importance of upholding the precepts by evoking the authority of Eisai, considered the founder of the Rinzai sect, and showed the way with large precept assemblies and many popular as well as more technical writings. Although Menzan's overall influence on Sōtō Zen is pervasive, his positions on the form and content of precepts were soon rejected. After a brief fling with mainstream ideas, Sōtō Zen returned to the esoteric way of using the precept ceremony as an initiation that confers transcendent benefit through the attainment of buddhahood. Although the esoteric view triumphed in early modern Japan, Menzan's position is much closer to the emphasis on practicing the precepts in modern Western Zen groups, and his work thus remains an important resource. Riggs describes his experiences of Sōtō precept ceremonies conducted at both Eiheiji and in the United States.

"Vocalizing the Remembrance of Dōgen: A Study of the *Shinpen Hōon Kōshiki*" by Michaela Mross, who conducted fieldwork combined with musical notation research on Sōtō rites in Japan for six years, examines the liturgical genre of *hōon kōshiki*, which has played an important role in Sōtō Zen since its very beginnings with the teachings of Dōgen. In the Edo period Sōtō monks began composing *kōshiki* ritual texts in memory of its founder. Mross discusses one of these: the *Dōgen Zenji Hōon Kōshiki* written by the scholar-monk Menzan. She argues that this *kōshiki* text was part of Menzan's activities in the sectarian reform movement and shows that even today this rite expressing gratitude for benefits received from the founder's teaching is performed annually at the Eiheiji monastery's branch temple in Tokyo, called the Eiheiji Betsuin (Chōkokuji) temple.

Menzan was very influential in the Sōtō reform movement of early modern Japan. His expanded and annotated edition of the fifteenth-century biography of Dōgen, the *Teiho Kenzeiki*, became the major source for the study of Dōgen's life. Furthermore his ritual manuals as well as ideas of monastic life were put into practice at Eiheiji temple. In the *Dōgen Zenji Hōon Kōshiki* we find elements of these two aspects of Menzan's activities: on the one hand, this *kōshiki* can be interpreted as a hagiography of Dōgen; on the other hand, it is a liturgy characterized by offerings, ritual actions, melodic chants, and the playing of musical instruments. Mross analyzes the text as a hagiography and examines how Dōgen is described in this ritual text in relation to the *Teiho Kenzeiki*, as well as contemporary modifications based on biographical as well as social issues. She also explains the performance of the *Dōgen Zenji Hōon Kōshiki*, especially the singing of *shōmyō*. Mross thereby illuminates new aspects of the ritual tradition of the Sōtō sect and its religious music.

Chapter 9, "Interpreting the Material Heritage of the 'Elephant Trunk Robe' in Sōtō Zen" by Diane Riggs, who has done extensive historical and fieldwork studies of Sōtō robe-making rites, shows that during the Edo period Japanese Buddhist sects met challenges about the laxity of their practice through renewed study of monastic rules and wrote numerous works on the proper form of Buddhist vestments by relying primarily on interpretations of the Chinese Vinaya master Daoxuan (596–667). In most schools Vinaya reformers achieved a blend of revised and traditional practice. Reform of the production and use of the robe (*kesa*) was complicated in Zen, however, by the existence of elaborate brocade *kesa* that were revered as a sign of transmission of the dharma in several lineages, including the Sōtō Zen sect. Many of these robes, dating to the Kamakura period, used the elongated and distorted shape of the "elephant trunk" *kesa*, which violated several Vinaya teachings about the robe.

Sōtō reformers could not rely solely on the Vinaya because of an increasing emphasis on the writings of Dōgen as a source of authority. Dōgen's criticisms of the visionary source of Daoxuan's writings on the *kesa* as well as his own occasionally elliptical comments complicated matters for the reformers. In the eighteenth century two Sōtō Zen scholar-monks, Gyakusui Tōryū (1684–1766), abbot of Daijōji, and Menzan, a scholar of Dōgen's writings, debated the appropriate form of the Sōtō Zen robe in a series of essays, in which each claimed to represent Dōgen's intentions. Their essays reveal methodological tensions over the use of the Vinaya to decide questions of practice and the significance of robes traditionally attributed to founding members of Sōtō

Zen. The various arguments fueled debates in the "three-robe controversy" that threatened sectarian unity in the nineteenth century. By investigating the arguments and methodologies proposed by Toryū and Menzan, Riggs raises broader questions about the role of the *kesa* in Sōtō ideology.

In the final chapter, "Embodying Sōtō Zen: Institutional Identity and Ideal Body Image at Daihonzan Eiheiji," Pamela D. Winfield, an expert on Japanese Buddhist religious imagery and iconography, especially in the premodern period, demonstrates that Eiheiji's monastic training center as it appears today, originally established by Dōgen and his band of followers in the 1240s, constitutes a sprawling complex of monastic buildings, memorial halls, and subsidiary structures that have accrued and been renewed throughout Eiheiji's sedimented architectural history. This chapter focuses on Eiheiji's visual displays of authenticity and tradition in terms of its material and visual "temple bodies," seen in contrast with the Sōtō sect's other main temple, or *daihonzan*, at Sōjiji temple, originally established by Keizan in the Noto peninsula and transferred to Tsurumi near Yokohama in the early twentieth century.

In particular Winfield considers the architectural body, Eiheiji's anthropomorphic seven-hall layout as opposed to Sōjiji's somewhat idiosyncratic temple layout, and the figural body, Eiheiji's sculpted Buddha bodies that signal the eternity of practice as opposed to Sōjiji's more historic emphasis on dharma heirs and specific temple founders. Taken as a whole, Winfield argues that Eiheiji has consistently constructed concrete material and visual markers to physically embody the dharma in Japan and that its anthropomorphic structures, sculptures, and other embodied displays of authority and authenticity have been instrumental to its institutional survival and success. Analyzing Eiheiji's ideal body types in this way offers a novel approach for understanding Sōtō's institutional identity issues and helps to cement the vital connection between the visibility and the viability of Eiheiji's self-consciously constructed "tradition."

A Note on Contributions

Two of the contributions were published previously in other outlets, and this volume offers an opportunity to bring these examples of scholarship with revisions to a wider audience: Steven Heine's chapter on Dōgen's poetry originally appeared as "When Dōgen Went to China: Chan Poetry He Did and Did Not Write," *Hsiang Lectures on Chinese Poetry* 6 (2012): 75–100, with revisions made for this volume (and is reprinted with permission); John C. Maraldo's chapter on death in Dōgen appeared online in the Nanzan Institute for Religion and Culture's series *Essays in Japanese Philosophy* 7 (n.d.): 89–121, and appears here with revisions.

The authors provide transliterations for titles in various ways; this is especially the case for fascicles of the *Shōbōgenzō*, which some authors place in quotation marks and others in italics, and which may have different romanized spellings. An editorial decision was made to let the discrepancies stand rather than force all the chapters to conform since various approaches are accepted in recent scholarship. Note that Sanskrit diacritics are not included in this volume.

NOTES

1. Steven Heine, ed., *Dōgen: Textual and Historical Studies* (New York: Oxford University Press, 2012).
2. Sōtō Zen Translation Project; http://scbs.stanford.edu/sztp3/.
3. Hubert Nearman, trans., *Shōbōgenzō: The Treasure House of the Eye of the True Teaching* (Mount Shasta, CA: Shasta Abbey Press, 2007), http://www.shasta-abbey.org/pdf/shobo/oo1bendo.pdf; Dōgen, *Shōbōgenzō*, 4 vols., trans. Gudo Nishijima and Chodo Cross (Charleston, SC: BookSurge, 1994); Dōgen, *Shōbōgenzō*, 2 vols., trans. Kazuaki Tanahashi (Boston: Shambhala, 2010).
4. Dōgen, *The True Dharma Eye: Zen Master Dōgen's Three Hundred Kōans*, trans. Kazuaki Tanahashi and John Daido Loori (Boston: Shambhala, 2005); Dōgen, *Master Dōgen's Shinji Shōbōgenzō: 301 Kōan Stories*, trans. Gudo Nishijima (Tokyo: Windbell Publications, 2003); Dōgen, *Dōgen's Extensive Record: A Translation of the Eihei Kōroku*, trans. Taigen Dan Leighton and Shohaku Okamura (Somerville, MA: Wisdom, 2010); Dōgen, *Gendaigoyaku Eihei Kōroku*, trans. Yokoi Yūhō (Tokyo: Sanikibō Buddhist Bookstore, 1978).
5. Steven Heine, *Did Dōgen Go to China? What He Wrote and When He Wrote it* (New York: Oxford University Press, 2006); Hee-Jin Kim, *Dōgen on Meditation and Thinking: A Reflection on His View of Zen* (New York: State University of New York Press, 2007); Gereon Kopf, *Beyond Personal Identity: Dōgen, Nishida, and a Phenomenology of No-Self* (Richmond, UK: Curzon Press, 2001); Taigen Dan Leighton, *Visions of Awakening Space and Time: Dōgen and the Lotus Sutra* (New York: Oxford University Press, 2007).
6. Steven Bein, trans., *Purifying Zen: Watsuji Tetsuro's Shamon Dōgen* (Honolulu: University of Hawaii Press, 2011).
7. Paula Arai, *Women Living Zen: Japanese Sōtō Buddhist Nuns* (New York: Oxford University Press, 1999); Duncan Williams, *The Other Side of Zen: A Social History of Sōtō Zen Buddhism in Tokugawa Japan* (Princeton, NJ: Princeton University Press, 2009); Richard Jaffe, *Neither Monk nor Layman: Clerical Marriage in Modern Japan* (Princeton, NJ: Princeton University Press: 2001).
8. Bernard Faure, *Visions of Power: Imagining Medieval Japanese Buddhism*, trans. Phyllis Brooks (Princeton, NJ: Princeton University Press, 1996).
9. Kawamura Kōdō and Ishikawa Rikizan, eds., *Dōgen* (Tokyo: Yoshikawa Kobunkan, 1985).

10. William M. Bodiford, *Sōtō Zen in Medieval Japan* (Honolulu: University of Hawaii Press, 2008); Bernard Faure, "The Daruma-shū, Dōgen, and Sōtō Zen," *Monumenta Nipponica* 42.1 (1987): 25–55.

11. Nara Yasuaki, ed., *Budda kara Dōgen e* (Tokyo: Tokyo shoseki, 1992).

12. Jamie Hubbard and Paul Swanson, eds., *Pruning the Bodhi Tree: The Storm over Critical Buddhism* (Honolulu: University of Hawaii Press, 1997).

PART I

Studies of Dōgen

Dōgen's Use of Rujing's "Just Sit" (shikan taza) and Other Kōans

T. Griffith Foulk

IN THE SUMMER of 2011, I participated in an international conference on the topic "*Ganhwa Seon*: Its Principle and Structure," which was held at Dongguk University in Seoul. *Ganhwa seon* is the Korean pronunciation of the Japanese expression *kanna zen*, or "Zen of contemplating sayings,"[1] which at present refers mainly to a method of meditating on kōans that is used in the Rinzai school of Japanese Zen and the Jogye order of Korean Seon. Both of those traditions regard themselves as heirs to a mode of "contemplating sayings" (Ch. *kan hua-tou*, Jp. *kan watō*, Kr. *gan hwadu*) that was first championed by Dahui Zonggao (1089–1163), an eminent monk of the Song dynasty who belonged to the Linji (Jp. Rinzai, Kr. Imje) branch of the Chan lineage. Dongguk University is a Buddhist institution that was founded by the Jogye order, and the audience at the conference was largely composed of monks and lay followers. The Korean scholars who gave papers and responded to the presentations of the visiting Western scholars, too, were mainly Jogye monks or members of the Dongguk University faculty.

The paper I gave at the conference, entitled "Rujing's 'Just Sit' (Ch. *qiguan dazuo*, Jp. *shikan taza*) and Other Kōans Used by Zen Master Dōgen," was an earlier draft of the present chapter. Translated into Korean, the paper stirred widespread indignation in the audience, and even anger from a couple of outspoken panelists. My utter ignorance and incompetence was clear to all, for as "everybody knows," the Sōtō (Ch. Caodong, Kr. Jo Dong) school that Dōgen founded in Japan rejected *ganhwa seon* in favor of "silent illumination" (Ch. *mozhao*, Jp. *mokushō*, Kr. *mukjo*), a heretical practice that Dahui himself had railed against. How preposterous it was for this American scholar to claim that Dōgen had used kōans!

In response to those Korean critics, I pointed out that Dōgen's commentaries on various kōans are found in virtually every chapter of his acclaimed masterwork, *Shōbōgenzō* (*Treasury of the True Dharma Eye*), and that his discourse record, the *Eihei Kōroku* (*Extensive Record of Eihei [Dōgen]*), shows that he routinely held up kōans as topics for analysis and commentary when instructing his followers at the monasteries where he served as abbot. I granted that Dōgen's use of kōans was different in some important ways from what is now called *kanna zen* in Japan or *ganhwa seon* in Korea, but I insisted that his engagement with the kōan genre of literature was, in many other respects, the same as that of Dahui and his epigones in the Linji school of Chan (Zen). That rejoinder was met with even more misunderstanding, and I felt like a member of a political party trying to explain to members of the opposition that our leaders actually share many of their fundamental values.

In the aftermath of that conference, I found myself wondering why Korean Seon Buddhists today feel such antipathy toward Dōgen. Was it because the Sōtō school was especially active in Korea during the period of annexation by Japan, from 1910 to 1945? There may be some residual resentment on that account, but the Rinzai school of Japanese Zen was also involved in "missionary" (*fukyō*) outreach to the Korean people in support of Japan's colonial policies, and the monk celebrated as that school's latter-day reviver—Hakuin Ekaku (1685–1768)—is now embraced as a spiritual role model by the Jogye order. Hakuin is in favor because he is understood to have championed the *kanna zen* of Dahui, while Dōgen is denigrated as an heir to Caodong monks who opposed Dahui and taught "silent illumination."

The Korean Buddhists I met had obviously not read any of the current scholarship on Dōgen written in English that discusses his use of kōans nor the works of Japanese scholars who have recently begun to acknowledge that aspect of Dōgen's teachings. The Koreans are hardly to be blamed for the stereotyped image of Dōgen they cling to, however, for that was created and perpetuated by several generations of Japanese scholars whose publications spanned the twentieth century. Because Western students of Dōgen, too, are still partly in thrall to that image, it is worth recounting its main features here.

Modern scholars of the Japanese Zen tradition have often drawn a sharp distinction between the approaches to Buddhist practice taken by the Rinzai school and those by the Sōtō school. The Rinzai school, which since the middle of the Meiji period (1868–1912) has been represented solely by monks who trace their dharma lineages back to Hakuin, is typically characterized as "kōan Zen" (*kōan zen*). It is said to stress the attainment and deepening of awakening (*satori*) through the practice of meditating on the "keywords" (*watō*) of kōans, an approach known as the Zen of contemplating sayings. The Sōtō school, which since the Meiji period has held up the "two ancestors" (*ryōso*) Dōgen (1200–1253) and Keizan Jōkin (1268–1325) as cofounders of the tradition, is said to stress "just sitting" (*shikantaza*).[2] That is explained as the practice of "sitting in meditation" (Ch. *zuochan*, Jp. *zazen*) with "nothing to be gained" (*mushotoku*)—that is, without any intention of gaining awakening—and without any object of contemplation other than the mind-ground (*shinji*) itself. The practice of *shikantaza* is said to be based on the doctrine of the "identity of practice and realization" (*shushō ittō*), according to which, practice (*shugyō*) is not a means of attaining awakening but rather a way of manifesting the buddha-nature (*busshō*) that is innate in all beings. The expression "Rinzai warrior Sōtō farmer" (*Rinzai bushi, Sōtō hyakushō*) is sometimes used to sum up these differences. The idea is that Rinzai monks are like samurai who put their lives on the line and mount a frontal assault on awakening, while Sōtō monks calmly and steadily cultivate the field of their own buddha-nature.

These modern characterizations of the two main branches of Zen in Japan have been endorsed by partisans of both schools, although their evaluations of each other's approaches tend to be either critical or dismissive. Members of the Rinzai school sometimes denigrate the Sōtō approach as a kind of "purposeless Zen" (*mui zen*) or "nothing-to-do Zen" (*buji zen*) that allows practitioners to remain smugly ensconced in delusion while believing that they are already awakened. Rinzai partisans also echo a criticism that Dahui leveled against the Zen of silent illumination promoted by Hongzhi Zhengjue (1091–1157), Zhenxie Qingliao (1088–1151), and other leaders of the Caodong lineage in Song China, to wit, that the Sōtō approach is quietist and results only in mental tranquility, not awakening. *Shikantaza*, they further suggest, smacks of the kind of "polishing the mirror of the mind" that the Sixth Ancestor Huineng (*rokuso Enō*) rejected as gradual awakening (*zengo*).

For their part, members of the Sōtō school criticize the Rinzai approach as a "Zen of waiting for awakening" (*taigo zen*), which involves the deluded reification of enlightenment as some kind of "thing" or experience that one can either "have" or "not have." Sōtō partisans also belittle the process of working through a number of kōans by calling it "step-by-step Zen" (*hashigo zen*), a term that implies gradual awakening. It is precisely *shikantaza*, they argue, that is consistent with the principle of sudden awakening (*tongo*) established by the Sixth Ancestor Huineng, because it is based on the insight that buddhahood is innate and that "from the start there is no single thing" (*honrai muichi motsu*) that might be gained through practice.

It is not my intention in this chapter to take sides in this polemical debate, which all too often has been driven by partisans who know their own branch of the Japanese Zen tradition well enough but are largely ignorant of the other.

Speaking as a practitioner who has trained in both Rinzai and Sōtō monasteries in Japan and as a scholar who has collected and studied the monastic rules,
liturgical texts, and ritual manuals used in both branches of the tradition,
I would rather point out that what the Rinzai and Sōtō schools hold in common with regard to Buddhist practice—both historically and at present—far
outweighs their differences.

The training monasteries (*sōdō*) of both schools today have virtually identi-
cal schedules of daily, monthly, and annual observances. Those include daily
services for chanting sutras (*fugin*) and dedicating merit (*ekō*) in support of
prayers to various buddhas, bodhisattvas, and protecting deities; annual and
monthly memorial services for ancestral teachers (*soshi*), former abbots, and
lay patrons; sermons on Zen texts; communal meditation; walking meditation (*kinhin*); manual labor (*samu*); and procedures (*sahō*) for ritualizing and
sanctifying all aspects of everyday life, such as sleeping at one's individual
place on the platforms (*tan*), taking meals, face washing, bathing, and going
to the toilet.

The features of organization and operation that serve to distinguish
present-day Rinzai institutions from their Sōtō counterparts are relatively
minor, but two such differences do pertain to the way kōans are studied. First,
Rinzai training monasteries have regularly scheduled times, always during
periods of zazen, when monks in training (*unsui*) can enter the abbot's room
(*nisshitsu*) for "individual consultation" (*dokusan*) concerning the kōans they
are working on. In Sōtō monasteries there is no such arrangement because
the study of kōans is not linked to the practice of zazen but pursued in the
context of formal sermons (*hōyaku*) and classroom lectures on Zen texts such
as Dōgen's *Shōbōgenzō*, Keizan's *Denkōroku* (*Record of the Transmission of the
Light*), and the *Congronglu* (*Congrong Hermitage Record*). Second, in Rinzai
monasteries there is only one Zen master (*shike*), usually called "Rōshi," who
is both the abbot (*jūji*) and the spiritual guide who gives individual instruction
to every trainee monk on the matter of contemplating kōans. In Sōtō monasteries there are, in addition to the abbot, a number of senior monks who hold
high office in the bureaucracy, are addressed as Rōshi, and serve as mentors
to individual monks in training, who seek them out in their private quarters.

The present chapter does not focus on contemporary Japanese Zen but
rather on the founder of the Sōtō lineage in Japan, Dōgen, and the approach
he took to Buddhist practice. I have raised the issue of the modern characterization of Rinzai versus Sōtō Zen only because such polemics have deeply, and
misleadingly, influenced the way the figure of Dōgen has been portrayed over
the course of the past century. Modern Sōtō scholarship has not only idealized
shikantaza as a mode of practice that sharply distinguishes Sōtō Zen from

the kōan Zen of the Rinzai school; it also has attributed the former practice directly to Dōgen and argued that it is a "pure" form of Zen consistent with Dōgen's rejection of "superstitious" beliefs and superfluous rituals. Those characterizations of Dōgen are misconceptions that I aim to dispel in these pages.

This chapter is a sequel to an earlier publication, "Just Sitting? Dōgen's Take on Zazen, Sutra Reading, and Other Conventional Buddhist Practices."[3] Some of the conclusions that I reached earlier are summarized herein, without revisiting all of the textual evidence that I adduced previously. Those conclusions function in the present context as premises on which I base some new arguments, supported by additional evidence. In my citations of primary texts (the writings of Dōgen), I have tried to keep repetition to a minimum, but a certain amount has proven unavoidable, for this chapter must also be able to stand on its own legs.

The first part of the chapter is dedicated to an overview of Dōgen's use of kōans, with an examination of the specific ways his approach was consistent with or different from other Chan and Zen masters of his day. In particular, I compare Dōgen's mode of meditating on kōans with the method of contemplating sayings attributed to Dahui and argue that the differences between them, while significant, are not as great as modern Japanese scholarship would lead us to expect. I also point out the ways Dōgen was unusual or unique in his treatment of kōans, such as his use of them to comment on and elucidate Indian Vinaya texts and Chinese monastic "rules of purity" (*shingi*).

In the second part of the chapter I demonstrate that, despite what "everybody knows" about Dōgen, he did not teach a method of meditation that he or his disciples called "just sitting." In his *Fukanzazengi* (*Universally Recommended Instructions for Zazen*) and other detailed written instructions for seated meditation, a practice that he clearly believed was an essential part of the Buddhist path, Dōgen never mentioned *shikantaza*. Whenever he did use the expression "just sit," he was actually quoting his teacher Tiantong Rujing (1163–1228). In almost every case, moreover, it is clear that he was using Rujing's dictum "just sit" as a kōan: a profound statement, uttered by an ancestral teacher, that was puzzling or opaque in some way and thus cried out for explanatory comment. In all of his extant writings there is but a single instance, in "Bendōwa" ("A Talk on Cultivating the Way"), where Dōgen used the words *simply sit* (*tadashi taza shite*) in a way that could possibly be taken literally as an injunction to devote oneself exclusively to zazen and forgo other conventional modes of Buddhist practice. Modern scholars have seized on the "Bendōwa" passage in question as proof that Dōgen taught what they call *shikantaza*, but it too is actually just Dōgen's translation into Japanese of Rujing's dictum, which in every other instance he quotes in the original Chinese and treats as a kōan. My analysis shows that the text of "Bendōwa" does not actually contain the teaching of *shikantaza* that latter-day scholars have tried to read into it.

Dōgen's Use of Kōans

Dōgen was familiar with the kōan collection compiled around 1141 by Dahui Zonggao entitled *Zhengfayanzang* in Chinese. He gave the same title to his own assemblage of three hundred kōans in Chinese,[4] as well as the now-famous set of approximately ninety-five essays that he wrote in classical Japanese, the *Shōbōgenzō*. It is clear from those writings and the *Eihei Kōroku* that, in many respects, his use of kōans followed a pattern already well established by numerous Chan masters in Song China who served as the abbots of major public monasteries.

For example, when he took the high seat in the dharma hall (*hattō*) for the rite of "ascending the hall" (*jōdō*), Dōgen frequently "raised" (*kyo*) kōans, posing rhetorical questions about those "old cases" (*kosoku*) that challenged his listeners to strive to penetrate their meaning and commenting on them to demonstrate his own understanding. He also wrote "verse commentaries on old cases" (*juko*) in the privacy of his own study, ninety of which are preserved in the form of a kōan collection that composes volume 9 of *Eihei Kōroku*. There are no records that show exactly how Dōgen employed kōans when instructing close disciples who entered his room in the abbot's quarters for individual consultation, but similar lacunae are the norm when it comes to the discourse records of most Chan and Zen masters of Song dynasty China and Kamakura Japan, including those who belonged to the Linji lineage in the generations following Dahui. It is clear nevertheless that Dōgen regarded kōan literature as a repository of wisdom left by the "buddhas and ancestors" (*busso*) in Bodhidharma's lineage, that he embraced and recommended the study of kōans as an essential part of Buddhist practice, and that kōan commentary was the principal device he used to instruct his own disciples.

Dōgen's numerous writings also leave no doubt that he distinguished between people who were "endowed with the eye" (*gugen*) of the dharma from those "not yet endowed with the eye" (*migugen*) and that he regarded the ability to "speak" (*dō*) or comment incisively on kōans as the best way of determining who had attained the way (*jōdō*) and who had not.

In those respects there is little to distinguish Dōgen from the many Chan masters of his day who employed kōan commentary as a device for instructing and evaluating others. There are other aspects of Dōgen's use of kōans, however, that do set him apart as an innovative thinker and teacher. In a number of chapters of his *Shōbōgenzō*, such as "Shinjin Gakudō" ("Studying the Way with Body and Mind"), "Kenbutsu" ("Seeing Buddha"), and "Shōhōjissō" ("True Marks of All Dharmas"), he illustrated and backed up points he wished to make by first citing a relevant passage from the *Lotus Sutra* (*Hokkekyō*). That he would rely on that scripture is not surprising, given its popularity in the Japanese Buddhism of the day and the fact that he and many of his followers had begun their careers as monks in the Tendai school. What is noteworthy about Dōgen's frequent use of the *Lotus Sutra*, however, is that he invariably explicated it by referring to Zen lore or by "attaching words" (*jakugo*) or "appending words" (*agyo*) that were drawn from kōans.

In "Kenbutsu," for example, he quoted a passage from the *Lotus Sutra*: "At that time, when the Buddha Sakyamuni was on Numinous Vulture Peak, Bhaisajya-raja Bodhisattva addressed the great assembly, saying: 'If one becomes close to the Dharma Master, one will attain the bodhisattva path. By practicing in accordance with this master, one will be able to see buddhas as innumerable as the sands of the Ganges.'"[5] Dōgen then commented as follows:

> The "becoming close to the Dharma Master" (*shingon hosshi*) that is spoken of [in the *Lotus Sutra*] is like the Second Ancestor's eight years of serving his teacher, after which he got the marrow of a whole arm; it is like Nanyue's fifteen years of pursuing the way. Getting the master's marrow is called [in the *Lotus Sutra*] "becoming close to" (*shingon*). When it [the *Lotus Sutra*] speaks of the "bodhisattva path" (*bosatsudō*), this is "I am also like this, you are also like this (*go yaku nyoze, jo yaku nyoze*)."[6]

"Getting the marrow" (*tokuzui* or *zui wo uru*) refers to the famous story in which Bodhidharma tested the understanding of his disciples and selected Huike (Eka) as the Second Ancestor (*niso*).[7] The expression "whole arm" (*zenhi*) is an ironic allusion to the well-known incident in which Huike demonstrated the sincerity of his way-seeking mind by cutting off his own arm and presenting it to Bodhidharma. The expression "I am also like this, you are also like this" (*go yaku nyoze, jo yaku nyoze*) is an allusion to a famous encounter dialogue that is said to have taken place between the Sixth Ancestor Huineng and his dharma heir, Nanyue Huairang (677–744).[8]

With this sort of commentary on passages from the *Lotus* and other Mahayana sutras, Dōgen consistently made the point that the Indian Buddha and the Chinese ancestral teachers, despite their different rhetorical styles, were all speaking about the same thing. In that respect his attitude toward the so-called teachings (*kyō*) that are named in the slogan "A separate transmission apart from the teachings" (*kyōge betsuden*) was similar to that of Chan masters such as Guifeng Zongmi (780–841), Yongming Yanshou (904–75), and Fori Qisong (1007–72), all of whom cautioned against taking the slogan as a literal rejection of sutra and commentarial literature.

Dōgen's use of kōans to comment on sutras was unusual in its frequency but not entirely unprecedented in the literature of Song Chan. He seems to have been unique, however, in his application of the same mode of commentary to monastic rules of the sort that are found in Chinese translations of the Indian Vinaya, commentaries on the Vinaya by Daoxuan (596–667), and the *Chanyuan Qingui* (*Rules of Purity for Chan Monasteries*), all of which he relied on to establish Song Chinese modes of Buddhist monastic discipline in Japan. The aforementioned genres of literature are entirely devoid of the sort of encounter dialogue (*kien mondō*) material that Chan is famous for, but that did not stop Dōgen from frequently citing kōans in his explanations of the ritual procedures laid out in those texts.

In his *Tenzokyōkun* (*Admonitions for the Chef*), for example, Dōgen interspersed direct quotations from the *Chanyuan Qingui* with famous kōans, as the following passage illustrates:

> The *Chanyuan Qingui* says: "If the six flavors are not refined and the three virtues are not provided, then it cannot be said that the chef has served the assembly." When examining the rice, first check for sand; when examining the sand [sifted from the rice], first check for rice. If you pay careful attention to detail, watching when coming and watching when going, then your mind cannot be scattered, and [the food] will naturally be replete with the three virtues and endowed with the six flavors. *When Xuefeng resided at Dongshan [monastery], he served as chef. One day when he was sifting rice [master] Dongshan asked him, "Are you sifting the sand and removing the rice, or sifting the rice and removing the sand?" Xuefeng said, "Sand and rice are simultaneously removed." Dongshan asked, "What will the great assembly eat?" Xuefeng overturned the bowl. Dongshan said, "In the future you will go and be scrutinized by someone else."* In the past, eminent men in possession of the way practiced in this way [as chefs], working energetically with their own hands. In this latter day, how can we who are so late getting started be negligent about this? The ancients said that chefs regard tying up their sleeves as the way-seeking mind. Lest there be any mistakes in the sifting out of rice and sand, you should examine it with your own hands. The *Chanyuan Qingui* says, "When preparing meals, one should reflect intimately on one's own self; [the food] will then of itself be pure and refined."[9]

The italicized part of this passage was often used as a kōan—a saying raised and commented on. That fact is clear from its appearance in the *Hongzhi Chanshi Guanglu* (*Extensive Record of Chan Master Hongzhi*), a record of the sayings of Hongzhi Zhengjue, and in the *Xutang Heshang Yulu* (*Discourse Record of Preceptor Xutang*), a record of the sayings of Xutang Zhiyu (1185–1269).[10]

Another passage from *Tenzokyōkun* exemplifies the way Dōgen seamlessly wove together explanations of monastic rules and comments on kōans:

> When cooking the vegetable side dishes for the morning gruel, also prepare the platters and tubs used for rice, soup, etc., as well as the various utensils and supplies that will be used for that day's midday meal. Wash them so that they are completely pure and clean, placing up high those that belong in high places and putting down low those that belong in low places. *High places high and level; low places low and level.* Treat utensils such as tongs and ladles, and all other implements and ingredients, with equal respect; handle all things with sincerity, picking them up and putting them down with courtesy.[11]

The italicized expression, "High places high and level; low places low and level," comes from a famous dialogue between Weishan Lingyou (771–853) and his disciple Yangshan Huiji (807–83) that appears, among other places, in the kōan collection *Congronglu*: "Guishan, inviting all [the monks to communal labor], was opening a field. Yangshan inquired, 'This part is so low, and that part is so high.' Gui said, 'Water can level things; we can just use water to level it.' Yang said, 'Water is unreliable. Preceptor, [we should] just [make] the high places high and level, and the low places low and level.' Gui assented."[12] Dōgen included this kōan in his collection known as *Shōbōgenzō Sanbyakusoku* (*Shōbōgenzō* in Three Hundred Cases), and we know from *Eihei Kōroku* that he raised and commented on it in dharma hall convocations. A slightly different version of the kōan was also used, in the same formal setting, by Dahui.[13]

In his Japanese-language *Shōbōgenzō*, too, Dōgen frequently used kōans to comment on standard practices such as sutra reading (Ch. *kanjing*, Jp. *kankin*), the holding of monastic retreats (*ango*), and leaving home to become a monk (*shukke*). In the chapter entitled "Senjō" ("Purifications"), which contains rules for using the toilet, he opened by stating: "There is a practice and verification (*shushō*) maintained and upheld by the buddhas and ancestors, which is called non-defilement (*fuzenna*)."[14]

Although written in classical Japanese, this is actually a paraphrase of the words attributed to the Sixth Ancestor Huineng in a famous "dialogue" (*mondō*) between him and his dharma heir, Nanyue Huairang, which Dōgen cited immediately following this opening sentence: "The [Sixth] Ancestor said, 'Precisely this non-defilement is the awareness that is maintained by all buddhas. You are also like this (*jo yaku nyo ze*), I am also like this (*go yaku nyo ze*), and the ancestors of India in the West are also like this.'"[15] Dōgen next quoted a Vinaya text: "The *Dabiqiu Sanqian Weii Jing* (*Sutra of Three Thousand Rules of Deportment for Fully Ordained Monks*) says: 'To purify the body is to wash after urinating and defecating, and to clip the nails of one's ten fingers.'"[16]

Then, having established the kōan as the frame of reference for explaining the Vinaya rules for purifying the body, Dōgen launched into his commentary, which begins, "This being so, even if body and mind are not defiled, there is a procedure for purifying the body and there is a procedure for the mind."[17] In other words, despite the fact that the buddhas and ancestors are fundamentally undefiled because they know that "there is not one thing" (*mu ichi motsu*), they still follow proper procedures for washing their bodies after using the toilet and proper procedures for regulating their minds as well.

In the chapter of *Shōbōgenzō* entitled "Kankin" ("Sutra Reading"), Dōgen quoted in their entirety and commented on ten different kōans that, in his view, shed some light on the significance of reading sutras and the attitude with which one should engage in that practice. The kōans in question include, for example, case 3 from the *Congronglu*, "The King of Eastern India Invites the Ancestor" (*Tōinshōso*); case 7 from the *Congronglu*, "Yueshan Takes the Dharma Seat" (*Yakusan Shinza*); and the story of Great Master Zhenji of the Kuanyin Cloister in Zhaozhou (*Jōshū Kannon'in Shinsai Daishi*) who "revolved the canon" (*tenzō*) by walking once around his own meditation seat, which is included as case 74 in Dōgen's *Shōbōgenzō Sanbyakusoku* and raised as a kōan in *Dahui Pujue Chanshi Yulu* (*Discourse Record of Chan Master Dahui Pujue*).[18]

To give an idea of how Dōgen dealt with such kōans, let us consider just one example from the "Kankin" chapter of *Shōbōgenzō*:

The Ancient Ancestor, Great Master Hongdao of Yueshan, ordinarily did not permit people to engage in sutra reading. One day he took hold of a sutra and perused it himself. A monk asked, "The reverend teacher ordinarily does not permit people to engage in sutra reading; why, on the contrary, are you yourself reading?" The master said, "As for me, I need only shield my eyes (*shagan*)." The monk said, "If I follow the method of the reverend teacher, will it work?" The master said, "If you were to read, even oxhide would be transparent!"[19]

Dōgen's commentary on this kōan reads as follows:

> This saying, "I need only shield my eyes," is the self-expression of one with shielded eyes. To shield the eyes is to forget the eyes; it is to forget the sutra; it is the shielding of the entire eye; it is to entirely shield the eye. To shield the eyes is to open the eyes while shielded; it is the living eye behind the shield; it is the living shield behind the eye; it is a layer of skin added to the skin of the eye; it is to hold up the eye behind the shield; it is the eye itself holding up the shield. Thus, if it is not the eye sutra (*ganzei kyō*), there is still no merit in shielding the eyes. As for "Even oxhide would be transparent," it is the hide of the entire ox; it is the ox of the entire hide; it is to hold up the ox and prepare the hide. For this reason, I regard the skin, flesh, bones, and marrow (*hi niku kotsu zui*), the horns on the head, and the nose as the livelihood of the cow. In following the method of the reverend teacher, to shield the eyes is for the ox to function as eyes. It is for the eyes to function as the ox.[20]

This is quite typical of Dōgen's exuberant style of kōan commentary. Whatever else we might say about his remarks, it is clear that he subscribes to the premise of this particular old case, which is that some people (like the Great Master Hongdao of Yueshan) can read sutras without deluded attachment, but others cannot.

To summarize Dōgen's dealings with kōans, he not only employed them in a conventional manner that had been established by numerous Chan masters in Song China, but he also used them without restraint in a way that was virtually unprecedented: as tools for commenting on Buddhist monastic rules. To the best of my knowledge, no other Chan or Zen master in China or Japan ever juxtaposed Vinaya texts and "rules of purity" with kōan literature in that way. That Dōgen did so is further testimony to his belief that the ancestral teachers in the lineage of Bodhidharma transmitted the true dharma of the Buddha Sakyamuni in its entirety, and that their distinctive mode of expression, couched in colloquial Chinese, embodied the same insights as those manifested in the sutras and Vinaya rules preached by the Buddha. Dōgen's mixing of genres helped to bring otherwise dry prescriptions of monastic procedure and etiquette to life and bestow them with spiritual significance. By the same token it familiarized his Japanese followers with the rhetorical conventions of the Chan dialogue literature, rendering that difficult material more accessible by placing it in concrete, practical contexts.

One thing that Dōgen did not do with kōans, however, was to use them as objects of contemplation in the manner recommended by Dahui. That Chan master advocated fixing the mind on the "keyword" of an old case, such as the single word "none" (*mu*) in the famous kōan "Zhaozhou's Dog" (*Jōshū kushi*), in which the master famously answered "None"—more precisely, "Does not have" or "There is none"—when asked if even a dog has buddha-nature. Dahui said that practitioners should concentrate on such a keyword without cease, in the midst of seated meditation and all other activities, until intellection is exhausted and all that remains is a great ball of doubt. They should then intensify that doubt until a breakthrough experience occurs—an awakening in which all doubts are said to be removed. Dōgen did not advocate such an approach, which modern scholars have dubbed "the Zen of contemplating sayings," nor did he ever speak directly against it. Indeed although Dōgen certainly knew Dahui as an eminent ancestor in the Linji branch of the Chan lineage who was worthy of emulation, there is nothing in his writings that suggests he was aware of any special meditation techniques attributed to Dahui. The evidence of one Japanese monk who visited Song China some sixty years after Dahui's death is hardly conclusive, but if the method of "intensifying doubt" was so widespread at the time, one wonders why Dōgen does not seem to have heard of it.

Modern Sōtō school scholars hold that Dōgen was critical of Rinzai monks who practiced Buddhism for the sake of an awakening experience, citing the following passage from the "Daigo" ("Great Awakening") chapter of his *Shōbōgenzō* as evidence:

> Recently, shavepates in the Land of the Great Song say, "Awakening to the way (*godō*) is the basic expectation (*hongo*)." So saying, they vainly await awakening (*itazura no taigo su*). Nevertheless, they seem not to be illumined by the radiance of the buddhas and ancestors. Given over to laziness (*randa*), they miss (*shaka*) the fact that they should just make inquiries (*sanshu*) of a true good friend. Even during the advent of the old buddhas, they would probably not have been liberated (*dodatsu*).[21]

The expression "await awakening" (*taigo*), as noted earlier, is used by Sōtō partisans today as a criticism of the Rinzai school's Zen of contemplating sayings, but it is highly unlikely that Dōgen himself actually had Dahui or his epigones in mind when he criticized Chinese monks who "vainly await awakening." After all, what Dahui emphasized was an intense, single-minded effort to induce awakening by focusing on the keyword of a kōan. What Dōgen scorned in the passage just quoted was not contemplation of the sayings (*kanna*) of the ancestors; it was laziness on the part of monks who failed to make inquiries of a good teacher and thereby missed the opportunity to gain liberation. As a matter of fact Dōgen very often used the verb "to inquire" as an exhortation to his disciples to investigate and penetrate the meaning of some phrase taken from a kōan. Thus, if anything, the passage above would seem to align Dōgen's approach with that of Dahui.

Rujing's "Just Sit"

In the chapter that stands as a precursor to the present one—"Just Sitting? Dōgen's Take on Zazen, Sutra Reading, and Other Conventional Buddhist Practices"—I present a detailed analysis of every instance in which the phrase "just sit" appears in Dōgen's extant writings and discourse records. One key point I make is that every time Dōgen used that phrase he was not speaking for himself but was in fact quoting his teacher Tiantong Rujing.

For example, in *Hōkyōki* (*Record of the Hōkyō Era*), Dōgen's record of his interactions with Rujing in China, he recalled the following exchange:

> The reverend abbot [Rujing] said, "Studying Zen is body and mind sloughed off (*sanchan zhe shenxin tuoluo ye*). Make no use of burning incense, prostrations, buddha-mindfulness, repentances, or sutra reading. Just sit and that is all (*qiguan dazuo er yi*)."
> I [Dōgen] respectfully enquired, "What is 'body and mind sloughed off'?" The reverend abbot said, "'Body and mind sloughed off' (Ch. *shenxin tuoluo*, Jp. *shinjin datsuraku*) is seated meditation. When one just sits in meditation (*qiguan zuochan*), one is separated from the five desires and rid of the five obstructions."[22]

Rujing's words in this context could perhaps be taken as a literal rejection of any conventional Buddhist practices other than seated meditation, but as I point out in my detailed analysis of *Hōkyōki*, Dōgen could not have construed them in that way.[23] Why not? Because in the very same exchange Rujing also stressed the importance of studying both Mahayana and the Hinayana sutras, which of course would entail sutra reading. In another dialogue recorded in *Hōkyōki*, moreover, Rujing explicitly criticized the name "Chan (Zen) lineage" (Ch. *chanzong*, Jp. *zenshū*) on the grounds that it wrongly implied the exclusive practice of zazen.

In that connection Rujing recommended that Dōgen read the *Shimen Linjianlu* (*Shimen's Record of the Monastic Groves*), a work completed in 1107 by Juefan Huihong (1071–1128), alias Shimen, a monk who belonged to the Huanglong branch of the Linji lineage. Huihong held that Bodhidharma was not merely a "practitioner of *dhyana*" (Ch. *xichan*, Jp. *shūzen*) but also a sage who embraced the full range of practices: the six perfections, of which *dhyana* was but one. In Huihong's view, what Bodhidharma transmitted was not any single practice but rather the buddha-mind itself: the awakening of the Buddha Sakyamuni. That Dōgen followed Rujing's advice to read the *Shimen Linjianlu*, and that he agreed with Huihong, is clear from his citation of and commentary on that work in the "Butsudō" ("Buddha-Way") chapter of *Shōbōgenzō*.[24]

Another, even more compelling reason to conclude that Dōgen did not take literally Rujing's injunction to "just sit" is the fact that all the practices named by Rujing as unnecessary—burning incense (Ch. *shaoxiang*, Jp. *shōkō*), prostrations (Ch. *libai*, Jp. *raihai*), buddha-mindfulness (Ch. *nianfo*, Jp. *nenbutsu*), repentances (Ch. *xiuchan*, Jp. *shusan*), and sutra reading—were explicitly endorsed and promoted by Dōgen in a number of his other works, often with much attention to their religious meaning and the ritual details of their performance. That is a fact that I thoroughly document under the heading "Conventional Buddhist Practices Embraced by Dōgen" in the chapter that stands as a precursor to the present one.[25]

A question that arises then is why, if Dōgen was not offering it as practical advice to his disciples, did he repeatedly invoke Rujing's admonition to "just sit"? He himself must have experienced that injunction as odd and startling when he first heard it during his stay in China, for all of the practices that Rujing seemed to dismiss as unnecessary were actually part of the ordinary routine at the Jingde Monastery (Keitokuji) on Mount Tiantong (Tendōzan), the place where Dōgen met and interacted with Rujing, who served as abbot between 1225 and his death in 1228. The practices in question were a matter of long-standing tradition within the Chinese Buddhist sangha, and they were stipulated by detailed monastic rules and procedural guidelines that Dōgen himself transmitted to Japan and implemented in the monasteries he founded there.

In my view the reason that Dōgen repeatedly cited Rujing's saying "Just sit" was because it was startling and enigmatic but at the same time necessarily imbued with some profound meaning, having issued from the mouth of an awakened Chan master. In short, Dōgen used Rujing's "Just sit" as a kōan, which he raised in various pedagogical contexts (including live debates and written works) as a topic for contemplation and interpretation. For instance, in volume 9 (case 85) of *Eihei Kōroku*, a collection of verse commentaries on old cases, Dōgen selected Rujing's saying as a kōan to be commented on.[26] In the chapter of *Shōbōgenzō* entitled "Bukkyō" ("Sutras [Spoken] by Buddha"), to cite but one other example, he quoted Rujing as follows: "My former master [Rujing] always said, 'In my place here, make no use of burning incense, prostrations, buddha-mindfulness, repentances, or sutra reading. Just sit, make a concentrated effort to pursue the way (Ch. *biandao gongfu*, Jp. *bendō kufū*), and body and mind will be sloughed off.' "[27] Here again the fact that Dōgen left the quotation in the original Chinese, which his Japanese disciples could read but would not have been able to understand if they heard it spoken, shows that he was treating it as an established old case. His subsequent comment, written in Japanese, reads as follows:

> Those who understand such words [of Rujing] are rare. Why is that? Because if one reads the words "sutra reading" and takes them to mean sutra reading, one butts one's head against them, but if one reads them and does not take them to mean sutra reading, one turns one's back on them.[28] "You must not have anything to say, and you must not lack anything to say. Speak quickly! Speak quickly!"[29] You should investigate this principle. It is due to this essential point that a man of old said, "For reading sutras one must be equipped with the eye for reading sutras."[30] You should know that if there were no sutras in the past or in the present there could be no words such as these. You should investigate the fact that there is "sloughed off sutra reading" and there is "sutra reading of which one makes no use."[31]

A point I wish to emphasize here is that Dōgen explicitly stated that Rujing's dictum, "Just sit ... etc.," is a saying that few people can comprehend and that it should be rigorously investigated (*sangaku*). In short, he urged contemplation (*kan*) of the saying (*wa*), up to the point when the practitioner can understand (*satoru*) it and "speak quickly" (*hayaku iu*) to demonstrate that understanding.

Given that Dōgen undeniably treated Rujing's "Just sit" as a kōan in these and other contexts, a question that remains is this: How did he interpret the meaning of the saying? As I show in my previously published analysis of Dōgen's commentary on the kōan that appears in the chapter of *Shōbōgenzō* entitled "Zanmai Ō Zanmai" ("King of Samadhis Samadhi"), he allowed that the verb "to sit" (Ch. *dazuo*, Jp. *taza*) had a number of different meanings.[32] In the first place there is the "sitting of the body" (*mi no taza*), which presumably refers to the physical posture of zazen. What he called "mental sitting" (*kokoro no taza*), then, would be a kind of concentrated state of mind that could be cultivated in any posture, whatever the practitioner is doing. When the practitioner is no longer attached to any physical or mental phenomena, however, that liberated or awakened state is referred to by Dōgen as the "sitting of the body and mind sloughed off" (*shinjin datsuraku no taza*). In light of this I conclude that Dōgen interpreted Rujing's admonition to "just sit" as an injunction to "just gain awakening." As such, to "just sit" would not preclude any particular

Buddhist practice but would be the correct understanding, free from attachment, with which to undertake all practices (including zazen).

Modern scholars who hold that Dōgen taught a particular mode of meditation practice called "just sitting" invariably offer up the evidence of a single
passage from "Bendōwa," a work that Dōgen wrote in Japanese in 1231, after
his return from China in 1227: "From the start of your consultation with a
wise teacher, have no recourse whatsoever to burning incense, prostrations,
buddha-mindfulness, repentances, or sutra reading. Simply (*tadashi*) sit (*taza
shite*) and attain the sloughing off of body and mind (*shinjin datsuraku suru
koto wo eyo*)."³³ This passage, of course, was not something that Dōgen came
up with on his own. It was rather his rendition into Japanese of the Chinese
saying that, in a number of other contexts, he explicitly attributed to his
teacher Rujing. The quotation of Rujing that appears in *Shōbōgenzō* "Zanmai
Ō Zanmai" provides a good basis for comparison: "My former master, the old
buddha (Rujing) said: 'Studying Zen is body and mind sloughed off. Just sit;
only then will you get it (*qiguan dazuo shide*). You do not need to burn incense,
make prostrations, recollect buddhas, practice repentance, or read sutras.' "³⁴
When Dōgen rendered the Chinese words *qiguan dazuo* into Japanese in
"Bendōwa," he translated them as "just (*tadashi*) sit (*taza shite*)." That is to say,
he took the word *qiguan* (Jp. *shikan*) as an adverb that modifies the verb "to sit"
and translated it using the Japanese adverb "just" (*tadashi*). My point here is
that Dōgen definitely did not understand the expression *shikantaza* as a single
noun (i.e., the name of a particular mode of meditation practice) of the sort
that we could accurately translate into English as "just sitting."

It is also significant that Dōgen understood Rujing to mean that "body and
mind sloughed off" is a particular state to be "attained" (Ch. *de*, Jp. *toku/eru*)
by sitting in meditation. That Dōgen took the expression "body and mind
sloughed off" as a noun is demonstrated by the fact that in "Bendōwa" he used
a gerundial form in Japanese—"the sloughing off of body and mind" (*shinjin
datsuraku suru koto*)—and marked it with the particle *wo* to identify it as the
object of the verb "to attain." In Dōgen's Japanese, moreover, the verb appears
in the imperative voice—"[you] should attain (*eyo*)"—which suggests that a
practitioner should sit in meditation with the intention (or for the purpose) of
gaining awakening. That, too, is not at all consistent with the modern scholarly definition of *shikantaza*.

One of Dōgen's aims in "Bendōwa" was to promote the practice of seated
meditation, which he extolled in the text as the "dharma gate that is easy and
joyful" (*anraku no hōmon*) and described as the "marvelous means" (*myōjutsu*)
used by all the buddhas and ancestors to "open awakening" (*kaigo*). The expression "mind and body sloughed off" (*shinjin datsuraku*), in Dōgen's usage, is a

synonym for *satori* or awakening (*go*). The main thrust of "Bendōwa," therefore, is not at all consistent with the modern notion that, in zazen as Dōgen taught it, there is nothing to be gained.

It is true that, elsewhere in "Bendōwa," Dōgen criticized the notion that "pursuing the way in seated meditation" (*zazen bendō*) is a means of gaining realization (*shō wo toru*) that can be dispensed with once a person has "clarified the buddhas' true dharma" (*butsu shōbō wo akirame*). Such an understanding, he said, is a "non-Buddhist view" (*gedō no ken*). The true teaching of the buddhas (*buppō*), he stressed, is that "practice and realization are coeval" (*shushō kore ittō*), which is to say, realization does not come after practice: it informs practice from the very start and is lost when practice ceases. Thus, Dōgen explained, even a beginner's pursuit of the way (*shoshin no bendō*) is the complete embodiment of original realization (*honshō no zentai*), and even the buddhas and ancestors do not stop pursuing the way in seated meditation.[35] However, just because Dōgen viewed practice and realization as coeval does not mean, as many modern scholars have assumed, that he denied any cause-and-effect relationship between them or that he disavowed realization as a goal of practice. The undeniable fact remains that, in "Bendōwa," he recommended the practice (*bendō*) of zazen as the marvelous means of opening awakening.

Among Dōgen's extensive writings on various aspects of Buddhist monastic discipline and religious practices, there are a few works that do not merely mention seated meditation or "sitting" (*taza*) in passing or treat it in the context of some broader discussion but focus directly and exclusively on that mode of practice. The works in question, which Carl Bielefeldt calls "Dōgen's manuals of Zen meditation,"[36] include two recensions of *Fukanzazengi*; the "Zazenhō" ("Procedures for Zazen") section of *Bendōhō* (*Procedures for Cultivating the Way*); and the "Zazengi" ("Principles of Zazen") and "Zazenshin" ("Lancet of Zazen") chapters of *Shōbōgenzō*. If, as modern scholars claim, "just sitting" was a distinctive mode of meditation practice taught by Dōgen, one would expect to find it featured prominently in those texts. In point of fact the word *shikantaza* does not appear in any of them.

Nevertheless there is a recurring phrase in Dōgen's meditation manuals that modern scholars have seized upon and made the centerpiece of their explications of "Dōgen's *shikantaza*." That phrase is "Do not figure to make a buddha" (*sabutsu wo zu suru koto nakare*).[37] Although the verb *sa* generally means "to make" or "to activate," in Dōgen's usage the idea is that one should not try to make *oneself* into a buddha—that is, one should not try to "become a buddha" (*sabutsu*)—by means of seated meditation.[38] To engage in zazen without "planning on" (*zu su*) becoming a buddha, modern scholars hold, is precisely what Dōgen had in when mind when he advocated "just sitting."

There is some merit to that view insofar as Dōgen used Rujing's dictum "Just sit" as code for an awakened state in which "body and mind are sloughed off" and one is free from deluded attachment to imaginary entities or outcomes even while actively engaged in a full range of Buddhist practices. It is quite another thing, however, to claim (as modern Sōtō scholars do) that Dōgen regarded "just sitting" in zazen as a practice that is entirely "without purpose" (*mui*) or in which there is literally "nothing to be gained." It is also a huge, unjustified leap to take Dōgen's remonstrations against awaiting awakening and "figuring to make a buddha" (*sabutsu wo zu su*) as attacks on the Rinzai practice of contemplating kōans in the midst of seated meditation. We have already seen that, in "Bendōwa," Dōgen described zazen as a "marvelous means" used by all the buddhas and ancestors to "open awakening" and that in *Shōbōgenzō Daigo* his criticism of monks who "vainly await awakening" was directed against their "laziness" and failure to gain liberation, not their use of kōans.

The modern conceit that Dōgen's criticism of "figuring to make a buddha" was an attack on the Rinzai use of kōans is also problematic for another, more ironic reason: that very expression is drawn from a famous kōan featuring an exchange between Mazu Daoyi (709–88) and his teacher Nanyue Huairang. As that story goes, Mazu was an assiduous practitioner of seated meditation. Nanyue, recognizing the young monk's great potential, asked him, "What are you figuring to do, sitting there in meditation?" Mazu answered, "I'm figuring to make a buddha" (*zu sabutsu*). Nanyue thereupon picked up a tile and began to rub it on a stone. When Mazu asked him what he was doing, he said, "I'm polishing this to make a mirror."[39]

Some modern scholars, mostly Rinzai school proponents of the Zen of contemplating sayings (e.g., Yanagida Seizan), have held this story up as evidence of an actual rejection of seated meditation by Buddhist monks who flourished during the "golden age" of Tang dynasty Chan, but the preponderance of historical evidence does not support such a conclusion. Dōgen cited the kōan frequently in his writings and commented on it at great length in *Shōbōgenzō Zazengi*.[40] His take, as one might expect from all the evidence adduced thus far in this chapter, was that the practice of zazen is essential to the Buddhist path, but there is a right way and a wrong way of understanding it. In Dōgen's explication, even Mazu's words "I'm figuring to make a buddha" are not necessarily a sign of deluded attachment: it all depends on the spirit in which they were uttered. Dōgen actually absolved Mazu of the error that he attributed to other Chinese monks who spoke of striving for buddhahood.

The term "await awakening" appears only once in *Shōbōgenzō*, in the passage from "Daigo" that I cite earlier. It does, however, occur again in *Eihei Kōroku*: "The seated meditation of the various schools makes awaiting awakening the norm. [They say that] it is like availing oneself of a raft to cross a great ocean: once one has crossed the ocean, one should let go of the boat. The seated meditation of our buddhas and ancestors is not like this; it is the activity of a buddha."[41] This passage, like the one from "Daigo," suggests that the real target of Dōgen's criticisms of awaiting awakening and figuring to make a Buddha were contemporary monks who held that zazen was a practice for beginners on the path, but that it was not necessary for those who had already attained the way.

That impression is confirmed in *Shōbōgenzō Zazenshin*, where Dōgen states:

> Let it be known: a mode of investigation established for practicing the way is cultivating the way in zazen. The essential point that serves as its emblem is [the understanding that] there is a practicing buddha who does not seek to become a buddha. Because a practicing buddha does not go on to become a buddha, this is a clear-cut case. An embodied buddha does not go on to become a buddha. When the nets and cages are ripped open, a sitting buddha does not go on to interfere with becoming a buddha. At that very moment, simultaneously with one thousand or ten thousand ages past, from the start there is the power to enter into Buddha or enter into Mara.[42]

The thrust of the argument here is that if zazen were merely a means of becoming a buddha, then a real-life "embodied buddha" (*shinbutsu*) or "practicing buddha" (*gyōbutsu*)—this must refer at least to Sakyamuni—would no longer practice zazen. The undeniable fact that Sakyamuni *did* practice zazen even after attaining buddhahood proves, in Dōgen's view, that zazen is more than just a means; it is the very "activity of a buddha" (*butsugyō*).

It does not follow from this, however, that pursuing the way in seated meditation was never a means for "becoming a buddha" in Dōgen's estimation. After all, until the "nets and cages are ripped open" (*rarō taha*), as Dōgen put it, the practitioner of zazen is still a deluded sentient being, not a "sitting buddha" (*zabutsu*). For beginners, Dōgen seems to be saying, zazen *can* be a means to attain awakening, even if it is not such a means for the buddhas who engage in it. There can be no doubt that Dōgen stressed a kind of "rigorous investigation" (*sankyū*) that called for great exertion at the outset. Without some notion of a goal to be attained, he suggests in his commentary on Mazu's "I'm figuring to make a buddha," very few people would rouse themselves to make such an effort. Mazu's saying, as Dōgen interprets it, can be seen as an expedient device, even if it is ultimately false. Moreover "a sitting buddha does not go on to interfere with becoming a buddha" (*zabutsu sara ni sabutsu wo saezu*). In other words, from the awakened point of view that Dōgen espoused, neither the aspiration to become a buddha nor its opposite, a rejection of the idea of becoming a buddha, had any ultimate validity, although either might prove useful as a motivational tool or corrective device.

Conclusion

A central point of this chapter is that Dōgen did not actually teach the practice of "just sitting" as that is understood and ascribed to him in modern scholarship. "Just sitting" is sometimes taken to mean a single-minded focus on seated meditation, to the exclusion of other conventional Buddhist practices, but that is certainly not what Dōgen taught. He did stress the importance of zazen, but only within the balanced framework of the three fundamental modes of practice (*sangaku*): morality (*kai*), concentration (*jō*), and wisdom (*e*). "Just sitting" is also characterized as a mode of Zen practice (the Sōtō brand) that does not make use of kōans and renounces the goal of attaining awakening or liberation, but neither of those are accurate descriptions of Dōgen's approach. He regarded sutras and kōan literature alike as the wise sayings of the buddhas and ancestors, and he urged his followers to read and contemplate them as a means of attaining awakening.

Citing Dōgen's own writings and discourse records as proof, I have demonstrated in this chapter and the one that precedes it that he used the saying in which Rujing admonished his follower to "just sit" as a kōan, not as any kind of practical advice that was meant to be taken literally. It is the failure to recognize "Just sit" as a kōan, of course, that has enabled modern scholars to construe "just sitting" as a mode of practice taught by Dōgen that rejects the contemplation of kōans. That conviction, in turn, blinds them to all the textual evidence that Dōgen not only used "Just sit" as a kōan but that he actually employed numerous kōans and used commentary on them (and by means of them) as a primary teaching device.

These findings cut the ground out from under much of the modern scholarly assessment of Dōgen's teachings and the role he played as the putative founder of the Sōtō Zen school in Japan. In my view neither the orthodox Sōtō vision of a Dōgen who rejected the contemplation of kōans and advocated the exclusive practice of zazen nor the Rinzai caricature of a Dōgen who was sunk in the torpor of "just sitting" and cared nothing for awakening succeeds in capturing the spirit of the lively, imaginative, cranky, and brilliant Zen master who jumps off the pages of *Shōbōgenzō* and the *Eihei Kōroku*.

I have demonstrated in this chapter that Dōgen did not teach the practice of "just sitting" as that is understood by modern scholarship, but I have not addressed the question of when that practice (or rather the conception of it) came into existence. I initially thought that it may have been formulated as part of the reinvention of Dōgen's Zen that took place in the Edo period, spearheaded by Sōtō monk scholars such as Manzan Dōhaku (1636–1715) and Menzan Zuihō (1683–1769). That was in fact a time when reform-minded proponents of both the Sōtō and Rinzai traditions began to argue that there was a significant disparity in their respective use of kōans. A preliminary search of Menzan's writings, however, suggests that he was not at all concerned with anything called "just sitting." Another hypothesis, which I have not attempted to confirm in any systematic way, is that the notion of "just sitting" may have been conceived during the Meiji and Taishō (1912–26) eras, a time when Sōtō scholars were not only inclined to distinguish Dōgen from his Rinzai contemporaries who used kōans but were keen to absolve him of any involvement in "superstitious" religious beliefs and practices.

NOTES

1. The expression was coined in modern Japan; it is not found in premodern Chinese sources.
2. I use the roman letters *shikantaza* (one word, a gerundive noun, no space) when the meaning is "just sitting," and the roman *shikan taza* (two words, an adverb and a verb, separated by a space) when the meaning is "just sit."
3. T. Griffith Foulk, "Just Sitting? Dōgen's Take on Zazen, Sutra Reading, and Other Conventional Buddhist Practices," in Steven Heine, ed., *Dōgen: Textual and Historical Studies* (New York: Oxford University Press, 2012), 75–106.
4. Modern scholars refer to this kōan collection, which is devoid of any commentary by Dōgen himself, as the *Shinji Shōbōgenzō* (*Shōbōgenzō* in Chinese Characters) or *Shōbōgenzō Sanbyakusoku* (*Shōbōgenzō* in Three Hundred Cases).
5. T 82.223b1–2.
6. T 82.223b4–8.
7. The first three disciples to speak are said to have gotten Bodhidharma's skin (*hi*), flesh (*niku*), and bones (*kotsu*), respectively. Huike, who bowed and said nothing, "got the marrow" (*tokuzui*).
8. The dialogue appears as case 101 in Dōgen's *Shōbōgenzō Sanbyakusoku* (*Shōbōgenzō* in Three Hundred Cases; DZZ-2 5:178, case 101):

> Chan Master Dahui of Mount Nanyue went to inquire of the Sixth Ancestor. The Ancestor said, "Where have you come from?" The Master said, "From the place of National Teacher An on Mount Song." The Ancestor said, "What sort of thing comes in this way?" The Master could not handle this [question], but he kept it

in mind and attended upon [the Ancestor] for eight years, during which time he reflected on the foregoing dialogue. Then he addressed the Ancestor, saying, "Huairang [I] have understood [the question] Your Reverence greeted me with when I first came here: "What sort of thing comes in this way?" The Ancestor said, "What do you make of it?" The Master said, "If I were to say it resembles one thing, I would thereby miss the mark." The Ancestor said, "Well then, would you provisionally allow 'practice and verification,' or not?" The Master said, "Even if 'practice and verification' are not non-existent, still I am not susceptible to defilement." The Ancestor said, "Precisely this non-defilement is the awareness that is maintained by all buddhas. You are also like this, I am also like this, and the ancestors of India in the West are also like this."

9. T 82.320b2–11.
10. T 48.34a7–13; T 47.1051b11–17.
11. T 82.320b14–19.
12. T 48.240b16–19.
13. T 47.824b9–16.
14. T 82.30a4–5.
15. T 82.30a8–10.
16. This is a direct quote of a line in the *Dabiqiu Sanqian Weii Jing* (*Sutra of Three Thousand Rules of Deportment for Fully Ordained Monks*), a Vinaya text translated by An Shigao, who was active from 148 to 170 CE (T 24.914a16).
17. T 82.30a13–14.
18. T 48.229a12–18; T 48.231b9–14; T 47.849b11–15.
19. This story, quoted by Dōgen in the original Chinese, appears in biographies of Yueshan found in the *Zutangji* (*Ancestors Hall Collection*), *Jingde Chuandenglu* (*Jingde Record of the Transmission of the Flame*); T 51.312b5–8), and *Zongmen Liandeng Huiyao* (*Collated Essentials of the Consolidated Flame* [*Records*] *of Our* [*Chan*] *School*); X 79.164a14–16). The story also occurs as a topic for commentary (i.e., a kōan) in the discourse records of a number of Song Chan masters, such as the *Fenyang Heshang Yulu* (*Discourse Record of Reverend Fenyang*; ZZ 120.122a1–3) and the *Xutang Heshang Yulu* (*Discourse Record of Reverend Xutang*; T 47.1005c1–3).
20. T 82.89c11–21.
21. T 82.115c18–23, translation by Carl Bielefeldt, Soto Zen Text Project, accessed July 3, 2013, http://scbs.stanford.edu/sztp3/.
22. My translation is based on the edition of the text found in Takashi James Kodera, *Dōgen's Formative Years in China: An Historical Study and Annotated Translation of the "Hōkyō-ki"* (Boulder, CO: Prajna Press, 1980), 236–37.
23. Foulk, "Just Sitting?," 88–91.
24. T 82.182c12–28.
25. Foulk, "Just Sitting?," 77–88.

26. For a translation of Rujing's saying and Dōgen's verse commentary, together with my analysis of the meaning of the latter, see Foulk, "Just Sitting?," 94–95.

27. T 82.195b1–3.

28. That is, by seizing on the literal meaning of "sutra reading" one commits an error of interpretation, but it is also a mistake to ignore the literal meaning.

29. This quotation comes from case 43 of the *Mumonkan* (*Gateless Barrier*, Ch. *Wumenguan;* T 48.298b19). The first sentence also appears in the *Tendōzan Keitokuji Nyojō Zenji Goroku* (*Discourse Record of Chan Master Rujing of Jingde Monastery on Mount Tiantong;* T 48:129a17).

30. This quotation comes from the *Yunmen Guanglu* (*Extensive Record of Yunmen;* T 47.572c4).

31. T 82.195b3–11.

32. Foulk, "Just Sitting?," 99–100.

33. T 82.15c28–16a1.

34. T 82.243c17–19.

35. T 82.18b22–c29.

36. Carl Bielefeldt, *Dōgen's Manuals of Zen Meditation* (Berkeley: University of California Press, 1988), 174–205.

37. The phrase appears in the *Kōroku* edition of *Fukanzazengi*, in the "Zazengi" chapter of *Shōbōgenzō*, and in slightly reworded form in the "Zazenshin" chapter of *Shōbōgenzō*, which speaks of "not seeking to make a buddha" (*sabutsu wo motomezaru*).

38. That *sabutsu* means "to become a buddha" is clearly attested from the contexts in which the term appears. In the Zen tradition the ultimate attainment for practitioners is often referred to as "becoming a buddha and making [oneself into] an ancestor" (*jōbutsu saso*). In that context the characters *jō* and *sa* are used synonymously.

39. Dōgen includes this kōan as case 8 in his *Sanbyakusoku* (DZZ-2 5:128). It appears in many Chan texts, including the *Jingde Record of the Transmission of the Flame* (T 51.240c19–124).

40. DZZ-2 1:103ff.

41. *Eihei Kōroku*, DZZ-2 4:164 (*hōgo* 11), translation by Bielefeldt.

42. T 82.117a2–9.

2

"Raihaitokuzui" and Dōgen's Views of Gender and Women

A RECONSIDERATION

Miriam L. Levering

WAS DŌGEN A "great manly hero" who proclaimed a profound affirmation to awakened persons of all genders? Or was he a Zen teacher who, when speaking of women's value, compared women to trees and walls? Dōgen's views of gender and women deserve another look.

In this chapter I look at Dōgen's teachings as they relate to women in three of his essays and in *Eihei Kōroku* (*Eihei Dōgen's Extensive Record*). One essay is an independent work, and the other two are from the various collections of Dōgen's writings that are called *The Treasury of the True Dharma Eye* (or *The True Dharma Eye Storehouse; Shōbōgenzō*). The first, the "Talk about Wholeheartedly Pursuing the Way" ("Bendōwa"),[1] should be considered an independent work, although it was belatedly included in the ninety-five-fascicle Honzan edition of the *Shōbōgenzō* compiled in 1815. The second essay, "Bowing [to a Teacher] and Getting [the Teacher's] Marrow" ("Raihaitokuzui"), has been included in most recensions of the *Shōbōgenzō*, although only the "short" version is attested by more than one manuscript; for this reason I will confine my discussion here to the short version and discuss in another essay the additional material in the long version.[2] Finally, the essay "The Merit of Leaving Home [and Becoming a Monastic]" ("Shukke Kudoku")[3] was included in the sixty-fascicle edition of which a 1381 copy exists, in the twelve-fascicle *Shōbōgenzō* (for which a manuscript copy dated 1420 exists), as well as in the Edo-period Honzan edition.

While *Eihei Kōroku* contains writings from all stages of Dōgen's career, the three essays are thought to represent different Dōgens from different periods. Where they touch on women and lay people they seem to contradict each other. In such a manner there are created the interpretive problems I address in this chapter.

In Steven Heine's schema in his book *Did Dōgen Go to China?*, "Bendōwa" belongs to Dōgen's very early writings; in fact it is very likely the first written record of his teachings.[4] "Raihaitokuzui" belongs to the "early middle" or "transitional" period. "Shukke Kudoku" is regarded as a revision of an earlier essay called "Leaving Home" ("Shukke"). Scholars date this and most—but not all—of the twelve essays included in the twelve-fascicle *Shōbōgenzō* (hereafter *Jūnikanbon*) to the last few years of Dōgen's life.

I have placed "Raihaitokuzui" at the center of this discussion because in my view it is the text in which Dōgen very deliberately presents his views on women and gender in a thoroughgoing manner. A comparison of "Raihaitokuzui" with each of the other texts will allow me to lay out a number of connected aspects of his views. I intend to compare Dōgen's views as expressed in the three essays and *Eihei Kōroku* with each other. But in all cases I will also trace his views to China and compare his versions with versions he most likely learned there.

"Raihaitokuzui" and "Bendōwa"

In an essay published in the *Journal of the International Association of Buddhist Studies* in 1999, I attempted to broaden the context of the discussion of Dōgen and women by pointing out in some detail that in the areas of China in which Dōgen (may have) spent four years studying Chan, a small but significant number of nuns and lay women had already won recognition within widely read Chan lineage genealogical literature as awakened dharma heirs.[5] A few nuns and laywomen had won recognition as Chan teachers, and those nuns had themselves produced widely recognized female dharma heirs. A larger number of nuns and lay women received "dharma instructions" (Ch. *fayu*, Jp. *hōgo*) from eminent male Chan teachers, a sign of a substantial teacher-disciple relationship in which the disciple is actually practicing Chan. Many more nuns and lay women visited the temples of and interacted with famous Chan teachers, forming a teacher-disciple relationship with them. I pointed out that Dōgen, who had traveled to China, could well have been aware of this, and that to him the Japanese sangha of his day—in which there were no fully ordained nuns and where Tendai and Shingon, the large, established practice schools, did not welcome women to their monasteries on Mount Hiei and Kōyasan—must have looked quite different from what he had seen and heard about in China.

After he returned from Song China in 1227 as an heir to Rujing's dharma, Dōgen stayed for a few years at Kenninji, the Tendai temple founded by Eisai, where he had originally become a disciple of the Zen teacher Myōzen. There he wrote "Bendōwa."[6] "Bendōwa" is a beautiful essay, setting out the reasons why Dōgen advocated seated meditation (zazen) as a new primary practice.[7] It includes (and in some versions entirely consists of) questions and answers, both penned by Dōgen. Women and gender come up only in the following exchanges.

The fictional questioner asks, "Can this practice [zazen] be done by men and women in lay life, or is it only suitable for monks?" Dōgen answers, "The [Indian and Chinese Chan] Ancestors have said in their teaching, 'When it comes to realizing the Buddha dharma, make no distinction between male and female, or between the exalted and the lowly.'" The fictional questioner asks, "By leaving home life behind, monks are quickly separated from all their various ties so that they have no impediments to diligently practicing seated mediation. But how can those of us involved in the daily pressures of lay life turn to doing training and practice so that we may realize the Way of the buddhas, which is unconcerned with worldly affairs?" Dōgen replies:

The Buddhas and Ancestors, out of their overflowing sympathy, have opened the great, wide gates of their compassion. They have done this so that they might help all sentient beings realize the truth and enter the Way. Who amongst those in the worlds of either the mundane [lay] or the saintly [monastic] could possibly be excluded from entering?[8] ... It simply depends on whether you have the determination or not: it has nothing to do with being a householder or a monastic.[9]

He also wrote:

In Great Song China, I never heard it said that present-day rulers and their ministers, gentry and commoners, men and women, had not fixed their hearts on the Way of the [Indian and Chinese Chan] Ancestors. Both those in the military and those in civil service were intent on seeking training in meditation and studying the Way. Among those who were intent, many undoubtedly illumined that which is the foundation of their hearts and minds.[10]

In "Bendōwa," Dōgen mentioned two women who appear in stories and were "rescued by their genuine faith and trust." The first is a "woman who came to understand what the Great Way is due to her playfully dressing up in a monk's robe in a previous life." In the story she is depicted as an arhat. The other, in a story from Song China, is a faithful lay woman who awakened upon seeing an ignorant old monk, to whom she had brought food daily, just dumbly sitting.[11]

As Dōgen stated clearly in "Bendōwa," the requirements for practice and awakening are great determination, great faith, and an awakened teacher. No one is excluded from possessing either faith or determination. Training, including centrally the practice of zazen, is also absolutely necessary for awakening.

When Dōgen wrote, "The [Indian and Chinese Chan] Ancestors have said in their teaching, 'When it comes to realizing the Buddha Dharma, make no distinction between male and female, or between the exalted and the lowly,'" he transmitted faithfully what had been said in Song China, according to our records. For example, Dahui Zonggao (Jp. Daie Sōkō, 1089–1163), the most famous of his generation's Linji (Jp. Rinzai) Chan lineage teachers, made the following statements in his public sermons. About Lady Tang, one of his most successful lay students, he said, "Can you say that she is a woman, and women have no share [in enlightenment]? You must believe that This Matter has nothing to do with [whether one is] male or female, old or young. Ours is an egalitarian Dharma-gate that has only one flavor."[12]

In another sermon Dahui said, "For mastering the truth, it does not matter whether one is male or female, high class or of low birth. One moment of insight and one is shoulder to shoulder with the Buddha."[13] Dahui's contemporary, Hongzhi Zhengjue (Jp. Wanshi Zenji, 1091–1157), an outstanding Caodong teacher during the Southern Song dynasty, was famous for his teachings on "Silent Illumination Chan." Describing the moment when one is free of all impediments and experiences reality, he wrote, "Everyone has this complete within himself or herself. At this moment there is no male or female or other distinction of mark [*xiang*]. Only a pure, single marvelous clarity."[14] Again Hongzhi wrote:

The real mark is the mark of no mark;
The real mind is the mind of no mind.
The real attainment is the no-attaining attaining.
The real activity is the no-activity activity.
In that condition, each and every phenomenon (dharma) is within my power; if all marks appear in my person, all marks are beautiful. At such a moment, one does not see that there are such distinguishing

marks as rich and poor, male and female, right and wrong, gain and loss. It is only because there are marks that you accept and marks that you reject that you are not able to join yourself to emptiness and experience equality with the Dharma realm [*Dharmadhatu*].[15]

Finally, Hongzhi wrote of the activity of the buddha-nature discovered at the moment of awakening: "Is it not that in this moment [of awakening] a monk or nun received the complete and sufficient activity [of the buddha-nature]? It is where you act, and where I act, and where all the Buddhas and patriarchs are at work; how could distinctions of monastic and lay, male and female, matter then?"[16]

Dōgen eventually developed his own distinctive understanding and expression of the relation of awakening, practice, and the activity of the Buddha and buddha-nature. But on the fundamental points, that form and *xiang*, and thus gender, are irrelevant to awakening, and that the buddhas and patriarchs understand the activity of buddhahood universally to pervade all phenomenal activity and save all beings, the Dōgen of "Bendōwa" was on the same page with the Chinese ancestors.[17]

Heine has indicated that he thinks that since answers to only three of eighteen questions of "Bendōwa" address whether women or lay people can practice zazen and attain awakening, those who appreciate Dōgen's "'refreshingly ecumenical' universal outlook embracing laypersons and women" and see a change in Dōgen's later works, as well as those who support women as practitioners and teachers, should not make too much of the universalism expressed in these lines.[18] I believe the opposite is true: there are reasons for the latter group to make much of Dōgen's ringing proclamation in "Bendōwa." "Bendōwa" is his way of setting the tone and the rules for his incipient practice community, his way of revealing who he is and will be as a teacher. As the American Zen teacher Myoan Grace Schireson writes of "Raihaitokuzui":

Raihaitokuzui was written early in Dōgen's teaching career (1240) and represents the foundational teaching in Dōgen's Zen that all beings, without exception, fully express Buddha nature. More specifically, in *Raihaitokuzui*, Dōgen uses gender equality itself as an example of the complete expression of Buddhism in all beings. In 1240, Dōgen was engaged in an attempt to build a community based on this very teaching. It was to be a community that not only taught equality, but also actually functioned based on respect for the equality of all beings, including women, as Buddhist teachers. Beginning with the Buddha himself, many great Buddhist teachers had to work around customs and laws of their times and cultures that placed women in the position of second class citizens. In this context, *Raihaitokuzui* was more than simply a statement of and about equality; Dōgen wanted to go further to establish an actual community based on this teaching. Without enacting his understanding of equality in his community, full and true expression of the Buddha's teaching would be compromised.[19]

Even more than "Raihaitokuzui" of 1240, "Bendōwa" of 1231, Dōgen's first surviving written statement, proclaimed the nature of the practice he intended to encourage in his new community and the Buddhist insights he thought essential to enact there. It is very significant that in "Bendōwa" he clearly states the instruction he has received from the ancestors: "When it comes to realizing the Buddha Dharma, make no distinction between male and female, or between the exalted and the lowly." This proclamation affirms the commitment of true Chan and Zen masters to teaching lay women and men and supporting their practice and declares it to be a necessary commitment for one who wants to teach and practice as the buddhas do. As Schireson writes, "Without enacting his understanding of equality in his community, full and true expression of the Buddha's teaching would be compromised." Following on this strong proclamation, in 1240 Dōgen took a further step in "Raihaitokuzui": he proclaimed awakened women to be fully equal to awakened men as teachers for those not yet awakened.

Reading "Raihaitokuzui" in Conjunction with Eihei Kōroku

Another set of texts that predates "Raihaitokuzui" is Dōgen's two, or possibly three, dharma instructions to his nun disciple Ryōnen. These were all probably written before "Raihaitokuzui," and they deploy language and themes that are developed at more length in that essay. Again we find in Dōgen's *hōgo* to Ryōnen references to stories and language that are brought up by Dahui and Hongzhi in support of women and their practice.

Around 1231 Dōgen left Kenninji and moved to Anyō'in, a small hermitage in the Fukakusa district on the outskirts of Kyoto to found an independent monastery. There his circle of students began to form, including followers of the Daruma-shū, a Zen school that was centered on the charismatic, self-certified Zen figure Nōnin and had been outlawed by the court of Go-Toba-Tennō in 1194. With this move Dōgen came under attack from the monks of Mount Hiei, the headquarters of Tendai.[20] He sacrificed his status as an "official monk" as well as his link to Tendai and Enryakuji. He became a "reclusive monk" (*tonseisō*).

At his hermitage in Fukakusa in 1235 and 1236 Dōgen raised money to build a monks' hall (*sōdō*), a characteristically Song dynasty Chan-style train-ing hall, and subsequently changed the name of his temple there to Kōshōji. In 1243, for reasons not revealed in extant sources, he left Kōshōji and led his disciples into the mountains of Echizen, where, with the help and protection of a prominent warrior-class patron, he built a new monastery.

Although we do not know a lot about Dōgen's early efforts to collect and teach a group of students before and during the thirteen years that he taught at Fukakusa, it is clear that Buddhist nuns were among his community of disciples and donors.[21] We learn the most about these nuns, who were studying with Dōgen at the time he gave the sermon on which the essay "Raihaitokuzui" was based, from contemporaneous material concerning them in *Eihei Kōroku*.

Dōgen wrote at least two and probably three dharma instructions to a nun, Ryōnen, whom he praised as a serious practitioner. In the first undated dharma instruction included in volume 8 of *Eihei Kōroku*, he wrote, "Wayfarer Ryōnen, you have the seeds of transcendent wisdom [*prajna*] from former lives, intently aspiring to the great way of buddhas and ancestors. You are a woman, but have the strength of will of a great manly person [*daijobu*]."[22] In the third dharma instruction for Ryōnen, for which we have a manuscript copy in Dōgen's own hand dated 1231, he wrote, "This mountain monk regards the sincerity of the aspiration for the way of wayfarer Ryōnen, and sees that other people cannot match her."[23]

The nun Ryōnen is listed in the Zen lineage chart in the Zen dictionary published in Japan in 1985 by the Sōtō School as Dōgen's dharma-heir.[24]

Let us pause a minute to think about what Dōgen says to and about the nun Ryōnen. In light of "Raihaitokuzui," where it is said that one's truly awak-ened teacher "is not in the form of a man or woman but rather will be a person of great resolve"—literally a *daijobu*—we can see that Dōgen in his praise of Ryōnen was saying that she had what it takes to become a true Zen teacher; perhaps she was of teacher caliber already. We should not think of the nun Ryōnen as a marginal hanger-on in a sangha where the attention was mostly given to the male students on whom the future rested. First, Dōgen is com-mitted to teaching all based on their equal capacity to express buddha-nature. Second, Dōgen tells her (and us) that "other people cannot match her."

In 1234 a nun named Egi joined his community as one of a group of Daruma-shū disciples. Both Ryōnen and Egi reappear in records we have from his Echizen period, which suggests that they remained in Dōgen's circle for a long time. If Ryōnen had wanted to set out on her own as a teacher, there would not have been institutional support.

The Daruma-shū group to which the nun Egi belonged also included the monk Ejō, who between 1235 and 1237 wrote down excerpts of Dōgen's talks and responses to questions, forming a text called the *Record of Things Heard* (*Shōbōgenzō Zuimonki*).[25] One exchange in this text features an unnamed nun asking Dōgen a question, which makes it evident that nuns attended his informal teaching sessions. Dōgen's circle included women who gave financial support as well; in 1237 the aristocratic nun Shōgaku donated a lecture hall for Kōshōji.[26]

In 1240, during this Kōshōji period, Dōgen also delivered the sermon later included in the seventy-five-fascicle *Shōbōgenzō* entitled "Raihaitokuzui." The sermon begins with the theme of how to choose a teacher and how to obtain his or her most profound teaching, namely, awakening. But it becomes in large part a sermon on how awakened nuns and lay women, though lower in status in the sangha than monks, should be honored by monks and lay men and are worthy of being their teachers. In this sermon Dōgen tells several important stories of awakened women Chan ancestors and the men who bowed to them and received their teaching. He makes clear to a predominantly male audience that the moral of these stories is that seeing oneself lightly and seeing everyone and everything as potentially one's teacher, including women and lower status people, is the attitude of a truly admirable dharma student.

Some scholars have suggested that Dōgen's real purpose in giving this sermon was to make the point that true students of the Way would be willing to take *him* as a teacher.[27] Monks in Japan were divided into "official monks" (*kansō*) and "monks in retreat" (*tonseisō*). The first group was restricted to monks of aristocratic birth; their role was to perform ceremonies and give dharma instruction to the court. The great institutions of the Tendai and Shingon sects were administered by such monks. The greatly sought-after teachers there taught inner circles of monks who, like themselves, were of aristocratic origin. Dōgen could have participated in all this; he was of aristocratic birth as the son of the Great Minister of the Center (*naidaijin*) Minamoto no Michichika, who died in 1202, and he had been ordained at Enryakuji, the headquarters temple of the Tendai school. However, in 1230 he had given up the status of an official monk and had become a monk in retreat, incurring a considerable loss of status.[28] The monks who joined Dōgen at Kōshōji similarly cut themselves off from the traditional route to monastic fame and leadership. They may indeed have been low-status monks.[29]

This line of interpretation has some plausibility and force. Yet to suggest that Dōgen talked about awakened women and the men who entrusted their practice and education to them solely in order to talk indirectly about himself goes a step too far. We should not forget that women were active as disciples in his early sangha; surely the audience listening to this sermon was not exclusively male. We must not forget Dōgen's sincere praise of the nun Ryōnen's practice and attainment in the dharma instructions recorded in *Eihei Kōroku*. Most likely there were awakened women present in his sangha ready or nearly ready to serve as teachers for his students, if the students could bring themselves to submit to them. Even though in "Raihaitokuzui" Dōgen often seems to be addressing male students, as he talked he may well have had in mind women whom he could recommend as teachers or, equally likely, some women audience members who were personally interested in the question of whether women could teach. In the texts of Yuanwu Keqin, Dahui Zonggao, and others in Song dynasty Chan, one can usually find a close correlation between a master's mention of the possibility of a woman becoming awakened through Chan practice and the recorded presence of a woman either as intended audience for a dharma instruction, letter, or poem in which the point is made or as sponsor of the sermon containing the point.

Some point out that at the beginning of "Raihaitokuzui," women are being compared to foxes and stone pillars. Heine writes, "[In addition to affirming the role of women,] the *Raihaitokuzui* also suggests, perhaps ironically, that demons, pillars and foxes are worthy representatives of the Dharma."[30] To this reader, though, the apparent irony in comparing women to foxes and pillars lessens, and even disappears, if one knows to what Dōgen refers when he brings up foxes and pillars, and if one reminds oneself about Dōgen's oft-used level-shifting, paradoxical, ever challenging "kōan-like" writing strategy. Most important, Dōgen's message surely was that every single thing, however unremarkable or apparently mundane, can be one's teacher.

"Getting the Marrow by Doing Obeisance": A Close Reading

The essay "Raihaitokuzui" is found in two versions. The short version is attested by many manuscript versions, while the long version, which contains the short version plus additional material, is attested by only one. This additional material is found in the *Secret [Himitsu] Shōbōgenzō* in twenty-eight chapters housed at Eiheiji temple. Since the creation of the ninety-five-chapter Honzan edition of the *Shōbōgenzō* in the early nineteenth century, the long version has been included in many subsequent editions and in English translations. William M. Bodiford argues that the contemporary, almost universal inclusion of the additional material gives us a false idea that the additional material was important and well-known in the premodern period and creates a chapter that disturbs the flow of the larger *Shōbōgenzō*.[31] Because of limits of space and in order to present a close reading of the short version, I will treat here the short version only.

Dōgen begins his sermon with the topic of the difficulty of finding a true teacher and the importance of dropping everything to study with such a teacher when found.[32] The point he wishes to make is that true teachers may take any form: even a youth, a lay person, or a woman may be a true teacher. With this theme in mind, the short version of the essay can be divided into two parts, each of which reflects different aspects of Dōgen's approach to the Chinese story from which the title is taken. The first part reflects Dōgen's approach to the story as a whole, while the second part may be triggered in part by the unexpected fact that the story includes a nun among the four chief disciples of the monk Bodhidharma, the putative transmitter of the Dhyana (Chan/Zen) lineage from India to China.

The story as found in the early Song dynasty genealogical history of the Chan school, called the *Transmission of the Lamp the Jingde Era*, shows the Indian monk Bodhidharma, soon to return to India, asking his four chief disciples—Daofu, Daoyu, Huike, and the nun Zongchi—to express their deep insight in verse. When the first one does, he says, "You got my skin." When the second one, the nun Zongchi, does, he says, "You got my flesh." When the third one does, he says, "You got my bones." When the fourth one does, he says, "You got my marrow." The Chan tradition since the Song dynasty has seen the one who got his "marrow," the monk Huike, as Bodhidharma's only true heir. In "Kattō," a later essay in the *Shōbōgenzō*, Dōgen famously refused to sanction ranking the understanding transmitted to each disciple according to intimacy or thoroughness, saying that seeing one of them as Bodhidharma's dharma-heir and the others as unequal would be a mistake.[33]

In the first several paragraphs of "Raihaitokuzui," Dōgen's focus is on the difficult task of finding a teacher and the trusting, devoted, energetic response to the teacher's instruction that should ensue. He writes, "A true teacher has nothing at all to do with such characteristics as male and female and so on, but the teacher must be one who is a great man [Ch. *dajangfu*, Jp. *daijobu*], must be 'such a person' [i.e., one who is intimately acquainted with *satori*]."[34]

It is particularly significant that Dōgen's essay begins with a sentence the first part of which is a quotation from the famous statement of the nun Chan teacher Moshan Liaoran to a male Chan student named Zhixian. In the story of their encounter, Zhixian is wandering about in search of a teacher. He hears that a nun has set herself up as abbess and teacher, and he is both curious and skeptical about her implied claims. Zhixian decides to test her; if she fails to demonstrate awakened mind, he will "overturn her teaching platform." If she impresses him, he will stay and study with her. When he enters the Abbess Liaoran's temple at Moshan (Mount Mo) and meets her, Zhixian flunks the first coded dialogue. Subsequently his test question to her is "What is the person in the mountain [i.e., Mount Mo] like?" Reading his mind perhaps, she replies, "It is not [a matter of] male or female form and so on." After another exchange, defeated and impressed, he stays, and later acknowledges that at least half his accomplishment is due to her teaching. (He receives dharma transmission from his next teacher, Linji Yixuan [Rinzai Gigen].) So while Dōgen's mind is on the important story of the nun and three monks who are Bodhidharma's dharma-heirs, his mind is also making a connection to the story of Moshan Liaoran, the story of a woman who teaches a male disciple, and the story of a male disciple who stays on to study with her after he has found her to be a true teacher. Apparently her deep insight into the irrelevancy of form and characteristics (*xiang*) to the awakened mind of the true teacher has impressed him deeply.

The second part of Dōgen's sentence says that the teacher must be a *daijobu* (Ch. *dajangfu*), a "great manly person." Behind this term lies a passage from the *Nirvana Sutra* (i.e., *Sutra on the Final Nirvana of Sakyamuni*), fascicle 9, the "Rulaixing" chapter, which says, "If one is able to know that he has the Buddha nature, I say that he has the characteristics of a man [*jangfu*]. If there is a woman [who knows], then she is a man [*nanzi*]."

The rhetoric of gender equality in Chinese Chan in the Song dynasty draws heavily on the concept of *daijobu*, someone who, whether a man or a woman, has the characteristic fierce strength and determination of a great manly person, or someone who cuts through all delusion with a single stroke and, upon awakening, is beyond the limitations, including the gender limitations, of the unawakened. In Japan too in the late Kamakura period Dōgen is not alone in using this term to argue for gender equality, at least if the woman is capable of the decisive strength of will of which great manly persons are capable.[35] As the *Nirvana Sutra* passage makes clear, not all men are capable of being "great manly persons" either; in that way, there is equality, perhaps. Lori Meeks quotes the Vinaya master Eison, who was a close contemporary of Dōgen, as writing, "Even women, if they renounce the world now, pursue Buddhist learning and practice, take the tonsure and reach enlightenment, are all manly persons. Truly this is a reason to rejoice!"[36]

Dōgen's next offering in the essay "Raihaitokuzui" is this: "The teacher is not a person from the past or from the present. More likely it will be a fox spirit who will be the good friend. . . . The teacher will not be in the dark about cause and effect; the teacher may be you or I or someone else."

As for the student, she or he needs sincerity and the believing mind. She or he must prize the dharma and value herself or himself very lightly. She or he must flee the world and regard the way as her or his abode. If she or he does this, the master will be revealed to be inside the student. Dōgen writes, "The ancestor [Huike] who cut off his arm to get the marrow does not refer to another; the master who will teach you the sloughing off of body and mind [like his own teacher Rujing in China] is already within yourself." At this point in the essay his mind is on the true meaning, the takeaway moral, of the story of Bodhidharma and Huike.

With Huike, Zhixian and Moshan Liaoran, and the Chinese ancestors who also told these stories to encourage their women students no doubt still in mind, Dōgen turns to the task of expanding his examples of successful students beyond Huike. He says, "There is not just one instance of a person who had the determination to regard the dharma as something precious. . . . I shall present just a few examples here."

The reader or listener is now waiting for some straightforward human examples like Huike. But instead of offering those, Dōgen turns to the strange idea that one can preserve and prize the dharma in any form, "as a pillar, as a lantern, as all buddhas, as a little fox, a demon, a man or a woman." (This is the passage that Heine takes to be ironic.) And then he immediately introduces himself in a direct address to the listener: "If you have gotten my marrow . . . " Dōgen quotes an unidentified utterance of Sakyamuni Buddha that says that nothing about the teacher's appearance, caste, shortcomings, or behavior should weigh at all with a student seeking a teacher; what is important is that the student venerates and prizes the teacher's wisdom. This leads back to the "teachers" that can be found in the world—trees and rocks, pillars, walls, the little fox to whom the god Indra did obeisance and put questions about the dharma: "Long ago [the great god] Indra honored a wild fox as his own master and sought the Dharma from him, calling him 'Great Bodhisattva.' It had nothing to do with whether the teacher was in a high or low [noble or base] form because of past karma."

A Note on the Wild Fox and Indra

Does "Raihaitokuzui" use irony to put down women? Let us pause to consider whether the comparison between women and wild foxes is meant ironically.

Dōgen more than once brings up the story of Indra and the wild fox in his writings. In this story Indra realizes that he wants to take refuge in the three jewels, and he asks a wild fox trapped in a well to preach the dharma to him. The story is found in the *Unprecedented Causation Sutra*. In the sutra the fox in the well says to Indra, "You are the king of devas, but do not behave well. The Dharma teacher is down here and you are up there. You are asking for essential dharma without expressing respect. The Dharma water is pure and capable of saving beings. Why do you regard yourself as higher?"

We can see that the story of Indra and the fox is entirely on point in Dōgen's sermon. In Dōgen's view, Indra does well to ask the fox. The fox does well to demand respect from Indra if he wants dharma. The fox points out that, where dharma is concerned, worldly or cosmic status and form of rebirth mean nothing. If women, Dōgen, and the fox are all on a par as being socially and karmically viewed as inferior, and therefore treated without respect, but worthy of respect as dharma teachers, then women are not necessarily put down by being compared with the fox of the sutra.

In Chan, pillars and lanterns too have a long history of being dharma teachers. Dōgen no doubt was familiar with the following exchange in the record of Shitou: "A monk asked Shitou, 'Why did the first ancestor come from the West?' Shitou said: 'Ask the temple pillar.'"[37]

Based on this and many other examples from the records of Yunmen and others, I suggest that when Dōgen proposes that one seek the dharma from pillars and foxes, he does so on the basis of sutra stories or stories in Chan literature in which protagonists truly seek to learn or should seek to learn the dharma from such beings—in fact from all beings. Seen with the eye of true dharma, things are not what they seem to the worldly eye; one has to consider every possible angle if one wants to catch a glimpse of what the true dharma eye sees. Furthermore, leading the reader rapidly through several apparently conflicting views of a subject is Dōgen's constant strategy in his writings of the Early and Middle periods. This strategy unseats one's settled assumptions, opening one's eyes to the possibility of seeing buddhas in ordinary people and mundane things. Is this not what is going on here? No irony is intended.

With this we reach the end of section 1 of the short version. Dōgen has already beautifully and realistically portrayed the mental attitude the successful student must have. Further, he has followed earlier masters in undercutting with bizarre, even grotesque examples from Chan and Mahayana literature any expectations one might want to hold on to about the teacher. And he hints here that he is challenging the listener or reader to recognize wisdom in him, to recognize the challenge that he himself presents as a monk without much of a following who might nonetheless open up vast wisdom to one who can look beyond status or ecclesiastical accomplishment. He is just an eccentric, reclusive monk who dropped out of the rank of the official monks serving the state and emperor, the rank into which he had been ordained. He wears black robes, not the white ones of official monks.[38] He lacks significant patrons. Why would you study with him? Because wisdom can be sought from him by those who with fierce determination want to find the supremely valuable way and have the imagination and the resolve to inquire of a demon, a pillar, or a little fox.

In section 2 of the short version, Dōgen turns to the subject of how the best Song dynasty monks, the ones who really seek the Way, do not draw lines between people of high and low status and between women and men where the Way is concerned. The key criterion is wisdom. A female, monastic or lay, who has wisdom wins everyone's respect in Chinese Chan circles. According to Dōgen, a few Tang, Five Dynasties, and Song dynasty Chinese monk students were admirably willing to do obeisance to a woman who had attained the Way, and they awakened thereby. This contrasts with Japanese monks, who want to choose their teachers only from among those of equal or higher rank. In the Buddhist order nuns rank below monks, and in Japanese society the status of men of a given rank is greater than that of the women of that rank. Female monastics and lay women will certainly not be taken as teachers by Japanese monks. But this is a big mistake.

Dōgen writes, "Deluded people of high social status, age, seniority, monastic rank or accomplishment on the bodhisattva path, though, think that they cannot bow to those of lower status or rank and take them as their teachers, even if such lower ranking persons have acquired the Dharma." He then offers a long list of telling examples. For instance, some think to themselves, "I am the chief of the monk officials who govern monastic affairs, so I cannot bow to ordinary men and women, even if they have acquired the Dharma." Others think, "I have reached a very high stage of the bodhisattva path, and I cannot honor nuns and the like, even if they have acquired the Dharma." Dōgen points out that this is entirely the wrong attitude in one who truly seeks the dharma: "When a nun [who as a nun ranks lower than any monk] who has acquired the Way, and who has acquired the Dharma appears in the world [as an abbess], for the monk who seeks the Dharma and studies Zen to enter her assembly, bow to her in homage [as your teacher] and ask [her] about the Dharma, that is the mark of his excellence as a student. It [finding an awakened teacher] should be like finding drinking water when you are thirsty."

One might argue that Dōgen still has not left the subject of his own claims to be recognized as a teacher of great worth. But in fact his discourse in the second section is not like the first: it is consistently focused on the value of a woman, lay or monastic, who has attained the Way and stories of Chinese monks whose capacity for recognizing transcendent wisdom *in a woman* has led to their own awakening. In the root story of this essay, Bodhidharma recognized the awakened mind of the nun Zongchi. Dōgen tells the story of the monk Guanqi Zhixian, who during the Five Dynasties in China studied under the nun teacher Moshan Liaoran; this story is told in the *Jingde Chuandenglu* and is given in full below. He ends by saying, "Zhixian's bowing to and seeking the Dharma from Moshan showed the superiority of his determination [to attain the Way]."

He then tells how a nun named Miaoxin became the provisions manager of the ninth-century master Yangshan Huiji's (807–83) monastery because the monks at the monastery agreed that she was the most qualified. Her duty was to attend to donors, donations, and provisions, particularly of grain and food. Her cloister was apparently lower on the mountainside than the main compound that contained the dharma hall and abbot's quarters. Seventeen traveling monks from Sichuan who stopped for the night at her cloister on their way up the mountain to study with Huiji bowed to her as a sign of taking her as their teacher. This came about because, in the evening as they were resting, they had a discussion about the Sixth Patriarch's comment as recorded in the *Platform Sutra*, "It is not the wind that moves or the flag that moves, it is your mind that moves," which she overheard.

When her disparaging remarks about their discussion were reported to them, they did not brush them aside. Instead "they were ashamed that they had not been able to speak [dharma, as those who understood Chan would do]," and at once they put on their outer robes and performed the ceremonial etiquette appropriate to seeking an interview with a teacher. In the formal interview she said to them, "It is not the wind which moves, it is not the flag which moves, and it is not the mind which moves." When they heard this comment of hers, they had a realization and made bows of thanks and became her disciples. Then they returned to Sichuan, since they had found enlightenment and a teacher and did not need to climb the mountain the next day to see Huiji.[39]

The moral Dōgen draws from these stories of Chinese monks who have taken lower status people such as women as their teachers is that the Japanese monks in his audience should do the same. He says, "When the abbot of the monastery and the senior monk with whom he shares his teaching seat are not around, you should ask a nun who has acquired the Way to teach you." Don't prefer a monk, even a senior monk, if he has not acquired the Way.

In support of his point that in China male Chan students take enlightened women as their teachers, he makes a more general observation:

At present nuns enroll in the monasteries of the Song. When one becomes famous for her attainment of the Dharma, and receives the imperial edict from the government officials appointing her abbess of a monastery for nuns, then at [another, neighboring men's] monastery she "ascends the Hall" [Ch. *shangtang*, Jp. *jōdō*]. That is, she goes to the Dharma Hall in response to an invitation issued with great ceremony and ascends the high seat to teach by giving a formal sermon and answering questions, as the Chan teacher who is an abbot or who represents the abbot does on the most formal of teaching occasions. All of the monastic community [of the neighboring monastery] from the abbot down attend to hear her teaching, listening to the Dharma while standing formally in their positions. Among those who ask questions [of the woman master] about [old] sayings [Ch. *huatou*, Jp. *watō*] there are also male monks. This is a long-established practice.

Holding the inaugural ceremony in a nearby larger monastery would be especially necessary if one's new monastery were small, but in the case of male monastics it seems to have happened in China even when the monastery to which one was appointed was quite large. Regardless, Dōgen clearly means to tell his listeners that, on this occasion of her first sermon as abbess, her assembled audience of students included all of the monks of her host monastery from the abbot down, and the questioners included monks. His point is clearly that in Song China men students of Chan who were monks and members of the Chan lineage were willing to present themselves formally and ritually in the role of student in relation to a woman teacher.[40]

An important feature of this scene that Dōgen describes is that the woman teacher ritually takes the role of Buddha in relation to the assembled company as she takes her place on the high seat of the dharma hall and as she speaks the dharma from the standpoint of enlightened Mind. As we know, this contradicts the notion of the five hindrances that is found in many Mahayana texts, namely that a woman cannot in her present female body become a buddha or any of four other important cosmic figures.

Dōgen solves this problem, as those in Song China had done, by invoking the idea that an awakened woman should no longer be seen as a woman, for she is now something else, a *daijobu* (*mahapurusha*; a great manly person), a teacher of gods and humans.[41] When he tells the story of Miaoxin, summarized earlier, his narrative has Yangshan Huiji say to the other monks in recommending Miaoxin for the position, "Although [Miao]xin Huaizi is a woman, she has the determined spirit [*shiki*] of a *daijobu*."⁴² And immediately following his description of enlightened Song nuns becoming abbesses, he says:

> Because a person who has attained the Dharma is an authentic ancient Buddha, we should not greet that person in terms of what s/he once was. When s/he sees me, s/he receives me from an entirely new standpoint; when I see him/her, my reception of her/him is based entirely on today, [not on what she (or I) was in the past]. For example, in the case of a nun who has received the treasury of the true Dharma eye through transmission, if [the arhats of] the four fruitions, the pratyekabuddhas, and even the (advanced bodhisattvas) of the three wise stages and of the ten holy states pay homage to her and seek the Dharma from her, she should receive their obeisance.⁴³

The reason of course is that she is not to be thought of primarily as a woman any longer, and thus lower than any man and any monastic; she is not to be thought of primarily as a nun any longer, and thus lower in status than any monk; she is an awakened being, and thus from a Buddhist point of view higher than even arhats, pratyekabuddhas, and advanced bodhisattvas, and able to teach them. Dōgen concludes the shorter version of the "Raihaitokuzui" sermon as found in the seventy-five-volume version of the *Shōbōgenzō* by alluding to the seven-year-old dragon girl of the "Devadatta" chapter of the *Lotus Sutra*: "Even a seven-year-old girl who practices the Buddha Dharma and is enlightened in it is the leader and guide of the four-fold sangha, the compassionate father of sentient beings. For instance, the dragon [*naga*] girl in the *Lotus Sutra* achieved Buddhahood. Giving respect and homage to someone such as she is the same as giving it to all the buddhas."

The Status of Nuns and Women Buddhist Practitioners in Dōgen's Japan

When Dōgen gave this sermon Japan was not like China. Unlike China, there were no fully ordained Buddhist nuns in Japan for almost all of Dōgen's lifetime. Full ordination for women using the full set of 348 precepts, in a manner recognized by the male authorities of a Buddhist monastic institution in Japan occurred in 1249 in the city of Nara for the first time in more than four centuries.⁴⁴ There had been full ordination of nuns in the Nara period, but by the early years of the ninth century, during the Heian period, the court ceased to support monastic institutions for women and to invite nuns to participate in court ceremonies. Without state support, full ordinations for women stopped. Nonetheless women (and lay men) could enter into "home-leaver" (*shukke*) status, and many did. This fact, recently brought to light by the Japanese scholar Katsuura Noriko and, in English, by Paul Groner and Lori Meeks, should completely change how we read the *Shōbōgenzō* essay "Shukke Kudoku" ("The Merit of Home-leaving").[45]

In the late Heian and Kamakura periods, Meeks writes, the term *shukke* was ambiguous; it could refer to lay people, including lay women, as well as those who served in officially recognized clerical positions. *Shukke* was a recognized status and an expected life cycle event. Lay women (and men) took Buddhist names, wore Buddhist robes, and shaved, cut, or covered their tresses. They made a commitment to full-time religious practice. Priests commonly bestowed the precepts on women in private tonsure ceremonies. Because these women lived a life of renunciation and full-time religious practice, Dōgen and others called them, including Egi, who studied with Dōgen, "nuns" (*ama*). For a time the term *ni* (*bikuni*) was reserved for those who had shaved their heads, but by late Kamakura it too came to refer to all "lay monastics" or "privately professed nuns," including those who merely cut or covered their hair. Unlike lay men who entered *shukke* renunciant status, who often continued living with their wives and families, women left their families and abandoned their female names, their long hair and feminine clothing, as well as their sexual lives.

By the mid-Heian period most educated women expected to spend the final years of their lives as Buddhist lay renunciants. Due to the spread of Pure Land faith, in the Heian period this was usually considered a step necessary to the attainment of personal salvation, an aid to their preparations for death. By the mid-Kamakura period the timing of women's *shukke* had become more fixed and its signification more rigid: a woman was to take vows when she became a widow—no sooner and no later—and her *shukke* was to be understood as an act of allegiance directed at her late husband and his household.

In the mid-twelfth century women were still recognized as members of their natal families, and especially of their father's lineage. By the thirteenth century many elites had come to view women as members of their husband's lineage; and by the fourteenth century this new view of family had spread to commoners as well. However, whether or not they had received these ordination rituals, women were expected to be patrons of male priests, not their students.

"Shukke Kudoku" contains the famous passage in which Dōgen denies that the teaching that women can become buddhas in a female body is an authentic transmission of Sakyamuni's golden words.

"Shukke Kudoku" in Relation to *"Raihaitokuzui"*

Talk of Becoming a Buddha in a Female Body (*Nyoshin Jōbutsu*) Is Not an Authentic Transmission

Let us turn now to this famously puzzling passage, which seems to contradict what Dōgen sets out in his "Raihaitokuzui" essay:

> Among all buddhas of the three times and ten directions there are no buddhas, not even a single buddha, who become buddhas as householders [*zaike jōbutsu*]. Due to the existence of buddhas in the past, there is the merit of going forth from home and receiving the precepts [*shukke jukai*]. The gaining of the Way [*tokudō*] by living beings always depends on going forth from home and receiving the precepts. In essence, because the merit of going forth from home and receiving the precepts is itself the constant norm [*jōhō*] of all buddhas, that merit is incalculable [*muryō*]. Although within the holy/sage teachings [*shōkyō*] there is talk of becoming a buddha as a householder, that is not an authentic transmission [*shōden*]; although there is talk of becoming a buddha in a female body [*nyoshin jōbutsu*], that too is not an authentic transmission. What the buddhas and [Chan] ancestors authentically transmit [*busso shōden suru*] is becoming a buddha as a home-leaver [*shukke jōbutsu*].[46]

There is little to guide one's interpretation of this passage, as its next to last sentence is the only sentence in the essay, indeed in *Jūnikanbon*, that mentions the issue of women and buddhahood at all. It has been suggested that it is an interpolation, the work of a later editor. It has also been seen as showing that at the end of his life Dōgen did not escape the influence of interpretations of chapter 12 of the *Lotus Sutra* that were unfavorable to women. Speculation is unavoidable; I would like to reflect on such speculations briefly here.

The sentence in question makes the most sense when placed within the context of other "late teachings" of Dōgen that are inconsistent with earlier teachings such as "Raihaitokuzui." Ishikawa Rikizan's persuasive essay on this line places it in the context of *Jūnikanbon* essays as a whole, which display certain features new to Dōgen's writing.[47] As David Putney writes:

> Some of the key changes that we find in [Dōgen's] later writings [when compared with his earlier ones] include: (1) his severe critique of the

Rinzai (Linji) tradition … ; (2) his escalating critique of Chinese Chan Buddhism in general; (3) the emphasis on his own exclusive "transmission" of the Buddha Dharma; and (4) Dōgen's apparent "rejection" of lay Buddhism.[48]

Dōgen's one-line statement about the need for a woman to exchange her body for that of a man before she attains buddhahood could be associated with difference number 4, as the problems of the difficulty of practice and attainment experienced by women and that experienced by lay people were problems initially raised together in "Bendōwa," reflecting perhaps a general social attitude. But our one-line statement also belongs to category number 3, in that it could reflect Dōgen's late repudiation of the way Chinese Chan in the Song dynasty (and earlier) interpreted the story of the dragon princess in chapter 12 of the *Lotus Sutra*.

In "Raihaitokuzui" Dōgen agrees with the general Chan interpretation of the story of the dragon girl of the *Lotus Sutra*, which is a very subitist interpretation. To quote Hongbian, a ninth-century Chan teacher, "One wrong thought and Ananda falls into hell; one correct thought and the Dragon girl becomes a buddha." Awakening is not a gradual, step-by-step process. It is a sudden transformation.

This oft-expressed Chan interpretation of the story of the dragon princess could be said not to be in perfect harmony with the *Lotus Sutra* story itself. The story stresses that the dragon girl's attainment of buddhahood after hearing the *Lotus Sutra* preached and appearing before the Buddha and his disciples is very quick. It also stresses that it is a performance. But the story can also be read as not totally subitist, as it takes the dragon girl through every step of the transformation prescribed by orthodox Buddhism. She becomes male, she goes to another world, she becomes a monk, she performs all the bodhisattva practices, she manifests the thirty-two bodily marks and the eighty physical characteristics that indicate that a male will become a buddha, and she manifests as a buddha teaching the dharma to an assembly of listeners. All this is done speedily, but it is done.

Surely, however, the universalism of the *Lotus Sutra* is a major part of the story. In the *Lotus Sutra* buddhahood is predicted for every person. Even children who playfully build a stupa in the sand will become buddhas. Speed is another important part of the story; in chapter 16 of the *Lotus Sutra* the Buddha announces that his constant thought is how to help sentient beings quickly perfect their buddha bodies. In the assembly in chapter 12 someone asks whether Manjusrī's preaching of the *Lotus Sutra* has enabled any hearer to speedily accomplish buddhahood. Manjusri replies by describing the dragon girl. So to draw subitism out of this story, as the Chan teachers do, despite the detailed description of the stages of attaining buddhahood, is not a large stretch.

Dōgen concludes the shorter version of the "Raihaitokuzui" sermon as found in the seventy-five-volume *Shōbōgenzō* by alluding to the seven-year-old dragon girl (eight by Chinese reckoning) of the "Devadatta" chapter of the *Lotus Sutra*. He says:

> But when someone practices the buddha dharma and expounds the buddha dharma, though such a person be a girl seven years of age, that person is a guide and teacher for the four groups and a compassionate father for all sentient beings. Such a person may be compared to the daughter of the Dragon King who attained buddhahood. Offerings should be made and respectful homage paid equal to that accorded to the buddhas and tathagatas. This is an ancient rule in the buddha dharma. Those who do not understand this, or who have not received the single transmission are to be pitied.[49]

Dōgen's phrase "the daughter of the Dragon King who attained buddhahood" tallies with the way Tang and Song dynasty Chan teachers refer to the dragon princess. In their view her complete awakening is attained in a single instant of thought. Her performance demonstrates the emptiness of all obstacles to awakening, including those associated with being a nonhuman, a child, a female, and a nonmonastic. By contrast, in this line in "Shukke Kudoku" Dōgen seems to reject that subitist interpretation in favor of a more gradualist reading of the *Lotus Sutra* text of the story: "Although [in the sacred writings] there is talk of becoming a buddha in a female body [*nyoshin jōbutsu*], that too is not an authentic transmission. What the buddhas and [Chan] ancestors authentically transmit [*busso shōden suru*] is becoming a buddha as a home-leaver [*shukke jōbutsu*]."

Why does this change in Dōgen's thinking, apparently a change to a less subitist position, occur? Scholars who isolate this essay and try to answer this question have so far had little success. If, as Ishikawa does, scholars group this essay with apparently similar essays, some of which are late, and if we accept the grouping that occurs in *Jūnikanbon* in a way that ignores the problems with seeing a consistent set of characteristics among all those essays so grouped, they can hazard somewhat stronger interpretive theories.[50]

Let us consider the essay "Shukke Kudoku" by itself as a context for the problematic two lines. First, "Shukke Kudoku" begins with long quotations from sutras and shastras, prominently including the *Lotus Sutra*. The very first line is:

Nagarjuna Bodhisattva said,

Question: If the precepts of the home dweller enable one to be born as a deva, gain the bodhisattva path and attain nirvana, then what use are the precepts of those who go forth from household life [*shukkekai*]?

The essay thus begins with a question from a passage from the *Great Perfection of Wisdom Sastra* (Skt. *Mahaprajnaparamita-sastra*, Ch. *Dazhidulun*, Jp. *Daichidoron*),[51] a text that is attributed to Nagarjuna. Dōgen cited the passage because it explains the "merit" (*kudoku*) of "going forth from household life" (*shukke*). A person who receives the precepts of the lay person can gain the bodhisattva path and attain nirvana and perhaps also attain buddhahood; this is admitted in the question. But the passage goes on to say that though both can attain the Way, the obstacles on the lay path are immense. Dōgen comments, "From this we know that, for one who goes forth from household life [*shukke*], cultivating the precepts [*shukai*] and practicing the way [*gyōdō*] is very easy."

Yet, at the same time, attaining peace of mind as a home-leaver is very difficult, as leaving home is difficult. But, according to Dōgen, "the benefit of going forth from household life [*shukke no ri*] is merit that is incalculable [*kudoku muryō*]. Thus, although lay followers [*byakue*] have the five precepts [*gokai*], they are not like those who go forth from household life." Summing up, Dōgen writes, "Do not entrust your evanescent life to the winds of impermanence, wasting this excellent, superior body. Piling up life after life of going forth from home, let us store up good deeds and accumulate virtue."

Then, while discussing the centrality of receiving the full precepts in the Buddha's intention, he cites three vows made by Sakyamuni as recorded in the *Flower of Compassion Sutra* (Skt. *Karuna-pundarika-sutra*, Ch. *Peihuajing*, Jp. *Hikekyō*), translated by Dharmaksema.[52] Here are two of the vows he quotes:

Among the five hundred great vows of the Buddha Sakyamuni, vow number 137 is: In the future, after I have attained right awakening [*shōgaku*], if there are people who, in accordance with my dharma, wish to go forth from household life, I vow that they shall have no obstructions—which is to say, weakness, loss of memory, confusion, pride, lack of due caution, deluded lack of wisdom, many afflictions, and minds that are distracted. If that is not the case, then may I not attain right awakening [in the first place].

Also:

> Vow number 138 is: In the future, after I have attained perfect awak-
> ening, if there are women who, in accordance with my dharma, wish
> to go forth from home, study the Way, and receive the great precepts
> [Mahayana precepts, *daikai*], I vow to make them attain those goals. If
> that is not the case, then may I not attain perfect awakening [in the first
> place].

The first vow establishes that the Buddha wants people to be home-leavers
and has the intention and the power to help them succeed. The second vow
introduces the subject of the Buddha's support for the full ordination of
women. Surely this is a subject that, in the context of the whole essay, Dōgen
was not forced to bring up. He brings it up voluntarily. Why?

Perhaps, as he urges the importance of taking the Mahayana precepts for
full ordination, he realizes that while many men who left home in the Japan
of his time did so as lay men, they had the choice to seek full ordination with
the Mahayana precepts or the full 250 precepts. But women did not; no ordination as *bikuni* (Skt. *bhiksuni*) with 348 precepts was available to them, and
ordination with the Mahayana precepts was purely a private matter between a
woman and her male preceptor that conveyed no powers or religious status.
Here Dōgen subtly supported the proposition that there should be public, recognized ordination for women in Japan and a full-fledged nun's sangha.

As Meeks has made clear, in this Dōgen reflected one of the concerns of
his age. He joined a number of male Japanese monastic leaders, particularly
among Rinzai Zen and Vinaya monks, who deplored the fact that Japan, unlike
China, had no order of fully ordained female monastics.[53] In 1249 Eison of the
Vinaya school ordained twelve nuns who had revived an important convent in
Nara with the 348 precepts of the Dharmaguptaka Vinaya.

We must also note that, before quoting these two vows, Dōgen tells the
story, a favorite of his, of the woman entertainer who put on a monk's robe to
amuse her audience. The merit of even that insincere wearing of the monk's
robe propelled her in future lives to become a nun, and then an arhat. Dōgen
continues the story here, relating how she, now a nun, visited well-off, still
attractive women in their homes to persuade them to take ordination as a
nun. By telling this story, Dōgen added great support to his argument that
home-leaving produces much merit, but he also added support to the idea of
women leaving home attaining the Way.

Given the context provided by the other passages in "Shukke Kudoku," what
can we make of these two lines: "Although in the sacred writings there is talk of

becoming a buddha in a female body [*nyoshin jōbutsu*], that too is not an authentic transmission. What the buddhas and [Chan] ancestors authentically transmit [*busso shōden suru*] is becoming a buddha as a home-leaver [*shukke jōbutsu*]."

First, they are not clearly related linearly. Is Dōgen saying that nuns like his own successful disciple Ryōnen may and do become buddhas? In this and some other essays Dōgen shows himself to be at odds—shockingly—with Song dynasty Chan in the matter of recognizing awakening in lay people. Perhaps he means to say that lay women, like the dragon girl, must change their bodies before becoming buddhas, but not nuns.

Or perhaps the passage is about the dragon girl story in the *Lotus Sutra*. In other *Jūnikanbon* essays Dōgen expresses his reverence for the *Lotus Sutra*, even saying that it is the only sutra that expresses the truth; all others are "skillful means" (*hōben*). However, the subitist interpretation of the story may have become uncomfortable for Dōgen. Perhaps he merely wanted to express that discomfort by affirming here that the story does say that the dragon girl changed her body before becoming a buddha. His putative discomfort would have matched increasing interest in and commitment to the importance of cause and effect (and merit) displayed in this and other essays in *Jūnikanbon*.

Or perhaps Dōgen saw the need to align himself with other monks who found in the *Lotus Sutra* story of the dragon girl authority for the view that women could be saved, but only as the dragon girl was saved, by changing her body to a male body.

Speculation is endless. Whatever Dōgen intended here, if indeed he was the author of the offending line, is at least partially hidden.[54] In this and other chapters of *Jūnikanbon*, he copiously repudiated his earlier affirmation in "Bendōwa" of the possibility of awakening while in lay status. In a chapter that affirms women becoming nuns, as Dōgen had also done in "Raihaitokuzui" and in *Jūnikanbon* as a whole, only this one line appears that expresses his new gradualism in a way that qualifies women's hopes. These two lines are therefore hard to interpret. Perhaps Dōgen had reasons for agreeing briefly with those who had adopted this always ambiguous, ambivalent, hard to interpret, restricted application of the subitism of the *Lotus Sutra* to women, an application that offered women eventual buddhahood as well as the hope of leaving their female bodies behind.[55]

Meanwhile, in China, using the same language and citing the stories of Moshan Liaoran and the daughter of the Dragon King Sagara, Chan monks and nuns continued to assert that awakening and buddhahood did not depend on one's gender or monastic status. Chinese Chan never repudiated the subitist discourse of the irrelevance of maleness and femaleness with respect to awakening or attaining Buddhahood.

NOTES

1. DZZ-2 2: 460–81.

2. DZZ-2 1: 302–15. This fact is well known, but the implications for scholarship are very clearly stated by William M. Bodiford in "Textual Genealogies of Dōgen," in Steven Heine, ed., *Dōgen: Textual and Historical Studies* (New York: Oxford University Press 2012), 18. "Raihaitokuzui" is not in the sixty-fascicle *Shōbōgenzō* (see Bodiford, "Textual Genealogies of Dōgen," 31–32), but it is in the Honzan edition, and it is also in the twenty-eight-fascicle version that possibly dates from the mid-fourteenth century; it is in this version that the extra material appears that is often added to the "long version."

3. DZZ-2 2: 266–93.

4. Steven Heine, *Did Dōgen Go to China? What He Wrote and When He Wrote It* (New York: Oxford University Press, 2006).

5. Miriam L. Levering, "Dōgen's Raihaitokuzui and Women Teaching in Sung Chan," *Journal of the International Association of Buddhist Studies* 21.1 (1998): 77–110.

6. Heine, *Did Dōgen Go to China?*, 128.

7. Hubert Nearman, trans., *Shōbōgenzō: The Treasure House of the Eye of the True Teaching* (Mount Shashta, CA: Shasta Abbey Press, 2007), accessed December 10, 2013, http://www.shastaabbey.org/pdf/shobo/001bendo.pdf.

8. Nearman, *Shōbōgenzō*, 17–18.

9. Nearman, *Shōbōgenzō*, 18. I changed "monk" to "monastic."

10. Nearman, *Shōbōgenzō*, 18.

11. Nearman, *Shōbōgenzō*, 22.

12. *Dahui Pujue Chanshi Pushuo, Dainihon Zokuzōkyō* 1, 31, 5: 455a; hereafter cited as *Dahui Pushuo*. This and the following quotation from Dahui are also found in Miriam L. Levering, "The Dragon Girl and the Abbess of Mo-shan: Gender and Status in the Ch'an Buddhist Tradition," *Journal of the International Association for Buddhist Studies* 5.1 (1982): 19–35.

13. *Dahui Pushuo*, 433b.

14. *Hongzhi Chanshi Guanglu*, T 48:67c. This and the following two quotations from Hongzhi's *Guanglu* are found in Miriam Levering, "Lin-chi (Rinzai) Ch'an and Gender: The Rhetoric of Equality and the Rhetoric of Heroism," in Jose Ignacio Cabezon, ed., *Buddhism, Sexuality and Gender* (Albany: State University of New York Press, 1982), 137–56.

15. T 48.64.

16. T 48.65c.

17. While Dōgen did not recognize Dahui as a genuinely fully awakened teacher, Dahui's writings had a great influence on him. Gender was apparently a matter on which Dōgen agreed with Dahui; see Ishii Shūdō, "Raihaitokuzui kō," *Komazawa Daigaku Bukkyōgakubu Ronshū* 37 (2006): 69–90, 86a.

18. Steven Heine, "The Dōgen Canon: Dōgen's Pre-*Shōbōgenzō* Writings and the Question of Change in His Later Works," *Japanese Journal of Religious Studies*

24.1–2 (1997): 51; the quoted phrase is from Carl Bielefeldt, "Recarving the Dragon," in William R. Lafleur, ed., *Dōgen Studies* (Honolulu: University of Hawaii Press, 1985), 21–53.

19. Myoan Grace Schireson, *"Raihaitokuzui*: Dōgen's Seven Arguments for Empowering Zen Women," in Eido Frances Carney, ed., *Receiving the Marrow: Teachings on Dōgen by Sōtō Women Priests* (Olympia, WA: Temple Ground Press, 2012), 57–68.

20. Carl Bielefeldt, "Filling the Zen shū: Notes on the *Jisshū Yōdōki*," *Cahiers d'Extreme-Asie* 7 (1993–94): 235.

21. Technically these nuns were lay nuns, as full *bhiksuni* ordination for nuns had lapsed in Japan in the ninth century and was not restored until 1253. See Lori Meeks, *Hokkeji and the Reemergence of Female Monastic Orders in Premodern Japan* (Honolulu: University of Hawaii Press, 2010).

22. *Eihei Kōroku*, vol. 8, translated by Taigen Dan Leighton and Shohaku Okumura as *Dōgen's Extensive Record: A Translation of the Eihei Kōroku* (Boston: Wisdom, 2004), 506–7. I have retained the bulk of the translation here by Leighton and Okumura but have changed it to make it more literal. Leighton and Okumura's translation obscures the gendered term *daijobu* ("great manly person") and thus obscures the continuity of Dōgen's diction with that of his Chinese predecessors. Leighton and Okumura also obscure the term "former lives."

23. Leighton and Okamura, *Dōgen's Extensive Record*, 522–24, quotation on 524.

24. Chart 18 in *Zengaku Daijiten*, ed. Zengaku Daijiten Hensanjō (Tokyo: Taishūkan shoten, 1985), vol. 3 (Bekkan), 21.

25. On the *Shōbōgenzō Zuimonki*, see Heine, *Did Dōgen Go to China?*, 138–41. More detailed bibliographic information is given in Bodiford, "Textual Genealogies of Dōgen."

26. On the subject of women in Dōgen's sangha, see Tajima Hakudo, *Dōgen Keizan Ryo Zenji no Nisokan* (Nagoya: Sōtō-shū koto nigakurin shuppanbu, 1953); Tajima Hakudo, *Sōtōshu Nisoshi* (Tokyo: Sōtōshū nisōdan honbu sanyosha, 1955); Ishikawa Rikizan, "Chūsei Bukkyō ni okeru ni no iso ni tsuite: Toku ni Shoki Sōtō-shū Kyōdan no Jirei o chūshin to shite," *Komazawa Daigaku Zenkenkyūjo Nenpo* 3 (1992): 141–53; Paula Kane Robinson Arai, *Women Living Zen* (New York: Oxford University Press, 1999).

27. Morten Schlütter made this suggestion at a conference on Song Buddhism held at the University of Illinois in April 1996.

28. Kenji Matsuo, *A History of Japanese Buddhism* (Folkestone, UK: Global Oriental, 2007), 64.

29. William M. Bodiford, *Sōtō Zen in Medieval Japan* (Honolulu: University of Hawaii Press, 1993), 25. My summary of Dōgen's career in Japan after his return from China is indebted to Bodiford's account (22–26).

30. Heine, *Did Dōgen Go to China?*, 129.

31. Bodiford, "Textual Genealogies of Dōgen."

32. The term Dōgen uses might better be translated as "a mentor" or "a guide"; it is the same term that is used in China of teachers who direct one's doctoral research. Not only does this teacher instruct you in some subject, but she or he also guides you in your efforts to reach the goal. Hee-Jin Kim uses the term "guide" in his translation in his *Flowers of Emptiness: Selections from Dōgen's Shōbōgenzō* (Lewiston, NY: Edwin Mellen Press, 1985).

33. Ishii, "*Raihaitokuzui kō*," 62–63. This is also the theme of a dharma hall sermon (*jōdō*) in *Eihei Kōroku*, among other places; see Leighton and Okumura, *Dōgen's Extensive Record*, 109–10.

34. The first part of this sentence is taken from the statement of Moshan Liaoran to Zhixian that Dōgen quotes below. The second part of the sentence says that the teacher must be a *daijobu* (Ch. *dajangfu*). The notes in the *Nihon Koten Bungaku Taikei* edition of the *Shōbōgenzō* (vol. 81) cite the *Mahaparinirvana Sutra* (*Sutra on the Final Nirvana of Sakyamuni*), fascicle 9, the "Rulaixing" chapter, which says, "If one is able to know that he has the Buddha nature, I say that he has the characteristics of a man [*jangfu*]. If there is a woman [who knows], then she is a man [*nanzi*]." Kim's translation of *dajangfu* in *Flowers of Emptiness* is interesting: "What counts is that the guide be a being of virtue." This translation has the advantage of reflecting the way Mencius reinterpreted *dajangfu* to mean not a hero of great physical strength or political power but rather a moral hero, a man of virtue. The third part of the sentence refers to the story discussed by Dōgen in his "Immo" fascicle, the statement that if you want to know "such a thing," you must be "such a person."

35. I like Meeks's translation of *daijobu* as "great manly person" (*Hokkeji and the Reemergence of Female Monastic Orders*, 104–5). Meeks writes of contemporaries of Dōgen among Rinzai priests in Kyoto and Kamakura, and among Nara priests from others schools who had contact with those Rinzai priests, as impressed with Chan accounts of nuns active in Chan circles in China. Among those who similarly spoke of women as capable of being successful students of Chan and Zen if they were "manly persons" is Enni Ben'en's Chinese teacher Wuzhun Shifan (1177–1249). In describing a certain woman in the order, he says, "Even though she is a female priest [or "female monastic," a nun; *niso*], she can be regarded as a manly person [*jobu*]" (*Hokkeji and the Reemergence of Female Monastic Orders*, 105).

36. Eison quotes the *Sutra on the Final Nirvana of Sakyamuni*, fascicle 9, the "Rulaixing" chapter, just before making this statement about women (in Meeks, *Hokkeji and the Reemergence of Female Monastic Orders*, 105).

37. Andrew Ferguson, *Zen's Chinese Heritage: The Masters and Their Teachings* (Somerville, MA: Wisdom, 2000), 82.

38. Matsuo, *A History of Japanese Buddhism*, 26–27.

39. This story cannot be found in an extant Chinese text.

40. I am indebted for help with this passage to Joan Piggott of the University of Southern California and William Bodiford of the University of California at Los Angeles.

41. Dōgen's usage parallels that of the Chinese original, *dajangfu*, a "great hero" or a "great fellow."

42. *Huaizi* literally means "child, or son, of the Huai River"—perhaps a nickname for Miaoxin because she came from the Huai River region.

43. My translation here is largely based on that of Kim in *Flowers of Emptiness*, 290.

44. Meeks, *Hokkeji and the Reemergence of Female Monastic Orders*, 1.

45. See especially Lori Meeks, "Reconfiguring Ritual Authenticity: The Ordination Traditions of Aristocratic Women in Premodern Japan," *Japanese Journal of Religious Studies* 33.1 (2006): 51–74; Lori Meeks, "Buddhist Renunciation and the Female Life Cycle: Understanding Nunhood in Heian and Kamakura Japan," *Harvard Journal of Asiatic Studies* 70.1 (2010): 1–59.

46. Translation by Griffith Foulk.

47. Ishikawa Rikizan, "Dōgen no 'Nyoshin Fujobutsu Ron' ni tsuite—*Jūnikanbon Shōbōgenzō* no Seikaku o meguru oboegaki," *Komazawa Daigaku Zenkenkyūjo Nenpo* 1 (1990): 88–123.

48. David Putney, "Some Problems in Interpretation: The Early and Late Writings of Dōgen," *Philosphy East and West* 46/4 (1996): 497–531.

49. Stanley Weinstein's translation of "Raihaitokuzui" for the Sōtō Zen Text Project, accessed February 17, 2014, http://scbs.stanford.edu/sztp3/translations/shobo-genzo/translations/raihai_tokuzui/rhtz.translation.html.

50. Ishikawa, "Dōgen no 'Nyoshin Fujobutsu Ron' ni tsuite."

51. T 25.160c28–161b24.

52. T 3.211b6–9. In the sutra these vows lack numbers, as well as the formulaic expressions in which the vow is framed, starting with "In the future, after I have attained right awakening," and ending with "If that is not the case, then may I not attain right awakening [in the first place]."

53. Meeks, *Hokkeji and the Reemergence of Female Monastic Order*, 107–10. Meeks discusses Dōgen and this vow in "Shukke Kudoku" on 109.

54. Arai speculates that the offending line is an interpolation by a later editor in *Women Living Zen*.

55. It is worth comparing Dōgen and Song Chan to the case of Shinran and his followers explored by Galen Amstutz, "Ambivalence Regarding Women and Female Gender in Premodern Shin Buddhism," *Japanese Religions* 35 (2010): 1–32.

3

Dōgen, a Medieval Japanese Monk Well-Versed in Chinese Poetry

WHAT HE DID AND DID NOT COMPOSE

Steven Heine

On Dōgen's Chinese Writings and Poetry Collection

When Dōgen went to China as a young monk for a four-year stint from 1223 to 1227, he visited several temples in the area of the Southern Song capital of Hangzhou and gained enlightenment under the tutelage of the Caodong school master Rujing (Jp. Nyojō, 1163–1228) at Mount Tiantong (Jp. Mount Tendō).[1] This was previously the seat of master Hongzhi (Jp. Wanshi, 1091–1157), another prominent Caodong abbot who was known for his lyrical poetic compositions evoking the meaning of the experience of enlightenment.[2] From this training that abetted his reading of the entire Buddhist canon (Tripitaka), including voluminous Chinese works, prior to his travels while he was still studying in Kyoto on Mount Hiei as well as at Kenninji, the first Zen temple in Japan, Dōgen apparently became intimately familiar with a wide variety of Chan Buddhist textual materials.

Many of these texts included different types of poetry, such as cryptic comments on kōan (Ch. *gongan*) cases, lyrical verses celebrating a life of reclusion in nature, compositions with spiritual guidance for lay followers, and several additional categories. How knowledgeable was Dōgen in the intricacies of Chinese Chan verse, which followed rules of rhyme and tonal patterns and other elements of construction that were prescribed during the Tang dynasty and became typical of Song dynasty literature, including religious-oriented poetry? Was Dōgen able to utilize these regulations to his creative advantage in crafting eloquent Chan poems, or at least some examples that proved he was well-versed and skillful in the genre? If so, this must be considered a significant aspect of his oeuvre; if not, then how do we evaluate the significance of his lyricism other than for doctrinal or biographical reasons? Most Chinese verse (*kanshi*) that was widely recognized for its literary value in Japan was written by Rinzai (Ch. Linji) Zen monks and collected as Five Mountains literature (*Gozan bungaku*). Even though Dōgen and other Sōtō followers who composed poetry are almost entirely un(der)represented in those collections, this was an important literary activity that must be recognized as a context for assessing the history of the writings of Dōgen as an inheritor of the Chinese lineage and a founder of the Japanese sect.

According to an oft-cited passage in one of his sermons, Dōgen returned from China "with empty hands" (*kūshu genkyō*).[3] That is, he preferred to emphasize interior knowledge and wisdom gained during the journey, without the need to have accumulated many of the relics and regalia that were featured in the homecoming of most other Buddhist monks of this as well as earlier and subsequent periods, when collecting paraphernalia and external symbols of ritual attainment and authority was highly prized. As I have discussed previously, Dōgen's empty-handed return to Japan does not suggest that he was empty-headed, although he had a head "full of emptiness," to make a wordplay on the Buddhist metaphysics of vacuity (Ch. *kong*, Jp. *kū*).[4] Dōgen came back to his native country with an immense knowledge of and appreciation for the Chinese literary tradition and its multifarious expressions in various forms of Chan writings, including poetry, which he both emulated and transformed via engagement and integration with rhetorical styles of Japanese vernacular literature and different sorts of traditional Buddhist discourse.

Dōgen had a profound understanding of Chinese Chan prose sources, as evidenced by his ability to cite these materials extensively and with a great power of recall of the details of particular passages, while also challenging and changing their implications to suit his own conceptual needs or perhaps to reflect a creative misunderstanding of the source. This is the key to explaining the greatness of his two major writings. The first of these is the vernacular (*kana*) *Shōbōgenzō*, a collection of informal sermons (Ch. *shizhong*, Jp. *jishu*) composed in Japanese that are largely based on citations and reinterpretations of Chinese Chan texts, which he revises and modifies—some would say distorts, perhaps deliberately but also in some cases unwittingly—in order to convey his distinctive religious vision regarding the relation between practice and realization in the context of the world of impermanence and incessant change.[5]

The other major writing is the *Eihei Kōroku*, a ten-volume collection composed in Sino-Japanese (*kanbun*) consisting of formal sermons (Ch. *shangtang*, Jp. *jōdō*) and lectures in the first eight volumes and several styles of Chinese poetry in the final two volumes, to be discussed below.[6] Here again Dōgen often cites or alludes to, and at the same time innovatively critiques and refashions, a wide range of Chan textual materials, including those of Hongzhi and Rujing as well as several dozen other prominent masters, especially as extracted from the seminal transmission of the lamp text, the *Jingde Chuandenglu* (Jp. *Keitoku Dentōroku*). This was initially compiled as a reservoir of Chan narratives in 1004 and published five years later with a new introduction by a prominent poet, Yang Yi. Dōgen also clearly gained a high level of familiarity with at least several dozen other prominent Chan collections of sayings and kōan case commentaries from the Song dynasty.[7]

It is important to observe the historical irony that the vernacular *Shōbōgenzō* was compiled during the early period of Dōgen's career (1231–1243), while he was still in Kyoto, where many of his followers probably could understand Chinese fairly well. However, the Sino-Japanese collection of the *Eihei Kōroku* was primarily derived from the later period (1244–1253), when he was located at Eiheiji temple in the remote Echizen Mountains, where the vast majority of disciples who had not been with him in the capital would not have had a good comprehension of Chinese or knowledge of *kanbun* sources. On the other hand, it is clear that a prime motivation for Dōgen's transition from *kana* to *kanbun* writing was that, once he established a formal dharma hall (Ch. *fatang*, Jp. *hattō*) at his mountain temple in 1244, which was constructed in the seven-hall (*shichidō garan*) manner of what he experienced at Mount Tiantong and other Chinese monasteries, he was eager to follow the teaching model of his Chan mentors and predecessors. In any case, in both the *Shōbōgenzō* and the *Eihei Kōroku*, Dōgen often presents his own distinctive set of interpretations, which consistently modifies and critiques the mainstream view he had learned in China regarding various Chan sayings and dialogues.

Dōgen's Chinese poetry contained in the *Eihei Kōroku*, mainly in the ninth and tenth volumes, consists of over three hundred verses. In addition, quite a few of the sermons collected in the first eight volumes also include poems used to make commentaries on Chan sayings or anecdotes, including kōans, although it is sometimes difficult to discern if these are to be counted as verse or as a hybrid prose-poetry composition. Table 3.1 provides a detailed content analysis of the types and numbers of poems Dōgen composed.

Table 3.1 Dōgen's Chinese Poetry Collection

Eihei Kōroku	Subtotal	Total
Vols. 1–8, Jōdō (Ch. *Shangtang*)		57 (uncertain)
Vol. 1 (1236–43, ed. Senne)	9	
Vol. 2 (1245.4–1246.7, ed. Ejō)	1	
Vol. 3 (1246.7–1248.4, ed. Ejō)	6	
Vol. 4 (1248.4–1249.8, ed. Ejō)	3	
Vol. 5 (1249.9–1251.1, ed. Gien)	14	
Vol. 6 (1251.2–1251.10, ed. Gien)	7	
Vol. 7 (1251.12–1252.12, ed. Gien)	15	
Vol. 8, Hōgo (Ch. *Fayu*) (n.d., ed. Ejō)	2	
Vol. 9 (1235)		102
Juko (Ch. *Songgu*) on 90 Kōan (Ch. *Gongan*)		
Vol. 10		150
Shinsan (Ch. *Zhenzan*)	5 (4 irregular)	
Jisan (Ch. *Zizan*)	20 (12 irregular)	
Geju (Ch. *Jisong*)	125	
1–50 in China (1223–27)	50 (37 secular)	
51–76 in Kyoto/Fukakusa (1227–43)	26 (1 secular)	
77 in Kamakura (1248)	1	
78–125 in Echizen/Eiheiji (1243–53)	48 (1 secular)	
Also: Misc. (Bell, Silent Illumination, Death)	3	3
TOTAL		312 (plus?)

To sum up the contents briefly, there are four main categories of *kanshi* compositions:

1. The largest number of verses is contained in vol. 10 of the *Eihei Kōroku*, which includes 150 poems written throughout the various stages of Dōgen's career, including the only known writings (fifty poems) from his four-year stay in China. This section encompasses twenty-five verses on the enlightenment experience of the Chan patriarchs (*shinsan*) and of Dōgen himself (*jisan*), as well as 125 poems of various styles under the general heading of *geju*, primarily on lyrical and naturalistic topics as well as communications with lay followers (this is true only of the poems composed in China, where there was a strong tradition of Chan priests highly engaged with the concerns of nonclerics). There are also

verses dealing with monastic rituals, in addition to some of Dōgen's personal experiences and evocative reflections on the role of language versus silence and emotion versus detachment in the quest for spiritual realization. This includes some examples of "irregular" verses, or those that do not follow typical poetic patterns, and "secular" verses that do not deal explicitly with religious themes.

2. The second largest group in volume 9 of the *Eihei Kōroku* includes 102 four-line verses, or *juko*, on ninety of the spiritual enigmas or kōan cases that are the hallmark of Chan literature and practice (some of the kōans have two or three verse commentaries); all of these were composed in 1235, around the same time Dōgen was also working on the compilation of three hundred kōan cases in the *Mana Shōbōgenzō* (a.k.a. *Sanbyakusoku Shōbōgenzō*), which is a list of case records without any commentary produced in 1236. Both of the mid-1230s kōan collection texts seem to be part of a phase of preparation for Dōgen to gather in his mind relevant Chinese source materials before embarking just a few years later on his groundbreaking style of interpreting case records in the vernacular *kana Shōbōgenzō* and *kanbun* Sino-Japanese *Eihei Kōroku* sermons.

3. There are also verse comments that Dōgen integrated into his formal and informal *kanbun* sermons in the initial eight volumes of the *Eihei Kōroku*, which include dharma hall discourses before a public audience in volumes 1 through 7 and more informal preaching for a selected audience in volume 8. It is noteworthy that the number of poems increases significantly in volumes 5 through 7, which may mark a shift in Dōgen's approach in his later years or reflect the predilections of the editor Gien, who may have included more poetry than the previous editors did based on his own sense of their importance. However, the grand total of such poems is uncertain, since modern Japanese editions following traditional manuscript models of the text generally do not mark a distinction between where prose comments end and poetry begins in Dōgen's sermons.[8]

4. There are several prominent Chinese verses that appear elsewhere in Dōgen's collected works, including an example in which he rewrites one of Rujing's verses on the symbolism of the ringing of a bell and one that is a reworking of a famous verse by Hongzhi on silent illumination as a form of meditation, both of which are included in *Shōbōgenzō* fascicles, in addition to a poem at the time of his passing inspired by Rujing's death verse (*yuige*).[9]

Furthermore Dōgen composed a collection of sixty-six Japanese-style verses, or thirty-one-syllable *waka*, most of which were first included in the Sōtō sect's official biography, the *Kenzeiki*, published in 1472, over two hundred years after his death; of these, fifty-three verses are considered authentic

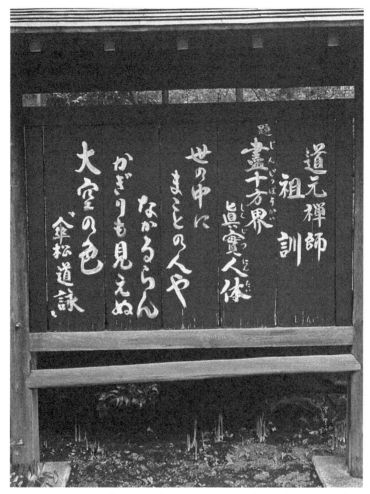

FIGURE 3.1 Dōgen's *waka* at Seishōji temple in Tokyo. Photograph by Steven Heine.

by modern scholars, and thirteen are deemed likely to be spurious.[10] There are a number of instances in which the *kanshi* and *waka* verses cover similar thematic territory or use comparable rhetorical styles. Figure 3.1 includes an example of Dōgen's *waka* on a signpost standing outside the modern Sōtō temple, Seishōji, located in central Tokyo, illustrating the importance of these works for sectarian practice today.[11]

In both the *Shōbōgenzō* and *Eihei Kōroku* in addition to numerous other writings, Dōgen produced a significant body of work that has been prized by traditional and modern commentators for developing a unique way of assimilating Chinese sources into Japanese contexts. However, some key aspects of Dōgen's ability to cite and write in Chinese forms adapted to Japanese were somewhat limited. An analysis of his prose and poetic texts in comparison with those of Chinese masters shows that there are certain styles typical of Song Chan poetry that he did not attempt to write, or only sparingly so, in that he either was forced by deficiency or preferred instead to use a form of expression to forge new discursive pathways while targeting his Japanese followers.

Perhaps the main example of this tendency is that, even though Dōgen commented extensively on dozens of Chan kōan records, he gave up writing four-verse *gatha* (Ch. *songgu*, Jp. *juko*) comments after an experiment with this style in 1235, included as volume 9 of *Eihei Kōroku*. He also generally did not try his hand at crafting poetic capping phrase (Ch. *zhuoyu*, Jp. *jakugo*) remarks on kōans, which was the rage among Chinese commentators at the time, especially in the *Blue Cliff Record* (Ch. *Biyanlu*, Jp. *Hekiganroku*) of 1128, the most prominent kōan collection that Dōgen apparently knew very well since he cites the same cases frequently and is said, according to some legends, to have been the one who brought the text to Japan.[12] In some cases, such as his interpretation of a famous verse by the Northern Song lay Buddhist poet Su Shi (1036–1101) that is featured in the "Keisei sanshoku" ("Sounds of Valleys, Colors of Mountains") fascicle of the *Shōbōgenzō*, Dōgen apparently favors the use of prose commentary rather than trying to compete with the literary giant's original composition.

The remainder of this chapter examines the kinds of Chan poetry Dōgen did and did not compose and their significance (or lack) for interpreting his oeuvre against the background of East Asian Buddhist literature. I focus on the following topics:

The overall impact of Dōgen's Chinese and Japanese poetry collections for understanding his career writings, as well as the way these have been received and appropriated over the centuries.

The issue, explored in some of Dōgen's verses, of whether literary imagery serves as a useful vehicle for expressing and enhancing, or as a distraction that detracts from, the realization of spiritual awareness.

How some of the poems convey autobiographical reflections in a way not otherwise revealed in Dōgen's prose writings, since these works are primarily doctrinal rather than personal texts with a few exceptions, such as "Bendōwa" and *Hōkyōki*.

The use of poetry to highlight and enhance Dōgen's Buddhist view of naturalism and an affirmation of phenomenal reality, as influenced by indigenous religiosity valorizing nature and everyday experience.

His prose rather than, for the most part, poetic commentary on Su Shi's prominent Buddhist verse on gaining enlightenment through an ecstatic experience of contemplating nature.

How Dōgen sometimes employed poetry to convey a philosophical message, but also why he did not utilize some typical Chinese Chan poetic
forms or instead chose prose commentary.

A concluding reflection on whether Dōgen does or does not appear to go
beyond didacticism in his poetic compositions.

As part of these discussions I will also consider and attempt to evaluate the
extent to which Dōgen was able to utilize Chinese poetic forms according to
their rules and regulations, especially the truncated four-line poetry known
as the *jueju* style (abbreviated from the prototypical eight-line form), with two
couplets consisting of five or seven characters each that have rhymes and tonal
patterns as well as caesuras internal to each line but without enjambment
linking the verse segments.

Overall Impact of Poetic Composition

In analyzing Dōgen's strengths and limitations as a creator of Chinese poems,
it is important to make a basic distinction between what he achieved as a writer
of prose commentaries, which reflect literary influences through a generic
sense of aesthetic embellishment and rhetorical flourish to enhance the ele-
gance and eloquence of his writing, and what he accomplished specifically
through verse compositions. While the vernacular narrative writings of the
Shōbōgenzō are greatly admired for their lyrical quality and are often included
in discussions of classical Japanese literature, this is far less the case with his
kanbun writings in the *Eihei Kōroku*.

Dōgen's Chinese poetry in particular has not been much appreciated
or studied due to a variety of factors regarding composition and its reception, in large part for sectarian reasons; literature and the arts were generally considered the domain of the rival Rinzai (Ch. Linji) sect in the highly
specialized world of Japanese religions. In Japan to a greater extent than in
China, government supervision traditionally pigeonholed Buddhist schools
in terms of the kinds of practices they were allowed to follow and related
restrictions, especially as a legacy of the hierarchy of the Edo era, during
which the Tokugawa shogunate required each Buddhist school to define its
agenda as separate from and not overlapping with that of any other schools'
approach to religiosity.

Let us consider the literary and naturalistic aspects of the prose writings of
Dōgen, who is known from the *Shōbōgenzō* for being the first major Buddhist
thinker to use Japanese vernacular writing, which at the time was almost exclusively the realm of literature exemplified by the Heian-era *Genji Monogatari* and

Kokin Wakashū, among many other masterpieces. This innovative yet eclectic text has been included in collections of classical Japanese literature, such as the *Nihon no Koten Bungaku*. There is also some evidence suggesting that Dōgen was a participant in *uta-awase*, poetry contests held among the court literati in Kyoto around 1230, a transitional phase of his career, and that he befriended Fujiwara Teika (1162–1241), the most renowned poet and literary critic of the era, who was the editor of the *Shinkokin Wakashū* poetry collection of 1205.

From a philosophical standpoint, Dōgen's probing and evocative approach to issues related to the transiency of reality has been associated with the medieval Japanese "metaphysics of impermanence" (*keijijōgaku no mujō*),[13] which is also expressed in such prominent Buddhist-influenced literary works as Kamo no Chōmeï's (1153?–1216?) *Hōjōki*, a personal essay on choosing a life of reclusion as a reprieve from the incessancy of change; the war epic *Heike Monogatari*'s comments on evanescence; and Yoshida Kenkō's *Tsurezuregusa*, reflections on monastic manners based on an appreciation of the shifting of the seasons. Dōgen's sense of naturalism evoking the pristine mountain setting of Eiheiji temple in Figures 3.2 and 3.3 reflects the view of Japanese aesthetics that combines the original enlightenment thought (*hongaku shisō*) of Tendai Buddhism with native animism.

In addition Dōgen's prose writings show stylistic and thematic features that draw on Japanese as well as Chinese literary traditions. These include his impressive use of calligraphy, as evidenced in the original script still available today of his meditation manual, the *Fukanzazengi*, supposedly the first text he wrote from the early 1230s after returning from China a few years earlier. The calligraphy in Figure 3.4 is recognized and highly prized for its formal handwriting technique, in contrast to the cursive style in Figure 3.5. Another aspect of literary flair is Dōgen's extensive manipulation in the *Shōbōgenzō* of linguistic meanings through philosophical punning and wordplay that highlights discrepancies in Japanese pronunciations and syntactical uses of Chinese characters.

Dōgen's *kanshi* poems, which are influenced by the Chan and broader Chinese literary traditions, demonstrate knowledge of the use of end-rhyme following the schemes AABA or ABCB, as well as level and oblique tonal patterns and the role of a caesura in the middle of each line, according to the *jueju* style. Moreover many of his poems, in addition to the prose commentaries consisting of interlinear comments on source texts, seem to follow the typical fourfold Chinese literary approach (*qi cheng zhuan he* [*jie*]) of offering an opening statement (*qi*), followed by explanatory development (*cheng*), a turnabout or inversion of meaning (*zhuan*), and a synthetic conclusion (*he* or *jie*). This seems to be crucial for understanding Dōgen's way of providing criticisms

FIGURE 3.2 Mountain setting of Eiheiji temple. Photograph by Steven Heine.

that change or reverse through subtle rewriting and wordplay the implications of prior interpretative approaches to Chan sayings and dialogues.

However, it is also the case that Dōgen's Chinese and Japanese poetry collections are not very well known or received. For one thing Dōgen himself disputes the role of elegant words used in poetic writings in favor of didacticism and pure dharma instruction in a prominent passage in a collection of evening lectures known as the *Shōbōgenzō Zuimonki* of 1236. Some scholars have also pointed out that his *waka* were not included in the *Kenzeiki* until over two centuries after his death and therefore may be an unreliable source, and that, with

FIGURE 3.3 Sacred water from Mount Hakusan offered at Eiheiji. Photograph by Steven Heine.

only one or two exceptions, the *kanshi* poems are not included in the prestigious medieval Japanese Five Mountains literature collections dominated by contributors from the Rinzai sect. (An exception is a lyrical verse about a hermitage in Fukakusa, discussed below.) It is further mentioned that the *Eihei Kōroku* was compiled early on but that extant editions were probably significantly edited in the Edo period in the intimidating context of the shogunate's strict oversight of religious sects, and therefore many components of the text's authenticity may be called into question.

Nevertheless the traditional skeptical view regarding Dōgen's poetry was altered significantly with the 1968 Nobel Prize acceptance speech of Kawabata Yasunari, "Japan, the Beautiful, and Myself," in which the novelist made an

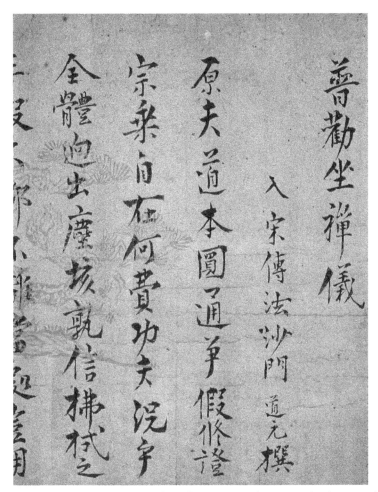

FIGURE 3.4 The prized calligraphy of Dōgen's *Fukanzazengi*. Photograph by Steven Heine.

opening reference to one of Dōgen's *waka* as being a major source of inspiration.[14] This caused the Sōtō sect to reevaluate the founder's view of poetry, and since that time both the Japanese and the Chinese collections have been examined more vigorously than at any phase since an eighteenth-century revival of scholastic studies. One major development was that a former abbot of Eiheiji temple provided an analysis of the rhyme scheme of the *kanshi* collection.[15] However, almost all of these newer studies have been conducted by sectarian scholars or priests, whose main goal is to explore Buddhist symbolism. For the most part literature scholars in Japan today still are not studying Dōgen's poetry for a fuller assessment of its aesthetic qualities as literary composition.

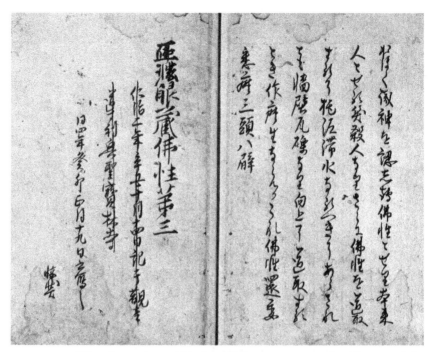

FIGURE 3.5 Dōgen's cursive writing in a *Shōbōgenzō* manuscript. Photograph by Steven Heine.

Literature as a Vehicle for or Distraction from Religious Experience?

Part of the reason for the continuing reluctance on the part of researchers to engage with and examine Dōgen's poetry is that he himself disavowed writing as an end in itself. Yet it is also clear he felt deeply that he could not help but be greatly influenced by the world of literature. A highly creative sense of ambivalence and uncertainty regarding words in contrast to the renunciation of language seen in relation to the spiritual quest is compellingly conveyed in a number of his Chinese and Japanese verses. Dōgen became a monk on Mount Hiei in 1213 and went to Mount Tiantong in China a decade later, and in both situations he entered into a cultural environment where there was profound interaction of Buddhism and the literati, many of whom were lay practitioners whose support was crucial to sustaining Chan/Zen temples, as well as an ongoing conflict yet underlying interdependency of pro- and antiliterary polemics.

This controversy is referred to as the debate between conceiving of Zen as a "special transmission beyond words and letters" (Ch. *jiaowai biechuan buli wenzi,*

Jp. *kyōge betsuden furyū monji*) and "literary Zen" (Ch. *wenzi chan*, Jp. *monji zen*), emphasizing silence versus speech in the context of making a commitment to live in and transform the mundane world while seeking solace through the path of utter detachment. In other words, should one who pursues the dharma with firm dedication remain in the realm of ordinary affairs and risk secularization or leave behind communication altogether for what may become a stubborn sense of isolation? Can such a seeker write about the religious quest in order to instructively evoke feelings of compassion and longing for the dharma, or must he give up pen and paper to emphasize the path of renunciation?

In the *Shōbōgenzō Zuimonki* Dōgen apparently draws a clear line between religion and art by warning his disciples against the pursuit of "style and rhetoric," which may distract from or impede their spiritual development. He conveys a "great doubt" about the need for writing while undertaking sustained meditative practice when he cautions, "The composition of literature, Chinese poetry and Japanese verse is worthless, and must be renounced." Furthermore, he insists, "Zen monks are fond of literature these days, finding it helpful to compose verses and write tracts. This is a mistake. ... No matter how elegant their prose or how exquisite their poetry might be, they are merely playing around with words and cannot gain the truth. ... Writing is a waste of time, and the reading of this literature should be cast aside."[16]

This harsh critique comes from a Zen master known for continually editing his graceful though challenging *Shōbōgenzō* prose throughout his career, even to his dying days. The distinction Dōgen makes between "art for art's sake" and the search for truth, or an idle indulgence in literature and an exclusive determination to fulfill the pursuit of the sacred, was played out in his personal life. His biography gives prominence to his departure from the elite world of the Kyoto court aesthetes, where he could have had a successful career based on his aristocratic birth and education. But despite pursuing the Buddhist path—or perhaps because of Buddhism's powerful connections with the literati in Japan and China—it is precisely an attraction to the realm of literature and to a shared sense of responsibility to construct compelling rhetoric about the spiritual quest that is captured, not only in the prose writings but also in his poetry.

Dōgen's Chinese and Japanese verse reveals that he is ever reminded that the frail beauty of nature arouses feelings that inspire spiritual striving expressed through literature in spite of, and while always recognizing, the inevitable limitations of emotional responses to transiency as well as the innate restrictions of language in trying to depict religious experience. In a verse contained in *Eihei Kōroku* 10.105c, he evokes the Buddhist struggle of being in the world and remaining mindful of the attraction of natural phenomena while straining to retire from feelings and the desire to compose, which is a form of attachment:

> *Living for so long in this world without attachments,*
> *Since giving up using paper and pen*
> *I see flowers and hear birds without feeling much,*
> *While dwelling on this mountain, I am embarrassed by my meager efforts.*

久舍人間無愛惜/文章筆硯既抛來/見花聞鳥風情少/乍在山猶愧不才.[17]

In the first line, if the verb "living" (*she*) in the second character contained the hand radical, which one commentator suggests may have been lost in the editing process, so that it becomes "abandoning" (*she*), this part of the verse would emphasize detachment even more strongly. Meanwhile the last line is filled with a sense of shame and misgiving about the choices he has made, as well as his inability to carry through fully with either side of the delicate balance between feeling and speaking in opposition to serenity and silence.

An analysis of the verse with Pinyin tones inserted—Jiǔ shè rénjiān wú aìxī / Wénzhāng bǐyàn jì pāo lái / Jiàn huā wén niǎo fēnqíng shǎo / Zhà zài shān yóu kuì bù cái—indicates that it adheres to an ABCB rhyme scheme, with the third character from the end of each line in the opposite tone from the final character. (Both characters are highlighted with italicized tone indicators in lines 2 and 4.)[18]

久舍人間無愛惜. 文章筆硯既抛來.
仄仄平平平仄仄. 平平仄仄仄平平.
見花聞鳥風情少. 乍在山猶愧不才.
仄平中仄平平仄. 仄仄平中仄仄平.

The poem also has a caesura after the fourth character in each line as well as the conceptual progression of opening-development-turnabout-conclusion. It is one of the most successful and satisfying—from a formalistic standpoint, at least—of Dōgen's Chinese verses.

The creative tension between speech and silence, engagement and detachment is similarly conveyed in a couple of Dōgen's Japanese poems. The first of these bears a title stressing renunciation that is contraindicated by the verse's content, featuring the potentially productive role of language:

> *"Furyū monji"*   *"No reliance on words or letters"*
> *Ii suteshi*   *Unlimited*
> *Sono koto no ha no*   *By language [petals of words],*
> *Hoka nareba*   *It is ceaselessly expressed—*

Fude ni mo ato o	*So too the way of letters*
Todome zari keri.	*Can display but not exhaust it.*[19]

The next example expresses Dōgen's own sense of uncertainty about his qualifications as either writer or renunciant:

Haru kaze ni	*Will their gaze fall upon*
Waga koto no ha no	*The petals of words I utter,*
Chirinuru o	*As if only the notes*
Hana no uta to ya	*Of a flower's song*
Hito no nagamen.	*Shaken loose and blown free by the spring breeze?*[20]

The following *kanshi* verse in *Eihei Kōroku* 10.71c uses an idiom in the third line that literally means "withered like chicken skin and crane's hair" so as to highlight Dōgen's ironic sense of becoming obsolete while feeling an ambivalence regarding the tension between withdrawal and engagement:

"Snowy Evening in Spring"
Peach and plum blossoms, snow and frost, have no attachment,
Green pines and emerald bamboos are shrouded in cloudy mist.
I am not yet dried up and over the hill,
Even though it's been several decades since I renounced fame and fortune.

春雪夜
桃李雪霜非愛処/青松翠竹幾雲煙/雞皮鶴髪縦無染/名利抛来数十年.[21]

One translator seems to overemphasize human subjectivity a bit by rendering the opening, "Peach and plum blossoms under snow and frost are not what I love."[22] This reading tends to personalize and thus modify the implications of having emotions in a passage that refers to being guided by transcendence amid impermanence, symbolized by the image of flowers enduring snow in late winter or early spring as well as the pines and bamboos remaining unaffected by the cloudy mist. The natural phenomena are aged but not withered, a lyrical image that seems to reflect the subjective sensations Dōgen feels rather than objective instances of nature.

Autobiographical Poems

One of the interesting features of both the Chinese and Japanese poetry collections is that they include several prominent examples commenting on Dōgen's emotions regarding key turning points in his life, thereby offering a rare glimpse into the thoughts and attitudes of a master known primarily for aloof metaphysical musings.²³ For example, the following *kanshi* verse in *Eihei Kōroku* 10.69c, one of six poems written in a hermitage, reveals Dōgen's thoughts around 1230, several years after returning from China but also three years prior to the opening of his first temple in Kyoto, when he no doubt felt a bit frustrated in trying to establish his new Zen sect in Japan:

> *How pitiful is birth-death with its constant ceasing and arising!*
> *I lose my way and find my path as if walking in a dream.*
> *Although there are still things I cannot forget,*
> *The deep grass of Fukakusa settles in the sound of the evening rain.*

生死可憐休又起/迷途覺路夢中行/雖然尚有難忘事/深草閑居夜雨声.²⁴

During this period Dōgen was staying in a retreat in the area of Fukakusa, to the southeast of the capital, that was favored by many of the literati as a pristine getaway from the turmoil of court life. Because the name of the town is literally "deep grass," this term was ripe for being the source of many puns in Japanese *waka* of the era reflecting on life in the city versus an escape to the countryside.

Here the vulnerability and instability Dōgen was experiencing is disclosed in a way that makes such attitudes productive for stimulating dedication to the religious quest. Many of the characters in the second line can also bear an explicit Buddhist connotation, including delusion (*mi*), awakening (*jue*), transcendence (*mengzhong* [literally, "within a dream"] or, conversely, unreality), and practice (*xing*), so that the passage could be rendered, "I practice within a transcendental realm while experiencing both delusion and awakening." This wording does not alter the meaning but highlights that the verse can be read as directly or indirectly evoking the effects of Buddhist discipline. Also, in considering the Pinyin tones for this verse—Shēngsǐ kělián xiū yòu qǐ / Mítú juélù mèngzhōng xíng / Suīrán shàng yǒu nánwàng shì / Shēn cǎo xiánjū yèyǔshēng—we find ABAB rhyme and the appropriate use of tones as well as caesura and conceptual progression:

生死可憐休又起. 迷途覺路夢中行.
平仄仄平平仄仄. 平平仄仄仄中平.
雖然尚有難忘事. 深草閑居夜雨声.
平平中仄平中仄. 中仄平平仄仄平.

Another *kanshi* poem with intriguing autobiographical implications deals with Dōgen's return to Eiheiji temple in the third month of 1248, after six months of travel (beginning in the eighth month of 1247) to the new capital of

Kamakura at the bequest of the shogun Hōjō Tokiyori, who offered him the opportunity to lead a new temple being built there; this eventually became Kenchōji, a leading Rinzai temple opened in 1253 and supervised by the renowned abbot Rankei Dōryū (Ch. Lanxi Daolong), who was imported from China. Before looking at the verse, let us consider a prose passage in *Eihei Kōroku* 3.251, which comments on the time of Dōgen's return, when he was apparently sensitive to criticism and skepticism from the monks who had been left leaderless at Eiheiji and may have feared that the master had changed his spiritual message to accommodate new lay followers involved in political power struggles and warfare.

Dōgen acknowledges that he had traveled "to expound the dharma for patrons and lay students," and that "some of you may have questions about the purpose of these travels."[25] But he goes on to argue for the ethical component of his teaching that is consistent with monastic training based on the doctrine of karmic rewards and punishments:

> It may sound like I value worldly people and take lightly monks. Moreover, some of you may ask whether I presented some Dharma that I never expounded, and that you have not heard before. However, there was no Dharma preached that I have not previously expounded, or that you have not heard. I merely explained that people who practice virtue improve and those who produce unwholesomeness degenerate, so they should clarify the cause and experience the results, and throw away the tile [mundane affairs] and only take up the jewel [dharma].

However, it seems that the focus on karmic causality was a new teaching that he developed in the late stages of his career, as is supported by analyzing the chronology of passages where it is explained in various sections of the *Shōbōgenzō* and *Eihei Kōroku*.[26]

Nevertheless, as was the case with the Fukakusa verse and other poems, in this sermon Dōgen can be found brooding about his missteps as he confesses, "How many errors I have made in my effort to cultivate the way! Today, I deeply regret how I have become like a water buffalo. This mountain monk has been gone for more than half a year. I was like a solitary wheel placed in vast space." Yet he concludes the sermon on a more upbeat note: "Today, I have returned to the mountains, and the monks [literally, clouds] are feeling joyful. My great love for the mountains has been significantly enhanced."

According to some of what can only be considered legends buttressed by a collection of twelve *waka* composed for the occasion, when Dōgen refused to accept the shogun's offer the Hōjō became enraged and threatened the Zen master's life, though his sword was dissuaded by the spiritual aura or force field generated by Dōgen's meditative prowess. In other versions the shogun paid tribute to Dōgen as he walked off with a sense of dignity and integrity still intact. In any case, as part of the celebration of the 800th anniversary of Dōgen's death in 2003, a new stele was installed across from Kenchōji commemorating the spot where he apparently took a stand for his commitment to just-sitting meditation (*shikan-taza*) at the expense of sacrificing the opportunity for practical worldly gain (see Figure 0.1 in the introduction).

The *kanbun* poem on the topic of the Kamakura journey is *Eihei Kōroku* 10.77c, which was composed in the third month of 1248, while Dōgen was still in Kamakura but making up his mind about leaving:

For half a year I've been taking my rice in the home of a layman.
The old tree's plum blossoms sitting amid frost and snow—
Awakened from my slumber by the crash of thunderbolts (BANG BAM
*   BOOM),*
In the capital [emperor's town], spring is brightened by red peach blossoms.

半年喫飯白衣舍/老樹梅花霜雪中/警蟄一雷轟霹靂/帝鄉春色桃花紅.[27]

In comparing himself to a plum tree known for symbolizing rejuvenation, Dōgen refers to his dismay at realizing suddenly, from the stirring effect of an early spring storm (the last three characters in line 3 form an onomatopoeia evoking the "bang bam boom" of thunder), that he had been lost in a kind of ritual hibernation, so to speak, while being entertained by a layman (the shogun). Now he longs for a return to Kyoto, which is close enough to Echizen to remind him of the life of monastic purity. However, as we have seen from the sermon delivered upon his return, he had to face another challenge in coming to terms with his followers' feelings of betrayal and alienation.

In this instance of Pinyin—Bànnián chī fàn bái yī shè / Lǎoshù méihuā shuāngxuězhōng / Jǐng zhé yì léi hōng pīlì / Dìxiāng chūnsè méihuā hóng—the ABAB rhyme is regular, along with the conceptual progression, but the tonal patterns and use of caesura are not, as shown in the following textual analysis:

半年喫飯白衣舍. 老樹梅花霜雪中.
仄平仄仄仄平仄. 仄仄平中平仄平.
警蟄一雷轟霹靂. 帝鄉春色桃花紅.
仄仄仄平平仄仄. 仄平平仄平平平.

Naturalism and Affirmation of Phenomenal Reality

Dōgen's primary interest in writing poetry was probably not to express either personal feelings or impersonal thoughts but to go beyond that distinction by evoking naturalism through images of seasonal changes, which had long been used in both Chinese and Japanese literature as a symbol of interiority and spiritual development ever tinged with ambivalent feelings. A prime example of this is that there are over forty references in *Eihei Kōroku* sermons and verses, especially from the late period of his career, expressing his appreciation for the imagery of plum blossoms, which bloom in late winter while there is still snow, as a symbol of renewal after a period of decline. This is seen in prose writings as well; for instance, *Shōbōgenzō* "Baika" ("Plum Blossoms"), written after three feet of snow fell on the sixth day of the eleventh month of 1243 at a hermitage in Echizen, suggests, "When an old plum tree blooms unexpectedly, just then the world unfolds itself with the flowering."[28] In *Shōbōgenzō* "Kūge" ("Flowers of Emptiness") Dōgen writes, "A plum tree that some days ago did not have flowers blooms, signaling the arrival of spring. When the time is right, it immediately blooms."[29]

Here and elsewhere Dōgen is no doubt influenced by Chinese literary works, such as a famed verse by the eighth-century Buddhist literati Wang Wei (699–759):

> *"Miscellaneous Poem"*
> *You, who have come from my hometown,*
> *Let me know what's been happening there!*
> *On the day you arrived, would the late winter plum blossoms*
> *Have opened yet in front of my silken window?*
>
> 雜詩
> 君自故鄉來／應知故鄉事／來日綺窗前／寒梅著花未.[30]

According to the naturalistic worldview this evokes, the very first whiff of the sweet fragrance of the plums heralds the advent of spring; indeed the new season is contained in, or its manifestation is coterminous with, the budding of the blossom. This sense of awakening is a cyclical event that occurs regularly on the same withered branch every year, but each time it is experienced as a spontaneous rejuvenation in the midst of decline and dejection. From a pantheistic standpoint, one single branch equals all branches, and the whole tree in that the here-and-now aspect of blooming generates the power of arising everywhere and at any time. Furthermore the purity of the white color of the blossoms amid the fallen snow ("silken window") creates a monochromatic spectacle that gives rise in the imagination to a display of manifold hues, thus combining the one with the many and the real with the illusory.

Dōgen may have also had in mind a specifically Chan symbolism suggesting that the five petals of the plum evoke the five branches of the fledgling Tang dynasty religious movement, of which the Linji and Caodong schools emerged as the main rivals by the time he arrived in Southern Song China. Dōgen was further influenced by the counterintuitive or inverted Buddhist notion suggested in a two-line verse by Rujing that the image of the plum might be as good as or better than reality, or represents a symbol of awakening since the time of Sakyamuni, in that it endures longer and appears unflawed:

> *Original face is not bound by birth-and-death.*
> *Spring abiding in the plum blossoms enters into a painting.*

本來面目無生死/春在梅花入畫圖.[31]

In *Eihei Kōroku* 7.481, in a poem that comprises the entire sermon from the time of the full moon of the first month of 1252, Dōgen expresses feelings of being captivated by the plum:

> *How is there dust in the snow-covered reeds?*
> *Who can recognize the Pure Land amidst so many people?*
> *The fragrance of a single late winter plum blossom bursts forth,*
> *There in the emptiness is held the awakening of spring.*

雪覆蘆花豈染塵/誰知浄地尚多人/寒梅一点芳心綻/喚起劫壺空處春.[32]

In *Eihei Kōroku* 7.530 (n.d.), the next to last formal sermon Dōgen delivered before falling into the illness that led to his death a year and a half later, he writes of the account in which King Prasenajit asks Venerable Pindola if he ever met the Buddha.[33] First Dōgen cites a Rujing verse interpreting this episode in light of plum blossom symbolism:

> *By raising his eyebrows he completed the dialogue,*
> *He met Buddha face-to-face and they did not hide anything from each other.*
> *Today he is worshiped in the four corners of the world,*
> *As spring occurs on the tip of a plum branch wrapped in a layer of white snow.*

策起眉毛答問端/親會見佛不相瞞/而今応供四天下/春在梅梢帶雪寒.[34]

An alternate translation of Rujing's verse that tries to preserve the AABA rhyme scheme of the original reads:

> *Raising his eyebrows to answer the question,*
> *Meeting Buddha there was nothing not mentioned.*
> *Worshiped today throughout the world,*
> *As spring inhabits a plum branch amid a snowy dimension.*

In commenting on his master's composition, Dōgen adopts the widely used strategy he frequently evokes of rewriting the words of his predecessors. Here he modifies the symbolism of nature to represent eternity rather than renewal through the image of flowers that do not fall. He further reinforces this innovative outlook by substituting the crane for plum blossoms in the last line as a similar but somewhat different indicator of happiness (*fu*) that suggests longevity instead of the ephemeral:

> *He met Buddha face-to-face and they exchanged words forthrightly.*
> *Raising his eyebrows, he tried not to conceal.*
> *In the field of merit, spring petals do not fall,*
> *In the jade forest, the wings of an ancient crane are still chilled.*

親會見仏語言端/策起眉毛欲不瞞/功德田春花未落/瓊林老鶴翼猶寒.[35]

The following is an alternate version of Dōgen's verse to capture the AABA rhyme:

> *His face-to-face meeting with Buddha is bold,*
> *The raising of eyebrows reveals what is told.*
> *The merit-field prevents spring petals from falling,*
> *In the jade forest a crane's wings grow cold.*

Commentary on Su Shi's Buddhist Verse

Unlike his rewriting of Rujing's poem, in his interpretation of a famous verse by Su Shi known as "Sounds of Valleys, Colors of Mountains" (Ch. "Xisheng Shanse," Jp. "Keisei Sanshoku"), Dōgen refrains from trying to compete with or surpass the source verse in kind, yet he vigorously maintains his style of challenging the implications of the literary giant in an extended prose commentary passage in *Shōbōgenzō* "Keisei sanshoku." According to Su Shi's evocative expression of his personal experience of sudden realization that

apparently occurred after he heard a rousing sermon regarding the enlightenment of sentient and insentient beings by a Chan master and reflected on this
while gazing all night at the natural landscape:

> *The valley stream's sounds are the long tongue [of Buddha],*
> *The mountain's colors are none other than the pure body [of Buddha].*
> *With the coming of night, I heard eighty-four thousand songs,*
> *But how am I ever to tell others in days to come?*

谿聲便是廣長舌/山色無非清淨身/夜來八萬四千偈/他日如何舉似人.³⁶

Dōgen remarks in "Keisei sanshoku," "While on a visit to Mount Lu, Su Shi was
struck by the sound of the valley stream rippling through the night, and became
enlightened. He composed the following poem about the experience, which he
presented to Changrong, who said in approval, 'Just so!'" However, Dōgen then
makes the ironic comment, "What a pity that the mountains and streams conceal sounds and colors, but you may also rejoice that colors and sounds emerge
through the mountains and streams. ... During past springs and autumns, Su
Shi had not seen or heard the mountains and streams." Dōgen continues to comment in a questioning manner regarding the poet's experience:

> Su Shi had this awakening experience shortly after he heard Changrong
> talk about a kōan case in which insentient beings are expressing the
> Dharma. ... But was it the voice of the stream or was it the sermon by
> the master that awakened Su Shi? ... Perhaps Changshe's comment
> that insentient beings express the Dharma had not yet ceased to rever-
> berate in Su Shi, and, unbeknownst to him, had intermingled with the
> sound of the stream's rippling through the night. Who can fathom the
> water; is it a bucketful or does it fill the whole ocean? In short, was it
> layman Su Shi who awakened [on viewing nature] or the mountains
> and streams that were awakened? Who today can clearly see the tongue
> and body of the Buddha?³⁷

Although he does not try his hand at rewriting the master's *kanshi* verse,
Dōgen's Japanese poetry collection includes a *waka* that, as one of a group of
five poems on the *Lotus Sutra*, celebrates Su Shi's experience without the irony
embedded in the prose comments cited above:

> *Mine no iro*   Colors of the mountains,
> *Tani no hibiki mo*   Streams in the valleys,
> *Mine nagara*   All in one, one in all

Waga Shakamuni no	The voice and body
Koe to sugata to.	Of our Sakyamuni Buddha.[38]

Furthermore, to briefly indicate how the intertextual dimension of Dōgen's prose and poetic commentaries reveals an intermingling of his views with those of various Chan records, in *Shōbōgenzō*'s "Mujō Seppō" ("Preaching of the Dharma by Insentient Beings") he cites a Chan master's intriguing verse in regard to the preaching of insentient beings like the mountains and rivers. This passage comments on the synesthesia implicitly involved in naturalism as an extension of Su Shi's spiritual experience by concluding, "Do not listen with the ears, but hear with the eyes!" However, Dōgen also cautions that this injunction should be taken not in a literal way to presume that all things automatically embody the Buddhist teachings but as a motivation to purify the mind in order to embrace natural phenomena as appropriate to one's own spiritual realization.

Doctrinal Poems

The topic of Dōgen's complex appropriations of Chan and Buddhist doctrines expressed in his groundbreaking interpretations of kōan cases via prose and poetic remarks, often based on reworking Chinese syntax through Japanese rhetorical appropriations, is tremendously complex and varied, so I will limit my discussion to his commentaries on the so-called Mu Kōan (Ch. Wu Gongan). In the version of this case that is most frequently cited in Chan texts, in response to a disciple's question of whether a dog has buddha-nature (Ch. *foxing*, Jp. *busshō*), since Mahayana Buddhist doctrine asserts that this is a universal endowment possessed by all beings, master Zhaozhou replies "No" (Ch. Wu, Jp. Mu), which literally means "It does not have" but can be taken to imply transcendental negation rather than absence or lack. However, there is an alternative version in which the negative answer is followed by an ironic dialogue and is also accompanied by a "Yes" (Ch. You, Jp. U) response, which literally means "It does have," and is followed by yet another brief dialogue. While the truncated no-only version of the kōan is taken to highlight the notion of absolute nothingness, the more complex yes-no version suggests the relativism of opposites.[39]

Following Hongzhi, who cited the complex version in his recorded sayings *Hongzhilu*, which became the basis of the *Record of Serenity* (Ch. *Congronglu*, Jp. *Shōyōroku*) kōan collection compiled by Wansong (Jp. Banshō) in 1224, Dōgen cites the complex version in the *Mana Shōbōgenzō* and several passages in the *Eihei Kōroku*, as well as in an extended passage in *Shōbōgenzō* "Busshō"

(Buddha-nature).⁴⁰ Note that in some cases in the citations of Hongzhi and Dōgen as well as other masters from the period the negative response precedes the positive, but in other instances this sequence is reversed. Also, on at least one occasion from early in his career, before his distinctive philosophical approach was fully developed, Dōgen cites the *mu*-only version in "Gakudōyōjinshū" ("Guidelines for Studying the Way").

The *Record of Serenity* resembles the *Blue Cliff Record*'s multilayered structure in containing one hundred cases that includes the main kōan along with capping phrase comments and additional verse commentary with its own set of capping phrases, and is also accompanied by wide-ranging prose remarks. I cite below two of the important sections featuring this literary style contained in case 18 (capping phrases are in parentheses) because of its intrinsic value and also to demonstrate that capping phrases, which are a uniquely Chan form of indirect, allusive, ironic rhetoric, are a key example of the kind of Chinese poetic expression that Dōgen generally did not attempt to construct:

Record of Serenity 18 Main Case (with capping phrases by Wansong)⁴¹

A monk asked Zhaozhou, "Does the dog have Buddha-nature, or not? (He blocked his way for a while).

Zhaozhou said, "Yes." (This did not add to understanding).

The monk said, "Since it has, why does it force itself into this skin-bag?" (As soon as you welcome someone, it immediately causes you to stick your neck out).

Zhaozhou said, "It knows better, but it willingly transgresses." (Meanwhile, he does not admit to talking about "you" [the monk]).

Another monk asked, "Does the dog have Buddha-nature, or not?" (They were born of one mother [or, "the apple does not fall far from the tree"]).

Zhaozhou said, "No." (This does not detract from understanding).

The monk said, "All sentient beings have Buddha-nature. How come the dog does not?"

(The foolish dog snatches a sparrow hawk).

Zhaozhou said, "Because it has karmic consciousness." (As usual, Zhaozhou seizes the occasion of small talk to wrap up the case).

僧問趙州狗子還有佛性也無 (攔街趁塊)
州云有 (也不曾添)

僧云既有為甚麼卻撞入這箇皮袋 (一款便招自領出頭)
州云為他知而故犯 (且莫招承不是道爾)
又有僧問狗子還有佛性也無 (一母所生)
州曰無 (也不曾減)
僧云一切眾生皆有佛性狗子為什麼卻無 (憨狗趁鵓子)
州云為伊有業識在 (右具如前據款結案).

Next follows Hongzhi's Verse Comment (with capping phrases by Wansong):

The dog has Buddha-nature; the dog does not have Buddha-nature (Beaten into one ball, melted into one lump)

A straight hook really seeks fish who've given up on life (Now these monks go belly up)

Wandering pilgrims [itinerant monks] follow the smell looking for incense (They don't even know that it has penetrated their nostrils)

The noisy chatter of idle speculation (Fighting and gnawing at dried bones—crunch! snap! howl! roar!)

Making quite a show (If you do not deceive them, your fellows will pipe down the chatter)

And feeling so comfortable (When talents are lofty, the speech sounds superb)

No wonder my family was confused from the start (As soon as a word is uttered, even wild horses can't pull it back)

Even if you only point out its flaws, you still try to grab the jade (Like a thief pointlessly trying to pick someone's pocket)

The King of Qin was not aware of Lin Xiangru (Even though it's right in front of him, he keeps walking by).

狗子佛性有. 狗子佛性無 (打做一團鍊做一塊)
直釣元求負命魚 (這僧今日合死)
逐氣尋香雲水客 (穿卻鼻孔也不知)
嘈嘈雜雜作分疏 (競齧枯骨哇喓嘷吠)
平展演 (沒蹺欺休廝諛)
大鋪舒 (材高語壯)
莫怪儂家不慎初 (一言出口駟馬難追)
指點瑕疵還奪璧 (白拈巧偷)
秦王不識藺相如 (當面蹉過).

The aim of the capping phrase commentaries on this complex, yes-no version of the Mu Kōan is to showcase that there is no single clear understanding to project and yet also no full misunderstanding to reject, since errancy and illusion lead circuitously to appropriating truth and reality, which in turn can never escape their opposites.

Dōgen's main commentary on the case is in the penultimate section of the fourteen-part "Busshō" fascicle, which elsewhere examines a variety of Chan sayings and dialogues about the meaning of buddha-nature in relation to sentient and insentient beings. The purpose of Dōgen's analysis resembles the *Record of Serenity* in overcoming the dichotomies of yes or no, positive or negative, have and have not, and right and wrong, but the rhetorical style varies significantly in relying on interlinear prose comments that allude to other Chan sources yet are tinged on occasion with a poetic flair.

To cite some key examples, in his comment on the disciple's initial query Dōgen highlights the transcendence of opposites from the standpoint of dedication to the religious quest:

> The meaning of this question needs to be clarified. ... The question does not ask whether the [dog] must have the Buddha-nature nor does it ask if the [dog] must not have the Buddha-nature. It asks whether a man of iron also studies the way. Although [the monk] may regret having stumbled upon a poisonous hand, this recalls the situation of meeting half a saint after thirty years [a reference to an obscure Chan dialogue].[42]

> この間の意趣、あきらむべし. 狗子とはいぬなり. かれに佛性あるべしと問取せず、なかるべしと問取するにあらず. これは、鐵漢また學道するかと問取するなり. あやまりて毒手にあふうらみふかしといへども、三十年よりこのかた、さらに半箇の聖人をみる風流なり.

Dōgen then remarks on Zhaozhou's positive response in order to move beyond conventional understandings of having or affirming realism:

> Zhaozhou said, "Yes." The meaning of this yes [or being or existence] is not the being of scholastic treatises or the being discussed by the Sarvastivadins [an early Buddhist school of realism]. The being of Buddha is the being of Zhaozhou; the being of Zhaozhou is the being of the dog; and the being of the dog is the being of the Buddha-nature.

趙州いはく、有. この有の様子は、教家の論師等の有にあらず、有部
の論有にあらざるなり.すすみて佛有を學すべし.佛有は趙州有なり、
趙州有は狗子有なり、狗子有は佛性有なり.

Furthermore, in his comment on the monk's follow-up question about why, if the dog has buddha-nature, it forces itself into the shape of a living being, Dōgen zeroes in on the philosophical meanings implicit in the term "already":

The monk's saying inquires whether it is present being, past being, or "already being," and although already being resembles the various kinds of being, already being clearly stands alone. Should already being imply forcibly entering or should it not imply forcibly entering? There is no merit in idly considering the effort of forcibly entering the bag of skin.

この僧の道得は、今有なるか、古有なるか、既有なるか
と問取するに、既有は諸有に相似せりといふとも、既有は孤明なり.
既有は撞入すべきか、撞入すべからざるか.撞入這皮袋の行履、いた
づらに蹉過の功夫あらず.

Although the discussion in "Busshō," the longest and most complex of the *Shōbōgenzō* fascicles and the one with the most sustained argumentation on a single topic, is his best-known writing on the topic, Dōgen also offers two *kanshi* verses on the case in *Eihei Kōroku* 9.73 (in addition to several other prose comments in the sermons in the first seven volumes):[43]

The whole body of dog, the whole body of Buddha—
It is difficult to discuss whether there is or is not [buddha-nature].
Selling off or gaining back through buying comes out the same.
Have no regrets over losses or partial gains.

全身狗子全身仏/箇裏難論有也無/一等売来還自買/莫憂折本又偏枯.

Yes and no as two sides of Buddha-nature
Do not determine the fate of sentient beings.
Even though it seems like milk turning into cream,
It leads to the complete extinction of thought in samadhi.

有無二仏性/不造衆生命/雖似酪成蘇/猶如滅尽定.

In both of these poems Dōgen reinforces the ideological message of "Busshō" by stressing the relativism of apparently contradictory answers to the case's core query. Given these verses, written in the early stages of his career over a half a decade before "Busshō," and despite the variety of ways he approaches interpreting the Mu Kōan, it is notable that he refrains from attempting the capping phrase technique.

In addition to the Mu Kōan, which Dōgen cites seven times in four different texts composed over the course of nearly twenty years, the next favorite dialogue he cites features Zhaozhou replying, "Cypress tree standing in the courtyard" to a monk's query about why Bodhidharma came from the west. Dōgen refers to this case on six different occasions, including *Mana Shōbōgenzō* case 119 and an entire fascicle in the *Shōbōgenzō* titled "Hakujushi" (Cypress Tree). The latter text cites a number of other sayings, including a poem in which Zhaozhou confesses:

> *Thinking of those who've left home in this realm,*
> *How many could there be with an abbacy like mine?*
> *An earthen bed with a tattered reed mat,*
> *An old elmwood headrest with no cover at all.*
> *At the icon, I don't burn the incense of Arsaces,*
> *In the ashes, I just smell the odor of cow dung.*[44]

思量天下出家人
似我住持能有幾
土榻牀破蘆發
老榆木枕全無被
尊像不燒安息香
灰裏唯聞牛糞氣.

Zhaozhou's cypress tree dialogue is also cited three times in the *Eihei Kōroku*, and each of these instances demonstrates a distinct interpretative style. For example, 9.45 in *Eihei Kōroku* features three verse comments, including one that reads, "A monk once asked old Zhaozhou about the way, / And he only spoke of the cypress tree standing in the courtyard. / His words in the end are quite marvelous, / Still I regret the delay in hearing about the ancestor's intention."[45] 有僧問道趙州老、只道庭前柏樹枝、端的之言雖是妙、但恨祖師来意遲. This suggests, probably tongue-in-cheek, that Zhaozhou can be faulted for not giving a more direct reply to the question.

The next two examples express capping phrase comments—a style, as we have seen, that Dōgen very rarely uses—to comment on two main features of the dialogue: the incongruity of Zhaozhou's reply and the fact that he repeats the phrase when challenged by his inquirer not to teach simply in terms of objects found in the external surroundings. In 7.488 Dōgen remarks that students who misunderstand Zhaozhou's words "are as numerous as rice, sesame, bamboo, and reeds," and he concludes by offering a naturalistic verse remark regarding the ineffable quality of Zen transmission:

> Now suppose someone asked me, "What is the meaning of the Bodhidharma coming from the west?" I would say: Crossing over the remote blue waves for three years. Suppose he said, "Master, do not instruct people in terms of objects in the environment." I would say: I am not instructing people in terms of objects in the environment. Suppose he again asked, "What is the master's expression that does not use objects to guide people?" I would say:
>
> How could blinking the eyes at Vulture Peak be a special occasion? Breaking into a smile has never ceased.
> Four or five thousand willows and flowering trees along the street, Twenty or thirty thousand musicians sitting in the balconies play string and wind instruments.[46]

> 今有人問永平、如何是祖師西来意. 向他道、蒼波迢迢涉三周. 他若道、和尚莫以境示人. 須向他道、吾不以境示人. 他又問、如何是和尚不以境人底道. 祇向他道、霊山瞬目豈時節、微笑破顔尚未休、四五千条華柳巷、二三万座管絃楼.

In 8.9s, a *shōsan* (Ch. *xiaocan*) or informal sermon given at the winter solstice that is cited here in full, Dōgen provides capping phrases as replacement words for every line of the original case, including questions to and answers by Zhaozhou, and concludes once again with an emphasis on naturalism:

> A monk asked Zhaozhou, "What is the meaning of Bodhidharma coming from the west?" Dōgen said: Your tongue is my tongue. Zhaozhou said, "The cypress tree standing in the courtyard." Dōgen said: It is difficult to reveal directly the function of dynamic activity, but [Zhaozhou] offered the ten-thousand-year-old Chan style of teaching for the sake of this follower.

> The monk said, "Master, do not instruct people in terms of objects in the environment." Dōgen said: He is forcing his eyes to try to see the North Star [behind his head]. Zhaozhou said, "I am not using objects to

instruct." Dōgen said: Without any sounds in the branches, the breeze carries the spring color.

The monk [again] asked, "What is the meaning of Bodhidharma coming from the west?" Dōgen said: Next year again there will be new branches profusely blooming; the spring wind never rests. Zhaozhou said, "The cypress tree standing in the courtyard." Dōgen said: Who can face this and still catch fish and shrimp? Today, I have something else to say. Do you not want to hear it? After a pause Dōgen said: In the cold of winter, I know the meaning of the green pine, and now I plant its spiritual root on the mountain peak.[47]

冬至小参.挙.僧問趙州、如何是祖師西来意.師云、舌頭是吾舌頭.州云
、 庭 前柏樹子. 師云、覿面難呈向上機、家風万古為人施. 僧云、和
尚莫以境示人.師云、剛突眼睛看北斗.州云、吾不以境示人.師云、不
鳴条風帯春色.僧云、如何是祖師西来意.師云、明年更有新条ノ、撩乱
春風卒未休.州云、庭前柏樹子.師云、誰向這頭魚鰕.今雖恁麼、更有
永平道取、要聴麼. 良久云、歳寒知得青松意、又把霊根峰頂栽.

This passage, especially the final comment, suggests that only direct personal understanding can solve the meaning of the case since truth is invariably shifting and provisional yet is actualized by concrete circumstances.[48]

Whither Dōgen's Poetry?

It is difficult to assess Dōgen's overall accomplishments as a writer of poetry in Chinese as well as Japanese because of two main interpretative disconnects, mentioned earlier. First, he repudiates poetry and literature yet composes several hundred *kanshi* verses in addition to over fifty *waka*, and the prose throughout his canon relies heavily on the use of poetic expressions. Second, his Chinese poems have been almost entirely excluded from major collections of medieval verse, while his prose as well as calligraphy are considered classics of Japanese literary arts from the early Kamakura era. Because of sectarian tendencies that have led to ignoring Dōgen's verse, with some modest exceptions, along with the highly specialized nature of scholarship in Japan, where Buddhology as primarily a field of textual historical studies varies from and does not interact much with other academic disciplines, such as literary critical methods, an ongoing lack of intersectarian and interdisciplinary approaches that could persuasively link religious thought and literature will probably remain in place. The verses of Dōgen, who may never have felt comfortable or confident as a "poet," if studied at all, will likely continue to be examined from historical-textual rather than literary perspectives.

Therefore the question of whether Dōgen's poetry goes beyond didacticism or is valuable for reasons other than those directly related to an evocation of the Buddhist dharma or of Dōgen's personal experiences will undoubtedly still linger. On the other hand, if we speculate regarding the way the master himself might respond to the situation, he would probably say that the intriguing element of his poetry is that it enables an appreciation for how literature contributes to a seamless understanding of his overall body of writing, which invariably captures and holds true to the creative tension of ambivalence regarding words and silence, or attachment and withdrawal.

From that standpoint Dōgen's Chinese and Japanese poetry collection should probably not be seen as the source of, but rather as the answer to one of the main hermeneutic issues in the contemporary field of Dōgen studies (*Dōgen kenkyū*) concerning the relation between literature and religion as influenced by Song and Kamakura cultural trends. Most of all it seems that Dōgen would prefer to be understood as one influenced by a poetic dimension that does not use rhetoric for its own sake but as a skillful means of challenging conventions and overturning assumptions in order to inspire students to think for themselves by reading between the lines yet not taking any particular theoretical or practice perspective at face value.

To conclude with another example of a Dōgen *kanshi* from *Eihei Kōroku* 10.100c:

Transmitting to the east the way the ancestors brought forward from the west,
Daily activities illuminated by the moon while shadowed by clouds, as in the
    ancient custom.
The secular dust of worldly behavior does not reach where I reside,
Secluded on a snowy evening in my grass-thatched hut deep in the mountains.

西来祖道我伝東/瑩月耕雲慕古風/世俗紅塵飛豈到/深山雪夜草庵中。[49]

NOTES

1. This chapter draws in part from several of my publications, especially *The Zen Poetry of Dōgen: Verses from the Mountain of Eternal Peace* (Mt. Tremper, NY: Dharma Communications, 2004), but all of the Chinese poems cited have been translated anew.

2. See Steven Heine, *Did Dōgen Go to China? What He Wrote and When He Wrote It* (New York: Oxford University Press, 2006).

3. *Eihei Kōroku* 1.48, DZZ-2 3:34.

4. Steven Heine, "Empty-Handed, but Not Empty-Headed: Dōgen's *Kōan* Strategies," in Richard K. Payne and Taigen Dan Leighton, eds., *Discourse and Ideology in Medieval Japanese Buddhism* (London: RoutledgeCurzon, 2006), 218–39.

5. For an Edo-period critique of Dōgen's approach by the Rinzai scholastic Mujaku Dōchū (1653–1744), see the discussion in Kagamishima Genryū, *Dōgen Zenji to Sono Monryū* (Tokyo: Seishin shobō, 1961), 215–89; see also Urs App, "Chan/Zen's Greatest Encyclopaedist Mujaku Dōchū (1653–1744)," *Cahiers d'Extrême-Asie* 3 (1987): 155–74.

6. DZZ-2 4:182–297. For a careful and generally outstanding translation of the entire *Eihei Kōroku*, see Taigen Dan Leighton and Shohaku Okumura, trans., *Dōgen's Extensive Record: A Translation of the Eihei Kōroku* (Boston: Wisdom, 2004). I have consulted extensively but in most cases departed from this translation.

7. For the influence on Dōgen of the relatively obscure 1093 text *Zongmen Tongyaoji* (Jp. *Shūmon Tōyōshū*), see Ishii Shūdō, "Kung-an Ch'an and the *Tsung-men t'ung-yao ji*," in Steven Heine and Dale Wright, eds., *The Kōan: Text and Context in Zen Buddhism* (New York: Oxford University Press, 2000), 110–36.

8. I am very much influenced by the textual analysis of this kind of writing in Andō Yoshinori, *Chūsei Zenshū Bunken no Kenkyū* (Tokyo: Kokusho kankokai, 2000).

9. See Frédéric Girard, *The Stanza of the Bell in the Wind: Zen and Nembutsu in the Early Kamakura Period* (Tokyo: International Institute for Buddhist Studies, 2007).

10. DZZ-2 7:152–79.

11. This verse reads, with the title cited in the first two lines:

"*Jinjippōkai*	"*True person manifest*
Shinjitsunintai"	*throughout the ten quarters of the world*"
Yo no naka ni	*The true person is*
Makoto no hito ya	*Not anyone in particular;*
Nakaruran	*But, like the deep blue color*
Kagiri mo mienu	*Of the limitless sky*
Ōzora no iro.	*It is everyone, everywhere in the world.*

12. Dōgen's version of the text, which was supposedly copied in a single night with the help of a local deity, as recorded in the master's sectarian biographies, and is stored at a Sōtō temple, Daijōji, has been documented by D. T. Suzuki, among others. But the account is curious because it is also said that the *Blue Cliff Record* was destroyed by detractors and kept out of circulation for about a century and a half, from the mid-1100s until around 1300, with Dōgen's supposed encounter with the text taking place just in the middle of that cycle. See also William Bodiford's chapter in this volume. On the other hand, some scholars, such as Griffith Foulk in his chapter in this volume, consider Dōgen's interlinear comments on Chinese anecdotes evident throughout fascicles of the *Shōbōgenzō* as capping phrases, but I am using the term in the formal sense of what is apparent in the genre of kōan collections such as the *Blue Cliff Record*.

13. Akane Shōichi, *Mujō no shisō* (Tokyo: Renga shobō shinsha, 1980).

14. Kawabata Yasunari, *Utsukushii Nihon to Watakushi*, trans. E. G. Seidensticker as *Japan, the Beautiful, and Myself* (Tokyo: Kodansha, 1969).

15. See Hata Eigyoku, "*Eihei kōroku—sono sodoku to chūkai*," *Sanshō* (1975–77).

16. DZZ-2 7:90.

17. DZZ-2 4:290. The following verse, on ambivalence regarding meditation and literary pursuit that recalls Dōgen, is by his eleventh-century Caodong predecessor Touzi Yiqing: "Though I am in the business of emptiness, / I cannot avoid being enslaved by my talents. / I have been studying and practicing Chan meditation, / but instead am preoccupied with literary content" 雖然所業空/免被才情役/忝曾學參禪/叨以習文義; cited with slight alteration from An-yi Pan, *Painting Faith: Li Gonglin and Northern Song Buddhist Culture* (Leiden: Brill, 2007), 27.

18. The following website provides an analysis of 仄 (inflected) and 平 (level) tones based on presumed pronunciation at the time (Song dynasty): http://sou-yun.com/AnalyzePoem.aspx.

19. DZZ-2 7:159.

20. DZZ-2 7:156.

21. DZZ-2 4:278.

22. Leighton and Okumura, *Dōgen's Extensive Record*, 628.

23. Additional Japanese poems comment further on the visit to Kamakura, where his primary teaching to the shogun was through a collection of a dozen *waka* verses. In a recent film, *Zen*, which is based on traditional biographies but is clearly fictionalized in some sections, Dōgen uses a couple of the *waka* to instruct the shogun on the meaning of Zen for overcoming his guilt and anxiety about conflict. In other accounts this typically feminine form of verse composition was a gift bestowed to the wife of Hōjō Tokiyori.

24. DZZ-2 4:276.

25. DZZ-2 3:166–68. See also Leighton and Okumura, *Dōgen's Extensive Record*, 246.

26. See Heine, *Did Dōgen Go to China?*

27. DZZ-2 4:280.

28. DZZ-2 2:71.

29. DZZ-2 1:133.

30. *Quan Tang shi*, 25 vols. (Beijing: Zhonghua shuju, 1960), 4: 1304.

31. DZZ-2 2:77.

32. DZZ-2 4:62.

33. This version of the legend is also found in *Shōbōgenzō* "Baika," but the encounter takes place with Asoka in the version of the story in *Shōbōgenzō* "Kenbutsu" (Seeing Buddha).

34. DZZ-2 4:106.

35. DZZ-2 4:106.

36. DZZ-2 1:274.

37. DZZ-2 1:275–76.

38. DZZ-2 7:163.

39. See Steven Heine, *Like Cats and Dogs: Contesting the Mu Kōan in Zen Buddhism* (New York: Oxford University Press, 2013).

40. It is interesting that Dōgen's travels in China overlapped with the production of this text, but since Wansong was located in Beijing then, when it was caught up in the turbulent transition from the rulership of the Jin Jurchen to that of the Mongols, it is unlikely that he would have been aware of the Caodong school master's publication. The *Record of Serenity* eventually became a fixture in Japan and was associated with the Sōtō sect, which frequently refers to it as "our version of the *Blue Cliff Record*."

41. T 48:238b–239a.

42. DZZ-2 1:39–41.

43. DZZ-2 4:232.

44. As translated by Carl Bielefeldt, accessed September 27, 2012, http://scbs.stanford.edu/sztp3/translations/shobogenzo/translations/hakujushi/pdf/translation.pdf (originally in X 68:90c).

45. DZZ-2 4:212; Leighton and Okumura, *Dōgen's Extensive Record*, 565.

46. DZZ-2 4:68–70; Leighton and Okumura, *Dōgen's Extensive Record*, 433–34.

47. DZZ-2 4:120; Leighton and Okumura, *Dōgen's Extensive Record*, 514.

48. As a symbol of particularity, both Dōgen and Zhaozhou (items 37–39 in the *Record of Zhaozhou*) refer to the notion of *saindhava* (Jp. *sendaba*), in which a king has faith in a trusty servant who knows to bring him exactly what he wants, whether salt, water, a bowl, or a horse, without needing to be asked or prodded.

49. DZZ-2 4:228–29.

4

Negotiating the Divide of Death in Japanese Buddhism

DŌGEN'S DIFFERENCE

John C. Maraldo

When you die, you want to die a beautiful death. But what makes for a beautiful death is not always clear. To die without suffering, to die without causing trouble to others, to die leaving behind a beautiful corpse, to die looking good—it's not clear what is meant by a beautiful death. Does a beautiful death refer to the way you die or the condition of your corpse after death? This distinction is not clear. And when you start to stretch the image of death to the method of how to dispose of your corpse as befitting your image of death, everything grows completely out of hand.

AOKI SHINMON, a Buddhist mortician

The Question

Many of us consider Dōgen to be the most profound of the philosophically minded Japanese Buddhist teachers in the classical period. But what, if anything, does Dōgen have to teach us about the meaning of a "beautiful death"? Can he take this matter that so easily gets completely out of hand and place it within our grasp?

The Divides

When it comes to the topic of death in Japanese Buddhism, it seems we encounter two disparate Buddhisms that rarely if ever meet. On the one hand, we find the Buddhism of the philosophers, including the Kyoto school and the Buddhist thinkers they quote, and on the other hand we encounter the Buddhism of the populace and of the scholars who study it.[1] The sense and significance of death differ so profoundly in these two approaches to Buddhist teachings and practices that one wonders whether death is a univocal phenomenon at all.

Philosophical Japanese Buddhism deals with the "great matter" of birth-and-death (shōji, samsara) and focuses on liberation through either rebirth in a Pure Land, the realization of one's birthless and deathless buddha-nature, or the transformation of one's own body-mind. In the esoteric tradition Kūkai (774–835) taught that we attain buddhahood with our present body and emphasized embodying to the (near) exclusion of dying. In the Zen tradition Dōgen wrote that seeking Buddha outside of birth-and-death is as futile as trying to travel south by heading north,[2] and other philosophers cite his words frequently when they explain the nonseparation of samsara and nirvana. Hakuin (1685–1768) wrote of the Great Death, the death of the illusions that sink one into the cycle of birth-and-death, and the Great Joy experienced at the awakening that frees one from this cycle.[3]

The twentieth-century Zen teacher Hisamatsu Shin'ichi (1889–1980) exclaimed, "I do not die," to proclaim his awakening from the delusion of being a self subject to birth and death.[4] In the Pure Land tradition, philosophers speak of birth and death or life and death together, on the same side, as opposed to the other side and the power of the Other to liberate the devotee. Hōnen (1133–1212) wrote, "The path to liberation from the cycle of birth-and-death at the present time is none other than birth in the Pure Land of Amida Buddha."[5] Shinran (1173–1263), contesting the view of the earlier Pure Land thinker Genshin (942–1017), wrote, "There is no need to wait in anticipation for the moment of death, no need to rely on Amida's coming. At the time true entrusting becomes settled, birth [in the Pure Land] too becomes settled; there is no need for the deathbed rites that prepare one for Amida's coming."[6] In the twentieth century Kiyozawa Manshi (1863–1903) wrote, "Life, that is not only who we are. Death is also who we are. We have life and death, side by side. But we do not have to be affected by life and death. We are a spiritual existence outside life and death."[7] Philosophical Buddhism places birth and death (or life and death) together on one side of a divide that distinguishes both from nirvana, even where nirvana is considered nothing but awakening within birth-and-death.

The Buddhism of the populace, on the other hand, concerns itself with a death that divides the departed from the living and focuses on the care of the corpse and of the spirit of the departed, who often is thought to care for or to curse the survivors. This Buddhism recognizes the fear and pain of death and offers rites of passage and of mourning. The depiction early in the *Tale of Genji* of the treatment of the death of Yūgao, Genji's lover, may be fictive, but it is not far from the long-standing truth about this Buddhism: "Outside the room where the body was laid out for the wake, two or three monks chatted between spells of silently calling Amida's Name. ... A venerable monk, the nun's own son, was chanting scripture in such tones as to arouse holy awe. Genji felt as though he would weep until his tears ran dry."[8]

Though the cause of his ailment is kept secret, the court has "rites, litanies, and purifications ... in numbers beyond counting" performed for the grief-stricken Genji, and later Genji has "images made every seven days for [Yūgao's] memorial services." The translator, Royall Tyler, notes that these images depicting Buddhist divinities were newly painted for each memorial service, "held every seven days during the first forty-nine days after death and at widening intervals thereafter," "to guide the soul toward a fortunate rebirth." The Buddhism of the people sees death as the departure of one who is born; it places the body of the departed in the care of clergy and family and imagines the spirit of the departed somehow, somewhere, on the other side of life.

Far from being merely one topic among others in the complex known as Japanese Buddhism, the topic of death forms the core of what, for a great many scholars, actually defines what Buddhism is really about. If we may speak of two disparate Buddhisms in Japan (and elsewhere), then the divide between the two over the sense of death marks a significant difference in interpretations of the nature of Buddhism. On the one hand, philosophically inclined Japanese Buddhists have criticized the fact that their religion became "funeral Buddhism" and a religion of rituals at the expense of the true teaching of liberation and the core practices of morality (Skt: *sila*), meditation (*dhyana*), and wisdom (*prajna*) to attain liberation. Some lament the "decline" of Japanese Buddhism to the extent of deeming predominant practices not true Buddhism at all.[9] On the other hand, scholars who would abstain from normative judgments argue that the practice of rituals for the dying and the dead, even if not confined to Japanese Buddhism, historically defines its most important social role.[10] Some find concern with death, the death opposed to life and the living, at its very core.

The eminent Buddhist scholar Sueki Fumihiko recently published a book that reexamines the history of Buddhism by focusing on death. He contends that arguments about the existence of the dead are irrelevant to what we can know about how the living relate to the dead, and what we know is that "the Japanese worldview allows for an ambiguous conceptual realm with an uncertain existence." The realm of the dead in this worldview includes deceased persons, Japanese and Buddhist deities, and even ghosts and spirits, to whom the living inevitably relate. For those living in the medieval period, this "other world" (*takai*) was dreamlike, not in the sense of being illusory but in its inherently ambiguous nature. Sueki argues that the relationship of the living to the dead defines the entire history of Buddhism, beginning with the passing of the Buddha and the consternation of his disciples over his absence. Practices of enshrining his relics were a way of keeping him present, as were practices of composing sutras. Pure Land sutras presented an Amida Buddha ever living in a realm into which one could be reborn, and the second half of the *Lotus Sutra* described how a relationship with the dead Sakyamuni Buddha was possible. Buddhism preeminently is a religion of dealing with the dead.[11]

Whatever differences there are among traditions of Buddhism in Japan, practices of dealing with the dead seem to run through all of them like a common thread. Jacqueline Stone states that, despite differences in the understanding of postmortem liberation, "the notion that a person's last hours should be ritually managed, as well as the basic techniques for so doing, cut across all divisions of 'old' and 'new,' 'exoteric' and 'esoteric,' in which we are accustomed to thinking of medieval Japanese Buddhism."[12] For the most part the great founders of various sects who did engage in philosophical reflection also paid special attention to the dying person and to deathbed rites. In general they taught that what the dying person did, and what was done for him or her, was crucial to liberation. Genshin exhorted the dying person to concentrate on Amida Buddha as his last thought (*nen*) to avoid rebirth in samsara. Kakuban (1095–1143) encouraged the dying to focus on union with the Buddha to realize, on the deathbed, buddhahood in this very body, which he considered synonymous with birth in a Pure Land. The "lotus samadhi" of Saichō (767–822), although not confined to the time of death, eventually came to define a rite for the dying. Nichiren (1222–82) taught followers to recite, once again on their deathbed, the name of the *Lotus Sutra* as a bridge to reach the Pure Land (of Sacred Eagle Peak).[13] Their concern with the dying represents the norm, the ordinary practice.

The extraordinary philosophical positions of Kūkai, Shinran, and Dōgen are apparent in their attitudes toward their own passing and their disregard for rites for the dead. Some legends depict Kūkai as never having died at all, as having simply entered samadhi in the Inner Shrine on Mount Kōya, where he still sits.[14] Although Shinran was probably cremated,[15] he is reputed to have told his congregation, "When my eyes close for the last time, place my body in the Kamo River, so the fish can feed on it."[16] Dōgen told his monks that the "body, hair, and skin are the products of the union of our parents. When the breathing stops, the body is scattered amid mountains and fields and finally turns to earth and mud. Why then do you attach to this body?"[17] The utter disregard on the part of Kūkai, Shinran, Dōgen, and later Zen philosophers was the exception, and a sign of a great divide between them and the teachers more representative of the Buddhism of the people. The messy matters of the deceased's body and the survivors' emotions are not taken into account in the Buddhism of the philosophers.

Several divides are discernible in this synopsis. The divide between Kūkai, Shinran, and Dōgen, on the one hand, and other Japanese Buddhist teachers, on the other hand, parallels the more general divide between the Buddhism of the philosophers and the Buddhism of the populace. The former side attends to liberation from birth-and-death, and the latter to death as a departure from life. Accordingly the former divides birth-and-death from something beyond birth-and death, even if found within it; the latter divides death from life.[18] But these divides are made visible by yet another, less studied division that throws them into relief. This is the more complicated divide of interests: the interests of history scholars as distinct from those of philosophers past and present, and both these sets of interests as opposed to the interest of practitioner-devotees in their own death or the death of others close to them. Historical scholars are interested in explaining predominant patterns of practice and in documenting their details; philosophers' interests turn to doctrinal interpretation that, for many of them, entails a universal soteriology; and practitioner-devotees are concerned with what happens to them and those close to them when they die. While these three groups of people may at times overlap in the focus of their attention, we can, without undue exaggeration, distinguish three points of view on the sense and significance of death. If "death" means something different for these three groups, then death in Japanese Buddhism is a polysemous phenomenon.

Points of View

One heuristic for clarifying the different senses of death emerges from a grammatical distinction that is usually evident in English, the language in which I write, but is often obscure in Japanese, the language of the people I am writing about. I am writing now and you are reading; were we together we might discuss what they, the others, talked about. "I," "you," "we," and "they" (and "she" or "he," etc.) name the "grammatical person." The category of grammatical person indicates the speaker, the addressee, or the other participants in an event. As a deictic reference, grammatical person requires a listener or reader to know the context of the situation in order to determine the referent. You, the reader, know that John Maraldo is the referent to "I" in the sentence above (although what sort of self "John Maraldo" refers to may be a matter of philosophical debate). In English, grammatical person is often coded in personal pronouns like "I," "you," "we," and "they"; other Indo-European languages may code grammatical person in the form of verbal endings. As you may know, however, indicators of grammatical person are more complicated in Japanese. Personal pronoun equivalents are much less often used than in English and are derived from words indicating location. Such words indicate social status in a relationship as much as they identify a speaker or addressee. In the written language of the Buddhist teachers I have referred to and in the *Tale of Genji*, such words are all but absent. When rendering Japanese into English, translators must interpret the context to generate the appropriate personal pronouns.

If grammatical person is so obscure in the language of Japanese Buddhists, why try to employ this category to clarify the senses of death? The reason is that death allows description from the perspectives of at least three grammatical persons—first person, second person, and third person—and the distinctions and interplay among these three bring clarity to the meanings of death in its various divides. I shall return to the question of whether yet another perspective is at work in some Buddhist philosophical accounts.

The *first-person perspective* presents the meaning and significance of death (and possibly liberation) for oneself. First-person perspectives on death are both a perennial concern of philosophical reflection and a matter of everyday anxiety for countless individuals. First-person perspectives imply some sense of self, of being oneself, that may be left ambiguous for the time being. We may note one remarkable parallel, however: the way translators generate pronouns seems to mirror the way a person's sense of self is generated to allow that person to refer to himself or herself. Although it is not a specific external agent, like a translator, that generates one's sense of self, that sense is discovered and (re)constructed out of a context wherein it did not previously exist as an experienced identity. Once a person's own point of view comes into being, it defines that person over and against other individuals and comes to articulate her own distinctive view of things.

This is the point of view so central to phenomenological analysis, which seeks to clarify matters as experienced from a first-person perspective.[19] It is also crucial to any reflection on death, insofar as death poses a limit to personal experience and existence. What death is for me, what *my* death means to me, and just how *my own death* defines a divide in my own existence— these are matters articulated in the first person, whether or not a grammatical indicator is evident. Since the "I," the "me," and the "my" refer to any and all of us in this case, we may shift to a more anonymous but less contextual formulation: what *one's own death* means *to oneself* and *for oneself*. The more anonymous formulation in terms of "oneself" is sometimes considered a third-person perspective, but I will define the third-person perspective on death as the viewpoint of commentators and observers who are more or less detached from what they describe or see.

One may of course imagine another person's first-person perspective on death, what death is to or for that person herself. A passage from Ōe Kenzaburo's novel *A Personal Matter* provides an example of both a third-person perspective and an imagined first-person perspective. The protagonist, nicknamed "Bird," ruminates on the pending death of his infant child, who he is told was born with a brain hernia that renders it (in the words of the doctor) a "vegetable," unable to respond like a normal human being:

> Bird shuddered ... and began thinking about the baby. ... The death of a vegetable baby—Bird examined his son's calamity from the angle that stabbed deepest. The death of a vegetable baby with only vegetable functions was not [according to the doctor] accompanied by suffering. Fine, but what did death mean to a baby like that? Or, for that matter, life? The bud of an existence appeared on a plain of nothingness that stretched for zillions of years and there it grew for nine months. Of course, there was no consciousness in a fetus, it simply curled in a ball and existed, filling utterly a warm, dark, mucous world. Then, perilously, into the external world. It was cold there, and hard, scratchy, dry and fiercely bright. The outside world was not so confined that the baby could fill it by himself: he must live with countless strangers. But, for a baby like a vegetable, that stay in the external world would be nothing more than a few hours of occult suffering he couldn't account for. Then the suffocating instant, and once again, on that plain of nothingness zillions of years long, the fine sand of nothingness itself.[20]

In this passage Ōe depicts Bird in the third person, from the perspective of a more or less detached observer, albeit an "omniscient" observer that can read the mind of the protagonist. Bird's own mind tries to imagine the experience of a severely disabled infant, to imagine what birth, life, and death might be like for his infant son. He tries to imagine the infant's first-person perspective on life and death. The difficulties involved in doing so are staggering, and Ōe has deliberately piled one difficulty on top of another. Ōe implicitly acknowledges the general difficulty of imagining *another person's* experience: he has

Bird asking himself questions and examining this "personal matter" from a particular angle. But Ōe adds to this general difficulty two more limitations: any person's own limitation in imagining her own death, and the limitations of an infant, a brain-damaged infant at that, to imagine or experience anything at all. The omniscience of the novelist runs up against an utterly unknowable personal matter, which he describes as a "plain of nothingness zillions of years long." This unknowability breaches the first-person perspective and necessitates an interplay with a third-person view of "the bud of an existence that appeared on the plain of nothingness."

If the first-person perspective commands the attention of all us mortals, philosophers or not, *the third-person perspective* presents things from the standpoint of an observer who is disengaged from the world that is described. It is the perspective Murasaki Shikibu takes in *The Tale of Genji*, and it defines the narrative stance of many works of fiction. It also represents the practice of most historical scholars who aim to be objective, disinterested, and purely descriptive as opposed to normative or ideological (despite postmodernist challenges to this aim). The scholarship on death and the afterlife in Japanese Buddhism generally employs the third-person perspective. The historical scholar usually assumes the viewpoint of a detached observer. Yet the scholar often links her research with more or less universal human interests, to show that the research has broader relevance or to identify herself as one of us who have a shared interest in the matter of life and death.

Karen Gerhart, for example, writes her enormously informative book, *The Material Culture of Death in Medieval Japan*, from the third-person perspective for the most part, but in her opening passage she makes the link to this sense of shared identity and uses the first-person plural grammatical form: "Death is an event of cataclysmic separation," and for this reason "we use ritual and ritual objects to help bridge the gulf, suture the wound to the collective body of family and of community, and overcome a sense of powerlessness in the face of death."[21] Gerhart is commenting here about people of all cultures to introduce her specialized study of medieval Japanese death rituals. Her study is an example of the kind of detailed historical research on Japan that is not found prior to the Meiji era on a topic, death, that in earlier Japan was rarely if ever presented from the disinterested, third-person stance of the scholar. But she too initially speaks of the separation that death means in a manner that connects this third-person perspective with concerns all of us have: "*we* use rituals and ritual objects to help bridge the gulf." The third-person perspective on death gains relevance from its interplay with first-person experience, a point of view that scholars of history must recognize if they are to describe the meanings of matters like death for others.

In many languages the grammatical first person also comes in a plural form, as in the English words "we" and "us" and "our." The plural form may indicate an extension of the singular first-person perspective to a community of people who share similar experiences or viewpoints, or it may define an in-group as opposed to outsiders. In the matter of death, however, "our death" can refer only to the death of each of us, individually, whether that death means a departure from life or an entrance into nirvana. The philosophers who divide birth-and-death from something beyond it (yet possibly within it) often imply a first-person plural perspective insofar as liberation is conceived of as universal, for all of us, but even there liberation comes by way of the work of or on behalf of the individual practitioner, each of us. When it comes to death, the first-person plural perspective derives from the first-person singular.

The *second person* invokes the perspective of someone who can address me, hear me, respond to me, challenge me, or engage me. The engagement with me can occur even when you are not at the moment speaking or writing; it may occur simply by your presence or by the signs of your presence in your artifacts or your remains. The convention in English grammar of calling this perspective the "second" person may conceal a bias toward self-centered consciousness but need not imply that the "second person" is less important than the "first." As James G. Hart writes, this "you" is "the second first person."[22] The imperative grammatical form implies the second person: "[You should or must] do this!" The person so addressed may be a general "anyone"; indeed, in contemporary English "you" often substitutes for the generic "one," meaning anyone. Here, however, I will confine the second person to the forms of speech and speech-acts that are directed at specific persons known to the speaker rather than at anonymous others. My use of the term differs from so-called second-person narratives, a form of literary fiction and nonfiction that also occurs in advertisements and musical lyrics, where second-person personal pronouns or other grammatical indicators are employed to address an anonymous reader. The novel *If on a winter's night a traveler* by the Italian writer Italo Calvino is an example of a (rather complex) second-person narrative. Invoking an anonymous, imagined reader, the book begins, "You are about to begin reading Italo Calvino's new novel, *If on a winter's night a traveler*. Relax. Concentrate. Dispel every other thought."[23]

The three major perspectives according to grammatical person may be summarized as follows:

- The first person refers to "my" (one's own) perspective on matters, including my own experience and what is at the limit of my own experience: my own death. Japanese Buddhist philosophers often, though not always, take this perspective in reflecting about matters such as life and death. So do practitioner-devotees.

- The second person refers to others known to and addressed by the writer or speaker. Buddhist teachers often invoke this form in performing rites and giving instruction to others they know, even if without explicit mention of the addressee (such as the mention of "you" in English).

- The third person intends to give someone's perspective on others, their experiences, their activities, their practices, or on anything at all, from a detached and often unidentified viewpoint. Contemporary scholars of Buddhism usually use this perspective in presenting their work.

It is important to keep two points in mind when applying the heuristic of the perspectives of grammatical person to clarify the notion of death. First, although the use of personal pronouns in English explicates these perspectives, they are not limited to a language like English that requires personal pronouns for clear communication. First-person, second-person, and third-person perspectives are present—are ways of presenting things—for speakers and writers of Japanese as well, and probably of most languages.

Dōgen's Japanese is a case in point. His writing is rarely marked by pronouns, referential nouns, or honorifics that might indicate the status of the speaker or the addressee. In autobiographical remarks he uses the word *yo* to refer to himself as the present speaker or writer or as the protagonist of stories he tells about himself.[24] He also uses the word *ware*, sometimes as a personal pronoun, sometimes in the sense of the general noun "the I" or "das Ich."[25] He also uses grammatical terms that translate as imperatives and imply the grammatical second person, such as *shirubeshi* (しるべし, "you should know") and *nakare* (なかれ, "do not ... "). Moreover Dōgen uses *ware* and the imperative forms in writings and talks concerned with death, in some sense of the word. The meaning of death for Dōgen will become clearer when the perspectives implied in his writing emerge more clearly. The second point to keep in mind is that the explicit or implicit use of grammatical person does not necessarily entail any particular philosophical concept of self. Dōgen's philosophy, for example, articulates a very specific notion of self and nonself, but he does not appeal to this notion every time he uses the word *jiko*, much less when he uses an imperative grammatical form that implies a "you," that is, the monks he is addressing. Perspectives according to grammatical person remain open-ended with regard to philosophical concepts of self.

With these grammatical perspectives in mind, it is possible to differentiate, at least tentatively, three senses of death:[26]

- *Autobiographical death* is my death, in each case one's own death. It means death as the ending of my life, my departure or passing from life. It is independent of whatever beliefs I and others may have regarding an afterlife, a world beyond (*takai*), or a life before this present life, a repeated or reincarnated life in a great cycle (*rin-ne*). I may imagine my death as the end of an interim, but this interim is still going on. Others may experience my death, but I myself cannot imagine or conceive this ending, for an end would stop the very act of imagining or conceiving. I may imagine myself continuing on in some form in an afterlife, but I cannot imagine or conceive my own death. Autobiographical death poses a limit to my experience. It is death in—and perhaps death of—a first-person perspective. This is the sense of death that the divide between birth-and-death and liberation seems to entail, at least initially.

- *Biographical death* refers to the death of an individual as perceived and conceived by other people in general. The dates on a gravestone mark one's biographical birth and death. Biographical death signifies the end to an interim that began with the individual's birth. It is the demise of persons that anonymous observers can witness and scholars can describe; it is death in the third person. When we divide life from death, literally or metaphorically, we appeal to this sense of death.

- *Your death, death of the second person*, is the biographical death of someone personally known, someone in one's family, congregation, or community. It is death for those left behind, the survivors (*izoku, ide*). Two features characterize this sense of death: your death means your absence from others who knew you, and it leaves your body for others to take care or dispose of. This is the death that is of central concern to the Buddhism of the people, to the priests who perform rites for the dying and the dead and the survivors. This in particular is the death of no concern to Kūkai, Shinran, Dōgen, and the philosophical Japanese Buddhist teachers. As we saw, they seemed to have little if any regard for death in the third person as well. (Dōgen, for example, frequently cites the patriarchs of old as models for the monks of his day; it is of no concern that they are no longer living. For Dōgen the patriarchs are still present insofar as their words and admonitions live.) The divide between "us survivors" and the death of "one of us" evokes the notion of the death of the second person.

In a crucial sense the death of the second person makes possible the sense of speaking of my death. I come to an awareness of death for me when I experience the death of others I know. My death approaches me—even if it never becomes accessible to me—via your death; the death of someone I personally

know evokes in me the prospect of my own death. Death in its autobiographical sense, distinct as it is, derives from the death of the second person. In this
sense the death of the second person always comes first.

These distinctions are crucial if we are to understand the disparate ways that
the matter of death is treated in Japanese Buddhism. Yet something, some aspect
still seems missing when we try to understand what death means in the matter
of birth-and-death, as the Buddhist philosophers think of it. Birth-and-death,
life-and-death, touches on the matter of *my* death and the liberation of (or from)
me, and thus has to do with autobiographical death more than with biographical
death or with death for the second person. The Buddhist philosophers, however,
might be speaking of the death *of* a first-person perspective. Not only that: it is as
if their utter disregard were directed at all three perspectives, as if these perspectives were more or less equivalent. Insofar as they function equivalently, I will
refer to all three perspectives as *personal death*.

The Death of Dōgen

Biographically Dōgen was born in 1200 and died in 1253. In his early twenties
he went to China and experienced an awakening under the direction of the Zen
master Rujing. After his return to Japan he taught monks that single-minded
zazen (which could include sitting with a kōan) was the only practice that
could realize buddhahood. But Dōgen also led lay worship ceremonies, reput-
edly often accompanied by miraculous events such as the appearance of flowers over altar statuary, and he performed rituals of popular appeal such as
precept recitation and worship of the sixteen arhats who protect Buddhism.[27]
Whether or not his and his monks' performance of lay rituals was an increasing concession to gather financial support by patrons, it is evident that he
continually used and adapted Chinese monastic rules and regulations for
the monastic communities he led; in other words, Buddhist practice for him
meant a meticulously regulated and ritualized lifestyle that facilitates zazen.
In the final period of his life Dōgen devoted his writing to commentaries on
Chan monastic codes compiled as the *Eihei Shingi*. Although these writings do
stress proper attitude more than the outward form of rules and rituals,[28] there
is no question that ritual was part and parcel of Dōgen's Zen.

Given all this attention to ritual, it is surprising that Dōgen left no record
of performing services for the dead.[29] His monastic codes give no guidance
for the treatment of deceased monks or laity, and his Japanese *Shōbōgenzō*
and other writings do not deal with what I have called the death of the second
person, marked by the dead body and the absence of the person, much less
biographical death.[30] He apparently was not concerned with the treatment of

the deceased, and in any case would have rejected rites to transfer merit and ensure one's fortune in an afterlife.[31] Dōgen left it to his disciples to deal with his death when he died in Kyoto at the age of fifty-four. He had been ill for nearly a year and had already appointed his main disciple, Ejō, as abbot of Eiheiji, but we can imagine that the community was both distraught and at a loss as to its future direction. William Bodiford notes how little we know about the treatment of Dōgen's body. The body was cremated, and Ejō recited the *Shari Raimon*, a verse on attaining all perfections through the power of the Buddha.[32] Otherwise the records are silent on the topic.

However, Dōgen did leave a few indications of his attitude toward the prospect of his imminent death in three poems he composed in his final days. Disciples had urged him to travel to his hometown, Kyoto, to seek medical help, and on the way there he composed two short Japanese poems (*waka*) that suggest a clear sense of his impending demise. It is possible to read in them a hint of a turn from a plaintive sense of passing to being absorbed in the presence of what was happening then and there. In one poem Dōgen seems to feel frail and momentary as a blade of grass as he passes through the mountains, then is swept up by the presence of mounting clouds. In another poem he seems to long to see the autumn moon again—the celebrated moon of the fifteenth day of the eighth lunar month—which then leaves him sleepless in the presence of its beauty.[33] A third poem, a *yuige* verse composed in Chinese just before he died and alluding to the legendary abode of the dead, seems to explode all ambivalence; Dōgen's "entire body" or person (身) fully lives even at the brink of the abyss of death:

> *Fifty-four years lighting up the sky*
> *A quivering leap smashes a billion worlds.*
> *Hah!*
> *Entire body looks for nothing.*
> *Plunging alive into Yellow Springs.*[34]

五十四年照第一天/打箇勃跳觸破大千/ 咦 /渾身無覓活陷黄泉.

Even in his own case Dōgen turns our attention away from thoughts of personal death as a coming to end of life.

Dōgen's relative lack of concern with personal death is all the more surprising when we recall stories of his childhood experience with death that motivated him to study the Buddha Way in the first place. His mother died when he was only seven. It is said that a profound sense of impermanence overcame the young Dōgen as he watched the smoke of incense rise during her funeral.[35] He never abandoned his concern with impermanence, even after identifying it as the place of awakening, and he frequently exhorted his monks to practice while they had the chance in this short life of ours, to practice as if their hair were on fire, casting aside body and mind.[36] Yet his own awakening had left personal death in the dust, had cast it into the realm of distractive and illusory concerns. The comment in the *Shōbōgenzō Zuimonki* quoted earlier, about attaching to one's body-mind, reflects his seeming indifference toward the significance of personal death in his own case as well. If we take this stance as a sign of his own liberation from birth-and-death, then it does seem to pertain to his own death, death for the first person. But it is notable that this liberation took place during his lifetime, not at the end of it, that he had, so to speak, already died to personal death.

What precisely do Dōgen's teachings about life-and-death have to do with death in the first person? Dōgen's directives and sermons to his followers make it abundantly clear that each must practice and manifest realization for himself, that the Buddha Way is a "personal matter," a matter of one's own life-and-death. Dōgen's teaching must pertain to autobiographical death, death in the first person, in some way. An examination of some passages in the *Shōbōgenzō* reveals some possible connections.

The fascicles of the *Shōbōgenzō* that treat of birth-and-death (or life-and-death), composed over a decade,[37] display a remarkable consistency. We may begin with the earliest of these, the profound study of perspectives known as *Genjōkōan*. Whether the perspectives in Dōgen's various studies coincide with those in the category of grammatical person, that is, whether they are perspectives on personal death, remains an open question at this point.

Genjōkōan begins by stating three doctrinal perspectives and then returning them to an ordinary, everyday stance, which I interpret freely and extract from the relevant passages:

> A common Buddhist perspective on things posits birth and death— samsara—along with delusion and enlightenment. A contrasting, self-less perspective on things discovers neither birth/life nor death/ cessation. These two perspectives converge in the Way that speaks of birth and death, delusion and enlightenment, at all. Be that as it may, the flowers we cherish will perish and the weeds we despise will arise.

諸法の佛法なる時節、すなはち迷悟あり、修行あり、生あり死あり、諸佛あり。万法ともにわれにあらざる時節、まどひなくさとりなく、諸佛なく衆生なく、生なし滅なし。佛道もとより豊儉より跳出せるゆゑに、生滅あり、迷悟あり。生佛あり。しかもかうのごとくなりといへども、華は愛惜にちり、草は棄嫌におふるのみなり。[38]

The grammar of the original Japanese does not clearly indicate the perspective of grammatical person from which Dōgen's statements are expressed, but the first three sentences seem closest to the third-person point of view. These three statements seem to be made by an anonymous authority taking up a kind of detached metaviewpoint on three perspectives.

Yet a hint of a category other than grammatical person appears in the way Dōgen has phrased the matter, explicitly in the first two statements and by extension in the third: the three perspectives are taken up at different junctures in time (*jisetsu*); they are perspectives held temporarily. Birth-and-death, and the enlightenment that liberates them, appear as temporal perspectives. Dōgen presents perspectives as temporal rather than spatial. The fourth statement of the everyday stance reflects the temporal, transitory occasions of our (yours and my) cherishing and despising transitory things. This concluding statement, even without the interpolated "we," suggests that the doctrinal temporal perspectives must connect to one's personal being in a deep sense. The attachments of cherishing flowers while despising weeds arise as personal matters, like one's own preference for life over death. Yet even there (or then) too they are temporal, transitory matters: Dōgen's language suggests that lovely flowers fall and despised weeds flourish "only" in our loving the one and hating the other.[39]

A later passage makes more explicit Dōgen's view of the divide of life and death. An analogy with firewood and ashes recapitulates the temporal perspective, which I interpret freely:

> We speak of firewood turning to ashes and not returning again to firewood. But it is not quite right to say something is first firewood and afterwards ashes. There is a "before" the firewood and an "after." What is before is not firewood and what is after is not firewood. Firewood takes up its own temporal position, has its own phenomenal status. (Like every other phenomenon, firewood is an existential moment, an *uji*.[40]) While we speak of there being a "before" and an "after," for the time being "before" and "after" are divided. The same is true of ashes. Analogously, after a person dies she does not return to life. But it is not quite right to put it this way. A person's life is just that, a person's life. It is not followed by the person's death. There is no such thing as a person who undergoes birth/life and then death, and then life again. The right way is not to say that life becomes death, that something that was alive is now dead. The right way is to say "all is arising"; there is nothing but arising, being born, living. To turn that around, there is nothing to which to contrast birth or life; there is "no birth or life, no

arising." (And no life after death.) Life is its own existential moment, its own time-being. The right way is to say that death does not become life, that something that was dead is not alive again. So we say "all is perishing"; there is nothing but perishing, dying. And again to turn that around, there is nothing to which to contrast death or perishing; there is "no perishing." (And no death after life.) Death is its own existential moment, its own stage of time.

たき木ははいとなる、さらにかへりてたき木となるべきにあらず。しかあるを、灰はのち薪はさきと見取すべからず。しべし、薪は薪の法位に住して、さきありのちあり、前後ありといへども、前後際断せり。灰は灰の法位にあり、のちありさきあり。かのたき木、はひとなりぬるのち、さらに薪とならざるがごとく、人のしぬるのち、さらに生とならず。しかあるを、生の死になるといはざるは、佛法のさだまれるならひなり、このゆゑに不生といふ。死の生に成らざる、法輪のさだまれる佛転なり、このゆゑに不滅といふ。生も一時のくらゐなり、死も一時のくらゐなり.⁴¹

Consider again the question of grammatical person, the perspective from which these statements are made. Mention of "after a person dies" is made from the external third-person perspective of those who remain in this world talking about others who do not. But what perspective allows the view that there is no perduring person who undergoes birth and life? If no person perdures, it cannot be the perspective of an anonymous third person who perdures throughout the lives and deaths of others. The view seems to be from a first-person perspective, my perspective of myself, in which (my own) conscious life is not something that can be extinguished, in which I can speak of my own not-being-born and not-perishing. Others experience someone dying (or being born); I cannot experience my own birth or death.⁴² Yet a statement that immediately precedes this passage challenges the first-person perspective: "If fully engaged in daily activities we come back to this right here and now, the truth that there is no 'I' accompanying things will be evident" もし行李をしたしくして簡裏に歸すれば、萬法のわれにあらぬ道理あきらけし. Evidently it is a conditional perspective that allows us to see life and death as independent temporal positions that are not states of a perduring self; the necessary condition is a return of consciousness to the situation at hand, this right here (簡裏 = このところ), leaving self-consciousness behind.

Since this passage refers to the established teachings of Buddhism (佛法の定まれる習い, 法輪の定まれる佛転), Dōgen's words *fushō* (unborn) and *fumetsu* (unperishing) here most likely allude to the Indian Buddhist doctrine of the nonarising (Skt: *anutpanna*) and nonperishing (*aniruddha*) of all things, due to their fundamental emptiness, as stated in the *Heart Sutra*, the *Nirvana Sutra*, and other scriptures.[43] But there is a twist in Dōgen's interpretation. The negations *fushō* and *fumetsu* traditionally describe buddha-nature, the body of the Tathagata, nirvana, or other names for unconditioned reality; in some texts *fushō* serves as a synonym for emptiness or for nirvana. The *Heart Sutra* applies the negative descriptions to proclaim the emptiness of the five skandhas and of all phenomena (all dharmas; *zeshohōkū*); all are nonarising and nonperishing (*fushō-fumetsu*). Likewise there is no aging and no death (無老死) and no extinction of aging and death (and suffering; 亦無老死尽).[44] The *Nirvana Sutra* proclaims that "non-arising and non-ceasing are precisely what liberation is" (不生不滅即是解脱).[45] But Dōgen turns around the sense of this statement. For him, the unborn and the unperishing do not refer one-sidedly to unconditioned nirvana apart from arising and perishing (or to an unborn mind or buddha-nature, as we find later in Bankei).

In taking life and death as separate time-being, and thus severing the link between them, Dōgen may be playing off of Nagarjuna's teaching that since all phenomena are empty of self-nature, causal links between them are undermined. More concretely Dōgen applies the words *fushō* and *fumetsu* to conditioned dharmas, temporal phenomena like firewood and ashes, and also like our life and death. It is not that nothing truly arises or perishes but that when we see all things as arising, then arising exhausts the being of all things; when we see all things as perishing, then perishing exhausts the being of all things. When it comes to our life and death, in other words, life is completely life and death is completely death. Life does not become death; thus we speak of absolute life. And death does not become life; thus we speak of absolute death.[46] When we face the divide between life and death, Dōgen offers no passage.

The pronoun "we" and the temporal-conditional "when" in this restatement are not present in the original Japanese, of course, but reflect the conditional perspective introduced by the statement that immediately precedes the passage "if ... we come back to this right here and now ... there is no 'I.'" This statement suggests that absorption in the "here and now" merges the first person, the subject of the sentences ("when we face" and "when we see") with the object ("all things as arising" or "all things as perishing"). The grammar as well as the content of Dōgen's statements suggest that in this temporal condition the person who views her own life is absolved, liberated, into that life, into living. (The phrase もし ... 箇裏に歸すれば could also be read as 若しここにまかせば, "if one yields to the present situation") This perspective on life is "absolute" (絶対) in the sense that it absolves or frees us from any contrast or opposition (対を絶する), not only between life and death but between the person living and that person's life. Yet how is it possible to say that the person who "views" her own death is absolved or freed into that death, into dying? What meaning of death or dying lies here?

The fascicle of the *Shōbōgenzō* called *Shōji* approximates an answer. Dōgen begins by saying that seeking Buddha apart from life-and-death is like facing south to see north, and this only intensifies the idea of samsara and loses sight of the way of liberation. When we take to heart that our very life-and-death itself is nirvana, and neither detest one as samsara nor desire the other as nirvana, then, for the first time, it is clear how to detach from life-and-death (and presumably from nirvana as well): "Only at the time that you detach from life-and-death … "このときはじめて、生死をはなるる分あり … [47] Then, echoing a statement in *Genjōkōan*, Dōgen says, as I interpret freely:

> To imagine there is a passage from life to death is a mistake. Be aware that, as its own time-being, life has a "before" and an "after." (What is before is not one's life and what is after is not one's life.) So the right way is to say: in the time that is life there is nothing but living, and there is no [contrast to] living. Similarly, as its own time-being, death has a "before" and an "after." Accordingly, we say: in the time that is death there is nothing but death, and there is no [contrast to] death. When it comes to living, just give yourself to life; when it comes to dying, just give yourself to death. Do not detest, do not desire.

> 生より死にうつると心うるは、これあやまり也。生はひとときのくらゐ　にて、すでにさきあり、のちあり。故、佛法の中には、生すなはち不生といふ。滅もひとときのくらゐにて、又さきあり、のちあり。これによりて、滅すなはち不滅といふ。生とふときには、生よりほかにものなく、滅といふとき、滅のほかにものなし。かるがゆゑに、生きたらばただこれ生、滅来らばこれ滅にむかひてつかふべし。いとふことなかれ、ねがふことなかれ.

In this passage Dōgen invokes the authority of the teachings of Buddhism (*buppō*) and implicitly includes himself as an authority, shifting grammatically from a third-person description of how things are to a kind of first-person perspective indicated in my free interpretation by the word "we." He speaks to his followers, and at the end implicitly addresses them in the second person: "[You should] not detest or desire." Although the Japanese text contains no words that translate as "I," "we," or "you," the imperative verbal form that

Dōgen uses (いとふことなかれ、ねがふことなかれ) clearly implies a directive issuing from a first-person voice and addressed to some "you."

The category of grammatical person, however, is hermeneutically insufficient without the grammar and references related to time. Grammatically Dōgen writes his words in the present tense, and now that they are written, a common hermeneutical practice is to interpret them as released from the particular time or occasion of their being written.[48] Contrary to this common practice, we may place Dōgen's writing in the present that he invokes both in the tense of his statements and in his references to time. There are two modes of referring to time in the passages I have quoted. In the last-mentioned passage, for example, Dōgen is telling whoever his audience is to be aware (心える), now, of life or of death, each as its own time-being (生はひとときのくらゐ,生とふとき … 滅もひとときのくらゐ,滅といふとき).

One mode of reference here is to time (or temporal position, 時のくらい) for the first person, for me and each of us, even as each of us is to give ourselves over completely to the occasion of one time. Borrowing a word from *Shōbogenzō Uji*, we may interpret this part of Dōgen's message by restating, "This living moment [*nikon*] of being-time is all there ever is to life, and to death."[49] Another mode of reference is the conditional formulation: "when, at the time that you … " The phrase "Only at the time that you detach from life-and-death … " (このときはじめて 生死をはなるる分 …) occurs near both the beginning and the end of the *Shōji* fascicle. The dimension of time or, better, the presencing of time is necessary to understand the perspective from which Dōgen makes his pronouncements.

The *Zenki* fascicle offers some final clues that intimate the meaning of death for Dōgen and the perspective from which he speaks. Similar to *Genjōkōan* and *Shōji*, *Zenki* often interprets the samsaric compound birth/life-and-death by treating the lexical elements *shō* (life) and *shi* (death) separately but equally. What is said of one is also asserted of the other. To summarize some points: life completely liberates life, and death completely liberates death; life is the presencing of the "whole works" (*zenki*), and so is death.[50] Life does not get in the way of death, and death does not get in the way of life. All reality (the entire earth and the whole empty sky) is contained in life but is likewise contained in death. Life and death, like earth and sky, are not one but not different, not different but not the same, not the same but not many.[51] How, then, do they relate?

Scholars often claim that Japanese Buddhism emphasizes and values death equally with life, contrary to a Western emphasis on life.[52] According to this view of Japanese Buddhism, life and death entail one another so completely that in speaking of life, we may as well say death; in speaking of death, we

may as well say life. There is life if and only if there is death; there is death if
and only if there is life. Thus to live in accord with the teachings of Buddhism
we should, while living, always keep death in mind as well. Dōgen seems to
reflect this view at one point, when his equivalence of the terms "life" and
"death" implies that in speaking of life, we may as well say death; in speaking
of death, we may as well say life. But I think this view as a whole is the view of
ordinary Buddhism, in contrast to Dōgen's relatively extraordinary perspective
on life and death. Dōgen clearly implies that life and death are each complete
in themselves—not that they are of equal value and entail one another.[53] Life
and death interchangeably are samsara and are the occasion of nirvana.

I think of myself as alive, not yet dead—how could one think of oneself
as dead? Dōgen encourages me to give myself over completely to being one
existential moment (*uji*) of living at a time. In *Zenki* he encourages me to
investigate a time like this very one (この正當恁麼時を功夫參學すべし),
and he writes of the "I that is life, the life that is I" (生なるわれ、われなる
生).[54] He does not follow this with a parallel comment concerning death, as if
he could speak of "the I that is death"—how could he?—but he does follow it
with a quotation from the Song dynasty Zen master Yuanwu to the effect that
life is the presencing of the whole works and so is death.[55] Dōgen's formulation implies that there is no self separate from birth/life and no self separate
from death. It is not that I am born, live, and die, as if there were some person
undergoing these events separate from them. Rather this I *is* the being-born,
living, dying—yet even that manner of speaking spreads the self over time. In
practice I am to give myself over completely to each and every moment right
now (in some texts *nikon*, a common Chinese expression for "now," is the
word Dōgen uses).

A Foregone Conclusion

What, then, does Dōgen have to say about personal death? Nothing directly
about biographical death, the death of others described by a detached, anonymous observer. Little about the death of the second person, the others he personally knows, save for a few words of admonition and encouragement, such
as "Do not detest death, do not desire life." These two perspectives already
imply some divide between life and death, but Dōgen places between life
and death an even deeper divide. As for autobiographical death, this death of
oneself becomes for Dōgen the death *of* the first person and *of* a first-person
perspective. The sense of death that he defines absolves or liberates one into
the moment. The divide between birth-and-death and liberation that initially
characterizes autobiographical death in much of philosophical Buddhism is

healed; there is no divide here. Several Mahayana traditions already identify samsara with nirvana. Dōgen adds a difference: constantly practicing the perspective of the all-engulfing moment.⁵⁶

Philosophically what we may gain from this perspective is the insight that the meaning of personal death, that is to say, one's intentionality directed to death, is inevitably directed to another time, not this time, not now. When I speak of the death of anonymous others I mean a time past; when I speak of your death, I think of a future time; when I think of my own death, I intend a future time too, perhaps about to come, but not right now. Dōgen shifts these meanings, this intentionality, to a different sense of death, death in the right now. *Death, more clearly than anything else, makes present the element of time.* Practically the practice of absorption into a momentary right now gives rise to serious ethical problems that would need to be addressed elsewhere. When it comes to a beautiful death, however, attention to the moment at hand, in whatever degree possible, may be the only way to go.

NOTES

1. A distinction in terms of philosophical Buddhism and the Buddhism of the populace is a tentative suggestion. Scholars have contrasted doctrinal with popular or folk Buddhism, and the Buddhism of the elites with that of nonelites, but these sets of distinctions pose historical problems of their own. See Susannne Formanek and William R. LaFleur, eds., *Practicing the Afterlife: Perspectives from Japan* (Vienna: Verlag der Österreichischen Akademie der Wissenschaften, 2004), 24–25, 34. Whatever the terms, the point is to contrast a major difference in two ways that Buddhists and scholars both have presented Japanese Buddhism, while recognizing that monk elites and illiterate laity shared many beliefs, and the keepers of doctrine also performed rites for common folk.

2. *Shobōgenzō Shōji*; see Norman Waddell and Masao Abe, trans., *The Heart of Dōgen's Shōbōgenzō* (Albany: State University of New York Press, 2002), 106.

3. *Orategama Zokushū*; see Philip B. Yampolsky, trans., *The Zen Master Hakuin: Selected Writings* (New York: Columbia University Press, 1971), 145.

4. Learning of the death of Hisamatsu, Sally Merrill recalled, "Speaking in an interview, Hisamatsu Sensei once said, 'I tell my family I do not die. I say that I am the formless Self. Therefore I do not die. In fact, death never even crosses my mind. I have some work to do.'" In Merrill, "Remembering Hisamatsu Sensei," *Eastern Buddhist* 14.1 (1981): 129.

5. "The Philosophy of Nenbutsu," trans. Mark L. Blum, in James W. Heisig, Thomas P. Kasulis, and John C. Maraldo, eds., *Japanese Philosophy: A Sourcebook* (Honolulu: University of Hawaii Press, 2011), 243. The original text is *Jōdoshū Ryakushō, in Shōwa shinshū hōnen jonin zenshū* (Kyoto: Heirakuji shoten, 1974), 590.

6. *The Collected Works of Shinran*, ed. Gadjin M. Nagao (Kyoto: Jōdo shinshū hongwanji-ha, 1997), 523, cited in Ōmine Akira, "The Genealogy of Sorrow: Japanese View of Life and Death," *Eastern Buddhist* 25.2 (1992): 26.

7. Kiyozawa Manshi, "Absolute Other Power," trans. Mark L. Blum, in Heisig, Kasulis, and Maraldo, *Japanese Philosophy*, 270. The original text is "Zettai Tariki no Daidō," in *Kiyozawa Manshi zenshū* (Tokyo: Iwanami shoten, 2002–3), 6: 110–13.

8. Murasaki Shikibu, *The Tale of Genji*, trans. Royall Tyler (New York: Viking, 2001), 72–73, 75.

9. Watanabe Shōkō is an example of a scholar who documents but harshly criticizes the "decline" of Buddhism in Japan into formalized religious ritual and the loss of its true mission: the "seeking of *bodhi*-mind above (*jōgu-bodai*) and the saving of beings below (*geke shujō*)." The religion that lacks these aspirations "is not [truly] Buddhism." Watanabe Shōkō, *Nihon no Bukkyō* (Tokyo: Iwanami, 1968), 207; Watanabe Shōkō, *Japanese Buddhism* (Tokyo: Kokusai bunka shinko-kai, 1970), 125.

10. Watanabe Shōkō considers rituals on behalf of the dead as a defining characteristic of what happened to Buddhism particularly in Japan (*Japanese Buddhism*, 41). Jacqueline I. Stone and Mariko Namba Walter, eds., *Death and the Afterlife in Japanese Buddhism* (Honolulu: University of Hawaii Press, 2008), 1, stress that services for the dead represent "the major social role of Buddhist priests and temples in Japan today." Other scholars would extend that characterization to most of the history of Japanese Buddhism. Gregory Schopen has given evidence of the central role of rituals and concern for the dead in Indian Buddhism from its very beginning in his *Bones, Stones, and Buddhist Monks: Collected Papers on the Archeology, Epigraphy, and Texts of Monastic Buddhism in India* (Honolulu: University of Hawaii Press, 1997). For evidence of the centrality of death in all Buddhism, see Bryan J. Cuevas and Jacqueline I. Stone, eds., *The Buddhist Dead: Practices, Discourses, Representations* (Honolulu: University of Hawaii Press, 2007).

11. See Sueki Fumihiko, "Rethinking Japanese Buddhism," *Nichibunken Newsletter* 76 (2009): 3–4; Sueki Fumihiko, *Butten Wo Yomu: Shi Kara Hajimaru Bukkyōshi* (Tokyo: Shinchōsha, 2009).

12. Jacqueline I. Stone, "With the Help of 'Good Friends': Deathbed Ritual Practices in Early Medieval Japan," in Stone and Walter, *Death and the Afterlife in Japanese Buddhism*, 71.

13. On the practices of Genshin and Kakuban see Stone, "With the Help of 'Good Friends,'" 61, 70; on the practices of Saichō and Nichiren, see Mariko Namba Walter, "The Structure of Japanese Buddhist Funerals," in Stone and Walter, *Death and the Afterlife in Japanese Buddhism*, 252, 259.

14. George J. Tanabe Jr., "The Founding of Mount Kōya and Kūkai's Eternal Meditation," in George J. Tanabe Jr., ed., *Religions of Japan in Practice* (Princeton,

NJ: Princeton University Press, 1999), 358–59. According to Walter, "The Structure of Japanese Buddhist Funerals," 253, Kūkai did compose and recite a text at the death of a close disciple, his sister's son. As far as I know, however, his writings pay no attention to such practices.

15. Teachers on both sides of the divide were evidently cremated. *Emaki* picture scrolls depict Hōnen's and Shinran's cremations, as well as Nichiren's, to name only a few figures. See the colored plates in Karen Gerhart, *The Material Culture of Death in Medieval Japan* (Honolulu: University of Hawaii Press, 2009).

16. As translated by Wayne Yokoyama, in Aoki, *Coffinman*, 45. In an unpublished manuscript, Yokoyama provides a more literal translation: "When the eyes of this fellow [*soregashi*; Shinran] close, let [his body] be committed to the Kamo river to be given over to the fishes." The source of this statement is Kakunyo's *Gaijashō* of 1337 in *Teihon Shinran Shōnin Zenshū* (Kyoto: Hōzōkan, 1969), 4; and in *Jōdo Shinshū Seiten* (Kyoto: Jodo shinshu hongwanji-ha, 2003), 937.

17. *A Primer of Sōtō Zen: A Translation of Dōgen's Shōbōgenzō Zuimonki*, trans. Reihō Masunaga (Honolulu: East-West Center Press, 1971), 62. Dōgen makes it clear in other talks in *Shōbōgenzō Zuimonki*, as well as in "Bendōwa," that he is not opposing the mortal body to some supposedly eternal mind or spirit; body and mind (*shinjin*) are undivided in practice.

18. The divide between these two Buddhisms in Japan is not repeated throughout Asian Buddhism. The divides between life and death on the one hand and samsara and nirvana on the other intersect in the *parinirvana* of Sakyamuni depicted for example in early Indian Buddhist literature, since *parinirvana* refers both to the final, definitive liberation of the Buddha and to his death as a departure from this world.

19. Philosophers of many persuasions have reflected on the meaning of death from the first person, but probably none more thoroughly than phenomenologists. One of the most systematic and enlightening investigations is James G. Hart, *Who One Is* (Dordrecht: Springer, 2009), vol. 1, chapters 7 and 8, and vol. 2, chapters 1 and 2. Martin Heidegger's *Being and Time* defines the authentic self as the self resolutely open to its own death. Paul Ricoeur considers death and birth as the limits of personal experience: as important as our birth and death may be to others, especially our family and friends, we do not experience them ourselves; for each of us birth is an "already happened" event and death a "not-yet occurred" event. "If 'learning finally how to live' is to learn to die, to take into account absolute mortality without salvation, resurrection, or redemption, I share all the negatives here." Ricoeur, *Living up to Death*, trans. David Pellauer (Chicago: University of Chicago Press, 2009), 85.

20. Ōe Kenzaburo, *A Personal Matter*, trans. John Nathan (New York: Grove Press, 1969), 30; Ōe Kenzaburo, *Kojinteki taiken* (Tokyo: Shinchō bunko, 1964), 45–50.

21. Gerhart, *The Material Culture of Death in Medieval Japan*, 1.

22. "The 'you' is a 'second first-person' made present by analogizing first-person experience" (Hart, *Who One Is*, 1: 213).

23. Italo Calvino, *If on a winter's night a traveler*, trans. William Weaver (San Diego: Harcourt, Brace, 1981), 3. In the original Italian, the second person is indicated by verb endings and the imperative form as well as by personal pronouns: "Stai per cominciare a leggere il nuovo romanzo *Se una notte d'inverno un viaggiatore* di Italo Calvino. Rilassati. Raccogliti. Allontana da te ogni altro pensiero." Calvino, *Se una notte d'inverno un viaggiatore* (Torino: Edizione Einaudi 1979), 3.

24. In *Shōbōgenzō* and "Bendōwa," for example.

25. In *Shōbōgenzō Zenki*, Dōgen uses われ as a personal pronoun, for example, われふねにのりて "riding a boat, I [or 'we'] ... " Most translations of *Genjōkōan* interpret われ as 我, *atman*, a substantial, self-subsisting self that has its own independent nature (*jisei*). A few translations render われ more ambiguously, simply as "an I," which can refer to this kind of objectified, substantial self or to a subject that can characterize or examine phenomena, in expressions like われにあらざる,われにあらぬ,自心自性は常住なるかとあやまる. Thomas P. Kasulis argues that われin Dōgen is solely a first-person reference, a personal subject who can take a standpoint; it does not refer to a self-subsisting *atman* or 我. See Kasulis, "The Ground of Translation: Issues in Translating Premodern Japanese Philosophy," in James W. Heisig and Rein Raud, eds., *Classical Japanese Philosophy (Frontiers of Philosophy 6)* (Nagoya, Japan: Nanzan Institute of Religion and Culture, 2010), 24. In my free interpretation, I prefer the more ambiguous reading. In contrast, the word *jiko* (自己) in the *Genjōkōan* and other texts can refer simply to oneself as a self-consciousness subject, as in the famous phrase 自己をならふといふは、自己をわするるなり ("to study the self means to forget the self").

26. For a similar distinction among three perspectives regarding death, see the section "La mort en troisième, en seconde, en première personne," in Vladimir Jankélévitch, *La Mort* (Paris: Falmmarion, 1966), 21–32.

27. William Bodiford, *Sōtō Zen in Medieval Japan* (Honolulu: University of Hawaii Press 1993), 14, xii, 32.

28. Bodiford, *Sōtō Zen in Medieval Japan*, 31. For a translation of the *Eihei Shingi*, see *Dōgen's Pure Standards for the Zen Community*, trans. Daniel Leighton and Shohaku Okumura (Albany: State University of New York Press, 1996). Leighton emphasizes Dōgen's intent to convey the proper attitude to benefit community practice (21).

29. Bodiford, *Sōtō Zen in Medieval Japan*, 192.

30. Bodiford, *Sōtō Zen in Medieval Japan*, 191. Bodiford notes that Dōgen's recorded sayings in Chinese include no funeral sermons. On the other hand, Steven Heine reminds me that Dōgen did occasionally give memorial sermons, especially for his teacher in China, Rujing. The collection of formal sermons in the Sino-Japanese *Eihei Kōroku* contains seven such sermons; see Heine, *Did Dōgen*

Go to China? What He Wrote and When He Wrote It (Oxford: Oxford University Press), 182–83. The collection of Chinese verses Dōgen composed while in China also includes examples of mourning on behalf of lay followers—a common practice for Song Chan masters, sometimes done by writing letters. Dōgen apparently abandoned this practice after he returned to Japan (personal communication from Heine, July 29, 2013). Dōgen also occasionally refers to relics; Heine lists as Dōgen's first writing a text of 1226, shortly after he returned from China, called *Shari Sōdenki*, on preserving his teacher Myōzen's relics (*Did Dōgen Go to China?*, 2). For all that, something Dōgen says in *Shōbōgenzō Zuimonki* removes the specialness of reverence for the dead and care for the grieving, and places these in a larger context: "The masses on mourning days and the good deeds done during *Chūin* [the seven weeks' mourning] are all employed by laymen. Zen priests must truly be aware of their deep gratitude to their parents. All my deeds should be like this. Do you suppose it is the Buddha's idea to practice prayer just on a special day to special people?" (cited in Watanabe, *Japanese Buddhism*, 73; the original text seems to be "Shōbōgenzō zuimonki," in *Jōyō Daishi Shōgyō Zenshū*, ed. Eiheiji [Tokyo: Eiheiji shutchōsho, 1909], 84).

31. Dōgen was an exception in the history of Japanese Zen with regard to funeral rites and spirit cults. Duncan Ryūken Williams, "Funerary Zen: Sōtō Zen Death Management in Tokugawa Japan," in Stone and Walter, *Death and the Afterlife in Japanese Buddhism*, 213, notes that the first Sōtō Zen funeral did not occur until the third generation after Dōgen, at the death of Gikai in 1309. Contrary to the myth of "traditional Zen," Bodiford characterizes Zen practices as mingled with spirit cults and rituals, notes the widespread performance of Zen funeral rites, and claims that these rites were the major source of all Japanese Buddhist funeral rituals (*Sōtō Zen in Medieval Japan*, 1–2). Using Bodiford's research, Gerhart, in *The Material Culture of Death in Medieval Japan*, summarizes the nine special rites typically used at a funeral for a Zen abbot (17). First the body was carefully bathed and dressed and then placed in the coffin (*nyūgan*). It was then transferred (*igan*) from the room where the priest had died to the lecture hall, and three rites were performed while the body lay in state in the hall: the coffin lid was closed (*sogan*), the deceased's portrait was hung above the altar (*kaishin*), and a wake in the form of a priest's consultation with the deceased was held (*tairyō shōsan*). The coffin was then moved to the cremation grounds (*kigan*), where libations of tea (*tencha*) and hot water (*tentō*) were offered. The final rite was the lighting of the funeral pyre (*ako, hinko*).

32. Bodiford, *Sōtō Zen in Medieval Japan*, 192. Bodiford surmises that the "death of Dōgen presented the Eiheiji community with a loss from which it could not easily recover. Dōgen had been the community's source of spiritual authority. After Dōgen's death, his disciples faced the new task of directing their communal life without the external support of their master's supervision and guidance" (35).

33. *Genbuntaishō Gendaigoyaku Dōgen Zenji Zenshū, vol. 17: Hōgo Kashō*, ed. Kagamijima Genryū et al. (Tokyo: Shunjūsha, 2010), 47, 49. In free translation these poems read:

> *A frail blade of grass I pass*
> *over Mt. Kinobe,*
> *my feelings all a cloud drift.*
> 草の葉にかどでせる身の木部山雲にをかある心地こそすれ
> *Thinking to see it again in the fall,*
> *such a wistful time—*
> *the moon tonight*
> *robs me of sleep.*
> また見むと思ひし時の秋だにも今夜の月にねられやはする

For other translations, seeSteven Heine, *A Blade of Grass: Japanese Poetry and Aesthetics in Dōgen Zen* (New York: Peter Lang, 1989), 85–86, and Heine's commentary, 8–9, 79.

34. Dōgen, *Moon in a Dewdrop: Writings of Zen Master Dōgen*, trans. Philip Whalen and Kazuaki Tanahashi, ed. Kazuaki Tanahashi (San Francisco: North Point Press, 1985), 219 (slightly modified). For the original Sino-Japanese, see DZZ-2 7:307.

35. Hee-Jin Kim, *Flowers of Emptiness: Selections from Dōgen's Shōbōgenzō* (Lewiston, NY: Edwin Mellen Press, 2004), 19.

36. In the *Gakudōyōjinshū* and *Shōbōgenzō Zuimonki*. See, for example, *A Primer of Sōtō Zen*, 83 and passim.

37. *Genjōkōan* dates from 1233 but was revised as late as 1252; *Zenki* dates from 1242. Scholars have found no colophon for the piece titled *Shōji*; it is not included in the seventy-five-fascicle version of the *Shōbōgenzō*, but I accept the Sōtō sect's treatment of it as authentic. Ejō recorded Dōgen's talks collected in *Shōbōgenzō Zuimonki* between 1235 and 1237. In examining Dōgen's statements about death, we should keep in mind that they were made relatively early in his teaching career, perhaps before he would have had to deal with the deaths of disciple monks or lay patrons.

38. DZZ-2 1:2. My interpretations draw upon several excellent translations of *Genjōkōan* and other chapters of the *Shōbōgenzō*, without adhering to any one published translation.

39. In a note to their translation of *Genjōkōan*, Norman Waddell and Masao Abe point out that in chapter 1 of the *Eihei Kōroku*, Dōgen wrote that "flowers fall *because of* our longing, weeds flourish *because of* our hatred" (my emphasis; *The Heart of Dōgen's Shōbōgenzō*, 40).

40. I owe to Rein Raud the term "existential moment" to translate Dōgen's famous term *uji*. See Raud, "The Existential Moment: Rereading Dōgen's Theory of Time," *Philosophy East and West* 62.2 (2012): 153–73.

41. DZZ-2 1:3–4. A translation more literal than my free interpretation would be:

    > Firewood cannot return to being firewood once it turns into ash. Be that as it
    > may, we cannot take ashes as "after" and firewood as "before." Firewood resides
    > in its own phenomenal position, and while we speak of there being a "before"
    > and an "after," a prior and a subsequent, for the time being "before" and "after"
    > are divided. Ashes are in the phenomenal state of ashes and have an "after" and
    > a "before," [yet for the time being "before" and "after" are divided.] Just as this
    > firewood, turning to ash, does not become firewood again, a person after dying
    > does not live again. That being so, it is an established teaching of Buddhism that
    > life cannot be said to turn into death, and for this reason it is called non-born,
    > non-arising. It is an established teaching that death does not become life, and
    > for this reason it is called non-perishing. Life is one stage of time, and death too
    > is one stage of time.

42. Note that if this "I" is not extinguished, then Dōgen's position on perishing is
    not nihilist, advocating the annihilation of the self. Similarly "nonarising" does
    not entail an eternalist position, an eternal self. Dōgen makes no pronounce-
    ments about the survival of a perduring self. His concern is the manifestation
    and the erasure of a personal, position-taking ego.

43. We know that Dōgen was familiar with the *Nirvana Sutra* from his *Shōbōgenzō
    Busshō*, where he transforms the sutra's statement "All beings have
    Buddha-nature" to "All beings are Buddha-nature." The sutra states, "All sen-
    tient beings universally possess Buddha-nature without exception" (一切衆生
    悉皆佛性, usually read in Japanese as *Issai shujō wa kotogotoku busshō o yusu*).
    Dōgen reads this as "All sentient beings, all existence, Buddha-nature" (*Issai
    shujō shitsuu busshō*). Thanks to Victor Sōgen Hori for this translation. Dōgen
    also transforms the sense of *hō-i*: in the *Lotus Sutra* and other scriptures it refers
    to the incomparable, necessary truth of the dharma, according to Nakamura
    Hajime, *Bukkyōgo Daijiten* (Tokyo: Tōkyō shokan, 1973), 1218. In the passage of
    Genjōkōan, *hō-i* means the transitory status that defines a particular dharma or
    phenomenon.

44. Similarly the *Vimalakirti Sutra* speaks of the patient "recognition that nothing
    really arises or perishes" (*mushōnin*, Sanskrit: *anutpattika-dharma-ksanti*).

45. Mark L. Blum's translation of the phrase in the Chinese version of *Mahayana
    Mahaparinirvana-sutra*, T 12.396a18. Blum notes that the *Nirvana Sutra* not only
    negates the view that things arise and perish; it also complements this nega-
    tion with an affirmation of "the permanence, joy, self, and purity" of "buddha,
    nirvana, and by extension the buddha-nature within everyone." "Despite our
    experience, there is thus another 'great self' [*daiga*] within us and the sutra even
    uses the term *true atman*." Blum, "Nirvana Sutra," in Robert E. Buswell et al.,
    eds., *Encyclopedia of Buddhism* (New York: Macmillan Reference), 606.

46. This interpretation of *fushō*, literally "nonarising," may be controversial, but it is supported by the passage from the fascicle called *Shōji* cited in the following paragraph in this chapter. It is also supported by the entries for *fushō* and *fumetsu* in Nakamura, *Bukkyōgo Daijiten*, 1163, 1173, which give "absolute" (*zettai*) for the meaning of 不 in these words in *Genjōkōan*. According to these entries, *fushō* does not mean "unborn" or "nonarising" but rather "absolutely everything is arising" (全体は生であること), and 不滅 means "absolutely everything is perishing" (全体滅ばかりで、生に対するものがないこと), with precedents in the *Lankavatara Sutra*.

47. DZZ-2 2:528. Many translations have "are free *from* life and death." Kim has "free *in* birth-and-death," which seems more appropriate, in *Flowers of Emptiness*, 166. Thomas Cleary has "some measure of detachment (はなるる分) from birth and death." *Shōbōgenzō: Zen Essays by Dōgen*, trans. Thomas Cleary (Honolulu: University of Hawaii Press, 1986), 122.

48. The European practice of romanticist hermeneutics in the nineteenth century was to try to relive the original occasion of the writing. In the twentieth century philosophers criticized this attempt as misguided, and the practice turned to liberating the text from any surmised intention of the author in his time. Paul Ricoeur writes, "Writing tears itself free of the limits of face-to-face dialogue and becomes the condition for discourse itself *becoming-text*. It is to hermeneutics that falls the task of exploring the implications of this becoming-text for the work of interpretation." Ricoeur, "On Interpretation," trans. Kathleen McLaughlin, in Alan Montefiore, ed., *Philosophy in France Today* (Cambridge, UK: Cambridge University Press, 1983), 191. A hermeneutics related to the romanticist practice is at work in current homilies by Zen teachers when they quote Zen masters like Dōgen as if the master's words were timeless, immediately applicable to the present audience. Scholars of Zen criticize this hermeneutics as part of a naïve "rhetoric of immediacy," a fabricated sense of spontaneity and immediacy found both in the original text and in its current use. While I too want to hear what Dōgen has to say to us here and now, in this day and age, concerning death, I appeal not to timeless words but rather to the temporal grammar of Dōgen's text that indicates an occurrence taking place within a present: the mutual presence to one another of the quoted speaker or actor and his audience. In Dōgen's writing that occurrence hardly seems fabricated.

49. This is the restatement of Bret W. Davis, "The Presencing of Truth," in William Edelglass and Jay L. Garfield, eds., *Buddhist Philosophy: Essential Readings* (Oxford: Oxford University Press, 2009), 255.

50. I use here Thomas Cleary's innovative translation of the word *zenki*, the dynamic and interdependent activity of all phenomena (*Shōbōgenzō: Zen Essays by Dōgen*, 43).

51. 一にあらざれども異にあらざれども即にあらず、即にあらざれども多にあらず. The order of contrasts here differs from the usual sequence, which is

not one and not many, not different and not same. The Kyoto school philosopher Tanabe Hajime interprets this sentence as an example of a unity of opposites. Tanabe Hajime, "The Philosophy of Dōgen," trans. Ralf Müller, in Heisig, Kasulis, and Maraldo, *Japanese Philosophy*, 686. The original text is "Shōbōgenzō no tetsugaku shikan," in *Tanabe Hajime Zenshū* vol. 5 (Tokyo: Chikuma shobō, 1963–64).

52. Sueki Fumihiko writes that in the modern (post-Christian) Western worldview that determined the conventional understanding of Buddhism, "only 'life' was considered of value and with death all value is lost" ("Rethinking Japanese Buddhism," 3).

53. Kim interprets the *Zenki* as saying that birth/life is all-inclusive, totally independent and self-sufficient, and presumably the same holds true for death as well (*Flowers of Emptiness*, 245n.7).

54. DZZ-2 1:220. Buddhist dictionaries say 正當恁麼時 means 正如此時: "just like this time" or "truly like this very moment."

55. Dōgen quotes the line 生也全機現、死也全機現 from a poem by Yuanwu (T 47.1997, 793). See *Shōbōgenzō: Ausgewählte Schriften*, trans. Ryōsuke Ōhashi and Rolf Elberfeld (Tokyo: Keio University Press, 2006), 183n.138; Dōgen, "*Shōbōgenzō Zenki*: 'Total Dynamic Working' and *Shōji*: 'Birth and Death,'" trans. Masao Abe and Norman Waddell, *Eastern Buddhist* 5.1 (1972): 71.

56. Dōgen's concentration on the all-engulfing moment at any time thus differs from what was once the focus in much of Japanese Pure Land Buddhism on the moment of death as the particularly momentous time of liberation, when one should die with a fervent hope for birth in the Pure Land. I noted how Genshin exhorted the dying person to concentrate on Amida Buddha as his last thought (*nen*). Carl Becker notes that this thought has precedents in many sutras that stress the importance of wholesome thoughts at the moment of death. "Buddha declared that the crucial variable governing rebirth was the nature of the consciousness at the moment of death." Becker refers to texts from the Pali canon, the *Petavatthu* and the *Vimanavatthu* (Stories of the Departed), and to *Majjhima Nikaya* II, 91; III, 258; and *Samyutta Nikaya* V, 408. Becker, "Buddhist Views of Suicide and Euthanasia," *Philosophy East and West* 40.4 (1990): 547.

5

"When All Dharmas Are the Buddha-Dharma"

DŌGEN AS COMPARATIVE PHILOSOPHER

Gereon Kopf

Dōgen as Philosopher

Scholars familiar with the Japanese Buddhist traditions usually identify Zen master Dōgen (1200–1254), in addition to the other famous founders of the Japanese Buddhist schools and perhaps Hakuin Ekaku (1686–1769), as major representatives of Japanese Buddhist philosophy.[1] Philosophers with little knowledge of Buddhism in Japan, however, seem to focus almost exclusively on Dōgen when discussing Japanese Buddhist contributions to philosophical discourse. The reason for this is twofold. First, Dōgen entered the canon of the "non-Western" philosophers when the philosophers of the Kyoto School learned about him from Watsuji Tetsujirō (1889–1960) through his essay *Shamon Dōgen*, published in 1926, and from Kimura Uno's *Dōgen to Nihon Tetsugaku* (1937).[2] Under the influence of Kyoto school thought, Abe Masao (1915–2006) popularized Dōgen in the English-language literature.[3] Second, in its English translations—and discussions in comparative philosophy are mostly held in English—Dōgen's writings seem to be especially predestined for an introduction to the philosophical discourse as they address major themes such as metaphysics, ethics, and, even if less obvious, epistemology.[4] Among the ontological themes one can find in Dōgen's conceptual opus *Shōbōgenzō* are the questions of selfhood and time.[5] Accordingly the appropriate fascicles have been quoted and requoted by philosophers, sometimes even without regard for their context or knowledge of the Japanese versions.

Thus the question arises: How are we to read Dōgen? How can we, if at all, put Dōgen into a dialogue with thinkers outside of his tradition? Interestingly enough, Dōgen scholars themselves are not in agreement on this issue. Concretely there seems to be a tension between various approaches in Dōgen studies. In a recent essay Rein Raud identifies four approaches to Dōgen's work: philological, historical, religious, and philosophical. Raud explains:

> A philologist would want to compare all the variable versions of the text in order to determine which of these is the correct one. ... A historian ... traces the influences, the threads of thought, developments, as well as reactions and rebuttals to other authors, and shows us how and why the individual contributions of an author have taken place by following its lifeline right down to its genesis. ... A religious reader is not necessarily bothered by the correct semantic meaning of the text, nor its intellectual genesis, but first and foremost by the relevance it has for the reader's own experience of the world. ... For the philosophical reader it does not matter so much whether the text she has is actually the only truly correct version. ... What matters is interpretations, their quality, their productivity for further thought.[6]

What distinguishes these four approaches are their methods and goals. The philologist applies textual methods, known in biblical studies as literary, textual, redaction, and form criticisms, in order to identify the original text and approximate the intent of the author. The historian strives to approximate the intent of the author by reading a specific text in the historical context reconstructed by archaeological, so-called material, and textual evidence. The religious reader uses as method, regardless of whether or not this method is consciously reflected upon, a text's significance for her life and practice in the contemporary world. Finally, the philosopher explores the argument and concept structures in a text in order to gauge the contribution and import of specific texts to wider issues. In all of this it is obvious that the location, method, and goal of the reader significantly influence the outcome of the hermeneutical exercise.

Especially intense seems to be the conflict between a textual-historical approach called Buddhology and the readings of Dōgen provided by comparative philosophers.[7] Often this tension is portrayed as the conflict between the rhetoric of authenticity and that of meaning and relevance. The former approach has been accused of reductionism, and the latter of "overinterpreting" or of "reading into" Dōgen's text ideas alien to the author and his times. However, both approaches have to confront the notions of "authorship" and "text" thematized by the textual-historical approach, on the one side, and the reason we study Dōgen's texts in the first place, on the other. Similarly both approaches have to acknowledge that the very constructions of "Dōgen" and, given the existence of multiple manuscripts and compilations, the "*Shōbōgenzō*" as well are problematic.[8] It seems unrealistic to imagine the "historical Dōgen" and his intent as much as it is unfeasible to identify the essence of Dōgen's thought.[9] One could argue that in the same sense in which it is meaningless to call a completely decontextualized Dōgen "Dōgen," it is also impossible to interpret Dōgen from any standpoint other than that of the twenty-first century. Even historians ask questions characteristic of their perspectives rather than Dōgen's historical, geographical, and discursive location.

Any reading of Dōgen requires what Hans-Georg Gadamer calls a "fusion of the horizons" (*Horizontverschmelzung*). Gadamer maintains that "understanding is always the process in which horizons that are presumed to be in-themselves are fused."[10] It seems obvious but nevertheless bears repeating that in the act of reading Dōgen, the twenty-first-century scholar understands Dōgen's text and situation through the lens of a twenty-first-century scholar, while the thought of the scholar does not remain unaffected by this reading. Thomas P. Kasulis makes the same point using Dōgen's own terminology: "To read the *Shōbōgenzō* is to be ensnared in the vines of the words (*kattō*), yet at the same time, its very complexity reveals Dōgen's own personal presence and gives us the opportunity to entangle our own entanglements with his entanglements."[11] The assumption as to what Dōgen thought is as disingenuous and misleading as is the appeal to the spirit of a text. While both approaches differ in method and scope, they are equally based on the assumption of an identifiable substrate. The former assumes an identifiable intent of the author, the latter an identifiable spirit or essence of the text. Either approach constructs its own "Dōgen": the philologist constructs the author Dōgen, the philosopher the thinker Dōgen, and the historian Dōgen as a *zoon politikon*.

Therefore I believe that an understanding of Dōgen as a person, religious teacher, sectarian founder, and creative thinker requires that the reader asks questions about the historical context as well as the current significance of the text, all the while being aware that authentic historicity as well as essences and consistent systems of thought are unattainable ideals beyond the grasp of any scholar. In other words, philologists, historians, and philosophers all contribute to our general understanding of Dōgen. The four ways of reading Dōgen are distinguished by the hermeneutical method they employ and by the willingness of the scholar to be "entangled" with the text in question. What makes a reading of Dōgen a philosophical one is that it is based on an "open encounter" with the text that emphasizes the argument and conceptual structures in the text and puts them into a dialogue with arguments and conceptual structures today.[12]

When I call Dōgen a philosopher, I do not use the term "philosopher" as an exclusive category that precludes his role and value as a founder or religious teacher but rather in order to describe one aspect of his life and work. Like Kevin Schilbrack, "I am not suggesting that Dōgen ... is 'really' a philosopher, as opposed to a religious teacher or the founder of a school. I claim not that I am presenting the essence of Dōgen, but only that, among other things Dōgen makes"—and now I am paraphrasing Schilbrack—"philosophical claims."[13] I am also not using the category "philosophy" to superimpose external criteria on Dōgen's work. As Kasulis already observed, "Dōgen is not doing Western [*sic*] philosophy; in fact, he is not doing modern Japanese philosophy. Still, he is *philosophizing*; he is thinking through questions of his own society and his own personal context. To appreciate Dōgen as philosopher, we must meet him on his turf not ours."[14] And again, "In the pragmatist's terms, one should examine the common problematic situation out of which Dōgen's text, hermeneutics, and one's own philosophical reflection arise."[15]

Ralf Müller and Raud take this approach to "meet him on his own turf" one step further. The former suggests a way of philosophizing based on Dōgen's use of the term "expression" (*dōtoku*), while the latter develops something like a "grammar" of Dōgen's texts in his recent "Thinking with Dōgen: Reading Philosophically into and beyond the Textual Surface." The themes raised by these philosophers, Schilbrack's emphasis on philosophical claims in Dōgen, Kasulis's reminder to meet Dōgen on "his turf," Müller's suggestion that Dōgen himself provides a terminology for and an outline of philosophy, and Raud's "grammar of Dōgen" illustrate why I think it is helpful to classify certain aspects of Dōgen's work as philosophy and will accompany us throughout this essay.

I explore how, not whether, Dōgen's work qualifies and functions as "philosophy."[16] How can we study Dōgen's work as philosophy? To clarify my method of inquiry, I would like to propose four principles of Dōgen studies:

1. Awareness of one's own hermeneutical horizon and methodological prejudice.
2. Identification of the referent we imagine when we employ the signifiers "Dōgen" and the "*Shōbōgenzō*."[17]
3. Encounter with Dōgen "on his own turf" and an appreciation of "his standpoint and horizon."[18]
4. Forthrightness about the role a particular interpretation plays in today's scholarship and landscape of ideologies.

Concretely this means that I read the *Shōbōgenzō* at the beginning of the twenty-first century as a philosopher who is familiar with the Japanese Zen Buddhist tradition, has some background in religious studies, and has experienced contemporary forms of Zen Buddhism in most East Asian cultures and in the United States. In this chapter I read selected excerpts from the *Shōbōgenzō* within the historical and, especially, textual horizon of Dōgen's work. In this process I strive to distinguish among Dōgen's texts, his sources, and the various interpretations thereof in order to fashion an image of Dōgen as a philosopher. When I employ phrases such as "Dōgen said," I refer to the Dōgen of the *Shōbōgenzō* and not some transcendent author. My goal is to show that a reading of Dōgen as a philosopher enriches both our understanding of Dōgen as well as our understanding of philosophy and the philosophical method.

In particular I will take clues from Dōgen, who himself creatively interpreted texts from various cultures across a period of at least one thousand years, and his interpreters throughout the ages and across different cultures on how to conduct comparative philosophy. I employ a definition of philosophy as self-discovery, clarification of conceptual language, and "translation of an idiom" that I construct from sources within the European and Japanese philosophical traditions.[19] I will base this definition on the thought of Plato (429–347), Nishitani Keiji (1900–1990), John Maraldo, Ueda Shizuteru, Ludwig Wittgenstein (1889–1951), and Dōgen himself. Using this definition as a heuristic device, I will reflect on Dōgen's approach to three themes that are equally important to his writing in particular and philosophy in general, namely self-discovery, standpoint analysis, and the subversion of conceptual language. This chapter introduces Dōgen's description of the "Buddha-way" (*butsudō*) as a journey of self-discovery and his treatise on the *tathagatagarbha* doctrine, "Busshō," as case studies of his philosophical activity and project.

Philosophy as Self-Discovery

One of the ways to commence a discussion of Dōgen as a philosopher is, of course, a definition of philosophy. While the term "philosophy" itself was alien to Dōgen as well as to the tradition in which he wrote and which influenced him, the philosophical project, and this is a point worth repeating, was not. So what is philosophy? There are multiple definitions formulated at different times and in various contexts. The definitions are so diverse that it is safe to say that even Plato, often recognized as one of the "fathers" of the European and American philosophical traditions, would not qualify as a philosopher given some of the narrow definitions of philosophy advanced in the analytical tradition. Two of the most general but also most commonly accepted definitions describe the goal of the philosophical project as the "examined life" and "the attempt to understand the nature of the world and our place and destiny in it."[20]

The Japanese philosopher Nishitani, who was himself influenced by Dōgen's writings, suggests that this examination of life and the understanding of "our place and destiny" in the world is nothing but an exercise in self-awareness. In his famous essay *Zen no Tachiba*, Nishitani draws a parallel between the heirs to the Cartesian project—most prominently the successors of Edmund Husserl (1859–1938) often referred to as the phenomenological movement—the philosophies of the Yogacara school of Buddhism, and the discourses and theories developed by Chan teachers and practitioners.[21] All these practices, whether they are philosophical or contemplative, commence with the self-conscious self and advance through a process not unlike the Husserlian reductions (*Reduktionen*) toward the deep structure of the self that Müller, using philosophical language, refers to as the "constitutive relationship between self and world."[22]

To Nishitani the philosophical project is best articulated by the words of the Japanese Zen master known as Daitō Kokushi (1282–1337), "the investigation of the matter of the self" (*koji kyūmei*), and more broadly by the third and fourth of the so-called four principles of Chan Buddhism as transmitted by *The Records of Chan Master Linji Huizhao* (*Linji Huizhao Chanshi Yulu*): "Point directly to the heart of the person, and become a buddha by seeing your nature."[23] Nishitani believes that these two lines illustrate the goal of philosophy, namely to clarify the notion of self, our cognitive processes, and ultimately "the nature of the world and our place and destiny in it." To Nishitani it is the goal of philosophy to engage in "the investigation of the matter of the self" and to "point directly to the heart of the person, and become a buddha by seeing your nature." The discursive expression of this self-discovery constitutes the core of philosophy.

Like Nishitani, Dōgen locates self-discovery, or at least self-exploration, at the center of his project. As is well known, Dōgen declares, "To study the Buddha-way is to study the self; to study the self is to forget the self; to forget the self is to be actualized by the ten thousand dharmas; to be actualized by the ten thousand dharmas is to cast off body and mind of self and other; the traces of awakening disappear and the awakening whose traces have disappeared goes on forever."[24] Of course, it was not "philosophy" Dōgen was interested in but the "Buddha-way," that is, following the Buddha. However, even a cursory reading of Dōgen's work reveals that, to him, the way of "all buddhas and all ancestors" (*shobutsu shoso*) is all-encompassing and also includes "philosophizing"

or, as he would say, "expression." In "The Incomparable Philosopher," Kasulis
suggests that this paragraph outlines the overall framework of Dōgen's sense
of "philosophizing." While I agree with Kasulis in general, I would like to take
a step back and approach this passage from three angles: the philosophical
discourse, Buddhist conceptions of no-self, and Dōgen's text itself. Most of
all, however, I want to show that there is no one interpretation but that our
reading is determined by the lens we use. Various readings reveal the multiple
facets of the text that are created by an ever-evolving intertextuality.

A philosopher would identify similarities between Dōgen, on the one side,
and Husserl and Vasubandhu (fourth or fifth century), on the other. Like the
main thinkers of phenomenology and Yogacara Buddhism, Dōgen provides a
description of the cognitive apparatus that commences with self-consciousness
and then advances to deeper and preconscious levels of what we call the "self."[25]
And like the other two thinkers, Dōgen roots self-consciousness in the larger
world and in the moment of intersubjectivity. To Husserl the place of the self
is the external "life world" (Lebenswelt);[26] to Vasubandhu, one of the foundational thinkers of Yogacara Buddhism, it is the internal world of the "storehouse consciousness" (alayavijnana). Similarly, and despite the accusations
of idealism and occasionally solipsism that have been leveled at times against
each of them, both thinkers identify the relationship between self and other as
central to the formation of consciousness. Husserl identifies intersubjectivity
as the most central problem of consciousness in his later work, especially in
his Ideas 2 (Ideen 2), whereas Vasubandhu addresses the question of alterity in
his Twenty Verses (Vimsatika). Dōgen refers to the "world," following the tradition of Daoism and Chan Buddhism, as the "ten thousand dharmas" (manbō)
and uses the terms self and other to describe the intersubjective relationship.

While these three terms as well as compounds such as the "benefit
of self and other" (jitari) occur ample times in the Buddhist canon, Dōgen
seems to be one of the few authors who use the phrase "oneness of self and
other" (jita ichinyo).[27] Such a conception of the self-other relationship would,
of course, give the phrase "cast off body and mind of self and other" a special meaning, but I will return to this notion later. For now it is important
to note that a comparative philosopher would recognize the binary structure
of self-consciousness that Dōgen's text shares with various philosophers of
consciousness from other traditions.[28] This consciousness is grounded in a
deep structure that is revealed by a progressive practice, speculative or contemplative, of what Dōgen calls "forgetting" (wasureru) and that seems to have
some similarities to the practice of "bracketing" (ausklammern) used during
the Husserlian reductions.[29] The phrases Dōgen employs to describe this deep
structure imply that the dichotomies between self and world, self and other,

and "mind" (*shin*) and "body" (*shin*) characteristic of self-consciousness have given way to an ambiguity wherein the opposites separated by consciousness into dichotomies seem to coexist.

A thinker familiar with the Buddhist tradition, on the other hand, will be reminded of the Buddhist conception of "no-self" (*anatman*). Of course, Dōgen does not use the Japanese translation of *anatman, muga*, in this passage. Neither does he use it in the rest of the *Shōbōgenzō*, as even a cursory reading of that volume reveals. This is rather interesting given his penchant for quoting the Buddhist canon. However, the passage under discussion reflects three of the basic characteristics of the theory of no-self in the Buddhist scriptures: (1) the belief that the realization of selflessness leads to liberation; (2) the rejection of any kind of essentialism regardless of whether it is expressed in the affirmation or denial of the existence of the self; and (3) the pairing of selflessness with a detachment from the body. Let us consider these three elements:

1. There are many passages asserting that all of reality is devoid of an essence.[30] But their function is not to merely make metaphysical claims. Rather, according to the scriptures, the knowledge of this inherent and fundamental selflessness constitutes the key to liberation. As the *Flower Garland Sutra* (*Buddhavatamsaka Mahavaipulya Sutra*) famously states, "I know that I have no self, no humanity, no eternal life, and no self-nature; I am neither active nor passive. This understanding of emptiness immediately precedes the entrance into the gate of liberation."[31]

2. Many Buddhist texts go one step further and suggest that any kind of assertion, whether affirmative or negative, and belief, whether positivism or nihilism, reifies conceptual language and reveals a "delusion about" reality. When asked about the nature of the self, Sakyamuni later explained his silence to his disciple Ananda by saying, "If I had said that there is a self, he would have formed the view of the self. If I had said that there is no self, he would have been even more confused."[32] The *Commentary on the Mahaprajnaparamita Sutra*, or *Mahaprajnaparamita-sastra*, for example, similarly suggests that "the claim 'the five skandhas are impermanent, empty, and without a self' means that in the perfected wisdom, the five skandhas are neither permanent nor impermanent, neither empty nor non-empty, neither with a self nor devoid of a self."[33] The *Treatise of the Path to Attain Liberation* (*Vimoksamarga-sastra*) also points out the inherent relation between opposite ideologies. It says, "Based on the view of impermanence one judges the theories of permanence, based on the view of suffering one judges the theories about happiness, based on the view of no-self one judges the theories of the self."[34]

3. Finally, there is a third set of passages in the Mahayana scriptures that, on first sight, are puzzling and shocking. For example, one passage in the *Diamond Sutra* reads, "When King Kalinga cut up my body I realized that I do not possess the characteristic of a self, a human, common people, or a person who will live a long life."[35] Similarly, in a rather macabre story of which there are multiple versions in the Buddhist canon,[36] a wanderer attains selflessness after two *yaksa* rip off his body parts and replace them with the corresponding parts taken from a corpse. Monks who meet him after this ordeal rejoice and exclaim rather unexpectedly, "See, this person knows selflessness; he is capable of attaining deliverance."[37] The *Commentary on the Mahaprajnaparamita Sutra* adds a heuristic tool when it suggests that, "if there is permanence, there is impermanence, self-existence no-self existence, activity no activity, form formlessness. These are many forms of non-attainment."[38] In short, attachment to views, regardless of which belief it is, indicates delusion, while detachment from them already results in attainment. The detachment that leads to liberation rejects not only theories but also essentialized beliefs about oneself, such as "This is my body" or "This is not my body," "I am this" or "I am that."

These are some of the characteristics of the early Buddhist theory of the "no-self." How do these passages help with interpreting Dōgen's passage about "studying the self"? First, in Dōgen's account, the soteriological function of realizing selflessness is rather apparent: it is the "forgetting of the self" that results in the experience of "actualization." Second, Dōgen negotiates opposites such as "studying" and "forgetting," "self" and the "ten thousand dharmas," "body" and "mind," as well as "self" and "other." And, not unlike the passages cited earlier, Dōgen equally refuses to either affirm or resolve dichotomies and ambiguities. Actually, as I will show in subsequent paragraphs, this ambivalent attitude toward dichotomies and ambiguities is an important feature of Dōgen's thought. While the current passage is not as obvious in its deconstruction of dichotomizing categories in particular and dualism in general, just a few lines earlier Dōgen eschews both positivism and nihilism and thus rejects the reification of the notion of a "self" and "no-self" equally. As I have suggested elsewhere, to Dōgen the correct understanding of personhood lies somewhere between the theories of selfhood and selflessness and requires a third term as paradigm. Finally, this paragraph reverberates with the violent description of extreme detachment from the body, even hinting at a certain level of disembodiment that in some of the cited passages precede the realization of selflessness when Dōgen refers to the attainment of liberation as "casting off of body and mind" (*shinjin datsuraku*).[39]

So far we have learned from the comparative philosophers that the process of self-discovery reveals a deep structure of consciousness where self and world, self and other, and body and mind are not separate. The philosopher familiar with the Buddhist tradition has added to this discussion the notion that selflessness implies not a denial of the self but rather a rejection of essentialism as well as dualism and thus requires a detachment from identification of the self with physical and, one can probably safely add, psychological features of the form "I am this" and "I am not that" as well as a rejection of ideologies.[40] In addition both readings suggest a process of an epistemic transformation that results in a deep insight. It is of course obvious that Dōgen's passage about "studying the self" echoes some common Buddhist sentiments.[41]

What makes this passage interesting and unique is not that Dōgen eschews dualism and subverts the dichotomies between self and world, as well as self and other, but how he does it. He does not simply resolve the difference between self and world or self and other but puts these seemingly opposite terms into an intimate relationship. Concretely he describes selflessness as "to be actualized by the ten thousand dharmas" and as "to cast off body and mind of self and other." The self is not dissolved in the "ten thousand dharmas" but "actualizes" them. The term used to describe the relationship between self and world as well as self and other and to undermine dualism and essentialism is "to actualize" (*shō suru*).[42] But what does it mean to "actualize" something or everything? To understand how this phrase works, we need to return to Dōgen's text *Shōbōgenzō* "Genjōkōan."

To understand Dōgen's contention that the self is "actualized by the ten thousand dharmas," we need to have a closer look at how he uses the term "actualization" in the first place and how he imagines the relationship between the "self" and the "ten thousand dharmas" in this fascicle. In some sense "actualization" is the main theme of the *Shōbōgenzō* fascicle "Presencing of the Kōan" ("Genjōkōan"). While not unlike the term that gave this fascicle its name, it does not necessarily constitute a neologism of Dōgen;[43] in addition both terms, "actualization" and "presencing the kōan" (*genjōkōan*) or simply "presencing" (*genjō*), share a similar function in Dōgen's overall system as the activity that actualizes or presences the "absolute" à la the "buddha-dharma" (*buppō*) or the totality" à la the "ten thousand dharmas."[44] However, he does seem to give it a new conceptual function within its specific text and his overall thought. In the Buddhist canon the character 證 is frequently used in compounds such as "practice-and-actualization" (*xuizheng*), "presencing actualization" (*xianzheng*), and "attainment of actualization" (*zhengde*).[45]

In "Genjōkōan," Dōgen uses the character 證 in five ways: (1) as the verb "to actualize"; (2) in the compound "practice-and-actualization"; (3) in the phrase "actualizing buddha" (shōbutsu); (4) as the verb "to actualize thoroughly" (shōkyū); and (5) in the phrase "to actualize through experience" (shōken). For the most part Dōgen employs the former two variations on the theme of actualizing in order to destabilize a dualistic framework of thought by introducing a third term. As is well known, he struggled with the seeming contradiction between the notions of "acquired enlightenment" (shigaku) and "original enlightenment" (hongaku) while practicing on Mount Hiei and proposed to resolve this tension with the phrase "practice-and-actualization are one" (shushō kore ittō nari) in his fascicle "Negotiating the Way" ("Bendōwa").[46] Similarly he commences the fascicle "Genjōkōan" by resolving the dichotomy between "delusion" (mayoi) and "awakening" (satori), "birth" (shō) and "death" (shi), and "all buddhas" (shobutsu) and "sentient beings" (shujō) by introducing the concepts of "delusion-and-awakening" (meigo), "birth-and-death" (shōji), and "sentient beings-and-buddhas" (shōbutsu) as a third term,[47] and thus asserts an existential ambiguity over a clear-cut either-or dichotomy. The phrases "practice-and-actualization" and "actualizing" function in the same way. It is not that the self merges into the ten thousand dharmas, but it actualizes them in one moment of self-consciousness. At the end of "Genjōkōan," Dōgen uses the example of Zen Master Baoche from Mount Mayu. When asked why he fanned himself despite the "permanent nature of the wind," the Zen master replied to the student, "While you know that the nature of wind is permanent, but you still do not understand the idea of the wind reaching everywhere."[48] The nature of the wind does not make the act of fanning unnecessary. In the same way awakening, "original enlightenment," and the ten thousand things have to be actualized in practice.

In addition in the first half of "Genjōkōan," Dōgen dedicates quite some space to the relationship between the self and the ten thousand dharmas. And as is the case in his description of self-discovery, he considers the notions of "actualization" and "practice-and-actualization" to be correct and to describe this relationship as a moment of "actualization." The key passage to this topic precedes Dōgen's description of self-discovery: "Delusion is to practice and to actualize the ten thousand dharmas in the horizon of the self. Awakening is to practice and actualize the self in the horizon of the ten thousand dharmas.[49] All buddhas are greatly awakened about delusion, while sentient beings are greatly deluded about awakening."[50] What distinguishes buddhas from sentient beings is not the kind of activity they engage in, both practice and actualization, but their perspective and horizon. Those who focus on the self are limited in their perspective and thus incapable of actualizing or even understanding the ten thousand dharmas. Under the horizon of the ten thousand dharmas, the practitioner is able to understand and actualize the self.

A few passages later in the same fascicle Dōgen provides the analogy of a boat sailing along the coastline to drive home the same point. Those who focus on the self see nothing but the self. However, the perspective of the ten thousand dharmas opens up an understanding and actualization of the self. Since every actualization or practice-and-actualization of the ten thousand dharmas is particular, two fundamental characteristics of this practice-and-actualization as well as practice of actualization follow. In Dōgen's words, "If one aspect is illuminated, another one is hidden" and even actualized buddhas "proceed to actualize buddhas endlessly."[51] The same sentiment of "continuous practice" (*gyōji*) is reiterated in the last line of Dōgen's description of self-discovery: "The awakening whose traces have disappeared goes on forever."

Philosophy as Actualization

Our examination of Dōgen's conception of self-discovery has revealed his understanding of the self as an "actualization of the ten thousand things." The next step of our inquiry will need to clarify if and in what way actualization can qualify as philosophy. Obviously not all forms of actualization can be considered philosophy, but neither are all examples of an "examined life" or all attempts "to understand the nature of the world and our place and destiny in it." Dōgen lists as examples of actualizations the actualization of the "foundation of great liberation," the "practice-and-actualization of communicating with gods," the actualization of a "dream inside a dream," "actually disseminating the teaching of millions of buddhas," "actualization of a picture," "the actualized effect," and the "thorough actualization of the depth of non-expression as the depth of non-expression."[52] And I am sure practices such as the tea ceremony (*sadō*) and calligraphy (*shodō*) would qualify as moments of actualization as well. Similarly, other forms of expression, such as poetry, music, arts, diaries, and even social activism or commitment to charity work, can easily reveal and witness an "examined life" or "the attempt to understand the nature of the world and our place and destiny in it." This means that additional criteria may be helpful. Therefore I would like to suggest Wittgenstein's definition of philosophy as the "battle against the bewitchment of our intelligence by means of language."[53] Philosophy, to Wittgenstein, is some kind of linguistic and discursive practice or even "self-cultivation" (*shugyō*).[54] This definition has the advantage of including the discursive dimension of academic philosophy that, as I implied earlier, focuses on the analysis of arguments and conceptual structures and corresponds to Dōgen's understanding of "expression" as one instance of actualization.

The assertion that there are Zen thinkers such as Dōgen, who are not only interested in the clarification of the conceptual language we use but believe that "letters and words" (*monji*) can express the buddha-dharma as well as silence, still comes as a surprise to many readers. The reason for this lies in the rhetoric of silence embraced by many Zen teachers and expressed in the so-called flower sermon popularized in the *Gateless Barrier* (*Wumenguan*). The story imagines a time when Sakyamuni sat in silence while his disciples waited for him to teach. When the disciples got impatient he explained, "I possess the treasury of the true dharma eye; it is the heart of nirvana, and the mysterious dharma gate without form. It does not rely on letters or words but constitutes a special tradition outside of the scriptures. I have just transmitted it to Mahakasyapa."[55] The core lines of this passage that reiterate the first two of the four principles of Zen, "There is a tradition outside of the scriptures, do not rely on words," attributed to Bodhidharma and transmitted by the *Records of the Chan Master Linji Huizhao*, have often been interpreted to privilege silence over language and especially speculative thought as the superior expression of the buddha-dharma. However, Dōgen wholeheartedly disagrees with this analysis and rejects this rhetoric of silence with this nonchalant comment about the flower sermon: "If The-World-honored-One hated using words but loved picking up flowers, he should have picked up a flower at the latter time, too."[56] As Müller has pointed out, "Dōgen succeeds in exactly that [developing his own linguistic practice] insofar as he engages in a reflexive relationship to language on multiple levels. Based on his understanding of Buddha's teaching he assigns language a positive, nay, necessary function in the constitutive relationship between self and world as well as in the interpretation of verbal and non-verbal symbols."[57]

Dōgen maintains that conceptual expressions, be they philosophical, poetic, liturgical, or instructional, do actualize the buddha-dharma and the ten thousand dharmas. He designs the concept of expression in the fascicle with the same title, in such a way that its use reverberates with the definition of "actualization" in the fascicle "Genjōkōan." I will show that (a) expression is the activity that manifests the dharma of "all buddhas and the all ancestors"; (b) while any expression manifests the buddha-dharma fully it is never complete since "if one aspect is illuminated, another one is hidden" and even "actualized buddhas" "proceed to actualize buddhas endlessly";[58] and (c) therefore expression is never comprehensive and concluded: "The awakening whose traces have disappeared goes on forever." To examine these points more fully:

(a) Dōgen commences his fascicle "Expression" with the wry assertion that "all buddhas and all ancestors constitute expression."[59] Expression is nothing less than the shibboleth of "all buddhas and all ancestors" as they "certainly ask whether or not someone is able to express themselves."[60] At this point it merits mentioning that the phrase translated here as "expression" literally translates into "attaining/gaining" (*toku*) the "way" (*dō*). The term "expression" thus identifies the activity of "all buddhas and buddha-ancestors" as well as the activity that reveals a practitioner's "actualization" and, as I will discuss below, "buddha-nature."

(b) However, as in the case of actualization, while expression is always full and never partial, it never can be complete.[61] Due to the predicament of particularity characteristic of samsara, any expression highlights one aspect and de-emphasizes all other dimensions of buddha-dharma. Dōgen explains, "When expression is expressed, non-expression is not-expressed. Even when one recognizes expression in expression, as long as one fails to actualize non-expression as non-expression thoroughly, one has not yet attained the face as well as the bones and marrow of the buddha ancestors."[62] And a few lines later: "Within us there is the depth of expression and the depth of non-expression. Within him there is the depth of expression and the depth of non-expression. In the depth of expression there is self and other. Within the depth of non-expression there is self and other."[63] Here Dōgen even evokes the intimate relationship between self and other that he identified as characteristic of the activity of actualization in "Genjōkōan," to express the existential ambiguity and, one could add, even the basic soteriological dilemma all religious thinkers face who suggest that the absolute and infinite enters, in one way or another, the world of temporality and particularity. Dōgen even coins the phrase "expression-and-not-expression" (*dōtokufudōtoku*).[64] One could even say that, not unlike Martin Heidegger's (1889–1976) truth, expression simultaneously reveals and obstructs and subsequently should be noted as expression.[65]

(c) While Dōgen emphasizes the importance of "continuous action" not as much in this fascicle as he does in his essays on meditation and morality, he does contend that even buddha-ancestors need to express their attainment in the present despite preceding acts of expression when he suggests that, "within this expression, they thoroughly actualized practice in the past and negotiate the way with all their effort today. ... This expression constitutes their effort of three, eight, thirty, forty years. It is an expression of inexhaustible power."[66]

Dōgen's commitment to conceive of linguistic and philosophical expression as expression and expression-and-non-expression in order to articulate the sentiment that, "if one aspect is illuminated, another one is hidden" has

three important reasons. To Dōgen conceptual language, like any other particular form of expression, verbal or nonverbal, constitutes a full expression
of buddha-nature and yet is itself incomplete. The reason for this lies in the
fact that, as particular expressions, concepts illuminate one aspect and hide
another. Ultimately conceptual expressions manifest a particular standpoint
rather than the buddha-dharma or the ten thousand things.[67] Nowhere does
Dōgen explore this perspectivism as clearly as in the fascicle that can be translated as "Existential Moment."[68] The Japanese phrase used in the title of the
"Uji" fascicle is usually translated as "being-time"; however, I prefer Raud's
translation, "Existential Moment."[69] Elaborating on the phrase "existential
moment," Dōgen explains, "At a certain time meaning arrives but phrases do
not. At a certain time, phrases arrive but meaning does not. At a certain time,
both meaning and phrases arrive. At a certain time neither of them arrives."[70]

Evoking the form of the famous tetralemma of Nagarjuna in the second
century, Dōgen explores the phrase "existential moment," which also can be
read "at a certain time," by proposing a perspectival view of language. He also
seems to imply that the relationship between "phrase" and "meaning," or
"signifier" (signifiant) and "signified" (signifié), as we would say today, is not
a necessary one. Obviously it would be a stretch to read a mature theory of
signification into Dōgen's text, but I think this passage does provide a glimpse
of his theory of language: the relationship between "phrase" and "meaning"
is contextual insofar as this relationship is established "at a certain time."[71] To
paraphrase Dōgen's observation, we could say that the meaning of a phrase is
neither necessary nor permanent. In a certain context phrases are meaningless, and in a different context meaning cannot be expressed verbally. Finally,
there are contexts in which phrases express a meaning and those in which any
linguistic description is inappropriate.

Dōgen applies heuristic devices such as the tetralemma, suggests creative
readings of phrases such as "existential moment," destabilizes concepts such
as the very term "expression" itself not to reject language but to remind the
reader that linguistic expression, like any form of actualization, is perspectival
and thus context-driven. Once you take a phrase out of its context, it changes
its meaning. Dōgen introduces this way of thinking in the opening paragraph
of his fascicle "Genjōkōan":

> When all dharmas have buddha nature, there is delusion and awaken-
> ing, there is practice, there is life, there is death, there are all buddhas,
> there are sentient beings. When neither dharmas nor self exist, there
> is neither delusion nor awakening, there are neither buddhas not sen-
> tient beings, there is neither life nor death. Because the Buddha-way is

originally beyond fulfillment and lack, there is birth and destruction, delusion and awakening, sentient beings. Nevertheless, flowers fall in regret, grass grows in dismay.[72]

In this paragraph, which I have discussed at length elsewhere,[73] Dōgen introduces four sets of belief about the nature of topics central to Zen practice such as delusion, awakening, birth, death, practice, actualization, sentient beings, and buddhas. Each of these beliefs is preceded by a phrase that identifies as its locus, its episteme, if you will, a belief system. The belief systems portrayed shift from an affirmation of discrete and real entities, such as "buddhas" and "sentient beings," via their negation, the postulation of a third term beyond affirmation and negation—what D. T. Suzuki calls "higher affirmation" and Nishida "negation-and-yet-affirmation" (*hitei soku kōtei*)[74]—to the declaration of impermanence. In some sense, of course, this paragraph provides a discursive context for Dōgen's notion of self-discovery: "studying the self" affirms the self, while "forgetting" negates it. The "actualization of the ten thousand dharmas" in the self transcends this dichotomy of studying and forgetting insofar as it expresses the self-and-the-ten-thousand-dharmas. Nevertheless self-awareness is never completed since "the traces of awakening disappear and the awakening whose traces have disappeared goes on forever."

Frequently at least three of these four epistemes have been taken to outline the spiritual process during meditation.[75] However, not only is such an interpretation difficult to reconcile with the fourth line of the paragraph; it also does not take into account Dōgen's belief that, "if one aspect is illuminated, another one is hidden." Using as a heuristic device the notion that every expression implies a nonexpression or that every ~~expression~~ simultaneously reveals and obscures, I would like to rephrase this paragraph: At a certain time, there are buddhas and sentient beings, because in certain situations the distinction between buddhas and sentient beings, nirvana and samsara, awakening and delusion is necessary. Without it religious practice and ethical rhetoric seems meaningless. At a different time there are neither buddhas nor sentient beings because there are situations when it is important to emphasize that both actualize buddha-nature and "because all buddhas are actualization, all things are actualization."[76] At a certain time there are buddhas-and-sentient-beings because only a philosophical nondualism can prevent the fallacies of either dualism or monism. In reality nothing persists and even the most beautiful flowers disappear when the winter arrives. Similarly even nondualism cannot be essentialized without falling into the trap of the "Senika heresy" (*senni gedō*). The doctrine of impermanence as well has to be protected from essentialism. The same applies, of course, to the four dimensions of self-discovery, studying, forgetting, actualizing, and the endless "awakening whose traces have disappeared goes on forever" as well. Each attitude or belief system provides a glimpse that highlights one aspect, expresses one standpoint, and bypasses or ignores all the others. Early Buddhist thinkers call this attachment to one view "ignorance" (avidya).

Thus Dōgen clearly rejects any form of essentialism. He not only rails against the essentialism of the so-called Senika heresy in his fascicles "Negotiating the Way" and "This Mind Is the Buddha" ("Sokushin Zebutsu").[77] He also critiques "heresies" or non-Buddhist theories, and he "corrects" or subverts Buddhist doctrines as well, most famously the doctrine of buddha-nature (tathagatagarbha). As I suggested in my "Zen, Philosophy, and Emptiness: Dōgen and the Deconstruction of Concepts," Dōgen reads the dictum of the Mahaparinirvana Sutra (Da Banniepan Jing) that "all sentient beings have buddha-nature" to mean "all sentient beings completely are buddha-nature."[78] In this fascicle Dōgen uses anecdotes recorded in the Platform Sutra (Liuzu Dashi Fabaotan Jing) and the Records of the Transmission of the Lamp (Xu zhuangdeng lu) to modify the notion of buddha-nature (busshō) as "being-buddha-nature" (yūbusshō), "non-being-buddha-nature" (mubusshō), "emptiness-buddha-nature" (kūbusshō), and "impermanence-buddha-nature" (mujōbusshō).[79]

Abe, who introduced Dōgen's reinterpretation of buddha-nature to the English literature on comparative philosophy, understands Dōgen's nonsubstantial conception of buddha-nature exclusively metaphysically as "de-anthropocentric," "dynamic," and "impermanent."[80] "For Dōgen, impermanence is preaching impermanence, practicing impermanence, and realizing impermanence."[81] And again: "Apart from this thorough realization of impermanence, there is no realization of buddha-nature."[82] Here Abe clearly reinforces Schilbrack's observation that Dōgen may not have been a metaphysician, but sure enough he makes "metaphysical claims."[83]

While Abe's interpretation of Dōgen's nonsubstantial conception of buddha-nature certainly adds to the concept of personhood in contemporary philosophical discourse, it also de-emphasizes important aspects of Dōgen's fascicle, that is, his subversion of Buddhist terminology. In short, Dōgen's conception of buddha-nature is multifaceted. He does not replace the notion of buddha-nature as "being-buddha-nature" with "impermanence-buddha-nature" but supplements it. The doctrine of buddha-nature expresses not only a basic Buddhist dictum but a central thesis of Dōgen's thought insofar as he believed that all beings share a common existential feature: all beings, sentient beings as well as buddhas, constitute an instance of actualization "because all buddhas are actualization, all things are actualization." The notion of "non-being-buddha-nature" serves as a warning not to succumb to essentialism in the same way in which the conception of "emptiness-buddha-nature" is designed to eschew dualism.[84] And even "emptiness-buddha-nature" cannot escape the fundamental existential predicament that "flowers fall in regret, grass grows in dismay." After all, this is the reason that "the traces of awakening disappear and the awakening, whose traces have disappeared, goes on forever." Yet none of these four variations of buddha-nature can stand on its own. Each highlights one aspect and obscures another. Subsequently "buddha-nature" should be written as ~~buddha-nature~~, "non-being-buddha-nature" as ~~non-being-buddha-nature~~, "emptiness-buddha-nature" as ~~emptiness-buddha-nature~~, and "impermanence-buddha-nature" as ~~impermanence-buddha-nature~~. The same methodological subversion can be applied to Dōgen's conception of "delusion," "awakening," "sentient beings," "buddhas," "self," and "other."

The greatest value of Dōgen's philosophy, however, lies in its importance for comparative philosophy. First, Dōgen's own hermeneutics reveal him as a comparative philosopher long before this category was in vogue or even meant anything. Who is a comparative philosopher if not the author who interprets Indian texts for a Japanese audience using a heuristic device borrowed from Chinese Buddhist scriptures? As Raud observes, Dōgen's "is a philosophy that transcends the boundaries of the tradition."[85] However, just as important as Dōgen's function as a role model for comparative philosophers is the fact that his philosophy provides the blueprint for comparative philosophy. The creativity of the interpretations that give rise to Dōgen's unique thoughts and ideas is his use or, one might say, exploitation of the ambiguity of language. Dōgen was not only aware that the relationship between phrases and meaning depends on their context; he was further able to create new understandings and applications, that is, new meanings of previously employed phrases. In his fascicle "Buddha-nature," he is able to expand and enrich the notion of buddha-nature by reading this concept through a variety of contexts, specifically the *Mahaparinirvana Sutra*, the *Platform Sutra*, and the *Records of the Transmission of the Lamp*.

This de- and recontextualization of "phrases and meaning" is possible since concepts function as "expressions-and-non-expressions" insofar as "if one aspect is illuminated, another one is hidden." By doing that Dōgen demonstrated that philosophy constitutes, as Maraldo has said, the "translation of an idiom." Philosophy emerges when one introduces a concept developed "at a certain time" to a new context. Concretely this "translation of the idiom" brings to the fore what previously had been hidden. The first condition for this practice of philosophy is self-awareness, that is, awareness of one's own discourse as well as of the locus in which the subject matter of analysis is located. The second condition is an understanding of what a text or concept expresses and what it does not convey. The application of one concept to a new context in the act of what Gadamer calls the fusion of horizons requires the "translation of an idiom." In Dōgen's words, it creates a third "time wherein there are phrases as well as meaning." The goal of comparative philosophy is, then, to use the abyss that opens up between "expression" and "nonexpression" in order to supplement the already full but incomplete expression of the buddha-dharma and to approximate, albeit in an "asymptotic fashion," the actualization of the ten thousand dharmas.[86] In other words, philosophy is the discursive expression of the totality under the horizon of the ten thousand dharmas.

Afterthought: Dōgen in Comparative Philosophy

I would like to add a few remarks on how Dōgen's thought has been and can be used in comparative philosophy. In the same way in which this whole chapter was not so much an analysis of Dōgen's thought as an exploration of how his thought translates into the language of comparative philosophy, the following examples demonstrate how a few contemporary comparative philosophers were inspired by Dōgen's philosophizing: Kasulis's phenomenology of zazen, Nishida's modern-day *panjiao* system,[87] and my own reading of Dōgen's hermeneutics as subversive philosophy. All these readings translate Dōgen's conceptions into a different "certain time" or "existential moment" in order to highlight what has been "hidden" and express what formerly has been "not-expressed." There are three elements:

1. In *Zen Action / Zen Person*, Kasulis analyzes Dōgen's "Instructions for Seated Meditation" ("Zazengi"), specifically interpreting the three key phrases of Dōgen's instruction "think [*shiryō*] about not-thinking [*fushiryō*] ... by means of without-thinking [*hishiryō*]."[88] However, he does not suggest that use to understand these three phrases as stages on the meditative process but believes that they identify three existential comportments: "thinking" is a "positional" attitude that takes "conceptualized objects" as its "noematic content"; "not-thinking" is equally "positional" in that it is the modality of "thinking as its "noematic content"; "without-thinking" is "non-positional" and takes as its "noematic content" the "pure presence of things as they are."[89]

2. Nishida developed what could be best called a modern-day *panjiao* system.[90] I have argued elsewhere that, in his first work, the *Inquiry into the Good (Zen no kenkyū)*, Nishida divides the responses provided by the philosophical tradition to any philosophical problem, regardless of whether it

belongs to ontology, ethics, or philosophy of religion, into three categories: "objectivism" (*kyakkan shugi*), "subjectivism" (*shukan shugi*), and a
nondualism based on the "self-identity of the absolute contradictories"
(*zettai mujunteki jiko dōitsu*).[91]

3. I believe that Dōgen's practice of subverting the key concepts
of his philosophical system applies to contemporary philosophies
as well, even though it will be difficult to emulate the skill he exhib-
ited in his "buddha-nature." In the same way that Dōgen modified
~~buddha-nature~~ as ~~non-being-buddha-nature~~, ~~emptiness-buddha-nature~~, and
~~impermanence-buddha-nature~~, I believe it is beneficial if we conceive of
each concept delineating the horizon of human cognition, experience, and
philosophy similarly as, for example, ~~totality~~, ~~absolute~~, and ~~infinity~~. It would
also enrich our conceptions that refer to particulars or are defined in relation
to its opposite if they are understood nondualistically within their discursive
horizon as body-and-mind, self-and-other, as well as birth-and-death. Finally,
since the horizon of human experience and thus philosophy is ever elusive
and requires an infinite number of expressions, a philosopher in the foot-
steps of Dōgen cannot but evoke the "continuous practice" of philosophy
that "is haunted by the gulf that separates particular expression and the totality of experience, a gulf which he seeks to bridge not by speculative constructions but by intermediate phenomena, though never quite completely."[92]

NOTES

1. *Japanese Philosophy: A Sourcebook* is probably the first book published in a
   European language that extends the term "philosopher" to a larger number
   of Buddhist thinkers in Japan, past and present. James W. Heisig, Thomas
   P. Kasulis, and John C. Maraldo, eds., *Japanese Philosophy: A Sourcebook*
   (Honolulu: University of Hawaii Press, 2011).

2. Watsuji Tetsujirō, *Shamon Dōgen* (1926; Tokyo: Ryūbunkan, 1987); Uno Kimura,
   Dōgen to Nihon Tetsugaku (Kyoto: Chōjiya shoten, 1937).

3. Masao Abe, *A Study of Dōgen: His Philosophy and Religion*, ed. Steven Heine
   (Albany: State University of New York Press, 1992).

4. On metaphysics, see Kevin Schilbrack, "Metaphysics in Dōgen," *Philosophy East
   and West* 50.1 (2000): 34–55. On ethics, see Douglas K. Mikkelson, "Who Is
   Arguing about the Cat: Moral Action and Enlightenment According to Dōgen,"
   Philosophy East and West 47.3 (1997): 383–97.

5. See Steven Heine, *Existential and Ontological Dimensions of Time in Heidegger
   and Dōgen* (Albany: State University of New York Press, 1985); Joan Stambaugh,
   Impermanence Is Buddha-Nature: Dōgen's Understanding of Temporality (Honolulu:

University of Hawaii Press, 1990); Joan Stambaugh, *The Formless Self* (Albany: State University of New York Press, 1999).

6. Rein Raud, "Thinking with Dōgen: Reading Philosophically into and beyond the Textual Surface," *Philosophizing in Asia*. APF Series 1, ed. Tsuyoshi Ishii and Wing-keung Lam (Tokyo: UTCP—Uehiro Booklet, 2013), 27–28.

7. Ralf Müller, *Dōgen's Sprachdenken* (München: Verlag Karl Alber, 2013), 29–31, identifies the Yanagida Seizan (1922–2006), Carl Bielefeldt, and Bernard Faure as representatives of the former, and Hee-jin Kim, Thomas Kasulis, Carl Olson, and Rolf Elberfeld as representatives of the latter approach.

8. Matsumoto Shirō, *Dōgen Shisōron* (Tokyo: Daizō shuppan, 2000) distinguished between the Dōgen of the seventy-five-fascicle and the Dōgen of the twelve-fascicle *Shōbōgenzō* and suggests that the former supported the "theory of original enlightenment" (*hongaku shisō*), while the latter was critical of it. William Bodiford, "Textual Genealogies of Dōgen," in Steven Heine, ed., *Dōgen: Textual and Historical Studies* (New York: Oxford University Press, 2012), 25–31, reminds us that the *Shōbōgenzō* was transmitted in multiple manuscript versions and fifteen compilations.

9. Scholars involved in the quest for the historical Jesus, which started with Albert Schweitzer (1875–1965) in 1906, are still struggling to construct an "authentic" image of Jesus between history and myth. For the latest scholarship on the subject, see Thomas L. Thompson and Thomas S. Verenna, eds., *"Is This Not the Carpenter?" The Question of the Historicity of the Figure of Jesus* (Sheffield, UK: Equinox, 2012). Roland Barthes, *Image-Music-Text*, trans. Stephen Heath (New York: Hill and Wang, 1977), 142–48, argues for the impossibility of reconstructing the intent of the author and suggested treating the text independent of its author.

10. Hans-Georg Gadamer, *Gesammelte Werke Band 1: Hermeneutik I: Wahrheit und Methode* (Tübingen: J. C. B. Mohr, 1990), 311.

11. Thomas P. Kasulis, "The Incomparable Philosopher: Dōgen on How to Read the *Shōbōgenzō*," in William R. LaFleur, ed., *Dōgen Studies* (Honolulu: University of Hawaii Press, 1985), 93–94.

12. Raud, "Thinking with Dōgen," 29.

13. Schilbrack, "Metaphysics in Dōgen," 35.

14. Kasulis, "The Incomparable Philosopher," 87.

15. Kasulis, "The Incomparable Philosopher," 95.

16. John Maraldo, "Defining Philosophy in the Making," in James W. Heisig, ed., *Japanese Philosophy Abroad* (Nagoya: Nanzan Institute for Religion and Culture, 2004), 220–45, provides a very convincing argument as to why Dōgen and other Japanese Buddhist philosophers should be included in the philosophical canon.

17. This formulation of the principle emerged from an informal conversation with Aleksi Järvelä.

18. Gadamer, *Gesammelte Werke*, 308.

19. John Maraldo, "Tradition, Textuality, and Trans-lation: The Case of Japan," in Charles W. Fu and Steven Heine, eds., *Japan in Traditional and Postmodern Perspectives* (Albany: State University of New York Press, 1995), 233.

20. Plato, *Plato's Apology of Socrates: An Interpretation, with a New Translation*, trans. Thomas G. West (London: Cornell University Press, 1979), 44; Maurice Cornforth, *Science versus Idealism* (New York: International Publishers, 1962), 219.

21. Nishitani Keiji, *Nishitani Keiji Chosakushū*, 26 vols. (Tokyo: Sōbunsha, 1986–95), 11: 3–257. Dan Lusthaus, *Buddhist Phenomenology: A Philosophical Investigation of Yogacara Buddhism and the Ch'eng Wei-shih Lun* (New York: RoutledgeCurzon, 2003), points out similarities between the philosophers of Yogacara Buddhism and the phenomenological movement and suggests referring to Yogacara philosophy as "Buddhist phenomenology."

22. In *Ideas* (*Ideen*), Husserl introduces the "phenomenological" (*phenomenologische*), "eidetic" (*eidetische*), and "transcendental" (*transcendentale*) reduction as the methods of exploring the working and structure of consciousness.

23. T 47.1985.495.

24. DZZ-1 1: 7–8. Dōgen mentions the importance of "gaining a disciple" (DZZ-1 1: 266) and frequently picks up the trope of Bodhidharma referring to his disciples as his "skin, flesh, bones, and marrow" (DZZ-1 1: 332). Kasulis uses this theme to interpret the line "to cast off body and mind of self and other" ("The Incomparable Philosopher," 92–93).

25. Buddhist thinkers, for the most, endorse the theory of no-self (*anatman*), which questions the assumption that the signifier "self" refers to a real referent. The classical formulation of this nominalism can be found in the *Conversations of King Menander* (*Milindapanha*).

26. Nishida Kitarō (1870–1945) famously formulated the "logic of place" (*basho no ronri*) to theorize this predicament. In his later work Nishida identified as the place of self-consciousness the "historical world" (*rekishiteki sekai*).

27. DZZ-1 1: 767.

28. For Husserl "self-consciousness" is structured by the relationship of positing self-conscious intentional act (*noesis*) and posited intentional object (*noema*). Vasubandhu identifies "self" (*atman*) and "constituents of experience" (dharma) as the basic elements of consciousness.

29. The two authors who suggest this comparison most explicitly are Kasulis and David Edward Shaner. See Thomas P. Kasulis, *Zen Action / Zen Person* (Honolulu: University of Hawaii Press, 1981), 72–75; David Edward Shaner, *The Bodymind Experience in Japanese Buddhism: A Phenomenological Perspective of Kūkai and Dōgen* (Albany: State University of New York Press, 1985).

30. Section 959 of the *Sutra of Miscellaneous Sayings* (*Samyuktagama sutra*) reports a dialogue in which the mendicant Vachagotta asks Buddha whether there is a self. Buddha responds with silence (T 2.99.34.245). Other texts clearly state that

"there are two ways of no-self: the ego is devoid of a self and the dharmas are devoid of a self" (T 19.996.523).

31. T 10.279.37.194.
32. T 2.99.34.245.
33. T 25.2509.117.
34. T 31.1648.700.
35. T 8.235.750.
36. The most well-known of the various versions of this story can be found in the *Mahaprajnaparamita-sastra* (T 25.1509.12.148) and the *Various Metaphors in many Scriptures* (*Zongjingzhuan-zapiyu*) (T 4.208.531–42).
37. T 4.208.3.532; T 25.1509.12.148.
38. T 25.1509.12.148.
39. Steven Heine, *A Dream within a Dream: Studies in Japanese Thought* (New York: Peter Lang, 1991), 14, suggests that "casting off" implies "nothing other than the perpetual process of casting off."
40. Interestingly enough, Husserl himself describes his reductions as a rejection of preexisting "beliefs" (*doxa*).
41. Using Guoan's (twelfth century) version of the "ten ox pictures" (*siniutou*) or the "ox-herding pictures" (*muniutou*) as a heuristic device, it is possible to argue that "to study the self" describes a process of mediation (pictures 1–6); "to forget the self" identifies the state of detachment from preconceptions also known as "emptiness" (*sunyata*; pictures 7–8); "to be actualized by the ten thousand dharmas" evokes the "wisdom" (*prajna*) of "seeing things as they are" (*yathabhuta darsana*; picture 9); and "to cast off body and mind of self and other" evokes the bodhisattva or Chan master who returns to the village out of "compassion" (*karuna*; picture 10).
42. According to the *Digital Dictionary of Buddhism*, the term *zheng* is the Chinese translation of to "actualize" (*adhigama*), "witness" (*saksat karoti*), "attain" (*praap*).
43. For example, the term *genjōkōan* can be found in the *Records of Yuanwu, the Zen Master of the Buddha Fruit* (*Yuanwu Foguo Chanshi Yulu*; T 47.1997.12.769).
44. Dōgen suggests a parallel between the activity of "actualizing" and that of "presencing" (DZZ 1:210) in his fascicle "Painted Rice Cakes" ("Gabyō").
45. T 19.945.8.141–42. In the *Suramgama Sutra* the term is used to refer to the practice-and-actualization of the Buddha in samadhi (T 19.945.8.141) as well as that of practitioners (T 19.945.8.142). "Presencing actualization" appears in T 18.865.207–8. "Attainment of actualization" appears in T 16.676.4.703. In the *Sutra on the Understanding of the Deep Secret* (*Samdhinirmocana Sutra*), it is frequently used in the phrase "power of the attainment of actualization" (T 16.676.4.703).
46. DZZ-1 1:737.
47. In his fascicle "Painted Rice Cakes," Dōgen similarly contends, "Because all Buddhas are actualization, all things are actualization. Despite this, they do not

share the same nature or heart/mind. However, at the time of actualization, the separate moments of their actualization is presenced without interference" (DZZ-1 1: 210).

48. DZZ-1 1: 10.

49. This translation is, of course, influenced by the language of Husserl and Gadamer. The original reads, "Delusion is to practice-and-actualize the ten thousand dharmas carrying the self. Awakening is to practice-and-actualize the self by advancing the ten thousand dharmas."

50. DZZ-1 1: 7.

51. DZZ-1 1: 7. In "What Is on the Other Side? Delusion and Realization in Dōgen's Genjōkōan," in Steven Heine, ed., *Dōgen: Textual and Historical Studies* (New York: Oxford University Press, 2012), 73–74, Heine suggests that "momentary perceptions, which cross the gaps between partiality and wholeness, as well as possibility and impossibility, transcend specificity and enable a level of spiritual awareness that penetrates and even leaps beyond, yet without claiming to deny, the inevitable presence of the horizon."

52. DZZ-1 1: 731, 14, 243, 277, 214, 277, 302.

53. Ludwig Wittgenstein, *Philosophical Investigations*, trans. Gertrude Elizabeth Margaret Anscombe (Oxford: Blackwell, 1953), 47.

54. In *Du mußt dein Leben ändern* (Frankfurt am Main: Suhrkamp, 2011), Peter Sloterdijk suggests that philosophy constitutes a "practice" (*Übung*) that aims at the transformation of the self.

55. T 49.2005.293.

56. DZZ-1 1: 394.

57. Müller, *Dōgen's Sprachdenken*, 249.

58. In his later work Nishida analyzes reality into two basic elements: the oneness of the world and the infinity of individuals. The former he refers to as the "one" (*itsu*) and the latter as the "many" (*ta*). I think Nishida suggests that the "one world" is *fully* expressed (*hyōgen*) in each individual moment of self-awareness; the complete expression of this totality, however, requires an infinite number of individual expressions and is thus "deferred infinitely."

59. DZZ-1 1: 301.

60. DZZ-1 1: 301.

61. Müller argues that expression is, at the same time, "complete" (*vollkommen*) and "incomplete" (*unvollkommen*). To articulate that a particular expression of the buddha-dharma cannot capture its totality, I prefer to say the expressions are "full" rather than "complete." "Dōgen points out the situatedness of the complete expression and thus indicates that the delimitation of each expression does not lessen its completeness" (Müller, *Dōgen's Sprachdenken*, 299). Müller explains that Dōgen "does not want to give up the moment of articulation but wants to hold on to the notion of a positive yet delimited expression" (300).

62. DZZ-1 1: 302. Müller paraphrases this quote as follows: "Expression always leaves something unsaid. Those who do not understand this fact, do not understand expression" (*Dōgen's Sprachdenken*, 298).

63. DZZ-1 1: 302.

64. DZZ-1 1: 305.

65. Martin Heidegger, *Vom Wesen der Wahrheit* (Frankfurt am Main: Klostermann, 1949). Heidegger crossed out the terms "is" and "Being" to indicate the inconceivability of Being (*Sein*), and Jacques Derrida did this to indicate the ambivalence of linguistic sign. I adopt Derrida's usage in Gereon Kopf, "Language Games, Selflessness, and the Death of God; A/Theology in Contemporary Zen Philosophy and Deconstruction," in Bret Davis, Brian Schroeder, and Jason Wirth, eds., *Continental and Japanese Philosophy: Comparative Approaches to the Kyoto School* (Bloomington: Indiana University Press, 2010), 176.

66. DZZ-1 1: 301. Similarly Dōgen suggests that both "seated meditation" (zazen) and "avoidance of all evils" (*shoakumakusa*) are ongoing practices and require "utmost effort" (DZZ-1 1: 284). See Gereon Kopf, "Meditation as Moral Training: Reading Dōgen's 'Shoakumakusa' in the Light of His Meditation Manuals," in Charles Willemen and Ven. Khammai Dhammasamai, eds., *Buddhist Meditation: Text, Tradition and Practice* (Mumbai: Somaiya, 2012), 350.

67. I believe the particularity of any discursive location can be illustrated with Risaku Mutai's (1890–1974) notion of the "specific" (*shu*). It is defined as "particular totality" (*tokushuteki zentai*; 4:84), "particular orientation" (*tokushuteki hōkō*; 4:83), and "small world" (*shōsekai*; 4:59). Risaku Mutai, *Mutai Risaku Chosaku shū*, 9 vols. (Tokyo: Kobushi shobō, 2000–2002).

68. Brett Davis, "The Philosophy of Zen Master Dōgen: Egoless Perspectivism," in William Edelglass and Jay L. Garfield, eds., *The Oxford Handbook of World Philosophy* (New York: Oxford University Press, 2011), 349, suggests that "rather than an overcoming of perspectivism, enlightenment for Dōgen entails a radical reorientation and qualitative transformation of the process of perspectival delimitation."

69. DZZ-1 1: 189–94. Rein Raud, "The Existential Moment: Reading Dōgen's Philosophy of Time," *Philosophy East and West* 62.2 (2012): 158, explains his translation as follows: "We can tentatively assume that, just as there is a difference in meaning, pointed out by many, between the Sinified and Japanese readings (u and *ari*) of the character 有, there is a similar difference between *ji* and *toki*, the two readings of 時. Just as in the case of 有, where *ari* refers to the less loaded usage and *u* is the philosophical concept, we can read the *ji* of *uji* to be specific and distinct from what would normally be called *toki*."

70. DZZ-1 1: 194. In his unpublished "Theorizing Japanese Literature: Memories, Evocations, Ghosts: On Reading the *Shōbōgenzō*. Allusive Networks as Context," Aleksi Järvelä introduces this passage as an example of the Chinese influences on Dōgen.

71. If we were to translate the characters 有時, following Dōgen's own suggestion, as "existence-moment" rather than "at a certain time," the context of phrases and meaning would be the existential predicament of the reader.

72. DZZ-1 1: 7.

73. Gereon Kopf, "Zen, Philosophy, and Emptiness: Dōgen and the Deconstruction of Concepts," in JeeLoo Liu and Douglas Berger, eds., *Nothingness in Asian Philosophy* (London: Routledge, 2014).

74. D. T. Suzuki, *An Introduction to Zen Buddhism* (New York: Grove Press, 1964), 66; Kitarō Nishida, *Nishida Kitarō Zenshū* [hereafter NKZ], 20 vols. (Tokyo: Iwanami shoten, 1988), 11: 374.

75. The opening paragraph of the "Genjōkōan" shows strong similarities with a famous passage from the *Records of the Transmission of the Lamp*: "Thirty years ago, when I had not yet started meditation, I saw that mountains were mountains, waters were waters. After I had begun meditating and gained some knowledge, I saw that mountains were not mountains, waters were not waters. But now as I achieved a place free of desire, I see that mountains are just mountains and waters are just waters" (T 51.2077.614). The preambles to various versions of the statements about the nature of mountains and water clearly identify as their context the transformation of the practitioner's episteme in the process of meditation.

76. DZZ-1 1: 210.

77. DZZ-1 1: 42–45.

78. T 12.374.522. In "Thinking with Dōgen," Raud has shown that the method of creatively playing with the ambiguity of Chinese characters Dōgen himself applied in fascicles like "Buddha-nature" and "Existential Moment" was a practice known in Song China (38).

79. The first version is from DZZ-1 1: 14. The second is from DZZ-1 1: 18–19. Rereading conversations between the Fourth and Fifth as well as the Fifth and Sixth Patriarchs (T 48.2008.348, T 51.2076.222), respectively, Dōgen rereads "not having buddha-nature" (*mubusshō*) as "non-being-buddha-nature" (*mubusshō*). In the third version Dōgen relies on the claim of various Zen records or Chan *yulu* that "buddha-nature is empty" (*busshōkū*; DZZ-1 1: 19, T 31.1589.70). The fourth phrase is based on the saying in the *Platform Sutra* that "impermanence is buddha-nature" (DZZ-1 1: 21; T 48.2008.359).

80. Abe, *A Study of Dōgen*, 42, 57.

81. Abe, *A Study of Dōgen*, 62.

82. Abe, *A Study of Dōgen*, 60.

83. Schilbrack, "Metaphysics in Dōgen," 35.

84. Here Dōgen actually anticipates and already precludes the basic claim of Hakamaya Noriaki's *Critical Buddhism* (*Hihan Bukkyō*) (Tokyo: Daizō shuppan, 1990), that most of Japanese Buddhism had been seduced by the lure of "the thought of original enlightenment."

85. Raud, "Thinking with Dōgen," 30.

86. This abyss can be compared to Derrida's *différance*. Jacques Derrida, *Margins of Philosophy*, trans. Alan Bass (Chicago: University of Chicago Press, 1982), 11. Ueda Shizuteru, *Ueda Shizuteru shū*, 11 vols. (Tokyo: Iwanami shoten, 2001–3). In *Zen to sekai*, Ueda defines as "philosophical Zen" (*tetsugakuteki zen* 5:13) systematic thought that develops the Zen idiom under the horizon of the "one world" (*hitotsu no sekai*; 5:48; Nishitani).

87. Thinkers of the Tiantai, Huayan, and Shingon schools of Buddhism developed the so-called *panjiao* systems to rank all belief systems known to them by their assumed level of achievements so as to outline the cognitive transformation engendered during Buddhist practice.

88. DZZ-1 1: 89. Kasulis translates the phrase *hishiryō* that is usually rendered "non-thinking" very appropriately as "without-thinking" (*Zen Action / Zen Person*, 72).

89. Kasulis, *Zen Action / Zen Person*, 73.

90. One could make the argument that both are inspired by the famous line on mountains and waters from the *Records of the Transmission of the Lamp* (T 51.2077.614), cited earlier. However, both thinkers admit to being influenced by Dōgen's writings.

91. He identifies as ontological prototypes the "abstract concept" of "nature" (*shizen*; NKZ 1:82), the "idealism" of the "spirit" (*seishin*; NKZ 1:88), and the conception of "god" as the "spiritual unity" (*seishinteki tōitsu*; NKZ 1:96). Nishida identifies three forms of ethics: "heteronomous ethics" (*taritsuteki rinrigakusetsu*), "autonomous ethics" (*jiritsuteki rinrigakusetsu*; NKZ 1:121), and "action theory" (*katsudōsetsu*; NKZ 1:142). He identifies as three basic forms of theology "theism" (*yūshinron*), "pantheism" (*hanshinron*; NKZ 1:175), and the conception of "god" as "unifying power" (*tōitsu chikara*; NKZ 1:179). On subjectivism, see NKZ 7:218. In his *Philosophical Essays Volume 2* (*Tetsugaku ronbunshū daini*), Nishida suggests that these three positions give rise to three worlds: the "world of physical laws" (*butsuriteki sekai*), the "world of living organisms" (*seibutsuteki sekai*), and the "world of history" (*rekishiteki sekai*). See Gereon Kopf, "The Self-Identity of the Absolute Contradictory What?—Reflections on How to Teach the Philosophy of Nishida Kitarō," in David Jones and Ellen Klein, eds., *Teaching Texts and Contexts: The Art of Infusing Asian Philosophies and Religions* (Albany: State University of New York Press, 2010), 129–48.

92. Here I paraphrase J. N. Mohanty, *Transcendental Phenomenology: An Analytic Account* (Oxford: Basil Blackwell, 1989), 18, who talks about the "tragic philosopher" "haunted by the gulf that separates philosophic reflection and unreflective experience, a gulf which he seeks to bridge not by speculative constructions but by intermediate phenomena, though never quite completely."

PART II

Studies of Sōtō Zen

6

Keizan's Denkōroku

A TEXTUAL AND CONTEXTUAL OVERVIEW

William M. Bodiford

THE *DENKŌROKU* (CONVEYING Illumination) is a short Zen text attributed to Keizan Jōkin (1264–1325; not 1268–1325). Its existence was completely unknown until 1857, when a Zen cleric named Busshū Sen'ei (1794–1864) published a two-fascicle woodblock edition. In the more than 150 years since its publication, the *Denkōroku* has attracted little attention. To date it has been read primarily by dedicated practitioners of Sōtō Zen, who value it because of its association with Keizan. He is important to them because the Japanese Sōtō School of Zen identifies Keizan as their Great Ancestor (*taiso*), the teacher who stands alongside their High Ancestor (*kōso*), Eihei Dōgen (1200–1253), as one of that school's two main patriarchs. Officially Keizan's *Denkōroku* ranks with Dōgen's *Shōbōgenzō* as the two fundamental texts (*konpon shūten*) upon which the Sōtō School bases its sectarian distinctiveness.[1]

The religious influence of these two texts, however, could hardly be more dissimilar. Dōgen's *Shōbōgenzō* exerts a pervasive influence over modern Sōtō discourse, especially descriptions of Sōtō orthopraxy. Even outside of Sōtō circles it is widely celebrated for its penetrating religious and philosophical insights. The *Denkōroku*, in contrast, remains largely ignored. There seems to be no place for it within modern Sōtō thought.[2] It is easy to imagine reasons why the *Denkōroku* has failed to attract much attention. I will mention a few of them. First, since more than four hundred years separate its initial appearance in print from its purported author, some Sōtō clerics have doubted whether it really is the work of Keizan. Second, it is written in an unconventional format, which mixes elements from disparate Zen genres without agreeing with any of them. Third, it appeared in print too late to play any role in the great eighteenth-century revival of interest in Dōgen and his writings. It was never cited by influential Sōtō clerics, such as Menzan Zuihō (1683–1769), who relied on the writings of Dōgen to distinguish Sōtō norms from other forms of Zen practice (whether Chinese or Japanese).³ As a result even today when people interpret Dōgen they almost never draw on the *Denkōroku*. Fourth, in comparison to other Zen literature the *Denkōroku*'s content and literary style can seem repetitive, if not flat and pedestrian. Unlike the *Shōbōgenzō*, it rarely soars with the kind of poetic imagery that resonates with readers outside the walls of monastic cloisters.

The *Denkōroku*, however, rewards closer examination. While it exerts less influence on modern Sōtō than its exalted official status might lead one to expect, its contents reveal much useful information regarding the literary culture of early Japanese Zen communities, the features of Japanese Zen literature, and the methods of Zen training that once flourished in medieval Japan. Limitations of space do not permit each of these topics to be addressed in depth, yet I hope a brief introduction to each one can highlight the scholarly value of the *Denkōroku* and dispel some of the confusion regarding its authorship, its unconventional format, and its literary style.

Textual History

The *Denkōroku* tells stories about the successive generations of Buddhist patriarchs. It begins with Sakyamuni Buddha and continues across twenty-eight generations of ancestors in South Asia, twenty-three generations in China, and two generations in Japan, concluding with Eihei Ejō (1198–1280), the second abbot of Eiheiji monastery. It presents these generations as the exclusive lineage (*tanden*) by which Zen teachers conveyed the brilliance of Sakyamuni Buddha to Japan. In the 1857 woodblock edition published by Busshū, the text is not divided into separate chapters or sections. No internal titles or special marks separate the stories. Nonetheless its textual format renders the beginning and end of each story perfectly clear. Each episode begins with a passage written in Chinese, which describes the next patriarch attaining awakening under the guidance of the previous patriarch. The Chinese passage is followed by a longer commentary, which is written mostly in Japanese with some Chinese portions. Finally, the commentary concludes with a verse written in Chinese.

In his preface to the woodblock edition, Busshū neither identifies the manuscript source on which he based his woodblock version nor mentions any emendations he made to the text. Yet it is clear that he must have corrected the text to agree with what he thought it should say. He rewrote many of the passages in Chinese. The passages tend to agree word for word with the editions of Chinese Buddhist texts published during the Tokugawa period (seventeenth to nineteenth century), which were available to Busshū—but not to Keizan. Upon close examination many passages in Chinese do not agree with the earlier Song-dynasty (tenth to thirteenth century) versions that would have been available to Keizan. For this reason almost as soon as the *Denkōroku* appeared in print some textual critics suspected it of being apocryphal, charging that it is a compilation by a later author to which Keizan's name was attached.

Other internal evidence, however, supports the purported link between the *Denkōroku* and Keizan. Editors of subsequent editions therefore attempted to correct Busshū's version to eliminate its textual anachronisms. Since they lacked access to any earlier manuscript versions, they could base their revision only on their own sense of whatever seemed most reasonable. Each new revised and corrected edition thus became less reliable than its predecessors. Noteworthy new versions appeared in 1885 (reprinted in 1985–87) with revisions by Ōuchi Seiran (1845–1918), in 1925 (reprinted in 1985) with revisions by Ishikawa Sodō (1842–1920), in 1934 (reprinted in 1937, 1942, 1956, 1967) with revisions by Kohō Chisan (1879–1967), and in 1940 (reprinted in 1944 and 1980) with revisions by Yokoseki Ryōin (1883–1973).[4] In 2005 the Sōtō sect published its own authorized revision of Ōuchi's 1885 version.

Each subsequent revision adopted and revised the changes introduced by the previous ones. For example, Ōuchi rewrote some Chinese passages in Japanese word order and used Chinese glyphs to replace phrases written in Japanese syllabary. Ishikawa converted all the Japanese syllabary from *katakana* to *hiragana* and indicated the Japanese pronunciations of Chinese glyphs.[5] Yokoseki introduced chapter divisions and subdivided each chapter into four sections: the kōan (*honsoku*), its circumstances (*kien*), examination (*teishō*), and verse summary (*juko*). This four-part subdivision has become standard, but revisions after Yokoseki usually use the label *nentei* for the examination.[6] For this reason the *Denkōroku* as it exists in print today represents the culmination of a modern editorial evolution.

In 1958 Tajima Hakudō discovered an early manuscript of the *Denkōroku* at the Kenkon'in (or Kenkōin, a Sōtō Zen temple in Aichi Prefecture). This manuscript in two fascicles was copied between 1430 and 1459 by Shikō Sōden (d. 1500), the third-generation abbot of Kenkon'in.[7] It preserves language and orthographic conventions that correspond to Keizan's own age. After Tajima's discovery, three other medieval (i.e., prior to 1650) manuscripts have come to light. They are the Ryūmonji (Ishikawa Prefecture) manuscript in five fascicles copied in 1547 by Tessō Hōken; the Shōzanji (Ishikawa Prefecture) manuscript in two fascicles copied between 1599 and 1627 by Yūzan Senshuku; and the Chōenji (Aichi Prefecture) manuscript in five fascicles copied in 1637 by Kidō Sōe. The discovery of these early manuscripts enabled scholars to establish the early textual history of the *Denkōroku* and has silenced most questions as to its authenticity. The Kenkon'in manuscript clearly is a copy of an earlier text.[8] While that earlier text has yet to be found, its inferred existence demonstrates that some version of the *Denkōroku* probably existed during the lifetimes of Keizan's disciples. Therefore it preserves teachings from the fourteenth century.

Comparison of Busshū's 1857 version of the *Denkōroku* with the medieval manuscripts reveals many radical discrepancies. It appears that Busshū prepared the text for publication by replacing Japanese-language passages with quotations from Chinese texts, by rewriting ambiguous lines, by adding additional materials, and by deleting some passages and abbreviating others. In short, he created a new version of the *Denkōroku*.[9] For these reasons neither the 1857 edition nor its subsequent revisions (which serve as the basis for the available foreign-language translations) should be used uncritically as an introduction to the teachings of the Keizan Jōkin, who lived and taught in the early fourteenth century, although they can be used as a guide to how his teachings have been conveyed in the late nineteenth and twentieth centuries.

Textual Format

The fact that Busshū extensively edited the *Denkōroku* for publication suggests that he regarded the original language and format of the *Denkōroku* as deficient. To understand why this would be so, it is useful to contrast the *Denkōroku* with the genres of Zen literature familiar to Keizan and to Busshū. The language of the earliest manuscript (the Kenkon'in text) in fact presents many difficulties. Passages that appear to be quotations from Chinese texts sometimes contain sections where the word order has been inverted to reflect the influence of Japanese-language patterns. Moreover in numerous lines homonyms (or near homonyms) replace standard vocabulary in ways that render some passages almost meaningless. For example, in one place the term "three jewels" (*sanbō*) is written as "three types of karma" (*sangō*). Significantly the visual forms of the Chinese glyphs for these terms—and for the many other mistaken homonyms in the text—do not resemble one another. It seems unlikely that a copyist looking at a written original could have mistakenly written one glyph for the other. The use of inverted word order in Chinese passages and the numerous homonyms suggest that the text of the *Denkōroku* originated as a transcription (*kikigaki*). In other words, the text was not written or edited by Keizan himself. Rather it seems to have been compiled by one or more students who took notes while listening to Keizan's lectures.[10] Other transcriptions of Zen lectures survive in manuscripts at Sōtō temples, but they typically date from the sixteenth and seventeenth centuries.[11] The *Denkōroku* appears to be an early forerunner of a method of compiling texts that became common much later in the Japanese Zen tradition.

One might assume that its transcriptions of monastic lectures locates the *Denkōroku* within the genre of Zen literature known as recorded sayings (*goroku*). In agreement with this assumption, the Kenkon'in manuscript of the *Denkōroku* actually begins with an inner title (*naidai*) that identifies its contents as Keizan's recorded sayings compiled by his attendants.[12] But even if the *Denkōroku* literally consists of sayings recorded by attendants it certainly does not conform to the usual conventions of the *goroku* genre in Japanese Zen.

Within the Sōtō lineage to which Keizan belonged we can point to at least four other early examples of this genre. They are *Eihei Gen Zenji Goroku*, the record of Dōgen (1200–1253) at Kōshōji and Eiheiji monasteries; *Giun Oshō Goroku*, the record of Giun (1253–1333) at Hōkyōji and Eiheiji monasteries; *Keizan oshō goroku*, the record of Keizan at Yōkōji monastery; and *Tsūgenroku*, the record of Tsūgen Jakurei (1322–91) at Sōjiji, Yōkokuji, and Ryūsenji monasteries. The content and structure of all four of these texts are remarkably similar to one another but differ greatly from the *Denkōroku*. The four texts of recorded sayings are episodic, consisting of brief comments written in Chinese to commemorate ceremonies conducted according to the liturgical calendar of the various monasteries. Frequently these ceremonies mention the occasion and especially the names of lay patrons or sponsors. Moreover the contents of the recorded sayings are assembled into specific categories, such as addresses delivered in the dharma hall (*jōdō*) or in the abbot's quarters (*shōsan*), dharma epistles (*hōgo*), inauguration remarks (*kaidō*), poems written on portraits (*san*), funerary remarks (*shōbutsuji*), and Buddhist verse or *gatha* (*geju*). All of these categories agree with the content of other texts labeled as recorded sayings that were produced in other Zen temples, whether in Japan or in China.[13] The consistent format and structure of these *goroku* texts serves to demonstrate that Zen practice in Japan maintains a linguistic continuity with its namesake in China. It is for this reason that Japanese Zen teachers endeavored to produce recorded sayings written in literary Chinese.[14]

The ability to write literate Chinese declined among Sōtō Zen clergy during the medieval period. Hardly any *goroku* survive from Sōtō teachers active during the sixteenth and seventeenth centuries, a period when the number of Sōtō clergy increased dramatically and Sōtō temples were built in every corner of Japan.[15] Recorded sayings written in Chinese did not become common among Sōtō Zen teachers until after the widespread revival of Chinese learning in the eighteenth and nineteenth centuries. Eventually they became so common that we can reasonably assume that almost every Zen teacher produced at least one. For example, Busshū—the Sōtō teacher who printed the woodblock edition of the *Denkōroku*—produced several *goroku* as Chinese-language records of the monastic events over which he presided at his temples.[16] When Busshū edited the *Denkōroku*, therefore, he must have been painfully aware of the poor impression that would be conveyed by the faulty Chinese passages in its manuscript versions.

Although the *Denkōroku* dates from the fourteenth century, when Zen teachers in Japan still wrote Chinese, it reflects a Japanese conversational style in which the word order of Chinese passages (subject-verb-object) would be adapted to Japanese speech patterns (subject-object-verb). Moreover it does not include any of the above-mentioned categories (*jōdō, shōsan, hōgo,* etc.) of monastic pronouncements. It fails to convey any sense of the routines and rhythms of Keizan's monastic life. In these respects it does not easily fit into the genre of recorded sayings.

The *Denkōroku* also resembles the Zen genre of genealogical hagiography known as flame (or lamp) records (*tōroku*).[17] It is impossible to determine with certainty which flame records the *Denkōroku* might have drawn upon for the stories of Zen patriarchs it recounts. The fact that the *Denkōroku* was preserved only as a transcription means that we cannot know when it corresponds precisely, word for word, with any original text that might have been read aloud during the lectures being transcribed. Nonetheless most of its hagiographical episodes could have come only from Chinese flame records. Moreover the *Denkōroku* cites three flame records by name: the *Jingde Era Transmission of the Flame* (Ch. *Jingde Chuandenglu*, Jp. *Keitoku Dentōroku*; ca. 1011), the *Jiatai Era Universal Flame Record* (Ch. *Jiatai Pudenglu*, Jp. *Katai Futōroku*; ca. 1204), and the *Combined Essentials of the Five Flames* (Ch. *Wudeng Huiyuan*, Jp. *Gotō Egen*; ca. 1252). During Keizan's day these texts would have been imported from China. Within a few decades after his death, all three were reprinted in Japan. They were reprinted repeatedly down to Busshū's time. Even today they constitute representative examples of Zen flame records.

In China the compilation, printing, and distribution of these flame records signified imperial recognition of Zen (Chan) as the official Buddhism of the realm. They were compiled by Buddhist clerics who enjoyed imperial patronage, who presented the texts to the throne, and who received imperial authorization to include them within the official editions of the Buddhist canon.[18] Each flame record presents the hagiographies of hundreds of Zen teachers, arranged in genealogical sequences that go back through India to the Buddha Sakyamuni. In this way they depict Zen as the only authentic Buddhism because it has been handed down in each generation by patriarchs (*soshi*) who constitute the Buddha's true religious family. This religious family functions conceptually like one of the aristocratic clans (*sō*) of ancient China, with several branch houses (*ke*). Each household collectively authenticates and transmits the same authentic religion. Buddhist clerics could attain recognition as a legitimate Zen teacher and receive appointment as abbot of a Zen monastery only if they were able to claim membership in one of these documented Zen lineages.[19]

Chinese flame records thus convey an overall impression of Buddhism as consisting of everlasting standards shared by all members of the Zen family regardless of geographical location or the passage of history. Both the *Jingde Era Transmission of the Flame* and the *Combined Essentials of the Five Flames* reinforce this sense of everlasting truth by identifying the origins of the Zen lineage not just with Sakyamuni Buddha alone but with the seven buddhas (*shichibutsu*) of the past. The seven buddhas are the last three buddhas of the previous eon (*shōgon kō*) as well as the first four buddhas of the present eon (*kengō*; Skt. *bhadra kalpa*), of which Sakyamuni is number four. Each eon is an infinitely long period of time during which one thousand buddhas appear, only one buddha appears at a time, and each new appearance is separated from the others by an incalculable number of years. In spite of the vast distance of time and space separating these seven buddhas, they all proclaim the same doctrines and practice. Moreover they transmit this truth from one buddha to the next via dharma transmission verses (*denpō ge*). Each generation of the Zen lineage, from the first buddha of the past down to Sakyamuni and continuing through all the patriarchs of India down to the thirty-third ancestor, Huineng (the sixth ancestor of China), chants a Buddhist verse (*ge*; Skt. *gatha*) that plays on the same doctrinal motifs as found in the verse chanted by the previous generation. Thereafter this model of seven buddhas and their dharma transmission verses became part of the standard image of Zen.[20] This emphasis on poetic expression of timeless truth served the religious agenda of the literary Zen (*monji zen*) that prevailed in elite monasteries during the Northern Song dynasty (960–1086).

The *Denkōroku* clearly aims to demonstrate that the Buddhism that Keizan inherited from his teacher is the same authentic Buddhism depicted by the flame records as having been handed down from generation to generation within the Buddha's true religious family. In this sense it shares the same worldview and religious agenda as the flame records mentioned earlier. In many other respects it differs from them. First, the *Denkōroku* presents only one genealogical line, the Sōtō Zen lineage. As a result its progression is strictly diachronic. It lacks any synchronic sense of Zen as a collective activity. Second, it does not attempt to present the same kind of hagiographic details as in the flame records. Unlike them, it does not attempt to present representative teachings, sayings, poems, or essays by the well-known figures it discusses. It concentrates solely on each generation's moment of awakening. Third, it ignores the seven buddhas of the past. It omits the mythological dimension of the Zen patriarchate as a universal entity standing outside of time and space. By ignoring the seven buddhas and starting with Sakyamuni, the *Denkōroku* locates the Zen lineage clearly within our world, our history, and our circumstances. It focuses on how each generation must achieve for itself the knowledge of the previous one. Rather than the static, unchanging nature of Zen as a religious organization, the *Denkōroku* emphasizes the inner journey by which one must encounter that truth. In this respect the *Denkōroku* differs in focus and purpose from traditional Chinese flame records. Fourth, instead of linking the generations together with dharma verses, the *Denkōroku* links them through kōan (pivotal events or words) that depict the crucial moment in each generation when the truth was fully authenticated (*shō*).

The word "kōan" has entered the English language. Nonetheless its connotations in Zen literature and its connotations in English are not necessarily the same. Here I adopt the "kōan as literary framework" definition proposed by T. Griffith Foulk. He stipulates that a kōan consists of "any text that combines, at a minimum, the following two formal features: (1) a narrative that has been excerpted from the biography or discourse record of a Chan, Son, or Zen master, and (2) some sort of commentary on that narrative." As Foulk notes, "to treat a particular passage from the patriarchal records as a kōan is precisely to single it out and problematize it as something profound and difficult to penetrate."[21] This is exactly what the *Denkōroku* does. It singles out a specific episode from the records of each generation of the Sōtō Zen lineage and comments on that episode as a demonstration of the process by which one attains insight into truth.

Since the *Denkōroku* consists of a series of lectures on patriarchal records, it also shares some characteristics with the Zen genre of kōan commentaries. The *Blue Cliff Collection* (Ch. *Biyanji*, Jp. *Hekiganshū*) stands out as the most widely studied example of this genre.[22] In modern times its popularity has declined among Sōtō clerics, but the situation once was just the opposite. It was especially popular among Sōtō circles. In medieval and early modern Japan it was reprinted repeatedly at Zen temples, including temples affiliated with the Sōtō order. Sōjiji, the monastery founded by Keizan and the headquarters of the largest network of Sōtō temples, published the *Blue Cliff Collection* in the 1490s.[23] Sōtō clerics such as Nan'ei Kenshū (1387–1459) and Daikū Genko (1428–1505) composed some of its earliest extant Japanese commentaries. For Japanese Zen audiences, even Sōtō audiences, the complexity of the *Blue Cliff Collection* would highlight the relative simplicity of the *Denkōroku*.

The skeleton of the *Blue Cliff Collection* consists of one hundred brief passages (kōan) from patriarchal records. Xuedou Chongxian (Jp. Setchō Jūken; 980–1052) selected this set of kōan and then wrote an accompanying verse in praise of each one. His collection of one-hundred kōan with verses was published in 1038. About seventy years later Yuanwu Keqin (Jp. Engo Kokugon; 1063–1135) lectured on Xuedou's compilation, and the *Blue Cliff Collection* purports to convey the content of his lectures. The resulting text introduces each kōan with Yuanwu's introductory instructions (labeled *jishu* or *suiji*). Next there appears the kōan originally selected by Xuedou. Each line of this kōan is accompanied by appended comments (labeled *chūkyaku* or *jakugo*) by Yuanwu. These appended comments clarify, criticize, and sometimes offer alternatives to the individual lines of dialogue in the kōan. Next the text presents Yuanwu's critical evaluation (*hyōshō*) of the kōan as a whole. Here Yuanwu discusses not just the text of the kōan but also its larger context and significance. Xuedou's verse appears next. Each line of the verse is interrupted by Yuanwu's appended comments. Finally, the text presents Yuanwu's critical evaluation of Xuedou's verse. While the appended comments tend to praise or criticize Xuedou's choice of words, the critical evaluation addresses the overall relationship between the verse and the kōan it accompanies.

These various layers of text combine to produce a whole greater than the sum of its parts. The *Blue Cliff Collection* gains its power through a complex interplay between its layers: the kōan and Yuanwu's appended comments, the kōan and Xuedou's verse, Xuedou's verse and Yuanwu's appended comments, as well as all of the above within the larger context of Yuanwu's introductory instructions and his two sets of critical evaluations. The intertextual impact provides readers with a multifaceted overview of the famous Zen personalities who appear in the kōan and the religious issues and concerns encapsulated by their stories. It also serves as an excellent textbook for learning the specialized vocabulary and discursive techniques characteristic of Zen language.

Keizan's lifetime (1264–1325) overlaps with a period when several other Zen (Chan) clerics in China compiled similar kōan commentaries. In 1224 Wansong Xingxiu (Jp. Banshō Gyōshū, 1166–1246) published the *Record of Serenity* (Ch. *Congronglu*, Jp. *Shōyōroku*), his appended comments and critical evaluations on one hundred kōan with accompanying verses by Hongzhi

Zhengjue (Jp. Wanshi Shōgaku, 1091–1157). In 1285 the *Empty Valley Collection* (Ch. *Kongguji*, Jp. *Kūkokushū*) was published. It is a collection of one hundred kōan with accompanying verses by Touzi Yiqing (Jp. Tōsu Gisei, 1032–83), with appended comments by Danxia Zichun (1064–1117) and critical evaluations by Linquan Conglun (Jp. Rinsen Jūrin, 1223–81). Ten years later, in 1295, the *Vacant Hall Collection* (Ch. *Xutangji*, Jp. *Kidōshū*) was printed. It is a collection of one hundred kōan with accompanying verses by Danxia Zichun with appended comments and critical evaluations by Linquan Conglun.

All the authors (Wansong, Hongzhi, Touzi, Danxia, and Linquan) represented by these subsequent kōan commentaries were members of the Sōtō (Caodong) lineage. It might seem therefore that if Keizan wanted to compile a kōan commentary he naturally would have joined the ranks of other Sōtō teachers who emulated the format of the *Blue Cliff Collection*. The historical record, however, does not support this assumption. The *Blue Cliff Collection* probably did not circulate in Japan until after 1300, when it was first reprinted in China.[24] That is the same year that Keizan delivered the lectures that formed the bases for the *Denkōroku*. The other kōan commentaries were reprinted in China as early as 1342, but that is long after Keizan's death.[25] Even then they probably did not circulate in Japan until the 1580s at the earliest. Moreover the *Denkōroku* contains no textual parallels that suggest the direct influence of any of these texts. The Sōtō patriarchs Yunyan Tancheng (Jp. Ungan Donjō, 782–841) and his disciple Dongshan Liangjie (Jp. Tōzan Ryōkai, 807–69), for example, appear prominently in both the *Blue Cliff Collection* (kōan nos. 43, 72, 89) and the *Record of Serenity* (nos. 21, 49, 89, 94). But the *Denkōroku* presents their attainments without mentioning even one of these kōan. For these reasons we cannot assume that Keizan drew upon the *Blue Cliff Collection* or its brethren.

The *Denkōroku* certainly makes no attempt to emulate the literary features or structure of the *Blue Cliff Record*. It does not provide introductory instructions for each episode. It does not offer line-by-line comments on each kōan. It does not suggest alternative answers or dialogue. Also the individual lectures regarding each kōan do not attempt a critical evaluation along the lines of the other kōan commentaries mentioned above. In those works the critical evaluation passes judgment on the quality of the repartee as a whole and on the religious implications behind each choice of words. This feature enables the kōan commentaries to function as textbooks of Zen rhetoric. The lectures of the *Denkōroku*, in contrast, do not display any fascination or curiosity with language, vocabulary, or rhetoric. Occasionally they might define terms, quote lines of verse, or introduce analogous dialogues. Even in these instances, however, the *Denkōroku* conveys very little sense of linguistic play or lyrical expressiveness. Its lectures seem to address rather different sets of concerns (regarding which, see below).

Rather than looking to the *Blue Cliff Collection* and similar texts as possible model for the *Denkōroku*, it probably makes more sense to compare it to the underlying text that gave birth to the *Blue Cliff Collection*. That text is the collection of one hundred kōan with accompanying verses by Xuedou. After Xuedou published his collection of kōan with verses in 1038, other Chinese Zen teachers emulated his example. Within a hundred years it became common for the published recorded sayings of Chinese Zen teachers to include a collection of kōan with accompanying verses. In Japan Dōgen's recorded sayings similarly include one section (in volume 9) that consists of ninety kōan with accompanying verses. During the sixteenth and seventeenth centuries, long after Japanese Sōtō Zen teachers ceased to compile recorded sayings in Chinese, they nonetheless continued to compose Chinese verse, especially Chinese verses that comment on individual kōan and on kōan that they compiled into collections. Frequently they composed alternative verses (*daigo*) for existing kōan collections. Indeed so many of these collections of verses for kōan survive that the historian Andō Yoshinori identifies the production of this genre of literature as one of the distinctive features of medieval Sōtō Zen. Andō suggests that the production and circulation of the *Denkōroku* presaged this development.[26]

The textual format of the *Denkōroku*, though, once again belies this suggestion. No other medieval Sōtō kōan collection follows a genealogical sequence. This emphasis on genealogy connects the *Denkōroku* more closely to flame records. Moreover each of the main kōan episodes in the *Denkōroku* are accompanied by a somewhat lengthy commentary in Japanese. The verses in Chinese that conclude each episode frequently reflect the contents of the Japanese commentary as much as they do the language of the Chinese kōan. For this reason one can interpret the meaning of the verses fairly easily. In the *Denkōroku* the appended verses generally are very short, with only two lines of seven glyphs per line (*shichigon niku*; in forty-six cases). Only a very few episodes have verses of four lines.[27] These verses amplify the main themes of the kōan under consideration and place them in a larger context by alluding to other passages in Chinese texts where related issues appear. But the verses are so terse that they would become enigmatic without the preceding prose commentary to identify main themes.

Other collections of Chinese verse comments on kōan produced by Sōtō Zen teachers in medieval Japan generally lack any prose commentary. The significance of their verses cannot be easily determined. The example of the *Denkōroku* serves to demonstrate how these kinds of terse and seemingly enigmatic Chinese verses could have conveyed meaning when provided with the proper context. Although the *Denkōroku* does not endeavor to provide the kind of thick linguistic commentary found in texts like the *Blue Cliff Collection*, its lectures nonetheless provide a discursive framework accessible to modern audiences, within which one can more easily appreciate the Chinese verses composed by Japanese Zen teachers to convey Zen teachings.

Its Japanese-language commentaries on each kōan distinguish the *Denkōroku* from the other genres of Zen literature discussed earlier. Unlike the typical recorded sayings, they do not provide a Chinese-language record of the lectures presented at monastic ceremonies conducted according to the liturgical calendar. Unlike the typical flame history, they do not present full-fledged hagiographies of the Zen patriarchs. Unlike a typical kōan commentary, they do not evaluate the language of each kōan. The Japanese-language sections of the *Denkōroku* do not ignore the Chinese models discussed earlier, but they do not try to imitate them either. Rather they combine features from each of these genres. While modern readers familiar with the standard genres might find their juxtaposition in the *Denkōroku* somewhat dissonant, the combination probably reflects the needs of the nascent Sōtō Zen community, which existed in relative isolation in rural Japan where knowledge of Chinese Zen would have been limited. It allows the text to introduce readers to a wide variety of literary tropes from Chinese Zen literature, to explain how those literary tropes relate to actual practices, and to address broader issues. Of these issues the most important ones were its religious identity as Sōtō and the significance of that imported Sōtō lineage for a new audience in faraway Japan.

Content and Style

The genealogical structure of the *Denkōroku* obviously focuses on the unique identity of the Sōtō lineage. As mentioned earlier, it tells stories about the successive generations of Sōtō patriarchs who conveyed the true teachings of Sakyamuni Buddha to Japan. Each story begins with a kōan in Chinese that links a new patriarch to the previous one, and through him to all the previous generations. The Japanese commentary presents the significance of the kōan for an audience far removed in time and space from actors depicted in the kōan.

Ever since the publication of the edition edited by Yokoseki,[28] it has become commonplace to divide the commentary into two sections: circumstances and examination. When I read the *Denkōroku* as preserved in the earliest manuscripts, I detect a more complex sequence. First, the commentary presents the briefest possible biographic summary of the new patriarch's background. For an audience in Japan, where Zen lore was relatively unknown, this biographical information must have been very welcome. Nonetheless overall the *Denkōroku* makes little effort to present the patriarchs as identifiable individuals with unique lives in their respective homeland. In the few cases where the commentary presents more than a bare-bones account, the background information primarily concerns the spiritual cultivation and virtuous qualities that prepared new patriarchs for their encounters with the previous patriarchs. The patriarchs seem to function mainly as generic role models. Each one serves to illustrate how one should approach Zen training and overcome spiritual obstacles.

The commentary typically discusses the kōan from at least three perspectives. It recounts the circumstances under which the patriarchs met and the sequence of events preceding the exchange that constitutes the kōan proper. Next it presents a conventional explanation of the contents of the kōan. This explanation frequently includes distinctive discussions of Buddhist doctrines, such as karma, or ritual activities, such as ordination. Sometimes it summarizes the ways that other Buddhists or Zen teachers might address specific aspects of the kōan. These passages in the commentary provide valuable information regarding the reception of Buddhist teachings in fourteenth-century rural Japan. Finally, the commentary will discuss the kōan again in terms of how the present audience should apply themselves to the kōan. In commentary after commentary the *Denkōroku* repeatedly admonishes its audience that the kōan refer not to other people, not to other, far-away places, not to another time long ago. Instead each kōan always refers to the members of the present audience, right here and now. Or rather the *Denkōroku* repeatedly reminds Zen students that they must transform each kōan into their own story, a story about themselves.

For example, this excerpt from the commentary on Sakyamuni's disciple Mahakasyapa takes this episode out of its historical Indian context and relocates it in contemporary Japan:

> Right now, today if you discern the Way, then Mahakasyapa will not be inside Cocksfoot Mountain [in India] but surely will appear here in Japan. Thus, even now you must keep Sakyamuni's flesh warm! Keep Mahakasyapa's smile fresh! Upon reaching such a field, you will become Mahakasyapa's successor and Mahakasyapa will inherit [the Zen lineage] from you.

只今日急辨道せハ迦葉非入鷄足正扶桑國ニ在出世スルフヲ得ン故釋尊ノ肉親今猶アタヽカニ迦葉微笑又更ニ新ン恁マ田地ニ到得ハ汝等却迦葉ニ紹迦葉却汝等ニ受ン[29]

This passage contains a key term, "field" (*denchi*), which occupies a prominent place in the commentary on almost every kōan. "Field" literally refers to the physical land on which one stands and stakes out a position. Figuratively it denotes a state of affairs or frame of mind. Metaphorically it symbolizes the human heart (or subconscious), where one plants karmic seeds and reaps karmic results (fruits), just as farmers plant seeds and harvest crops in fields of land.[30] Almost every commentary includes at least one exhortation to reach the same field attained by each patriarch. The *Denkōroku* does not provide step-by-step instructions regarding how this feat is to be accomplished, but it does discuss psychological factors (senses, perception, layers of consciousness, etc.) with a frequency and level of detail not typical in other kōan commentaries. While other kōan commentaries draw our attention to the linguistic features of Zen discourse, the *Denkōroku* describes each kōan as a psychological journey to a field where one encounters the Buddha, the patriarchs, and oneself.

The psychological journey depicted in the *Denkōroku* constitutes one of its most neglected and yet most intriguing features. It presents an approach to Zen kōan that seems rather different from the models that dominate modern scholarship. Most descriptions of kōan practice focus on the teachings of Dahui Zonggao (Jp. Daie Sōkō; 1089–1163)—especially his technique of observing the phrase (Ch. *kanhua*, Jp. *kanna*, Kr. *kanhwa*) in which one focuses on a single keyword (Ch. *huatou*, Jp. *kanna*, Kr. *hwadu*) to raise doubt—and their subsequent elaboration in the Japanese methods of Kōan Zen attributed to Hakuin Ekaku (1686–1769) and in Korean methods of Kanhwa Son (Ch. Kanhua Chan, Jp. Kanna Zen). The *Denkōroku* similarly emphasizes the importance of thoroughly mastering kōan, but in terms unrelated to Dahui. For example, "keywords" and "doubt" play no role. I wonder if the *Denkōroku* actually describes a different psychological approach to kōan study. Any attempt to address this question, though, must wait for a more careful study of the *Denkōroku* and related texts.

The repetitive format of the commentaries renders them somewhat predictable. Each kōan receives the same style of treatment in the same sequence of approaches. Each kōan concludes with the same kinds of exhortations to penetrate its spiritual core. This pedantic tone limits the appeal of the commentaries to a narrow readership. Yet this same pedagogical agenda provides the *Denkōroku* with a resolute purposefulness. Taken one at a time, each episode can be quite engaging. They not only introduce the Sōtō religious identity to a new audience but collapse the distance of time and space separating that audience from the Sōtō patriarchs of India and China. The *Denkōroku* explicitly rejects the narrative of Buddhist decline (*mappō*), according to which the spiritual abilities of people living today cannot measure up to those of earlier Buddhist patriarchs. It insists that people today confront the same spiritual issues faced by those patriarchs and can use the exact same Buddhist practices as they did to resolve them. Most significantly for devotees of Sōtō Zen, it provides that audience with an especially suggestive psychological guide to those practices.

Conclusion

In the eyes of many critics today, the *Denkōroku* presents an approach to Zen that seems out of step with the ethos of modern Sōtō Zen. It lacks the linguistic profundity of Dōgen's *Shōbōgenzō* and it does not advocate "just sitting" (*shikan taza*), which nowadays is regarded as the sine qua non of Dōgen's Zen.[31] It does not fit easily into any of the standard genres of Zen literature. When viewed within its own historical context, however, the very qualities that render the *Denkōroku* anomalistic also enhance its significance. It conveys an account of Zen from a time before the Zen traditions of Japan solidified into their present configuration. It contains invaluable information regarding a host of significant topics: the reception of Dōgen's writings and teachings during the first several generations following his passing, the earliest biographies of Dōgen and his disciple Ejō, as well as detailed descriptions of Buddhist doctrines, practices, and folklore. It is an important early source for investigating complex issues in the history of Japanese Zen, such as sectarian sensibilities, concepts of awakening and spiritual transformation, the reception of Chinese kōan language and practice, Buddhist notions of history, as well as how practitioners of Zen saw themselves and viewed other Buddhist traditions. Before the *Denkōroku* can contribute to our understanding of any of these topics, though, first it must escape from the confines of the anachronistic standards of early modern Zen that have led scholars both within and outside of Sōtō circles to overlook it.

NOTES

1. Arita Eshū, "Sōjo," in Shūten Hensan Iinkai, ed., *Taiso Keizan Zenji Senjutsu Denkōroku* (Tokyo: Sōtōshū shūmuchō, 2005), 2–3. This essay supersedes William M. Bodiford, "The Denkōroku as Keizan's Recorded Sayings," *Zen no Shinri to Jissen* (Tokyo: Shunjūsha, 2005), 640–20. I thank Mr. Tetsuya Ueda of Shunjusha Publishing Company for permission to incorporate parts of that essay here.

2. Takeuchi Kōdō, "Denkōroku to shūshi: Denkōroku wa shūshi kara dono yō ni tokareta ka?," *Shūgaku Kenkyū* 50 (2008): 87–92. Some sense of the disparity in

the reception of these two texts can be discerned by contrasting the number of times they appear in standard bibliographic databases. The Indian and Buddhist Studies Treatise Database (INBUDS DB; accessed September 1, 2013, http://tripitaka.l.u-tokyo.ac.jp//INBUDS/search.php) maintained by the Japanese Association of Indian and Buddhist Studies, yields 764 results for *shōbōgenzō* but only seventy for *denkōroku*. Likewise the Sōtōshū Kankei Bunken Mokuroku Onrain Sakuin (accessed September 1, 2013, http://www.sotozen-net.or.jp/tmp/kensaku.htm), the Sōtō school's own database of popular and scholarly publications related to Zen, yields 2,032 results for *shōbōgenzō* but only 174 for *denkōroku*.

3. David E. Riggs, "Meditation for Laymen and Laywomen: The Buddha Samadhi (*Jijuyū Zanmai*) of Menzan Zuihō," in Steven Heine and Dale S. Wright, eds., *Zen Classics* (New York: Oxford University Press, 2005), 247–74.

4. See Ishikawa Sodō, *Denkōroku Hakuji Ben: Daien Genchi Zenji Suiji*, ed. Arai Sekizen (1925; Yokohama: Daihonzan Sōjiji, 1985). For a complete list of the published editions of the *Denkōroku*, see Azuma Ryūshin, *Kenkon'in bon Denkōroku* (Tokyo: Rinjinsha, 1970), 138–142; Azuma Ryūshin, *Denkōroku: Gendaigoyaku* (Tokyo: Daizō shuppan, 1991), 58–61. He lists more than twenty editions, of which the 1934 version by Kohō Chisan is most widely read.

5. *Katakana* is the block form of Japanese phonetic glyphs that traditionally was used for formal or official texts, especially when accompanied by Chinese glyphs (*kanji*). *Hiragana* is the cursive form of Japanese phonetic glyphs that traditionally was used for informal texts but that in modern times has become the standard script.

6. The words *nentei* and *teishō* are synonyms. Both refer to the act of presenting a topic or raising an issue for examination. Frequently these words introduce a teacher's comments on a topic, a textual passage, or a kōan.

7. *Denkōroku*. 2 fasc. Copied by Shikō Sōden (d. 1500). Reprinted as *Denkōroku: Kenkon'in Shozōbon*, 2 vols. (Tokyo: Sōtōshū shūhō eiinbon kankōkai, 1994).

8. Azuma Ryūshin, *Denkōroku: Gendaigoyaku*, 48.

9. Azuma Ryūshin, *Kenkon'in bon Denkōroku*, 132.

10. Azuma Ryūshin, *Denkōroku: Gendaigoyaku*, 24.

11. William M. Bodiford, *Sōtō Zen in Medieval Japan* (Honolulu: University of Hawaii Press, 1994), 157–62.

12. Azuma Ryūshin, *Kenkon'in bon Denkōroku*, 5.

13. Tamamura Takeji, "Zen no tenseki," in *Nihon Zenshūshi Ronshū* (1941; Tokyo: Shibunkaku, 1981), 3: 117–39.

14. William M. Bodiford, "The Rhetoric of Chinese Language in Japanese Zen," in Christoph Anderl, ed., *Zen Buddhist Rhetoric in China, Korea, and Japan* (Leiden: Brill, 2011), 285–314.

15. Andō Yoshinori, *Chūsei Zenshū Bunken no Kenkyū* (Tokyo: Kokusho kankōkai, 2000), 33–46.

16. Yokoseki Ryōin, *Ibun Taikyo Shutten Sokō, Denkōroku Shōkai* (1940; Tokyo: Sanbō shuppankai, 1982), 84–85.

17. In translating *tō* as "flame" I am following the lead of T. Griffith Foulk, "Myth, Ritual, and Monastic Practice in Sung Ch'an Buddhism," in Patricia B. Ebrey and Peter N. Gregory, eds., *Religion and Society in T'ang and Sung China* (Honolulu: University of Hawaii Press, 1993), 200n20, who points out that the metaphor normally translated into English as "conveying a lamp" (*dentō*) can best symbolize the conveyance of wisdom (illumination) from one generation to the next only when it is conceived of as "the flame of one lamp [being] used to light another." To demonstrate that Zen texts refer to the flame (not the body) of the lamp, Foulk cites the following passage from the *Platform Sutra of the Sixth Patriarch* (*Rokuso Tanjing*): "Good friends, how then are concentration (*jō*) and discernment (*e*) alike? They are like the flame (*tō*) and its light (*kō*). If there is a flame there is light; if there is no flame there is no light. The flame is the substance (*tai*) of light; the light is the function (*yū*) of the flame. Thus, although they have two names, their substance is not of two types. The practices of concentration and discernment are also like this" (T 48.338b). See Philip B. Yampolsky, *The Platform Sutra of the Sixth Patriarch: The Text of the Tun-huang Manuscript with Translation, Introduction and Notes* (New York: Columbia University Press, 1967), 137, sec. 15; Chinese text, 6.

   Foulk explains: "If (following Yampolsky) one reads 'lamp' for 'flame' here, the statement becomes patently false, and the entire metaphor loses its force, since a lamp may exist (unlit) without there being any light."

18. Foulk, "Myth, Ritual, and Monastic Practice in Sung Ch'an Buddhism," 154.

19. Morten Schlütter, *How Zen Became Zen: The Dispute over Enlightenment and the Formation of Chan Buddhism in Song-Dynasty China* (Honolulu: University of Hawaii Press, 2008), 87.

20. The *Jingde Era Transmission of the Flame* reproduces the transmission verses found in the *Ancestral Hall Collection* (*Zutangji*; 20 fasc.) of 952. I cite the later text because after its publication in 1004 the *Jingde Era Transmission of the Flame* was included in the official versions of the Chinese Buddhist canon and consequently influenced all subsequent flame histories. The *Ancestral Hall Collection*, in contrast, circulated very little in China before becoming lost. It survived only in Korea, where it was published in 1245.

21. T. Griffith Foulk, "The Form and Function of Koan Literature: A Historical Overview," in Steven Heine and Dale S. Wright, eds., *The Kōan: Texts and Contexts in Zen Buddhism* (New York: Oxford University Press, 2000), 17, 27.

22. In modern Japan it is most commonly referred to as the *Blue Cliff Record* (*Biyanlu*; Jp. *Heikiganroku*).

23. Tajima Hakudō, "Noto Sōjiji 'Hekiganshū' no kenkyū," *Aichi Gakuin Daigaku Ronsō: Zengaku Kenkyū* 1 (1959): 1–22.

24. This conclusion is complicated by the existence of an early manuscript version of the *Blue Cliff Collection* owned by Daijōji monastery (Kanazawa City, Ishikawa Prefecture). This manuscript, titled *Yuanwu's Cracking the Barriers at the Blue Cliffs* (Ch. *Foguo Biyan Poguan Jijie*, Jp. *Bukka Hekigan Hakkan Gekisetsu*), is said to have been brought to Japan by Dōgen. It is popularly known as the "single night" (*ichiya*) text, since Dōgen supposedly copied it by hand in a single night. Because Daijōji is the monastery where Keizan presented the lectures that became the *Denkōroku*, one might well assume that he must have seen the single night manuscript owned by that temple. The Daijōji where Keizan lectured, however, was located in Kaga Prefecture. During the late sixteenth century it was destroyed by warfare. During the late seventeenth century (ca. 1690) Gesshū Sōko (1618–96) built a new Daijōji at its present location and became its twenty-sixth-generation abbot. The earlier history of the single night manuscript is undocumented. It played no role in the version of the *Blue Cliff Collection* printed in the 1490s at Sōjiji monastery (the other temple where Keizan taught) at a time when the original Daijōji still existed. Evidence for the possible use of this single night manuscript by Dōgen is ambiguous at best. Only four or five passages in Dōgen's writings seem to be derived from the *Blue Cliff Collection*. Of these, two are closer to the wording of the reprint edition of 1300, while two are closer to the wording of the single night manuscript. It is likely, therefore, that Dōgen saw another version of the *Blue Cliff Collection*, one that fits between the two extant versions. Or he could have seen another, as yet unidentified text that served as a source for the *Blue Cliff Collection*. See Kagamishima Genryū, *Dōgen Zenji to In'yō Kyōten-Goroku no Kenkyū* (Tokyo: Mokujisha, 1965), 162–80.

25. According to Shiina Kōyū, "Genban 'Shikeroku' to sono shiryō," *Komazawa Daigaku Bukkyō Gakubu Ronshū* 10 (1979): 227–56, the *Record of Serenity, Blue Cliff Collection, Empty Valley Collection,* and *Vacant Hall Collection* were reprinted as a set titled *Records of the Four Critical Evaluations* (Ch. *Sijia Pingchanglu*, Jp. *Shike Hyōshōroku*) in 1342. Japanese catalogues of Buddhist literature mistakenly identify this set as having originated with its reprint version, dated 1607. Because complete copies of this set are so rare, the cataloguers also fail to notice that it includes the *Blue Cliff Collection* as the second of the four critical evaluations.

26. Andō Yoshinori, *Chūsei Zenshū Bunken no Kenkyū* (Tokyo: Kokusho kankōkai, 2000), 35–46.

27. Seven cases, according to Tajima Hakudō, *Keizan*, Nihon no Zen Goroku, vol. 5, ed. Furuta Shōkin and Iriya Yoshitaka (Tokyo: Kōdansha, 1978), 46.

28. Yokoseki, *Ibun Taikyo Shutten Sokō, Denkōroku Shōkai.*

29. Azuma, *Kenkon'in Bon Denkōroku*, 7; see *Denkōroku*, Kenkon'in ms., fasc. 1, leaf 5a.

30. Tajima, *Keizan*, 244.

31. Recently Foulk demonstrated that a careful reading of all the passages where Dōgen mentions "just sitting" in his writings calls into question whether Dōgen actually taught a specific approach to Zen practice that can be characterized by that term. T. Griffith Foulk, "'Just Sitting'? Dōgen's Take on Zazen, Sutra Reading, and Other Conventional Buddhist Practices," in Steven Heine, ed., *Dōgen: Textual and Historical Studies* (New York: Oxford University Press, 2012), 75–106.

REFERENCES NOT CITED IN TEXT
Premodern Works (by Title)

Eihei Gen Zenji Goroku. 1 fasc. Ed. Wuwai Yiyuan. Printed 1358; reprinted 1648. In SZ 2, "Shūgen" 2.

Giun Oshō Goroku. 2 fasc. Printed 1357; reprinted 1715. In SZ 5, "Goroku," vol. 1.

Gyōji Jijo. Zenrinji temple (Fukui Prefecture) manuscript copied in 1376 by Fusai Zenkyū (1347–1408). Used by permission. Note: This 1376 copy of the *Gyōji jijo* is the earliest extant version of the monastic procedures that subsequently became known as the *Keizan Oshō Shingi* (see below).

Foguo Biyan Poguan Jijie. 2 fasc. Reprinted as *Bukka Hekigan Hakan Kyakusetsu (Ichiya Hekiganshū).* 2 vols. Tokyo: Sōtōshū shūhō eiinbon kankōkai, 1995.

Hekigan Daikūshō. 2 fasc. By Daikū Genko. Copied 1501 and 1681. Photomechanical reprint edited by Kagamishima Genryū. *Zenmon Shōmon Sōkan*, vol. 5. Tokyo: Kyūko shoin, 1975.

Hōonroku. Attributed to Keizan Jōkin. Komazawa University Rozan Bunko (Tokyo) manuscript, formerly owned by Eishōin (Yamanashi Prefecture) copied in 1474; photomechanical reprint edited by Yamauchi Shun'yū. *Zenmon Shōmon Sōkan*, vol. 17. Tokyo: Kyūko shoin, 1976.

Keizan Oshō Denkōroku. Woodblock edition. Busshū Sen'ei. 2 fasc. Kyoto: Ogawa tazaemon, 1857.

Keizan Oshō Goroku. 1 fasc. Daijōji monastery (Ishikawa Prefecture) manuscript copied by Kikudō Soei and recopied in 1432 by Eishū; reprinted by Ōtani Teppu, ed., *Daijōji Hihon Tōkokuki. Shūgaku kenkyū* 16 (1974): 245–47. Also included as *Keizan Kin Zenji Goroku* in *Jōsai Daishi Zenshū*, ed. Kohō Chisan, reprinted and enlarged. 1937. Yokohama: Daihonzan Sōjiji, 1976.

Keizan Oshō Shingi. 2 fascicles. Attributed to Keizan Jōkin (1264–1325). Ed. Manzan Dōhaku (1636–1714). Postscript by Gesshū Sōko (1630–98). Woodblock edition. Kyoto: Izumoji shōhakudō, 1681.

Tōkokuki. Attributed to Keizan Jōkin (1264–1325). Daijōji monastery (Ishikawa Prefecture) manuscript copied by Kikudō Soei and recopied in 1432 by Eishū; reprinted by Ōtani Teppu, ed. *Daijōji Hihon Tōkokuki. Shūgaku Kenkyū* 16 (1974): 231–48.

Tsūgenroku. 1 fasc. Printed 1940. In SZ 5, "Goroku," vol. 1, as *Tsūgen Zenji Goroku.*

Zenrin Shōkisen. 21 fasc. By Mujaku Dōchū (1653–1744). Printed 1741; reprinted with textual notes by Kōhō Tōshun (1714–79) and an essay and indexes by Itō Tōshin. Tokyo: Seishin shobō, 1968.

Zenseki Shi. 2 fasc. By Seiboku Gitai. Reprinted in *Dai Nihon Bukkyō zensho,* 1: 271–320, ed. Nanjō Bun'yū et al. 1716; Tokyo: Bussho kankōkai, 1912.

Modern Studies (by Authors)

Bodiford, William M. "Keizan's Dream History." In George J. Tanabe Jr., ed., *Religions of Japan in Practice.* Princeton, NJ: Princeton University Press, 1999, 501–22.

———. "Remembering Dōgen: Eiheiji and Dōgen Hagiography." In Steven Heine, ed., *Dōgen: Textual and Historical Studies.* New York: Oxford University Press, 2012, 207–22.

Buswell, Robert E., Jr., ed. *Encyclopedia of Buddhism.* 2 vols. New York: Macmillan Reference, 2004.

———. "The 'Short-cut' Approach of *K'an-hua* Meditation: The Evolution of a Practical Subitism in Chinese Ch'an Buddhism." In Peter N. Gregory, ed., *Sudden and Gradual: Approaches to Enlightenment in Chinese Thought.* Honolulu: University of Hawaii Press, 1987, 321–75.

Collcutt, Martin. *Five Mountains: The Rinzai Zen Monastic Institution in Medieval Japan.* Cambridge, MA: Harvard University Press, 1981.

Faure, Bernard. *Visions of Power: Imagining Medieval Japanese Buddhism.* Princeton, NJ: Princeton University Press, 1996.

Furuta Shōkin and Iriya Yoshitaka, eds. *Nihon no Zen Goroku.* 20 vols. Tokyo: Kōdansha, 1977–81.

Kagamishima Genryū, ed. Azuma Ryūshin, commentator. *Keizan Zenji Shingi.* Tokyo: Daihōrinkaku, 1974.

Kōchi Eigaku, Matsuda Fumio, Arai Shōryū. *Denkōroku kōkai,* by Keizan Zen. Vols. 1–4. Tokyo: Sankibō busshorin, 1985–87.

Kohō Chisan, *Jōsai Daishi Zenshū.* 1937; Yokohama: Daihonzan Sōjiji, 1967.

———. *Kanchū Denkōroku.* 1934, 1942; Tokyo: Kōmeisha, 1956.

Ōkubo Dōshū. *Dōgen Zenjiden no Kenkyū.* Revised and enlarged edition (*shūtei zōho*). 1953; Tokyo: Chikuma shobō, 1966.

Ōtani Teppu. "Tōkokuki: Sono Genkei ni tsuite no ichi shiron, Daijōji Hihon Tōkokuki o Chūshin ni shite." *Shūgaku Kenkyū* 16 (1974): 105–16.

Tajima Hakudō, "Shinshutsu Shiryō Kenkon'in bon 'Denkōroku' no Kenkyū." *Shūgaku Kenkyū* 2 (1960): 108–23.

———. "Shinshutsu Shiryō Kenkon'in Shozō Shahon no 'Denkōroku' ni tsuite." *Indogaku Bukkyōgaku Kenkyū* 8.1 (1960): 49–60.

Takeuchi Kōdō. "Shinshutsu no Zenrinji hon 'Keizan Shingi' ni tsuite." *Shūgaku Kenkyū* 32 (1990): 133–38.

Tamamura Takeji., *Gozan Bungaku: Tairiku Bunka Shōkaisha to Shite no Gozan Zensō no Katsudō*. Nihon Rekishi Shinsho. Tokyo: Shibundō, 1966.

Yasutani Hakuun, *Denkōroku Dokugo*. Tokyo: Sanbō kōryūkai, 1964.

Are Sōtō Zen Precepts for Ethical Guidance or Ceremonial Transformation?

MENZAN'S ATTEMPTED REFORMS AND CONTEMPORARY PRACTICES

David E. Riggs

BEYOND THEIR FUNDAMENTAL function as sets of injunctions prescribing particular standards of conduct, precepts are also the core text for a wide variety of Buddhist ceremonies, which confer a spiritual benefit or involve a change of status.[1] For example, becoming an ordained cleric involves a ceremony in which one takes the precepts (yet again). I will first give a general background of precepts in Zen and then describe in some detail Tokugawa-era controversies, when the idea of special precepts and ordinations unique to Japanese Sōtō Zen monks and laity was fully articulated, especially by Menzan Zuihō (1687–1763). Instead of having a text which has specific details of becoming a fully ordained cleric, the ceremony simply uses the general values of Mahayana Buddhist aspiration embodied in the text of the precepts. There are no additional rules specific to the station of the newly appointed cleric. The precepts thus have a central role as the main text in this ceremonial transfiguration of the new cleric, but in the contemporary Japanese ceremony the meaning of the precepts recited receives little or no attention. This habit of passing over the precepts in silence has not always been so and is not simply due to the desire to ignore them. There are much deeper reasons and impassioned controversies over the centuries that have led to the current practice.

To this historical background I will add a description of a modern precept assembly at Eiheiji and contrast this with the precept practices that have developed in Sōtō Zen groups in the United States (which are closer to the way advocated by Menzan). My interest here is neither in the question of whether or not people followed these precepts nor in what kind of moral direction the precepts supplied. Rather I am primarily concerned with the precept ceremony as an initiation or a consecration, and I will not be discussing the content of the precepts themselves. Sōtō Zen monks usually live in the extremely complex and rule-bound Japanese society and are also deeply embedded in the complex network of spiritual relationships of the Sōtō sect that govern both their personal lives and their place in Buddhist society. These relationships are formalized in ceremonies in which taking the precepts in one form or another is almost always central.

In China, Chan monks followed the same procedures for becoming a monk as did any other Buddhist, but in the seventeenth and eighteenth centuries in Japan the Sōtō school developed its own unique set of sixteen precepts. These precept ordinations came to be the crucial ritual that established a unique identity for Sōtō clerics. The same set of sixteen precepts was also used in funerals and in lay ordination assemblies to include the lay members of the Sōtō community in the lineage of the Buddha and to engage their loyalty and continued support. In the Tokugawa period the practice arose of calling this set by the name "Zen precepts" (*zenkai*), which were conferred in the Zen precepts assembly (*zenkaie*), thereby emphasizing their special quality in Zen. In modern times the more universal names of "receiving the precepts" (*jukai*) and "precepts-receiving assembly" (*jukaie*) are used. The tradition regards these Sōtō precepts as an uninterrupted transmission from the time of Dōgen, but the contemporary form of the ritual and the modern interpretation of the meaning of the precepts date only to the middle of the Tokugawa period. For over one hundred years they were the subject of an intense debate, and there was a wide variation in both the ritual and its interpretation. The position that eventually triumphed was a radical interpretation, which used only a set of sixteen precepts unique to Dōgen and which understood the taking of these precepts to entail awakening itself. Thus in Japanese Sōtō Zen the taking of the precepts became and has continued to be identified with the final goal of practice rather than the beginning of life as a Buddhist or strengthening the commitment to the Buddhist path.

The precepts used in Sōtō Zen are related to the precepts used by the Tendai school of Japanese Buddhism, but the exact form and arrangement apparently originated with Dōgen.[2] Modern Japanese Sōtō Zen has settled on the view that Dōgen brought back with him from China this true Zen set of only sixteen precepts, which are traced back to Bodhidharma and the Buddha himself, and that these make the other kind of precepts (such as the full 250 precepts) irrelevant. Unsurprisingly this is a historically untenable view, a fact clearly understood by the Sōtō clerics taking part in the Edo-period controversies. The scholar-monks who were carefully sifting textual evidence showing that Chinese Chan monks were taking the same precepts and ordinations as any Buddhist were also involved in the Sōtō polemics to establish the correctness and superiority of the special Dōgen precepts, as received in a direct line from his Chinese teacher Rujing.

Leaving aside the controversy over the origin of his special set, there is no doubt that Dōgen and his disciples assumed the right to ordain monks with these precepts without approval from either the government or from the established Japanese temples, and by so doing took a major step toward controlling their own affairs. Sōtō monks also conducted lay ordinations, and beginning in the medieval period, large assemblies were held that included an elaborate ceremony in which a famous teacher conferred the precepts upon the assembled laity from all social classes. In this way people from throughout the community could establish a connection with Sōtō Zen and with its teachers. These mass precept assemblies were a major factor in the propagation of Sōtō Zen throughout the country.[3]

The precepts represented more than simple admission to the Buddhist community. The ceremony and its accompanying transmission charts indicated a relationship with the Buddha and thus took on a powerful charisma.[4] This power can be seen in the frequent notices of Sōtō monks pacifying and converting local kami and spirits by administering the precepts to them.[5] The local spirit was understood to become a supporter of Buddhism because of the power of the precepts ceremony. Such tales often formed a crucial part of the conversion of a preexisting temple of another Buddhist affiliation to a Sōtō-lineage temple.

For all the importance of the precepts in these early Sōtō ceremonies, it is not at all clear exactly what the precepts were and upon what textual authority they were based. In the cases mentioned earlier, it is usually not specified what precepts were being administered. It is not that this was an obvious matter, and in fact the precepts were the focus of extremely heated discussion within the Buddhist community, perhaps never more so than in the mid-Edo period. In modern times, however, it has become at least reasonably clear which precepts Dōgen used in Japan when ordaining his monks. Three texts have been established as authentic and represent Dōgen's teachings concerning precepts. In order to establish a baseline in this complex discussion, I will first outline how precepts were used in China and Japan generally and then summarize the general content of Dōgen's three texts. It should be empha-sized however, that in early Tokugawa there was absolutely no such clarity about Dōgen's position on precepts: the sources that enable us to now speak so confidently were not generally available or were not universally accepted as authentic. In addition there were other texts being used that now cannot be demonstrated to be authentic. To first sketch the modern understanding of Dōgen's use of precepts is an anachronistic approach, but it has the advantage of quickly setting out the basic parameters of the rather confusing situation behind the discussion that follows. The pre-Tokugawa Japanese part of this overview is based primarily on William Bodiford's research and his summary of scholarship on the subject.[6]

The Chinese and Japanese Background

In China there was a standard set of precepts and procedures used to become a Buddhist cleric, regardless of affiliation with any particular lineage or kind of practice. I use the word "monk" or "cleric" interchangeably and limit my dis-cussion to male ordinations. The ordination to become a monk was based on the novice ordination, followed by the full ordination for monks as described in one of the texts of the Indian Vinaya. In China it was the norm to use the translation called the *Four Part Vinaya* (*Ssufen lu*) for the list of ten nov-ice and 250 full ordination precepts.[7] These precepts were given in elaborate ceremonies, at fixed times and in fixed locations at major monasteries, and resulted in the special position and privileges of a Buddhist monk. The change in status was recognized by the state (which required fees and documents), the entire Buddhist establishment, and of course lay society. Although the form and the details of the precepts were taken from the *Four Part Vinaya*, which was regarded as not Mahayana, the Chinese had long accepted these precepts as an integral part of their Mahayana practice by taking these precepts with a Mahayana attitude. Taking these precepts in this ceremony entailed the transition to fully ordained status in the eyes of the state and the Buddhist community.

Quite in addition to and entirely separate from this was another set of vows: the bodhisattva precepts. These precepts emphasized compassion and universal salvation, not the details of monastic life, and the Mahayana atti-tudes prescribed are appropriate for both householders and monastics.[8] There are several lists of such precepts in the sutra literature, but apparently the most common in China, and certainly in Japan, was the list of ten major and forty-eight minor precepts as found in the *Brahma's Net Sutra*.[9] These precepts

were taken at a variety of ceremonies along with other standard Buddhist
expressions of devotion, such as the three refuges, the three pure precepts,
and ritual repentances. There was no standardization, and since these precepts had no legal role to play, there was no requirement for them to be standardized. The key point is that these sets of precepts were not used to ordain
monks; they were devoid of the weighty social and legal implications of the full
precepts of ordination. It is true that after taking the full ordination precepts,
the newly ordained monks also went on to take the bodhisattva precepts, but
for them, as for the laity, these were precepts to express and strengthen their
religious devotion.

The same system was used in Japan until Saichō, after his return from
China with new teachings, attempted to set up his own way of ordaining
monks separate from the established temples. Eventually his Tendai community obtained the necessary state approval and in 823 ordained full status
monks recognized by the state. Their ultimate authority was the *Lotus Sutra*,
and they used the detailed precepts of the *Brahma's Net Sutra* but without also
using the full 250 precepts, as was the norm in both China and Japan.[10] This
new way was to be the normal ordination in Tendai, and it came to be used by
other groups as well, but it continued to be opposed by many Buddhist groups.
The vagueness of these bodhisattva precepts made them of little use for the
guidance of the daily life of monks, and over time other rules were composed
to fill the gap, but these rules lacked the universal authority of the full 250
precepts (which monks of the older Japanese Buddhist groups continued to
receive).

In this confusing situation the attitude toward the precepts of the early
Japanese Zen teachers reflects the full range of possibilities. Of particular
interest is Eisai's position upon his return from China in 1191, as seen in his
Kōzen Gokokuron.[11] Eisai was the first of the Kamakura-era visitors to China
to return with a Zen lineage, and he advocated strictly following the full 250
precepts as well as the bodhisattva precepts (the standard Chinese view) and
stressed the importance to Zen of beginning with a thorough grounding in
the precepts. This would seem unexceptional for an advocate of renewal for
Japanese Buddhism, freshly returned from his trip to China. Dōgen, however,
took the opposite tack in every way.[12] Dōgen's list of precepts is contained in
the "Jukai" chapter of the *Genzō*, and there are two other independent works
now accepted as authentic that give further ceremonial details and explain the
meaning of these precepts: the *Busso Shōden Bosatsukai Kyōju Kaimon* and the
Busso Shōden Bosatsukai Sahō.[13]

These works make clear that Dōgen not only rejected the full precepts of
the *Four Part Vinaya*, but he also regarded meditation as in effect trumping

all other kinds of practices, including following the precepts. Although there is no record of the content of the ordinations Dōgen received in China, we do know from these three texts that he administered to his own monks the first ten precepts of the *Brahma's Net Sutra* (but not the forty-eight minor ones, as was the practice in Japanese Tendai), plus the three refuges and the three pure precepts (which were commonly used in various ceremonies, as mentioned earlier). Dōgen claimed that the ceremony came from Rujing, but these sixteen precepts, although attested elsewhere individually, are apparently combined in this unique way by Dōgen himself, since no prior source has ever been discovered.[14] This is a summary of the result of modern scholarship, based on texts that were not available and accepted until quite recently.

Ōbaku Influence and the Revival of Precept Assembly Practice

Although these precepts have now come to be the norm for Sōtō, at the beginning of the Tokugawa period the whole question was still very open, and the textual clarity just described was simply lacking. It was not at all clear which precepts Dōgen had in mind because there was so little reliable textual evidence, and apparently there was no standard customary practice in Sōtō Zen. Between the time of Dōgen and the Tokugawa we know almost nothing about the details of Sōtō precept practices. Why was there such a sudden surge of interest in precepts in Sōtō Zen? As in so many other aspects of Japanese Zen of this period, one has to look to Ōbaku Zen to see where things got started. One might be inclined to think that, since Sōtō is a separate lineage from the shared lineage of Japanese Rinzai and Ōbaku, it was not really concerned with these Chinese monks who appeared in Nagasaki. But the Zen monks of this time were not so clearly split into Sōtō and Rinzai groups, and there was a great deal of movement back and forth for teaching and learning about different practices and rituals.

There were in fact many Sōtō monks that were extremely interested in whatever they could learn from the Chinese monks, and in a number of cases they studied for extended periods and then returned to their Sōtō temples, bringing what they had learned. They heavily modified the Sōtō practices to bring them more in line with the Ōbaku ways, which they saw as more authentic. The influence of Ōbaku monks on the Sōtō school of Japanese Zen begins with this initial attraction and even a wide-ranging adoption of many Ōbaku ideas and practices. The initial enthusiasm was followed by acrimonious struggles that continued into the nineteenth century. In most cases, and perhaps especially so with precepts, although the position that became the standard for Sōtō was quite in opposition to Ōbaku, a full appreciation of that position entails its contrast to the Ōbaku starting point. The main weapon used in this rejection of Ōbaku ways was the texts of Dōgen, and this use of his texts was an all-important part of the emergence of Dōgen as the source of Sōtō orthodoxy.

I will refer to this group of Chinese and Japanese monks as Ōbaku for convenience, but to do so is both anachronistic and a little misleading. In Japan the members of the lineage referred to themselves as the True Lineage of Linji Zen (Rinzai shōshū) until 1874, and in Sōtō writings of the period the group is often referred to simply as the Ming Chinese monks. There are times, however, when the term Ōbaku is used to distinguish between this recent Chinese lineage and the more established Rinzai and Sōtō lineages of Zen.[15] Be that as it may, the term Ōbaku will be used here, understanding that both the word and the connotations of a third stream of Japanese Zen in addition to Rinzai and Sōtō is problematic in many Tokugawa-era contexts.

The most important figure of these Chinese teachers was Yinyuan Longqi (Jp. Ingen Ryūki, 1592–1673), who was a major figure in Chinese Buddhist circles and an important reformer before coming to Japan.[16] When he arrived in 1654, the Chinese Buddhist community was already well established in Nagasaki, and Yinyuan was known in Japan, at least in certain circles, from his writings. It seems that when he arrived, the practice of holding precept assemblies had fallen into abeyance, and one of the most popular things he did was to hold eight-day-long precepts assemblies. In 1658 Yinyuan printed his own set of ordination rules (*Gukaihōgi*), in which he both prescribed the ceremonies and discussed the meaning of the precepts.[17] His work followed contemporary Chinese standards; even the title was something he borrowed from other works about precepts that appeared in the Ming canon. Apparently, in this area, Yinyuan was not the reformer he was in other aspects, but what he was doing must have been quite different from Japanese practice, judging from the distinguished crowds he attracted. When I asked about precept assemblies recently at the head temple, Manpukuji, the monks told me that this text was still the standard for their school and showed me hand-copied guides for precept assemblies, explaining that there were no printed materials. This is in stark contrast with the volumes of materials from Sōtō clerics written and printed beginning in the middle of the Tokugawa era.

The Ōbaku assembly encourages both lay and monk participation. In the first part of the event, everyone receives the three refuges, followed by the five precepts, the eight precepts, and the ten novice precepts. The second main stage is for the postulant monks to receive the classic 250 precepts of mainstream Buddhism and become full monks. At the end everyone takes the ten major and forty-eight minor bodhisattva precepts. In Yinyuan's 1661 assembly the precepts were conferred on hundreds of people, and it later became a standard practice by abbots of Manpukuji as well as its branch temples that continues to this day, albeit in a shorter form.

Many people received these extended precepts, which are the standard for any kind of Chinese Buddhism, from various Ōbaku teachers. Some prominent Sōtō monks participated in the assembly and stayed for long periods of practice, and then years later returned to the Sōtō fold. They had a profound effect. The Ōbaku abbot who was directly responsible for most of the ordination ceremonies involving Sōtō monks was Muan Xingdao (1611–84), the second abbot of the head temple of Manpukuji and the man responsible for training most of the Japanese Ōbaku monks.[18] Shōe Dōjō (1634–1713) received full precepts from Muan in 1668 and stayed in Ōbaku training until 1674, when he returned to help with the first retreat of Gesshū Sōko (1618–98) at Daijōji (an extremely important Sōtō training temple). Mokugen Genjaku (1629–80) also was ordained with full precepts by Muan in 1670 before returning to Daijōji. Spurred by the Ōbaku example, in 1671 Abbot Gesshū began to build what he called a lineage precepts platform (*kechimyaku kaidan*) at Daijōji. This practice continued at least until the next generation, as evidenced by the fact that Manzan Dōhaku (1636–1741), the champion of exclusive allegiance to the teachings of Dōgen, also received an Ōbaku ordination. This is revealed in his edition of Dōgen's *Kōroku*, published in 1673, which included a preface by Muan that indicates that Dōhaku (I will continue to call him Dōhaku just to avoid confusion with Menzan) received the full precepts from Muan, a fact not recorded in Dōhaku's own chronology.[19]

Apparently the influence was strong and persistent because some ninety years later Menzan Zuihō complained in the *Tokudo Wakumon* (1763), his set of questions and answers about ordinations, that most Sōtō monks were doing Ōbaku-style ordinations with too many rules and ceremonies, unlike the proper (i.e., Sōtō) Zen ordination.[20] The crucial point here is that the example of the elaborate Ōbaku ceremonies led first to imitation and then to serious research on the part of Sōtō monks into what their own lineage had to say on the subject. They found (apparently rather to their surprise) that Dōgen held that only his unprecedented set of sixteen precepts was necessary. It was only after unearthing previously obscure manuscripts and a great deal of wrangling that this conclusion was reached, and it was apparently due to the powerful example offered by Ōbaku that they began this research. It was not until the nineteenth century that the position that Sōtō Zen has its own special precepts came to be fully accepted.

Back to the Sources: The Development
of the Sōtō Precepts

The following discussion of the Sōtō response to this challenge draws on over-view articles that are not further cited, in addition to the sources cited below.[21] The first major work of the Sōtō reform movement concerned with precepts was the *Taikaku Kanwa*, written by Dōhaku and published in 1715, toward the end of his life.[22] In this text he claimed that his position came directly from his teacher, Gesshū (the abbot of Daijōji), who delivered many public lectures on the topic and administered precepts in what he described as the proper manner of the direct tradition of Rujing and Dōgen. Dōhaku maintained that the correct precepts for Zen, for which the term *zenkai* was now being used (Dōgen did not use this term), were the one-mind precepts (*isshinkai*). These had been transmitted to China by Bodhidharma and then to Japan by Saichō as part of his Zen lineage (which he received as well as his Tendai lin-eage). Dōhaku maintained that this lineage of precepts, despite the different name, had the same content as the Tendai perfect-sudden precepts (*endonkai*). Dōhaku also held that both Rinzai and Sōtō lineages originally had the same Zen precepts, but the ceremony and precepts were lost in China sometime after Dōgen returned to Japan, which explains why the contemporary Ōbaku Zen monks do not follow this form.

Before discussing the responses to Dōhaku's (very problematic) views, I will lay out the background for his arguments concerning the relationship between Zen precepts and Tendai, since this is the key point upon which years of dispute rests.[23] Dōhaku was arguing from passages coming at the end of the *Denjutsu Isshinkaimon*, which was written around 833 by Saichō's student Kōjō (779–858), who was defending the new usage of precepts under Saichō.[24] This text mentioned Bodhidharma in connection with something called the one-vehicle precepts (*ichijōkai*), the meaning of which was not explained. The text also referred to the bodhisattva precepts of the *Brahma's Net Sutra* as the one-mind precepts. Neither of these terms figure in later Tendai pre-cepts discussions, and in fact Bodhidharma and the Zen lineage were of little importance to Kōjō's arguments. Kōjō took the step (which Saichō did not) of entirely doing away with the full precepts even in a provisional manner and claimed that the one-vehicle precepts allow one to dispense entirely with the other precepts. Kōjō also equated precepts with the mind which perceives things as they are (*jissōshin*). This led in turn to the position that receiving the precepts entails mastery of meditation and wisdom, and thus entry into the ranks of the buddhas.

For Kōjō (unlike Saichō, who continued to emphasize strict adherence) the details of following the precepts were of little importance. Kōjō's arguments are a pastiche of quotations from Chinese writers, mostly of the Tendai lineage, but he arrived at his own conclusions. In short, compared to Kōjō, Saichō himself was relatively conservative in that he retained more of the forms of the precepts and he emphasized their place in practice as leading toward (but not encompassing) the goal. The same differences (between Kōjō and his teacher) were still to be seen in the two sides of the precepts dispute in Sōtō of the mid-Edo period. Despite strong arguments for a more conservative position, in the end the more radical position (which was apparently closer to Dōgen's) prevailed. Thus *zenkai* in Japan continued to mean much more than simply precepts that are observed by monks of the Zen lineage. The mainstream Sōtō lineage view came to be that to receive the precepts was to enter the lineage of the Buddha and without further endeavor to be ritually transformed to the status of the buddhas and ancestors.

To return to Dōhaku, his position was not accepted at the time by everyone even within Sōtō. It was roundly denounced in every aspect by Sekiun Yūsen (1677–?), a student of Dokuan Genkō (1630–98), who had been Dōhaku's great ally in the reform movement. Sekiun's position was very similar to the standard Chinese view, which might be explained at least in part by the fact that his teacher, Dokuan, was so close to Yinyuan's predecessor in Nagasaki, Daozhe Zhaoyuan (1602–62), that Dokuan was entrusted with the Chinese master's ritual implements (symbolizing his teaching authority) when he returned to China in 1658. Despite the friendship of his teacher with Dōhaku, in Sekiun's *Sōrin Yakuju*, printed in 1719, he followed the Chinese model of precepts (i.e., no special precepts for Zen) and emphasized the importance of following the precepts as an integral part of progress on the path.[25] Sekiun was a Sōtō monk, but he later took full precepts with a Shingon monk who was involved in the precepts revival of Shingon. Sekiun quite correctly wrote that Dōhaku's assertion about Zen precepts being lost was untenable in view of the fact that the standard Pure Rules texts (*shingi*) of the lineage clearly indicate that the full precepts are to be administered, followed by bodhisattva precepts.

Another major Sōtō figure of this time, Tenkei Denson (1648–1753), also took full precepts from the same lineage of Shingon teachers and held the same basic position as Sekiun. However, even Tenkei's own lineage did not continue to support this position, and Genrō Ōryū (1720–1813), although a member of the Tenkei lineage, argued in his *Ittsui Saiga* for using only Dōgen's precepts.[26]

Menzan's Middle Way

It is into this very confused and highly polemical situation that Menzan issued his voluminous and enormously learned tomes. Menzan is arguably the most influential and certainly the most erudite and prolific writer of the Sōtō reformers of this era. Although he grew up amid Sōtō priests who were strongly influenced by Ōbaku, he never took their precepts or trained in Ōbaku temples. Indeed he spent much of his life trying to eliminate Ōbaku influence, which he regarded as deviations from Dōgen and hence improper for a reformed Sōtō school. Menzan presided over assemblies in which he lectured on the precepts and conferred the precepts upon hundreds of people who had assembled for that purpose. In his three-volume major work on the precepts, *Busso Shōden Daikaiketsu* (1724), he asserted that the procedure Dōgen received from Rujing was to administer the novice precepts (*shamikai*), followed by the bodhisattva precepts, and that the full precepts had never been used in the lineage of Rujing.[27] The precepts are also to be given a second time, with full explanation in the abbot's room, when dharma transmission is bestowed to recognize the status of attainment as a teacher. Menzan relied on the *Busso Shōden Bosatsukai Kyōju Kaimon* and the *Busso Shōden Bosatsukai Sahō* as the sources of the early modern consensus on Dōgen's precepts.

However, Menzan also used another, much more problematic text that he had previously collated from various manuscripts, the *Eihei Soshi Tokudo Ryaku Sahō* (1744), also known as the *Shukke Ryaku Sahōmon* (1744).[28] He published this text as Dōgen's instructions for ordination, but now it seems unlikely that the text can be accepted as coming from Dōgen. It has a different series of precepts than the other texts mentioned earlier, and there are several different extant manuscript versions with different content, none of which is earlier than the fifteenth century.[29] At the time it was not clear which texts were authentic, and the rejection of Menzan's position did not depend on that question but rather on how the factions wanted precepts to be used, or not used, in the life of the lineage. Menzan did use texts that can no longer be accepted as supporting his choice of precepts, but his arguments about the meaning and use of precepts still stand.

Much later, in the short and accessible *Tokudo Wakumon*, Menzan stresses that the novice precepts are a necessary part of the ordination of monks because the bodhisattva precepts were concerned with the mind of awakening, and gave no guidance concerning the rules of proper conduct for monks.[30] It is also noteworthy that Menzan refers in this text to Eisai for authority for his assertion of the importance of upholding (not just receiving) the precepts.[31] He also addresses the problem of to what degree Dōgen is following the

Chanyuan Qingqui (Jp. *Zen'en shingi*), the standard set of Pure Rules for Zen monastics.[32] As Menzan and everyone else had come to recognize, Dōgen had not explicitly directed that the novice precepts should be taken. In the "Jukai" chapter, Dōgen quoted the *Chanyuan Qingqui* for his authority, as usual, but he ignored (even though he correctly quoted it) the part about taking the novice and full precepts.[33] Dōgen's extended discussion and detailed list of precepts is concerned only with the set of sixteen (now standard in Sōtō), inexplicably ignoring the other precepts in the passage he just quoted. Menzan's position was that Dōgen assumed that no further detail was necessary and that the precepts would be taken as usual. This was soon contested by Gyakusui Tōryū (1684–1766) of Dōhaku's lineage. In his *Tokudo Wakumon Bengishō* (1755), he claimed that there was a transmission from Jakuen (who was Chinese), which included the novice precepts and that Menzan mistook this Jakuen lineage ceremony for Dōgen's.[34] In any event, unless further manuscripts come to light, the question of the authenticity of this *Eihei Soshi Tokudo Ryaku Sahō* edition is doubtful, and on the basis of current evidence it seems that in this case Menzan was following the general Buddhist tradition more closely than he was following Dōgen's teachings.

Meaning of Precepts

I come back to what one might expect to be the main point regarding precepts: What happens after the precepts are received and what role does receiving the precepts play in the life of practice, whether of the laity or clerics? In mainstream Chinese Buddhism, and also in Eisai's writings (for example), the precepts are an all-important part, but only a part, of Buddhist practice. They are the crucial initial step upon which the later practices of meditation and wisdom depend. The other viewpoint holds that taking the precepts in some sense completes practice, which is what came to be the Sōtō position under the name of the unity of Zen and the precepts (*zenkai itchi*). This view is very similar to the Tendai notion that precepts are expressions of innate buddha-nature (*busshō*). The roots of this idea date back to the time of Saichō and his student Kōjō and were later developed in the Tendai tradition, until in Dōgen's time there were discussions of the precepts as the way to immediately realize buddhahood, indeed a way superior to meditation.[35] This view is also seen in *Zenkaiki* (1325) by the celebrated Rinzai monk Kokan Shiren (1278–1346).[36]

Although something like this notion can be seen as early as in the *Platform Sutra*, the idea becomes of central concern to Sōtō school writers in the

Edo period, who tend to equate the formless precepts of the *Platform Sutra* with their current Zen precepts. See, for example, Menzan's *Jakushū Eifuku Oshō Sekkai* (1752).[37] That is not to say, however, that this was a new idea in Sōtō: from the thirteenth century onward precepts were used to ordain lay people and even ghosts, who were thereby transformed without the need for further cultivation.[38] Despite its long pedigree, this use of precepts as a kind of initiation into a sacred lineage conveying immediate results (instead of precepts as either rules to follow or a change of status opening the opportunity for practice) was still controversial. In the Tokugawa period Sōtō writers were sharply divided on the question of whether to understand the precepts as this kind of initiation that entailed immediate results or as the basis of beginning to practice.

Although Dōhaku championed Dōgen's unique way, he did not accept the idea of the unity of Zen and the precepts. He maintained that precepts were in a secondary position to Zen; that is to say, they were a necessary condition but not in themselves the ultimate. Menzan held largely the same view. In general Menzan took the position that, as important as it was to take the precepts, the taking was a confirmation of practice, not its completion. Menzan's general attitudes are plainly laid out in his *Jakushū Eifuku Oshō Sekkai*, which are his lectures delivered in 1752 during a seven-day precepts assembly attended by six hundred people, including clerics and male and female laity.[39] Although he refers the audience to his recently printed *Busso Shōden Daikaiketsu* for the detailed evidence, he emphasizes very clearly that for all their importance, the precepts are only one of the three main parts of the triad of precepts, meditation, and wisdom, likening them to the three legs of a pot.[40] Menzan also emphasizes that the ceremony for monks should not be confused with the precepts assembly ceremony, which is for both monks and laity of both sexes.[41] Further the conferring of precepts as done in these ceremonies should not be confused with the transmission of precepts (*denkai*) done only in the private dharma-transmission ceremony. Contrary to the tendency seen in the medieval precepts assemblies, where it was believed that to receive the precepts was to attain buddhahood, Menzan emphasizes the different uses of the precepts for the two groups of people.

After Menzan, however, the trend was strongly toward the unity of Zen and precepts. Banjin Dōtan (1698–1775) based his position on the *Bonmōkyōryakushō* (1309), written in the first generation after Dōgen.[42] This all-important text explains Dōgen's *Busso Shōden Kyōjukaimon* in terms that make it clear that he regarded the precepts as not being bound by textual details and moral prescriptions but entailed awakening itself.[43] On the basis of his reading of this commentary Banjin claimed that Dōgen's view was that taking the precepts entailed buddhahood and that both Zen and the precepts were the eye of the true dharma. The question of following the precepts is of little importance; it is the ceremony of the precepts that entails the transformation.

For Banjin the transmission from the Buddha himself to Mahakasyapa was the basis for authority in the question of precepts, not Bodhidharma, much less any texts of mainstream Buddhism. Banjin's *Busso Shōden Zenkaishō* (1758) opens with an unusual list of rules, specifying that it is not to be shown outside of the group, and ends with the admonition that the blocks from which it was printed must be destroyed after fifteen years.[44] The preface opens with the statement that Zen and precepts are but two names for the true teaching passed down from the Tathagata to the Sōtō school. The content is simply parts of the *Bonmōkyōryakushō* that explain Dōgen's *Kyōju Kaimon*, leaving out the parts that discuss the remaining forty-eight precepts of the *Brahma's Net Sutra*. Despite the opening prohibitions and the fact that it is only a selection from a text that itself was a commentary, it was chosen to be included in the Taishō canon.[45]

The Modern Zen Precepts Assembly at Eiheiji

This transcendental view of the precepts as the text of an initiation or consecration ceremony is the position that came to prevail in Japanese Sōtō. The idea that simply participating in a ceremony is all it takes to become a buddha is not simply a fancy way of speaking. As can be clearly seen in the modern precepts assembly ceremony, which I describe below, that is exactly what is meant. Following the interpretation of Banjin, the precepts are not something to be carefully followed. Instead of considering how to observe the precepts in one's everyday life, one somehow keeps them without keeping them. I will skip over the intervening developments, as well as how this understanding was propagated in the modern era via the *Shushōgi*.[46] Instead I turn now to the annual precepts assembly at Eiheiji, the temple most closely identified with Dōgen and hence the touchstone for orthodoxy. This ceremony shows clearly the power of Banjin's position in uniting disparate groups of Sōtō followers but also highlights to what degree the precepts are detached from ethical considerations. I will describe events primarily from the viewpoint of a participant by bringing in comments from other participants and my own observations as a lay participant.

The precepts assembly lasts one full week but in other respects is utterly different from the traditional Chinese-style assemblies held by Ōbaku leaders in the seventeenth century. The precept list is the group of sixteen, as taught by Dōgen, and the event is open to participants, living or dead, with very little restriction. The deceased can participate by proxy and receive a lineage chart just as if they had been there. About two hundred people come for the week, with both men and women well represented, ranging in age from college students to retirees. Participants are often from Sōtō temple lay families, but people from other Buddhist denominations and others with no fixed affiliation are welcome. A significant minority come every year either to Eiheiji or to another Sōtō precepts assembly. Attendance is arranged by a simple application and the payment of a modest fee for room and board.

The ordinands (kaishi) live together for the week in one room, divided roughly in half, with men on one side and women on the other, leaving a wide gap in the middle in front of the altar. This means that there is exactly one tatami mat per person for sleeping, with the mats on all four sides occupied by fellow ordinands. Earplugs are highly recommended. All personal belongings are kept in rough wooden shelves around the edges of the hall. There is one toilet facility immediately adjacent, shared by men and women. The only concession to modesty is a small temporary hut to be used by women (only) for changing clothes.

This same hall is used not only for sleeping but also for eating and for many of the lectures given to the ordinands. All of the necessary arrangements of the room for meals, sleeping, and ceremonies, as well as meal clean-up, are done not by the ordinands but by the young monks in training, who are members of the great assembly (daishū) living in the nearby training hall. Their usual routine is to eat, sleep, and meditate in the monks' hall (sōdō), not unlike what the ordinands do during this week. At 9 p.m., when the ordinands return from their final evening lecture (held in a nearby modern Japanese-style tatami room), the monks have paved the hall with sleeping mats and pillows. The ordinands file into the room in separate parallel rows of men and women and simply take the bed position they stop at. When all have found their place for the night, they are released to affix their sheet and pillow case. After arising before 3 a.m., they go to another hall for morning meditation, and the bedding is put away by the monks.

This same hall, where ordinands sleep, eat, and have their piles of personal stuff, is the dharma hall (hattō), the main ceremonial hall of this most famous of Japanese training temples. This means that they get to see the daily round of ceremonies of the notables of the Sōtō sect and that they (and their disorderly stacks of junk) get to be seen by the unceasing flow of tourists, some in their Sunday best and others in their latest hip-hop apparel. The center of the room is an enormous main altar, behind which are the ashes of Dōgen, and it is this altar that is the focus of the week's activities, both for the ordinands and the monks, as well as the tourists, for whom space is somehow made in the already full hall. The more than one hundred monks in training of course have to participate in some of the daily services, but most of their time is devoted to looking after the needs of the ordinands. There is an approximately equal number of more senior clerics who are in some way or other teaching or taking care of the ordinands. This is all taking place in the midst of the usual flow of visitors to Eiheiji. It is not exactly a time of quiet retreat, but the ordinands display an impressive degree of quiet discipline and attentiveness.

The daily routine begins with a 2:50 a.m. wake-up, followed by a twenty-minute period of seated meditation, most of which is taken up with explanations about how to do meditation. The rest of the day is spent in various ways. First there are talks by either the Precepts Explaining Teacher (*sekkaishi*) or by an invited cleric flown in for the day from as far away as Hokkaido. Although the talks are ostensibly concerned with the precepts, in the ceremony I participated in they were mostly some variety of uplifting popular light stories with occasional Buddhist homilies and a brief summary of the life of Dōgen. Almost nothing was presented about the meaning of the ceremonies or about how to follow the precepts. Much of the remaining time is spent chanting the liturgy of the dharma hall or just watching from the edges. A few of the ordinands know the chants, but most of them do not even try to follow along in the handbook that is presented to each at the reception area. Several times each day there is group practice in the Sōtō slow melodic chanting (*baika ryūei sanka*), which has become very popular among some Sōtō groups. The text we chanted was the "Hymn to Receiving the Precepts" ("Ōjukai Gowasan"), led by young clerics. This is one activity where real training took place. To round out these events, twice a day for some twenty minutes the ordinands were led in a very slow procession around Eiheiji, chanting (in *baika* style), "Homage to the original teacher Sakyamuni the Tathagata" (*namu honshi shaka nyorai*). These activities left time only for eating and a daily afternoon bath.

For the ordinands as well as the other people visiting and those living in the temple complex, the focus of attention was the head of Eiheiji, which at the time of my visit was Abbot Miyazaki, universally referred to simply as Zen Master (Zenji sama). He was 104 and was rolled into the hall in an elaborate wheelchair, from which he conducted most ceremonies. He spoke without notes, slowly and softly. He gave short talks of up to ten minutes in the dharma hall, usually speaking to the ordinands about the meaning of what they were doing, teaching that Zen and the precepts are one and the same and that to receive the precepts is to become a buddha. In the ceremonies of the last two days, he repeated this message again and again.

The evening of the next to the last full day is the repentance ceremony (*sangeshiki*), for which the women make themselves up and dress in the formal clothes they have been holding in reserve. The ordinands are assembled in the dharma hall, joined by the monks in training, who will also be receiving the precepts. The hall has been completely curtained off with red cloth, forming an enclosed space around the altar with a pathway to an adjoining room. The ordinands are instructed in the procedure and then led in single file, in the order of the names in the registry, into a room adjoining the dharma hall. The entire route is lined with red cloth and dimly lit, in part with real candles. As each ordinand approaches the abbot, who is surrounded by all the major teachers of the assembly, he or she is handed a small slip of paper upon which is written "Minor infractions are endless" (*shōzai muryō*), which he or she then hands to the abbot as the ordinand chants this same phrase. This is the one time that the ordinand is required to give a solo performance, to say something for himself or herself; everything else is done as a group. The slip of paper is added to the growing mound in front of the abbot.

After all the ordinands have made this acknowledgment of their transgressions to the abbot and reassembled in the dharma hall, the abbot returns to the hall. The register containing the names of the ordinands is burned before the abbot in a brazier, and the abbot tells the ordinands that their transgressions have been entrusted to him and that he warrants, with his full authority, that those transgressions have been consumed in this fire.

The quiet and solemn nature of the ceremony is suddenly broken by very loud chants, ringing of hand bells, and shaking of staves as the assembly of clerics forms a circle and circumambulates the assembly of ordinands. They stop every twenty paces or so and bow to the ordinands in the center, and then take off again at a clip while chanting loudly, "Homage to the Original Teacher Sakyamuni Buddha" (*namu honshi shakamuni butsu*). The contrast with the solemn stillness that prevailed up until then is startling, and people are clearly very moved. Several of the ordinands tell me that they feel a great weight has been taken from them by the ceremony.

The following morning the abbot tells us that we have become buddha (*jōbutsu*) due to the connection made in this ceremony, and that he never tires of the great joy of this occasion. The morning lecture includes for the first time a few details about the precepts to a very tired but happy group of ordinands, of which perhaps half appear to be asleep. The mood of the group is indeed as if a cloud has been lifted. People are very cheerful and for the first time chat animatedly in the breaks between events. They again dress in their finest for the final evening ceremony, the receiving of the precepts along with the lineage certificate (*kechimyaku*) containing their Buddhist name. For those who have already participated in such a ceremony, their previous precept name (*kaimyō*) is used, but for others the abbot selects a name.

The central altar is again partitioned off with red curtains, and we are again presented to the abbot in the order of the name registry, separated into the usual four groups of male and female, cleric and lay. After many preliminary ceremonials, the ordinands approach the abbot, who is seated upon the altar with two brushes which he dips in water and then uses to anoint the heads of the ordinands, two at a time, leaning down from his position upon the altar. When all have been anointed, the abbot recites the precepts, and after each group the ordinands recite together, "I will preserve them well." At the end of this part the abbot tells the ordinands that from now on they begin again, living as a buddha, and that somehow they will keep the precepts even if they do not keep them.

Next the ordinands ascend to the center of the altar in groups of thirty. This is the main altar of the main hall, in the back of which are the ashes of Dōgen, a space usually reserved for the Zen Master and the statue of the Buddha. The assembled teachers circumambulate each group while shaking their staff and chanting that the ordinands have entered the rank of the buddhas, a position equal to that of the great awakening. After this has been done for each group, the ordinands approach the altar and receive their certificate, wrapped in a paper binder with their secular name on the outside. After a formal display of the lineage chart that all have just received, the ordinands repair to a nearby room where the certificates for the deceased ordinands (*mōkai*) are distributed to those who have arranged to have this done for their departed relatives. About one third of the participants have arranged for this. To everyone's evident relief we are told we can sleep in (until 3:40 a.m.), which is good because everyone is so excited and talkative that it takes some time before sleep descends.

After the usual morning ceremonies and a round of formal thanks, the assembly is dissolved and people return to their homes with an invitation to come back again as many times as they like. This ceremony clearly follows the line of thought that flows from Banjin's teaching. The ceremony itself is a complete religious event, which can be repeated, and yet one from which there can be no retreat, no defeat. Although the manual that was distributed to everyone at the beginning clearly says that to receive the precepts is to become a disciple of the Buddha, the ordinands have themselves become Buddha. They go forth in a new life, unburdened by either their past transgressions or the concern of trying to live up to a new standard.

North American Sōtō Zen Precept Assemblies

As might be expected, the Sōtō Mission temples in North America have precepts assemblies that follow closely the official head temple model. Zenshūji in Los Angeles has held five-day events that followed the same basic schedule as Eiheiji. According to the manual prepared for the occasion, the rituals include *baika* chanting, burning of the registry of names, and ascending the altar.

On the other hand, there are a number of independent Sōtō lineages that have developed in North America, which often primarily follow the lead of their own teachers. Even if those teachers are fully recognized by the Japanese hierarchy, they may not emphasize the teachings as understood by the mainstream Sōtō school. I will discuss only the lineage founded by Suzuki Shunryū in San Francisco. In his lectures about the precepts Suzuki clearly follows the idea of *zenkai itchi*, the unity of Zen and the precepts: "When I say precepts, what you will think of is something like Ten Commandments or grave prohibitory precepts. But Zen precepts are not like that. To start with, Zen precepts means to understand zazen. So another interpretation of zazen is precepts."[47] However, this community has come to see the precepts as an aid to deepening one's commitment and expressing one's intention to follow a more Buddhist style of life. In this aspect the style of this American Sōtō group is much closer to the practice advocated by Menzan and other, more mainstream thinkers of the Tokugawa. The belief that we are already Buddha is acknowledged in the beginning of the ceremony with the phrase "In faith that we are Buddha we enter Buddha's Way," but the focus is on the meaning of the precepts and on how to follow them.

For American Sōtō Buddhists, who are seldom born into a Buddhist family with ties to a particular lineage, receiving the precepts has become more like a rite of passage. Students must first develop a personal relationship with a Zen teacher and receive the teacher's permission to participate in a precepts ceremony. They must also sew their own miniature version of Buddha's robe, worn hung from the neck (*ryakusu*). This does not play a role in the mainstream Japanese Sōtō practice done at Eiheiji, but there are some Japanese Sōtō groups that follow a similar practice.[48] Before the ceremony takes place the ordinands are expected to attend classes about the precepts and to deepen their understanding and commitment. These preparations usually take several months, though they can take even longer.

Unlike the week-long event at Eiheiji, the precepts assembly itself is very short, usually one hour or so, though it may be held at the same time as another event, such as a weekend mediation retreat. The elaborate repentance and burning of the registry is compressed into a simple recitation of the repentance verse (*sangemon*), the same used in everyday ritual. The elaborate ritual preparations of the site for the ceremony done by the Japanese Sōtō school are absent. The repentance verse is immediately followed by the receiving of the precepts, and then the ordinands are presented with both their lineage certificate (as at Eiheiji) and also with the *rakusu* they have sewn, which has now been inscribed with their Buddhist name. There is no mounting of the altar, nor is there provision for ordination being received by the deceased.

When Eisai was working to establish the Zen lineage upon his return to Japan, he stressed the role of precepts in Zen, probably in response to a lack of such concern in much of Japanese Buddhism. He clearly meant following the precepts and taking the details seriously, so much so that Zen was also known as the Precepts School. The modern Sōtō school also has an idea of the importance of precepts, but it is expressed in the notion of the unity of Zen and the precepts, which has come to mean that taking the precepts trumps everything else. As discussed earlier, this position has an impeccable pedigree and has no doubt been of great importance to the social position of the school; the all-important funeral rites depend upon the idea of transforming the deceased through the conferring of precepts. With this in mind, one could make a case that the modern Sōtō lineage could also be called the Precepts School. Within a single name, however, is contained an enormous disparity of meaning.

Into this gulf steps the new American lineages, determined to both find their own way and also to follow the teachings of the lineage. Just as the set of precepts used by Dōgen is a new list out of old elements, so the American precepts practice makes something quite new out of very old elements. Although they keep Dōgen's list of precepts (certainly not following Menzan's insistence on the novice precepts), they approach precepts in a way quite different from their Japanese teachers: they emphasize personal commitment to attempt to follow the precepts in their own lives. This way, however, is much closer to the old ideas of mainstream Buddhism than it is to how Eiheiji takes what Dōgen wrote about precepts. Whether or not Menzan would have been pleased is impossible to know, but his example of precepts being only one of the three legs of the Buddhist life clearly applies much more to Zen practice at San Francisco Zen Center than at Eiheiji.

NOTES

1. Carl Bielefeldt, "Recarving the Dragon: History and Dogma in the Study of Dōgen," in William R. LaFleur, ed., *Dōgen Studies* (Honolulu: University of Hawaii Press, 1985), 21–24.

2. William M. Bodiford, *Sōtō Zen in Medieval Japan* (Honolulu: University of Hawaii Press, 1993), 169–73; Bernard Faure, *Visions of Power: Imagining Medieval Japanese Buddhism* (Stanford: Stanford University Press, 1996), 55–57.

3. Bodiford, *Sōtō Zen in Medieval Japan*, 179–84.

4. Bodiford, *Sōtō Zen in Medieval Japan*, 184; Faure, *Visions of Power*, 220–21.

5. William M. Bodiford, "The Enlightenment of Kami and Ghosts: Spirit Ordinations in Japanese Sōtō Zen," *Cahiers d'Extrême-Asia* 7 (1993–94): 267–82; Bodiford, *Sōtō Zen in Medieval Japan*, 173–79.

6. Bodiford, *Sōtō Zen in Medieval Japan*, 164–73; Paul Groner, *Saichō: The Establishment of the Japanese Tendai School* (Seoul: Po Chin Chai, 1984); Holmes Welch, *Practice of Chinese Buddhism 1900–50* (Cambridge, MA: Harvard University Press, 1967), 285–94.

7. T 22.1428.

8. Groner, *Saichō*, 215–20; Paul Groner, "The *Fan-wang Ching* and Monastic Discipline in Japanese Tendai: A Study of Annen's *Futsū Jubosatsukia Kōshaku*," in Robert E. Buswell Jr., ed., *Chinese Buddhist Apocrypha* (Honolulu: University of Hawaii Press, 1990).

9. T 24.1484.

10. Groner, *Saichō*, 272.

11. T 80.2543.

12. Bodiford, *Sōtō Zen in Medieval Japan*, 169.

13. DZZ-1 2:279–81; ZS Shūgen.

14. Bodiford, *Sōtō Zen in Medieval Japan*, 171.

15. SZ Hōgo 3:826.

16. Jiang Wu, *Enlightenment in Dispute: The Reinvention of Chan Buddhism in Seventeenth-century China* (New York: Oxford University Press, 2008).

17. *Zengaku Taikei*, vol. 7. Ed. Zengaku Taikei Hensankyoku (Tokyo: Ikkatsusha, 1915).

18. Helen J. Baroni, *Ōbaku Zen: The Emergence of the Third Sect of Zen in Tokugawa Japan* (Honolulu: University of Hawaii Press, 2000), 58–60.

19. Ōtani Tetsuo, *Eihei Kōroku: Manzanbon Sozanbon Taikō* (Tokyo: Issuisha, 1991), 31.

20. SZ Zenkai.

21. Kagamishima Genryū, *Dōgen Zenji to Sonno Monryū* (Tokyo: Seishin shobō, 1961); Kagamishima Genryū, "Edo jidai no tenkai: Shūgi," in Kagamishima Genryū and Tamaki Kōjirō, eds., *Dōgen Zen no Rekishi* (Tokyo: Shunjūsha, 1980); Watanabe Kenshū, "Kinsei in okeru Dōgen Zen no Tenkai: Zenkai Ron no Tenkai," in Sōtōshū shūgaku kenkyūjo, ed., *Dōgen Shisō no Ayumi* (Tokyo: Yoshikawa kobunkan, 1993).

22. SZ Zenkai.

23. William M. Bodiford, "Bodhidharma's Precepts in Japan," in William M. Bodiford, ed., *Going Forth: Visions of Buddhist Vinaya* (Honolulu: University

of Hawaii Press, 2005); William M. Bodiford, "Kokan Shiren's *Zen Precept Procedures*," in George J. Tanabe Jr., ed., *Religions of Japan in Practice* (Princeton, NJ: Princeton University, 1999).

24. T 78.2379; Groner, *Saichō*, 292–98.

25. SZ Zenkai.

26. ZS Shitchū.

27. SZ Zenkai, 87–88.

28. DZZ-1 2:272–78.

29. SZ Kaidai, 100; Bodiford, *Sōtō Zen in Medieval Japan*, 100; Kagamishima, "Edo Jidai no Tenkai," 177.

30. SZ Zenkai, 191–92.

31. SZ Zenkai, 194.

32. SZ Zenkai, 193–94.

33. DZZ-1 1:619; Kagamishima Genryū, Satō Tatsugen, and Kosaka Kiyū, *Yakuchū Zennen Shingi* (Tokyo: Sōtōshū shūmuchō, 1972), 13.

34. ZS Zenkai.

35. Jacqueline I. Stone, *Original Enlightenment and the Transformation of Medieval Japanese Buddhism* (Honolulu: University of Hawaii Press, 1999), 126–28.

36. Bodiford, "Kokan Shiren's *Zen Precept Procedures*"; *Zengaku Taikei*.

37. SZ Zenkai, 143.

38. Bodiford, *Sōtō Zen in Medieval Japan*, 172.

39. SZ Zenkai.

40. SZ Zenkai, 143.

41. SZ Zenkai, 174–75.

42. SZ Chūkai-2.

43. Bodiford, *Sōtō Zen in Medieval Japan*, 171–73.

44. SZ Zenkai, 455.

45. T 82.2601.

46. Steven Heine, "Abbreviation or Aberration: The Role of the *Shushōgi* in Modern Sōtō Zen Buddhism," in Steven Heine, ed., *Buddhism in the Modern World: Adaptation of an Ancient Tradition* (Oxford: Oxford University Press, 2003), 169–92.

47. Suzuki Shunryū, "Real Precepts Are Beyond Words," unpublished transcript of talk given July 2, 1971, San Francisco Zen Center.

48. Diane E. Riggs, "Fukudenkai: Sewing the Buddha's Robe in Contemporary Japanese Buddhist Practice," *Japanese Journal of Religious Studies* 31.2 (2004): 315–60.

8

Vocalizing the Remembrance of Dōgen

A STUDY OF THE *SHINPEN HŌON KŌSHIKI*

Michaela Mross

IT IS JANUARY 26. In all Japanese Sōtō temples Dōgen's (1200–53) birthday is celebrated. At the head temple, Eiheiji, in rural Fukui Prefecture, and its Tokyo branch, Eiheiji Betsuin (also called Chōkokuji), which is one of the official training centers of the Sōtō school, the *Hōon Kōshiki* (Buddhist ceremonial to repay benevolence) is performed. This ritual, belonging to the important liturgical genre of *kōshiki*, is one of the most musical, highly refined rituals of the Sōtō school. Monks sing beautiful, solemn melodies; various musical instruments are played; and offerings of tea, rice, and sweets in red lacquerware are made with highly stylized gestures.

Whereas monks at Eiheiji perform the *Hōon Kōshiki* composed by Menzan Zuihō (1683–1769), one of the most influential reformers of Sōtō Zen in the Tokugawa period, the monks at Eiheiji Betsuin perform the *Shinpen Hōon Kōshiki*, a heavenly revised version of Menzan's *kōshiki*. In this chapter I discuss the latter, which was edited in 2001 by Rev. Imamura Genshū. I will demonstrate the dynamics of founder worship and ritual change and show that the *kōshiki* is an enacted and vocalized form of remembrance.

As *kōshiki* have received little attention in Zen studies so far, I will first introduce their history and structure. This is followed by a brief introduction of *kōshiki* composed in remembrance of Dōgen. Next I will turn to Imamura's *Shinpen Hōon Kōshiki*: studying his intention and the content of the *kōshiki*. I will examine how Dōgen is remembered and venerated and how benevolence and the repaying of benevolence are defined and discuss the characteristics of the *kōshiki*. In the last section I analyze the musical side of the *Shinpen Hōon Kōshiki* in depth.

The Liturgical Genre of Kōshiki
A Brief History of *Kōshiki*

In the late tenth and eleventh centuries, Japanese clerics started to reform the liturgy and developed liturgical genres that were recited in Japanese.[1] This reform was the beginning of a liturgy in the vernacular language that strongly contributed to the spread of Buddhism in all social strata. The most important liturgical genre that developed during that time was *kōshiki*. The *Nijūgo Zanmai Shiki*, composed by the Tendai monk Genshin (942–1017), is acknowledged as the earliest work in this genre. Genshin composed this liturgical text for the monthly *Nijūgo Zanmai E*, a ritual that was performed by twenty-five monks who promised to help each other to attain rebirth in Amida's Pure Land. The *Nijūgo Zanmai Shiki* served as a model for the first *kōshiki* and was later revised as *Rokudō Kōshiki*, which became widely performed.

Approximately one century later the Tendai monk Meiken (1026–98) composed a *Seigan Kōshiki*, and the Sanron monk Yōkan (or Eikan, 1033–1111) composed an *Ōjō Kōshiki* (ca. 1079). The latter is acknowledged as *the* model for later *kōshiki* in terms of its structure. These early works were devoted to Amida Buddha and Pure Land belief. Together with the rise of Pure Land belief, *kōshiki* were performed at a wide variety of sites in many different local areas and became very popular. In the early medieval period, *kōshiki* spread throughout all Buddhist traditions and were composed and performed for a wide range of objects of veneration, such as buddhas, bodhisattvas, kami, eminent monks, sutras, as well as poetry and music. The composition of *kōshiki* reached a highpoint in the late twelfth and early thirteenth centuries with the Hossō monk Jōkei (1155–1213) and the Kegon-Shingon monk Myōe (1173–1232), who were the most prolific authors of *kōshiki*. Currently 372 *kōshiki* are listed in Niels Gülberg's *kōshiki* database, but probably more than 400 were composed.[2]

The history of *kōshiki* in the Sōtō school starts with its founder, Dōgen, who is credited with the composition of the *Rakan Kōshiki*, a *kōshiki* for the Sixteen Arhats.[3] Two fragments of a *Rakan Kōshiki* have survived that are recognized as Dōgen's handwriting and are assigned as national treasures.[4] Interestingly, in the Tokugawa period, when the high point in production of *kōshiki* had long since ended, Sōtō monks still composed or adopted *kōshiki*.

For example, they adopted the *Daruma Kōshiki* attributed to Kakua (1143–?) and Myōe, the *Busshōe Kōshiki* composed by Myōe for the celebration of the Buddha's birthday, and the *Kannon Kōshiki* written by Jōkei. Sōtō monks also composed new *kōshiki*, most of them in remembrance of Japanese Sōtō monks.

The subgenre of *kōshiki* composed in remembrance of eminent monks is called *hōon kōshiki*. Current sources suggest that the first *hōon kōshiki* composed for a Sōtō monk was the *Butsuji Kōshiki* for Keizan Jōkin (1264–1325), the founder of Sōjiji, in the early seventeenth century.[5] Later, *kōshiki* for Dōgen and Gasan Jōseki (1276–1366), the second abbot of Sōjiji, were composed.[6] Interestingly, the last *kōshiki* ever composed was by a Sōtō monk; it was the *Tōjō Dentō Kōshiki*, a *hōon kōshiki* for Keizan, composed by Bukkan Bonjō (?–1906) in Meiji 24 (1891).[7] Still today *kōshiki* continue to play a vital role in Sōtō liturgy. Several are performed annually in the head temples and training monasteries of the Sōtō school, and in some local areas *kōshiki* are performed during elaborate funeral services.

Defining *Kōshiki*

The first character, *kō*, of *kōshiki* describes a lecture that explains a sutra or doctrinal idea in an easily comprehendible manner. This character can also describe a group gathering for a certain purpose. In the case of a *kōshiki*, the character *kō* describes a group of devotees seeking to deepen their understanding and faith. The second character, *shiki*, describes a ceremony or the structure of a ceremony. Accordingly, a *kōshiki* is either a ceremony with a lecture at its center or the structure of this type of ceremony.[8]

Niels Gülberg, the most renowned scholar of *kōshiki*, distinguishes between a narrow and a wide definition of the term. In a narrow sense, a *kōshiki* is simply a text of a certain liturgical form consisting of a pronouncement of intention (*hyōbyaku*), usually an odd number of sections (*dan*), and verses (*kada*). This kind of text can also be called *shikimon* (central text of the ceremony). A central text of the ceremony is composed in *kanbun* (Chinese). The pronouncement of intention and the sections are recited in *kundoku* (Japanese) by the celebrating priest (*shikishi*), whereas the verses of the central text of the ceremony are usually sung in Sino-Japanese by the assembly (*daishū*). However, in a ritual centering on this kind of liturgical text, other texts are also recited. The wide definition of the term *kōshiki* includes all liturgical texts recited as well as the performance itself.[9] In this chapter I use the term *kōshiki* in a wide sense and call the specially composed text (i.e., *kōshiki* in a narrow sense) "the central text of the ceremony."[10]

A Brief History of Kōshiki Composed in Remembrance of Dōgen

The first known example of *kōshiki* composed in remembrance of Dōgen is the *Hokke Kōshiki*, which is attributed to Giun (1253–1333), the fifth abbot of Eiheiji.[11] This *kōshiki* remembers and venerates Dōgen, but the central text of the ceremony does not give an account of Dōgen's life; instead, it praises the *Lotus Sutra* and explains some of its doctrinal concepts. This *kōshiki* was performed in the first half of the eighteenth century during Dōgen's eight-day memorial service at Eiheiji.[12]

In Hōei 4 (1707), two *hōon kōshiki* for Dōgen were composed independently. One was the *Dōgen kōshiki* by the eighteenth abbot of Hōshōji (present-day Yamagata Prefecture), Zuihō Daiki (n.d.).[13] The other was the *Eihei Dōgen Zenji Kōshiki* written by Shōzen (n.d.) of Shinano Province (present-day Nagano Prefecture).[14] Why Daiki and Shōzen composed *kōshiki* in remembrance of Dōgen is unclear. Their compositions might have been inspired by the reform movement to revive the old style of the Sōtō school (*shūtō fukko undō*), lasting from around the middle of the seventeenth century until the middle of the eighteenth. The advocates of this movement intended to return to the old style of Dōgen's Zen. Consequently, Sōtō monks started to intensively study Dōgen's works, especially the *Shōbōgenzō*.

Around fifty years later Menzan Zuihō composed the *Eihei Kaisan Hōon Kōshiki* (hereafter *Hōon Kōshiki*) in commemoration of the 500th memorial year of Dōgen based on the *kōshiki* written by Daiki and Shōzen.[15] In his foreword, dated Hōryaku 3 (1753), he writes:

> The method of the holy one instructs that there are four sorts of kindnesses [*on*]. Three belong to the kindnesses of the world [i.e., the kindnesses of one's parents, of all sentient beings, and of the ruler]. One is the kindness of the dharma. If clerics know the kindness of the dharma, then they are branches and leaves. Earlier officer [Shō-]zen of the province of Shin [i.e., Shinano] and officer [Dai]ki of the province of U [i.e., Dewa] both wrote *Eihei Kōshiki* and these were conducted in the world. Surely, they knew the kindness of the dharma well. But [their] sentences have omissions and there are wrong characters [in their texts]. Further, a revision has not yet appeared. For this reason, the wide performance [of these *kōshiki*] is nearly afire. It is very regrettable.... I wish that [this new *kōshiki*] may become a medium to let novices of the Sōtō school know about the kindness of the patriarch.

This foreword clearly shows that the aim of the *Hōon Kōshiki* was the repaying of benevolence received. The last sentence also suggests that Menzan hoped that the *kōshiki* would serve a pedagogical function and help Sōtō clerics to deepen their understanding of Dōgen's virtue. Menzan's *Hōon Kōshiki* became the most widely circulated *hōon kōshiki* in the Sōtō school. In Meiji 14 (1881) Ōuchi Seiran (1845–1918), one of the most influential Buddhists during the Meiji era, slightly revised the *Hōon Kōshiki*. It remained one of the rituals performed during Dōgen's memorial service; however, through Western influence, birthday celebrations for the two patriarchs became important observances in the Sōtō liturgy, and since Meiji 33 (1900) all Sōtō temples celebrate the birthdays of Dōgen and Keizan.[16] As a result the *Hōon Kōshiki* was not performed during Dōgen's memorial service but during his birthday celebration.

Imamura Genshū's Shinpen Hōon Kōshiki
The Background of the New Edition

As recently as 2001 Rev. Imamura Genshū, the *tantō rōshi* of Eiheiji Betsuin in Tokyo at that time, revised Menzan's *Hōon Kōshiki* for the 750th memorial service for Dōgen, which was commemorated in 2002. Explanatory notes to the new edition illuminate Imamura's intentions. He writes:

> I think that Menzan's *kōshiki* and the *Teiho Kenzeiki*, which was published a year later, were made for a similar purpose. In other words, they were praises for the 500th memorial of the great ancestor and intended to repay the benevolence received. Thereafter, this *kōshiki* was mainly performed at the head temple [Eiheiji].... My intention is in line with the above-mentioned repaying of benevolence. However, this time I changed the central text of the ceremony into Japanese while respecting the traditional epic style of *kanbun* [Chinese]. I adopted older sources and trustworthy biographical sources of Zen master Dōgen such as the *Sanso Gyōgōki*, *Kenzeiki* (*Meishū* and *Zuichō* manuscripts) and *Goyuigon Kiroku* and so revised all sections of the old text. I thought that the structure of the fifth section needed to be completely revised. I considered an approach that addresses the human rights problem of our school and [therefore] avoided ornamentations concerning a particularly beautiful descent and honorary titles. I also left out obscure accounts and deeds.[17]

These notes give us important insights into the background of Imamura's edition. He briefly explains the history of the *Hōon Kōshiki* for Dōgen and states that his intention is the same as Menzan's: the repaying of the benevolence received. Imamura tried to adopt the *kōshiki* to contemporary historical circumstances and new insights about Dōgen's life. Usually the central text of the ceremony is written in *kanbun* but recited in Japanese. Imamura wrote the text in Japanese, presumably so it would be more easily understood by a wide audience as well as for convenience during the performance. However, he wrote it in the traditional style of how a *kanbun* text is read in Japanese; thus, during the actual performance a listener would not hear any difference.

He also changed the content of the central text of the ceremony. Menzan's *Hōon Kōshiki* was based on his edition of the *Kenzeiki*, the *Teiho Kenzeiki*. Until 1975 this edition was the only widely available edition of the influential Dōgen biography *Kenzeiki*, and all modern biographies of Dōgen were based on Menzan's edition. However, in 1975 Kawamura Kōdō published typographical reprints of six editions of the *Kenzeiki*, including medieval manuscripts.[18] This publication clearly shows that the *Teiho Kenzeiki* departs from medieval manuscripts and that Menzan had added many new accounts. Thus we now know that Menzan's *Teiho Kenzeiki* has to be considered carefully. As Bodiford wrote, "In remembering Dōgen, the time is ripe for someone to write a new, more accurate biography of Dōgen, one that sorts out what can be known and what was only remembered or invented by Menzan Zuihō and the artists of the illustrated version of Kenzei's chronicle."[19]

Imamura seems to have felt the need to sort out Menzan's additions to Dōgen's biography and therefore changed the central text of the ceremony based on older biographical texts, especially two medieval manuscripts of the *Kenzeiki*, the Meishū manuscript written in Tenbun 7 (1538) and the Zuichō manuscript written in Tenshō 17 (1589). Additionally, he consulted the *Sanso Gyōgōki*, a hagiographical work containing biographies of the first three abbots of Eiheiji, which was compiled before 1400 and is one of the oldest sources on Dōgen's life, and the *Goyuigon Kiroku*, which is said to have been compiled by Tettsū Gikai (1219–1309). This shows that the biographical image of eminent monks is fluid, and when research of scholars or scholar-monks yields new results, clerics try to establish the new insights in the collective memory.

Imamura mentions that he omitted honorary titles and avoided ornamentation of Dōgen's descent because of the human rights problem of the Sōtō school. Imamura refers here to the movement in the Sōtō school to end discriminatory practices. This movement was a reaction to the so-called Machida affair of 1979. At the Third World Conference on Religion and Peace, Rev.

Machida Muneo, the president of the headquarters of the Sōtō school at that time, declared that there would be no discrimination against members of "outcast groups" in Japan anymore. However, in the 1970s members of the *burakumin* still received discriminatory posthumous names (*sabetsu kaimyō*). Companies let private investigators check temple registers for the background of prospective executives in order to avoid hiring a member of a former "outcast" family.

Therefore, members of the Buraku Liberation League strongly protested after Rev. Machida's speech and openly denounced various discriminatory practices of the Sōtō school. In response the Sōtō school established a Human Rights Division, which initiated academic study on human rights in the Sōtō tradition and actions against discriminatory practices, such as the changing of discriminatory posthumous names given to *burakumin* and the exchange of the gravestones on which these names were engraved. Based on this tense background, Imamura decided to omit the posthumous names bestowed upon Dōgen when he edited the *Hōon Kōshiki* in 2001.[20] In a conversation, Imamura further said that Dōgen would have disliked worldly affairs, and therefore he omitted the honorary titles.

These three points show that Imamura's intention reflects contemporary issues and new scholarly insights. It further shows that *kōshiki* are neither a "relic" nor static; rather, *hōon kōshiki* continue to be adapted to the viewpoints of contemporary clerics.

The Central Text of the Ceremony

A close comparison of the central text of the ceremony of Menzan's *Hōon Kōshiki* with Imamura's *Shinpen Hōon Kōshiki* shows that both differ to a high degree.[21] Imamura used Menzan's structure of the central text of the ceremony and maintained the topics of the first four sections but changed their particular content. He further changed the content of the fifth section completely, as he indicated in his explanatory notes.

As was customary, the central text of the ceremony starts with a pronouncement of intention, which addresses the three treasures, all buddha patriarchs, and Dōgen. The text continues with a brief explanation of the transmission of the dharma, ending with a description of how Dōgen went to China, understood "the great matter of one's life" under Rujing (1162–1228), and then transmitted the true dharma to Japan. Then the text declares:

> Fortunately, we are connected by the blood [lineage] as dharma grandchildren. We should do our best to unendlessly repay [Dōgen's mercy].

Therefore, we now respectfully welcome the time of the 750th memorial service, and together with the pure monks of the whole mountain we offer humble offerings, devoting [our] faithful sincere heart we praise the deeds of [his] life and so answer the mercy received.

This paragraph explicitly states the intention of the ritual: to repay the benevolence received. The response to the benevolence received is described as the performance of the memorial service, the making of offerings, and the praising of Dōgen's deeds. Thus the ritual serves as a means to repay the benevolence received.

After the pronouncement of intention, five sections follow. The first section covers Dōgen's life from his birth until his entry into clergy. It starts as follows:

First, I will illuminate the gate of the birth and the leaving of the household. The master was of a son of a Koga, who was a descendant in the eighth generation of the Murakami Genji clan. When his mother was pregnant, there was a voice in the air, which said, "This child is a great holy sage who will have no equal in the next 500 years. He will be born and comes in order to bring the true teaching in Japan to prosperity." Then in Shōji 2 [1200] he was soon born. A wise man told his fortunes and said: "The seven places of his body [i.e., the two hands, two feet, two shoulders, and neck] are graceful, and he has deep eye pupils. The shape of his skull is rarely excellent. Common children are different. He is surely a holy child. However, perhaps his mother will not have a long life."

The first section thus explains that Dōgen was destined to become a holy man, and prior to his birth auspicious signs were seen. Imamura did not dwell on Dōgen's descent as a child of the Fujiwara family, as Menzan does. He mentions only that Dōgen's father was a Koga in the eighth generation, but he does not state the father's full name. The sources do not agree on who Dōgen's father was: medieval manuscripts of the *Kenzeiki*, the *Sanso Gyōgōki*, and Keizan's *Denkōroku* suggest that it was Koga Michitomo (1171–1227); the *Teiho Kenzeiki* suggests that it was Koga Michichika (1149–1202).[22] Thus Imamura avoided taking a stance on this issue.

The text then states that Dōgen was a highly gifted boy who read poetry collections and Confucian texts at a very young age. "In the winter of Jōgen 1 [1211], [his] mother passed away. When he saw the smoke of the incense he understood the impermanence of the world, and his great wish to deeply seek the dharma stood firm." The section explains Dōgen went to Hieizan when he was thirteen and was ordained one year later. The first section ends as follows:

> Because of karmic causes, we have now gratefully become dharma grandchildren. Eternally you should arise the great vow [to save sentient beings] that we have received. Therefore, you should intone a verse and perform a prostration. We sing a verse:
>
> > *Because of the final admonition and the kindness of his mother*
> > *He left the laity and rejected the honors of this world.*
> > *In his last incarnation*
> > *He left the household and realized the Buddha way.*
> > *Humbly prostrating we take refuge in the Great Ancestor [Kōso], the great venerable Dōgen.*

As in the subsequent sections, at "We sing a verse" the recitation of the celebrating priest ends. The cantor sings the first line of the verse solo, then all monks join the chanting. After the phrase "Humbly prostrating," which is chanted after each verse, the monks perform one prostration. Imamura maintains the verse of Menzan's *kōshiki*, a verse originally taken from the *Lotus Sutra*,[23] but changes "when the Buddha became a prince" in the first line to "because of the final admonition and the kindness of his mother" and so adjusted the verse to the content of the *kōshiki*.

The second section covers Dōgen's early years as a monk at Hieizan and Kenninji as well as his travel to China. It starts as follows:

> Second, I explain the gate of the entering of Song and the dharma transmission. After being ordained, the master intensively practiced the esoteric and exoteric essential teachings of the principles of the great and small vehicles. At the age of eighteen, he read the complete Buddhist canon twice. "The main principle of Tendai is that all [sentient beings] originally share the dharma nature and naturally have the body of self-nature," he went to ask Kōin of Mii[dera], a famous master of exoteric and esoteric doctrines, and [further] inquired, "If it is like this, why do all Buddhas make up their mind to reach perfect enlightenment and practice?" [Kō]in said, "This is easily asked, but cannot be answered. It is the profound teaching of our school, but I have not exhausted its meaning. I have heard that the correct doctrine that transmits the seal of the Buddha-mind exists in the great country of the Song. You should soon enter Song and seek [there]."

The *Shinpen Hōon Kōshiki* describes how Dōgen went to Kenninji and studied under Myōzen (1184–1225). Then Dōgen traveled to China with Myōzen in Jōō 2 (1223) and visited many famous masters. Because he was deeply disappointed by Chinese masters he considered returning to Japan. But then he met an elderly monk who told him about Rujing, who would be a truly awakened Zen master. Therefore, Dōgen went to see Rujing and started to intensively practice under him. The text continues:

> [When master Rujing] blamed a dosing monk and said: "Studying Zen is to let go of body and mind. Why do you only sleep?" The master [i.e., Dōgen] heard this and suddenly awakened. In the early morning, he entered the abbot's quarters, burned incense and performed prostrations. Master [Ru]jing asked, "Why do you burn incense?" The master said, "Body and mind have dropped off." Master [Ru]jing said, "Body and mind drop off, dropped off body and mind." The master said, "This is a temporal ability. Venerable master, you should not approve me without reason." Master [Ru]jing said, "I do not approve you without reason." The master said, "Why are you not approving me without reason?" Master [Ru]jing said, "Body and mind dropped off." Finally, the great matter of the Buddha dharma was transmitted.

Thus the second section describes in detail how Dōgen reached enlightenment under Rujing and how Rujing approved Dōgen. In this way the *kōshiki* legitimizes Dōgen and the Sōtō tradition as well as the performing clerics, who are described as standing in direct transmission of Dōgen's lineage throughout the *kōshiki*.

Afterward the focus changes and the assembly is addressed again:

> The later born descendants tasted the sublime dharma of the direct transmission of the great ancestor and every one should carry out the great practice in the same way. To follow the old style of the great ancestor is the same as to adore the past of the honorable Sakyamuni. To exert oneself in zazen and practice no-thinking are ways to repay the kindness of the dharma. For now, you should intone a verse and perform a prostration. We sing a verse:

> > *Because he longed for the correct teaching,*
> > *Body and mind were never tired.*
> > *For the sake of sentient beings*
> > *He expressed the profound meaning.*

Imamura again uses the verse of Menzan's *Hōon Kōshiki* but slightly changes it. This verse was originally taken from the *Lotus Sutra*.[24]

The third section describes Dōgen's return to Japan and the time until his move to Eichizen. It starts as follows:

> Third, I explain the gate of the return to the West and the propagation. When he told master [Ru]jing in 1227 that he would depart, master [Ru-]jing said, "After returning to your country do not stay close to kings and ministers. Do not live in villages and towns. Dwell in deep mountains and deep valleys. You do not need people of leisure who assemble like clouds. Many worthless are in reality not different from just a few. Select true followers of the way and make them your companions. If you obtain only one person or even half a person, the wisdom of the Buddha patriarchs will continue to be transmitted and you will raise the style of the house of the old Buddha." Then he gave [Dōgen] the monk's robe of Furong Daokai [1043–1118].

Interestingly, the *kōshiki* states that Rujing advised Dōgen to transmit the dharma to at least one person so that the dharma would continue to flourish. Then Rujing presented Dōgen with a robe. In the Zen schools a robe has traditionally been given to a dharma heir as an indicator of the correct dharma transmission; likewise, here it indicates the correct transmission of the dharma to Dōgen.

The *kōshiki* continues describing how Dōgen returned to Japan, and after staying at Kenninji he moved to Fukakusa to open a Zen temple. The text mentions that Dōgen wrote "Bendōwa," *Fukanzazengi*, and *Shōbōgenzō* and so elucidated the correct teaching of zazen, which the *kōshiki* describes as *the* central practice promoted by Dōgen. After ten years Dōgen is supposed to have remembered Rujing's instructions and decided to move to Eichizen to open a new temple, the future Eiheiji. The section concludes by addressing the monks of the assembly, stating that "the distant grandchildren fortunately bathe in this wave of kindness" and should therefore intone a verse and perform a prostration. This verse asks Dōgen to "turn the wheel of the dharma" and so save all suffering beings. Thus the verse suggests that Dōgen fully embodied the Mahayana ideal of a bodhisattva. Again Imamura maintains the verse of Menzan's *Hōon Kōshiki* but slightly changes it. This verse was also taken from the *Lotus Sutra*, and, as in the preceding sections, Menzan quoted it as exactly as in the sutra.[25]

The fourth section explains the transmission of the dharma. It starts by briefly describing how the dharma was transmitted from Bodhidharma to

Huike (487–593), and later from the fifth patriarch Hongren (601–74) to the sixth patriarch Huineng (638–713). Then the narration jumps to Dōgen and his disciples. More than half of the section explains Ejō's (1198–1280) career as a monk and his relation to Dōgen. Finally, the text lists the major disciples of Ejō, among them Keizan. In this way, the *kōshiki* explains how Dōgen's lineage was transmitted after his death. The section ends by changing the focus to the participants, addressing them as follows: "Now in this meeting, there is not a single person who is not a dharma grandchild of the great ancestor. Why should we not have the wish to repay the great mercy? Therefore, we should sing a verse and perform prostrations. We sing a verse." The following verse states that the number of clerics who have received the dharma transmission is uncountable as the dharma gate is wide. Here Imamura adopts and slightly changes the verse from the fifth section of Menzan's *Hōon Kōshiki*, again a verse from the *Lotus Sutra*.[26]

The fifth section covers Dōgen's final months in detail. It starts by describing how Dōgen became ill and in the first month of Kenchō 5 (1253) wrote "Hachidainingaku," his last chapter of the *Shōbōgenzō*. Imamura quotes the last paragraph of this chapter, which emphasizes the rarity of meeting the Buddha dharma and admonishes readers to develop the supreme truth of the bodhi and to instruct all sentient beings. When Dōgen's condition became critical, he went to the capital, where he passed away at midnight on the twenty-eighth day of the eighth month of Kenchō 5 (1253). The text then describes Ejō's sorrow and that Dōgen's relics were enshrined in a stupa at Eiheiji. The sections ends as follows:

Now, for 750 years the moon and the stars have moved and the world has changed, but the light of [Dōgen's] virtue increasingly shines brightly, around 10,000 dharma descendants fill the school. If [we] adore the remaining style of the great master day for day and practice day after day, the dharma body of the great master eternally exists and will not be extinguished. We wish to be protected by the buddhas and bodhisattvas of the true compassion of the Buddha and the patriarchs of the back of the great mirror, we raise the will to adore the old way of the Buddha patriarchs. Now, you should sing a verse and perform prostrations. We sing a verse:

> *The pure dharma body of the great master*
> *Exists here for eternity,*
> *If descendants practice zazen*
> *And thoroughly realize the bodhisattva way.*

As we have seen, the central text of the ceremony offers a sacred biography of Dōgen. This text is not an ordinary biography that was composed to be read in private; rather, it is recited by a celebrating priest during the performance of a ritual and is divided into sections interrupted by verses and prostrations performed by the assembly. The biography explains why Dōgen deserves veneration. The last paragraph of every section praises Dōgen, and the last sentence asks the monks to pay respect to Dōgen, sing a verse, and perform a prostration. The last sentences of each section therefore function as intermediate passages between the recitation of the sacred biography by the celebrating priest and the singing of the verses by the assembly. In this way, the narration of the sacred biography and the founder worship are completely intertwined.

After each verse, words of worship are sung and the monks perform a prostration. Thus the monks do not only praise Dōgen with their voices; they also embody their veneration by performing prostrations. Stanley Tambiah has argued that in rituals a message is transmitted simultaneously on different channels.[27] Likewise the veneration of Dōgen is conveyed by the chanting and the prostrations after each verse, and so two different channels are used: the voice and the body.

Through participation in the *kōshiki* the monks can remember and assure their own lineage. The pronouncement of intention as well as the second and fourth sections explain the dharma lineage. The performing monks are further addressed as Dōgen's dharma grandchildren. In this way, the *kōshiki* helps to make bonds stronger through the narration of the biography and through the communal performance of a ritual. Menzan's *Hōon Kōshiki* and Imamura's revision were both written when the Sōtō school was already well established—in contrast to the widely performed *Hōon Kōshiki* for Shinran (1173–1263) composed by Kakunyo (1270–1351) in Einin 2 (1294), which helped to form a district community of Jōdo-shin followers in the early stages of the school.[28] Nevertheless the *Hōon Kōshiki* for Dōgen also served to remember the tradition and raise the consciousness of the monks.

Interestingly, the last section emphasizes that the monks can repay the kindness they have received by practicing and that Dōgen will eternally live in this world if the monks practice zazen and realize the Buddha way. The second section also states, "To exert oneself in zazen and practice no-thinking are ways to repay the kindness of the dharma." Similarly, the *Hōon Kōshiki* for Shinran "situates the ritual participant in a relation of indebtedness, which can only be responded to through the practice of the *nembutsu* and faith."[29] Thus both *kōshiki* ask the ritual participants to respond with the practice recognized as central to the respective tradition: *nembutsu* for the Jōdo-shin school and zazen for the Sōtō school.

The Shinpen Hōon Kōshiki as Vocalized Founder Worship

The most important aspect in the performance of *kōshiki* is *shōmyō* (Japanese Buddhist chant). Music is a key component to the power of any ritual, and thus *shōmyō* has a long history in Japanese Buddhism. Already in the early stages of the introduction of Buddhism to Japan, Buddhist music was transmitted to Japan together with Buddhist doctrines and practices, first from the Korean kingdoms and later from China, and various styles of vocal and instrumental musical styles were introduced.[30] Buddhist ceremonies are not only colorful rituals but also offer a form of entertainment to the participants. The records of the eye-opening ceremony of the Great Buddha at Tōdaiji in Tenpyō 17 (752) give a lively picture of Buddhist music and report that more than 10,000 monks sang Buddhist chants, among them the *Shika Hōyō* (Four *Shōmyō* Melodies), which became a central part of the shared repertoire of Japanese Buddhist chants and are still performed today, also in Sōtō *kōshiki*. In Buddhist rituals the vocalization of texts is an essential part of the ritual; therefore, *shōmyō* has been an integral subject of the monastic curriculum in all Buddhist schools.

To aid memorization as well as to transmit the melodies more easily, Japanese monks invented musical notation systems for *shōmyō* (*hakase*); the earliest extant examples date from the eleventh century.[31] Sōtō monks have used musical notation since at least the medieval period. We find the oldest extant musical notation of Sōtō *shōmyō* in the Rinkō manuscript of the *Keizan shingi*, which was copied in Meiō 1 (1501).[32] Many later *kōshiki* handbooks with musical notation have been discovered, suggesting that Sōtō clerics were highly trained singers. The *Hōon Kōshiki* for Dōgen is a highly musical ritual, and all pieces sung by the assembly are notated with musical notation (see Figure 8.1).

Imamura wanted to produce a CD of the *Shinpen Hōon Kōshiki* to preserve the melodies for future generations, which would be important as the musical notation of the Sōtō school is not as exact as the one for *gagaku* or Tendai and Shinbone *shōmyō*, and so the melodies can easily be changed.[33] The CD was recorded in November and December 2001 in order to be released in time for the 750th memorial service for Dōgen. Along with a few priests, thirty-two monks, mainly from Eiheiji Betsuin, participated in the recording (Figure 8.2).

The CD was submitted to a performing arts competition organized by the Ministry of Cultural Affairs, but unfortunately it was not selected as one of the winners. Nevertheless that Sōtō monks participated in the competition reflects the monks' stance toward their musical tradition; they highly value

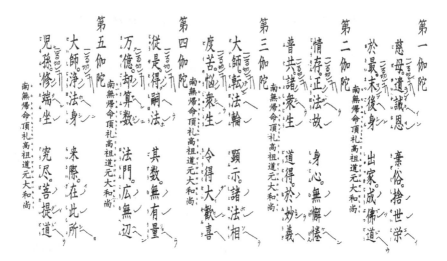

第一伽陀
慈母遺訓恩
於最末後身
南無帰命頂礼高祖道元大和尚
棄俗。捨世栄。
出家。成佛道。

第二伽陀
情存正法故
普共諸衆生
南無帰命頂礼高祖道元大和尚
身心。無懈惓
道得。於妙義

第三伽陀
大師転法輪
度苦悩衆生
南無帰命頂礼高祖道元大和尚
顕示。諸法相
令得大歓喜

第四伽陀
従是。得嗣法
万億。却算数
南無帰命頂礼高祖道元大和尚
其数無有量
法門広無辺

第五伽陀
大師。浄法身
児孫修端坐
南無帰命頂礼高祖道元大和尚
来際。在此所
究尽菩提道

FIGURE 8.1 *Shinpen Hōon Kōshiki*. Musical notation of the verses of the central text of the ceremony used at Eiheiji Betsuin. (The lines next to the characters indicate melodic movements.) Reprinted with permission.

FIGURE 8.2 Cover of the CD *Shinpen Hōon Kōshiki*. Reprinted with permission.

their *shōmyō* tradition and consider it an important style of Japanese traditional music. The liner notes underscore this standpoint. A note on the cover
by Nomura Yoshio, a renowned musicologist, claims that "the origin of the
marvelousness of Japanese music is the music of Zen, especially of one of
the Sōtō school." In the booklet the producer of the CD, Hashimoto Yūji,
expresses his hope that the CD will help to promote Sōtō *shōmyō* to a wider
audience and that the CD will become an indispensable resource for research
on traditional Japanese music.[34]

The CD of the *Shinpen Hōon Kōshiki* reflects the manifold musical landscape of *kōshiki* as the various pieces belong to different styles of *shōmyō*. In
the following, I will describe the performance of the *Shinpen Hōon Kōshiki*
based on the recording of the CD and my own fieldwork at Eiheiji Betsuin.[35]

The monks are called together by the playing of the *tenshō*, a hanging bell
that is played with a wooden stick. When the monks have assembled in the
hattō, the dharma hall, standing in two rows in the back of the hall facing each
other, the cantor (*kada* or *ino*) leaves the hall to invite the celebrating priest
to join them. He returns with the two assistants of the celebrating priest sol-
emnly ushering in the priest himself. They take their place in the two rows,
and all monks bow twice and enter the central area of the hall in a formal way.
When all monks stand at their assigned place in the main area of the hall, the
cantor plays a hand bell (*inkin*), which is a small sounding bowl on a stick, to
coordinate three prostrations of the monks.

Then the first chant follows. It is the *Song of Falling Flowers* (*Sange no Ge*):

> *Falling flowers decorate all ten directions.*
> *We scatter many precious flowers forming a curtain (chō).[36]*
> *We scatter many precious flowers in all ten directions*
> *And offer [these] to all Tathagatas.[37]*

The cantor plays a singing bowl (*keisu*) three times normally and once muted.
Then he sings the first line of the verse solo, adding long melodic lines to
some tones. The assembly joins the chanting, and at the end of each line the
monks sing melodic patterns. At the beginning of each line the cantor plays
the singing bowl once. As George Tanabe noted, "chanting often produces
sounds that cannot be recognized as a regular spoken language. The Heart
Sutra (*Prajnaparamitahrdaya-sutra*), for example, is popular in East Asia as a
Chinese text about emptiness, a fundamental Mahayana teaching, but when
it is chanted in Japan, each Chinese character is given a Japanese pronunciation without any change in the Chinese grammatical word order of the text.
The audible result is neither Japanese nor Chinese, but a ritual language unto

itself."[38] This can also be said of the *Song of Falling Flowers*, which is chanted in Sino-Japanese pronunciation in Chinese word order. During this chant three monks circumambulate the hall, sprinkle water, scatter flowers, and burn incense. The water is to clean the hall, the flowers to decorate the room, and the fragrance of incense to attract buddhas, bodhisattvas, and other deities.

Next comes the *zenbun* (introductory part) and the *chūbun* (middle part) of an instrumental play of cymbals (*hatsu* or *hachi*) and a small gong (*nyo*). The cymbals are played by two monks, who also lead the subsequent chanting. The cymbals are played in rhythmic patterns of long and short tones interrupted by the gong, which is played by the cantor. This instrumental play forms an introduction for the *Praise of the Four Wisdoms* (*Shichisan*), one of the oldest pieces of the Japanese *shōmyō* tradition, which was probably transmitted from China to Japan in the beginning of the ninth century. The *Praise of the Four Wisdoms* was originally a *sloka*, a Sanskrit verse consisting of two sixteen-syllable lines. The four wisdoms are the wisdom that reflects all phenomenal things as they are, the wisdom of observing the ultimate sameness of everything, the wisdom of discerning the distinctive features of all phenomena, and the wisdom of accomplishing what is to be done to benefit sentient beings.

In the *Praise of the Four Wisdoms* the four wisdoms are praised by invoking the names of the four directional bodhisattvas: Vajrasattva (east), Vajraratnah (south), Vajradharma (west), and Vajrakarma (north). Vajrasattva represents the wisdom that reflects all phenomenal things as they are; Vajraratnah represents the wisdom of observing the ultimate sameness of everything; Vajradharma represents the wisdom of discerning the distinctive features of all phenomena; and Vajrakarma represents the wisdom of accomplishing what is to be done to benefit sentient beings.[39] Through the invocation of the four directional bodhisattvas, a sacred space like a mandala is established, and the four directional bodhisattvas are thought to protect the room during the following ritual sequences. However, my fieldwork suggests that most Zen priests do not reflect on the meaning of their chants; rather, they "just sing," similar to their zazen practice of *shikantaza* (just sitting).[40] Because the text of the *Praise of the Four Wisdoms* is a transliteration and not a translation of the original Sanskrit mantra, the monks cannot understand the text when reading it. For them the text gains its meaning through the use of a sacred language. This chant differs from the previous chant to a high degree. Each syllable is sung several times on the same tone, each ending with a short pause; often the melody drops in glissando fashion when a syllable is sung for the last time. Occasionally a short melodic pattern is inserted. After the chanting, the cymbals and the gong are played again, offering a finale to the chant (Figure 8.3).

The third liturgical chant is the offertory declaration (*saimon*), which one monk recites solo. The offertory declaration of the *Shinpen Hōon Kōshiki*

FIGURE 8.3 Monks performing the *Praise of the Four Wisdoms* (*Shinpen Hōon Kōshiki*) at Eiheiji Betsuin, 2012. Photograph by Michaela Mross.

praises Dōgen and invites him to come to the ceremonial place. The fourth chant is the *sōrai no ge*, the communal obeisance. The cantor sings the first line, and then the assembly enters the chanting in unison:

> *The nature of us who worship and of the buddhas who are*
>   *worshiped is empty.*
> *The essence of us and of the others [i.e., the buddha patriarchs]*
>   *is not different.*
> *May we together with all sentient beings embody liberation,*
> *Give rise to the supreme aspiration to reach enlightenment and*
>   *return to the ultimate truth.*[41]

This verse is sung in a style similar to the opening *Song of Falling Flowers* and uses the same melodic patterns. During this chant the sounding bowl is played again to indicate the beginning of every line. After the chanting the hand bell is played in a prescribed way to signal prostrations.

The next ritual sequence is the *Shika Hōyō*. It functions as a symbolic feast for all attending: the object(s) of veneration, monks, nuns, and lay believers. This ritual sequence consists of four pieces. The first is a praise of the Buddha, entitled *Praise of the Thus Come One* (*Nyoraibai*). It is a highly melismatic chant and the most difficult piece of the Sōtō *shōmyō* repertoire. Therefore the two novice monks who are responsible for singing this chant need to intensively practice it. Its short text is: "Hail, Thus Come One, the marvelous!"[42] One of the two monks plays the hand bell three times before both sing *on nyo ra-i* in a soft voice, then the hand bell is played once, and with a strong voice the monks start singing many melismas on *me*; staccato tones, glissandi, and large vibratos interchange and build a dramatic, breathtaking performance.

After the *Praise of the Thus Come One*, the three pieces *Song of Falling Flowers*,[43] *Song of Sanskrit* (*Bonnon no Ge*), and *Song of the Shakujō* (*Shakujō no Ge*) are sung. The *Song of Falling Flowers* praises Sakyamuni and explains that the ritual participants offer incense and flowers to him. The *Song of Sanskrit* declares that the participants offer flowers to Sakyamuni and all bodhisattvas. The *Song of the Shakujō* describes how clerics dedicate themselves to Buddhist practice holding priest staffs in their hands. For each chant, one monk is in charge of singing certain lines solo and so leads the chanting. The three chants form a unity and are sung with similar melodies. During the last piece a *shakujō* is played by the monk leading the *Song of the Shakujō*. The *shakujō* is a priest staff on whose upper end six metal rings are attached. When it is shaken or hit on the ground it makes a metallic sound. The monks of Eiheiji Betsuin sing these chants slower than in other Sōtō temples, giving the song dignity and solemnity.

All these *shōmyō* pieces, from the opening *Song of Falling Flowers* to the *Song of the Shakujō*, constitute the preparatory ritual sequences for the central section of the *kōshiki*, the central text of the ceremony (Figure 8.4). It is divided into five sections, which the celebrating priest recites; after each section, the cantor sings the first line of a verse solo, and then the assembly joins the chanting. The melodic patterns of the verses are again nearly the same as in the opening *Song of Falling Flowers*. The central text of the ceremony is the longest text of the ritual; including the verses, its full performance takes around forty minutes. On the CD the complete central text of the ceremony is recorded, but during the actual performance this text is abbreviated, and only three of the five sections are recited in order to shorten the time needed to perform the ritual. Despite this abbreviation, the performance of the *kōshiki* still takes around two hours.

The ceremony closes with the *Universal Transfer of Merit* (*Fuekō*):

> *We wish that this merit*
> *Extends universally to all.*
> *May we and all sentient beings*
> *Together realize the Buddha way.*[44]
> *We take refuge in the dharma realm of self and others.*
>   *May we equally benefit.*

FIGURE 8.4 The celebrating priest recites the central text of ceremony. *Shinpen Hōon Kōshiki* at Eiheiji Betsuin, 2012. Photograph by Michaela Mross.

In many rituals this verse is recited to transfer the merit that is thought to have accumulated through the performance of the ritual. The cantor also leads this chant, which is sung with the same melodic patterns as the opening *Song of the Falling Flowers*. During this chant the sounding bowl is played again at the beginning of each line. The last line is sung by the cantor alone and ends with a tremolo between two tones getting softer and softer and so concludes the ritual in a calm mood. The monks perform three prostrations synchronized by the playing of the hand bell and then leave the hall.

The *Shinpen Hōon Kōshiki* is foremost a monastic ritual performed by the monks to celebrate the birthday of Dōgen. During my fieldwork at Eiheiji Betsuin, only three to four lay believers, if any, attended this elaborate ritual. However, as the doors of the dharma hall are widely open in the afternoon, when the *kōshiki* is performed, occasionally lay people do step into the hall, which offers a green oasis in downtown Tokyo, for a brief prayer; most of them are taken in by the ritual and stay for a while listening to the singing of the monks.

As we have seen, *kōshiki* are highly musical rituals that offer a colorful sonic landscape. Various musical instruments are played, but these are not used to accompany the singing. They "only" signal the start of a line in order to coordinate the singing of the monks or synchronize ritual actions. *Kōshiki* are vocal music. The monks learn to sing *shōmyō* pieces during their monastic training, and before the performance of a *kōshiki* they intensively practice. The music adds to the aesthetics of the ritual and offers the performing monks the enjoyment of singing in a "choir." In the case of the *Shinpen Hōon Kōshiki*, the music is a medium to express veneration to Dōgen and to remember him. In this way, the *kōshiki* is a vocalized form of remembrance.

Concluding Remarks

The *Shinpen Hōon Kōshiki* shows that the remembrance of eminent monks is influenced by the work of scholars or scholar-monks. As research yields new results on the life of an eminent monk, new biographies are written, and consequently monks feel the need to revise liturgical texts that narrate his sacred biography. Imamura's revision shows that rituals are not fixed or static; rather, they are molded by a changing tradition. These new liturgical texts shape the tradition and the collective memory of the school. Being aware of the discrepancy between the scholarly knowledge of Dōgen's life and Menzan's works, Imamura hoped that his new edition would also replace Menzan's *Hōon Kōshiki* at Eiheiji. However, to his disappointment, the monks of Eiheiji have not yet adopted the *Shinpen Hōon Kōshiki*.[45] It will be interesting to see whether they decide to perform this new version in the coming years.

This chapter has further aimed to illuminate a previously overlooked facet of the Zen tradition: *shōmyō*. *Shōmyō* is essential to our understanding of Zen as a "lived religion" because music is an integral part of the monastic training and clerics can be considered highly trained singers. The liturgical text of the *Shinpen Hōon Kōshiki* is brought to life through its vocalization, and during the performance of the ritual the vocalization expresses remembrance of Dōgen. We can therefore interpret the *Shinpen Hōon Kōshiki* as a vocalized remembrance of Dōgen.

The *Shinpen Hōon Kōshiki* for Dōgen is just one of several *kōshiki* performed annually at the head and training temples of the Sōtō school; in some local areas *kōshiki* are performed during elaborate funeral services, and new rituals are created using liturgical chants traditionally vocalized during *kōshiki*. Hence *kōshiki* continue to play a vital role in contemporary Sōtō Zen and hint at a long tradition—a tradition that originated with Dōgen himself.

NOTES

1. This historical outline is based on Yamada Shōzen, *"Kōshiki*: Sono Seiritsu to Tenkai,"* in Ito Hiroyuki et al., eds., *Bukkyō Bungaku Kōza 8: Shōdō no Bungaku* (Tokyo: Benseisha, 1995), 11–53; Niels Gülberg, *Buddhistische Zeremoniale (kōshiki) und ihre Bedeutung für die Literatur des japanischen Mittelalters* (Stuttgart: Steiner, 1999).

2. Niels Guelberg, Kōshiki Database, 1997, http://www.f.waseda.jp/guelberg/ koshiki/kdb/main/kousiki.htm (accessed February 15, 2014).

3. For an in-depth study of the historical development of *kōshiki* in Sōtō Zen, see Michaela Mross, "A Local History of Buddhist Rituals in Japan: *Kōshiki* at the Sōtō Zen Temple Sōjiji from the Seventeenth through Nineteenth Centuries," PhD diss., LMU Munich, 2013. For a detailed study of the *Rakan Kōshiki*, see Kirino Kōgaku, "Dōgen Zenji to Rakan Kuyō: Dōgen Zenji Sen *Rakan Kuyō Shikimon* Saikō," *Shūgaku Kenkyū Kiyō* 15 (2002): 61–95; Michaela Mross, "Das *Rakan Kōshiki* der Sōtō-Schule: Übersetzung und Analyze eines liturgischen Textes," MA thesis, University of Hamburg, 2007. For English translations of this liturgical text, see Marinus Willem de Visser, *The Arhats in China and Japan* (Berlin: Oesterheld, 1923), 182–96; Ichimura Shohei, trans., *Zen Master Keizan's Monastic Regulations* (Yokohama: Sōjiji, 1994), 145–83.

4. Archives of Daijōji (Kanazawa) and Zenkyūin (Toyohashi). For a typographical reprint, see DZZ-2 7:288–95. Facsimiles of these manuscripts are included in Daihonzan Eiheijinai Eihei Shōbōgenzō Shūsho Taisei Kankōkai, ed., *Dōgen Zenji Shinseki Kankei Shiryōshū* (Tokyo: Taishūkan shoten, 1980), 225–37.

5. For a study of the *Butsuji Kōshiki*, see Ozaki Shōzen, *"Butsuji Kōshiki* ni tsuite," *Shūgaku kenkyū* 41 (1999): 115–20; Michaela Mross, "Sōtōshū no *Hōon Kōshiki* ni Kansuru Kōsatsu: *Butsuji Kōshiki* to *Tōjō Dentō Kōshiki* ni tsuite," *Indogaku Bukkyōgaku Kenkyū* 58.2 (2010): 166–69; Mross, "A Local History," chapters 6, 8.

6. On the *Gasan Kōshiki*, see Michaela Mross, "Sōjiji no Nisoki ni Kansuru Kōsatsu: Jissōji Shozō *Gasan Kōshiki Saimon* to Shikimon," *Shūkyōgaku Ronshū* 32 (2013): 107–36; Michaela Mross, "Noto Sōjiji to *Gasan Kōshiki* ni tsuite 2: *Gasan Kō Kada* to *Ryōson Shōki tō Sajōchō* wo chūshin ni," *Sōtōshū Kenkyūin Kenkyū Kiyō* 43 (2013): 163–87.

7. For a study of the *Tōjō Dentō Kōshiki*, see Mross, "A Local History," chapter 7.

8. Yamada, *"Kōshiki,"* 13–14; Gülberg, *Buddhistische Zeremoniale (kōshiki) und ihre Bedeutung für die Literatur des japanischen Mittelalters,* 29.

9. Niels Gülberg, "Kōshiki to wa nani ka," in Tanaka Yukie, ed., *Nihon Kanbun Shiryō Gakushohen: Shōmyō Shiryōshū* (Tokyo: Nishōgakusha Daigaku, 2006), 30.

10. In the middle of the Tokugawa period Sōtō monks started to use the term *kōshiki* also for rituals that are not *kōshiki* in a traditional sense as they do not contain a central text of the ceremony, for example, the *Kannon senbō*, a highly musical

ritual for Kannon; the *Tanbutsue*, a ritual praising the Buddha; and the *Daifusatsu Bosatsu Shiki*, a repentance ritual. The common characteristic of these rituals is that during these *shōmyō* (Buddhist chant) is performed, that is, the texts are vocalized with elaborate melodies.

11. Postscript of the *Eiheiji Kaisan Kigyō Hokke Kōshiki* written by Engetsu Kōjaku (1694–1750), the forty-second abbot of Eiheiji, in Enkyō 4 (1747) (ZS 2:819–35).

12. *Kichijōzan Eiheiji Nenchū Teiki*. This *shingi* was compiled between 1716 and 1729, during the time of Eiheiji's thirty-ninth abbot, Jōten Sokuchi (1655–1744); see Ozaki Shōzen, "Honkoku Kishizawa Bunko Zō *Kichijōzan Eiheiji Nenchū Teiki*," *Tsurumi Daigaku Kiyō Dai Yon Bu Jinbun Shakai Shizen Kagakuhen* 37 (2000): 108–9.

13. *Dōgen Kōshiki*, Nukariya Bunko (library of Komazawa University); *Dōgen Zenji Kōshiki*, archive of Shōyōji (Yamagata Prefecture); *Buppō Zenji Kōshiki Ryaku*, archive of Daitokuji (Nagano Prefecture).

14. *Eihei Dōgen Zenji Kōshiki*, archive of the Research Institute for Japanese Music Historiography, Ueno Gakuen University; *Eihei Kōso Dōgen Zenji Kōshiki*, archive of Kōzenji (Tōyama Prefecture). For a typographical reprint, see Kasai Kōyū, "Shinshutsu Shiryō *Eihei Dōgen Zenji Kōshiki*: *Hōon Kōshiki* Senku Shiryō no Hitotsu toshite," *Shūgaku Kenkyū* 45 (2003): 97–102.

15. ZS 2:717–34.

16. Ōzaki Shōzen, *Watashitachi no Gyōji: Shūmon Girei wo Kangaeru* (Tokyo: Sōtōshū shūmuchō, 2010), 256.

17. Booklet of the CD *Shinpen Hōon Kōshiki* (Tokyo: Daihonzan Eiheiji Betsuin Chōkokuji, 2002), 20.

18. Kawamura Kōdō, ed., *Shohon Taikō Eihei Kaisan Dōgen Zenji Gyōjō Kenzeiki* (Tokyo: Taishūkan shoten, 1975).

19. William M. Bodiford, "Remembering Dōgen: Eiheiji and Dōgen," in Steven Heine, ed., *Dōgen: Textual and Historical Studies* (New York: Oxford University Press, 2012), 222.

20. For a study of this incident, see William M. Bodiford, "Zen and the Art of Religious Prejudice: Efforts to Reform a Tradition of Social Discrimination," *Japanese Journal of Religious Studies* 21.1 (1996): 3–36.

21. The text is included in the booklet of the CD *Shinpen Hōon Kōshiki*, 8–16.

22. On this issue, see, for example, Kagamishima Genryū, "Kawamura Kōdō chaku *Shohon Taikō Eihei Kaisan Dōgen Zenji Gyōjō Kenzeiki* ni tsuite," *Komazawa Daigaku Bukkyōgakubu Ronshū* 6 (1975): 141–42.

23. T 9:11c25–26.

24. T 9:34c20–21.

25. T 9:23c27–28.

26. T 9:26b29–c1.

27. Stanley Jeyaraja Tambiah, "A Performative Approach to Ritual," *Proceedings of the British Academy* 65 (1979): 113–69.

28. For a detailed study of the *Hōon Kōshiki* for Shinran, see Christopher Thane Callahan, *"Kakunyo and the Making of Shinran and Shin Buddhism,"* PhD diss., Harvard University, 2011.

29. Callahan, "Kakunyo and the Making of Shinran and Shin Buddhism," 101.

30. Tsutsuki Eishun, ed., *Tōdaiji Yōroku* (Osaka: Zenkoku shobō, 1944), 50.

31. For a detailed study of the development of *shōmyō* notation, see Arai Kōjun, "The Historical Development of Music Notation for *shoomyoo* (Japanese Buddhist chant): Centering on *hakase* Graphs," *Nihon Ongakushi Kenkyū* 1 (1996): vii–xxxix.

32. Archive of Yōkōji.

33. Mail conversation on December 20, 2013.

34. Booklet of the CD *Shinpen Hoon Kōshiki*, 23.

35. I was able to attend the *Hōon Kōshiki* at Eiheiji Betsuin in 2009, 2010, 2012, and 2013.

36. *Chō* is a curtain that hangs on both sides of the altar.

37. This verse is a variation of a verse of the *Avatamsaka Sutra* (T 9:435a5–6).

38. George J. Tanabe Jr., "Chanting and Liturgy," in Robert E. Buswell, ed., *Encyclopedia of Buddhism* (New York: Macmillan Reference, 2004), 137.

39. On the *Praise of the Four Wisdoms* see, for example, Watarai Shōjun and Sawada Atsuko, *Sōtō-Zen: Chōka, Senbō, Narashimono* (Tokyo: Tōshiba EMI), 20; Sakauchi Tatsuo, "Dentō Kōshiki," in Suzuki Bunmei, ed., *Shinpen Sōtōshu Jissen Sōsho* 3 (Tokyo: Dōhōsha, 2013), 260–62.

40. I have conducted fieldwork at Sōtō temples on Buddhist rituals and *shōmyō* in 2004–5 and 2007–13. During my extended stays in Japan, I was able to interview the most highly trained *shōmyō* specialists of the Sōtō school and observe many rituals as well as rehearsals of rituals at several temples. Further I have played saxophone in *shōmyō* Jazz ceremonies, in which many *shōmyō* specialists performed. I was involved in deciding the ritual structure of these ceremonies and participated in intensive rehearsals. In all cases I observed that most priests are not aware of the meaning and function of *shōmyō* pieces. Even among the *shōmyō* specialists I got to know, only very few priests were informed about the history or meaning of *shōmyō* pieces. Their main concern was the performance itself; in this way they just sang.

41. This verse is also called *Raihai no Ge*. It is supposed to have originated with Ennin's (794–864) *Jōgyō Sanmaidō Gyōhō*. Genshin (942–1017) also quoted this verse in his *Ōjō Yōshū* (T 84:48a6–8). It has been recited in many Buddhist schools and is part of the shared ritual vocabulary of Japanese Buddhism.

42. Originally the text was "The wondrous body of the Thus come one, [unequaled] in the world," but it was shortened with the edition of the *Shōwa Kaitei Shōmyō Kihan* (Tokyo: Sōtōshū shūmuchō, 1966). The text is the beginning of a verse of the *Srimala Sutra*. The whole verse is known under the title *Nyoraibaimon* and is sometimes sung instead of *Nyoraibai* (T 12:217a24–27). The complete verse is: "The body of the Tathagata, excellent in form, Is unequaled in the

world, Being incomparable and inconceivable. Therefore, we now honor you. The Tathagata's form is inexhaustible And likewise his wisdom. All things eternally abide [in him]. Therefore, we take refuge in you." Diana Y. Paul, *The Sutra of Queen Srimala of the Lion's Roar* (Berkeley: Numata Center for Buddhist Translation and Research, 2004), 10.

43. This *Song of Falling Flowers* has the same title as the *Song of Falling Flowers* in the beginning, but it is a different chant.

44. This verse is a quotation from the *Lotus Sutra* (T 9:24c21–22).

45. Mail from September 17, 2013. Nevertheless the monks of Eiheiji bought 2,000 CDs and distributed them as commemorative items.

9

Interpreting the Material Heritage of the "Elephant Trunk Robe" in Sōtō Zen

Diane Riggs

DURING THE TOKUGAWA period Japanese Buddhist schools met challenges about the laxity of their practice by studying monastic rules (Vinaya), relying primarily on interpretations of the Chinese Vinaya master Daoxuan (596–667). The Buddhist robe, as a physical sign of the earnestness of their practice, was a particular focus of reform in all the schools. This was a reformation based on texts, not on human example or the artistic and material witness that had shaped Japanese understanding of the robe for a thousand years. For the first time in the history of Japanese Buddhist vestments, reformers in the major Buddhist schools were trying to re-create the ancient customs and material culture of the Vinaya by studying texts and implementing their prescriptions.

Sōtō Zen reformers of this period could not rely solely on the Vinaya, however, because of the new emphasis on the writings of Dōgen. Dōgen's own elliptical comments and his criticisms of Daoxuan's visionary teachings about robes complicated reform efforts. To add to the confusion, brocade robes of an unusual shape called "elephant trunk" were attributed to founders of the school. In color, fabric, and shape, these robes violated Vinaya teachings (see Figures 9.1 and 9.2). Sōtō Zen clerics therefore had to consider the role of the Vinaya teachings while accepting the primacy of Dōgen's writings and respecting the authority of their material heritage. In this chapter I investigate the methodology and claims of two Sōtō Zen scholar-monks, Gyakusui Tōryū

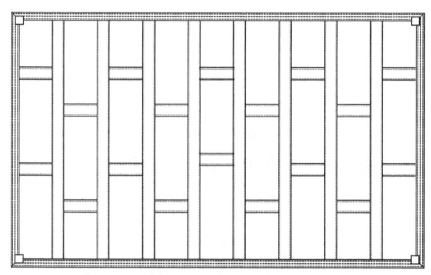

FIGURE 9.1 Illustration of the nine and twenty-five panel "great robe" that follows Vinaya regulations regarding the overall dimension and construction of the panels. Note that as the number of panels increases, their width decreases, so that both robes are approximately the same size. This illustration was created by David Riggs, based on a drawing from a reprinted edition of a handwritten copy of *Hōbuku kakushō*, privately published in 1937 by Kosaka Junni of Sengakuji, Tokyo.

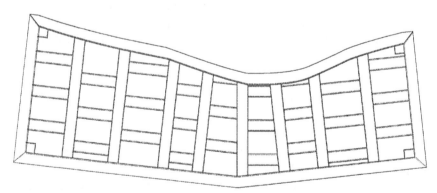

FIGURE 9.2 Illustration of an "elephant trunk" robe from Sōjiji sōin, attributed to Keizan Jōkin. Note the curved top line of the *kesa* and the variation in the size of each panel. In some robes of this style the panels themselves are not rectangular. Vertical dimension ranges from 138 cm at highest point to 98 cm at lowest point. The horizontal length is 298 cm. This illustration was created by David Riggs, based on a hand-drawn illustration from Sekiguchi Dōjun, *Nihon Sōtōshu shoki kyōdan ni okeru hōi no kenkyū* (Ichinomiya: Eirinji, 1992), 70.

(1684–1766), abbot of Daijōji, and Menzan Zuihō (1683–1769), who made the interpretation of Dōgen's writings the basis of his life's work.

Tōryū and Menzan addressed questions about the role of texts, art, and artifacts in resolving questions of form. Their different approaches reflect significant problems in the interpretation of Japanese Buddhist vestments. Since they arrive at diametrically opposed conclusions about the meaning of the "elephant trunk" artifacts and the meaning of Dōgen's teachings on the robe, their works demonstrate the challenges of using texts to interpret historical artifacts. Menzan and Tōryū were writing at a time when the form of robes was not so critical, but by the beginning of the nineteenth century, when Sōtō Zen had to distinguish itself from Rinzai and Ōbaku Zen in its doctrines, institutions, and religious forms (including robes), their arguments gained importance.

In order to explicate the issues raised in these debates, I first discuss relevant aspects of the history of Buddhist vestments in Japan. This allows us to see the work of these two Sōtō scholars as part of a continuum of perspectives on the Buddhist robe that began in the eighth century and continues to the present. The problem of interpreting artifacts through texts is as relevant today as it was then. Their debates therefore can be seen as a step toward modern thought and practice.

Perspectives on the Material Culture of Japanese Buddhist Vestments

Menzan and Tōryū began writing in the mid-eighteenth century, 150 years after Vinaya reforms had begun. The first Sōtō Zen essay on reforming robe practice was written in 1703 by Tokugon Yōson (fl. 1640–1730), so Sōtō Zen writers entered the field of robe reform rather late.[1] Numerous works on Buddhist vestments had already been written, and the characteristic plain robes of gray or brown linen and cotton of Vinaya reformers were recognized by the government.[2] Although the initial goal of Vinaya reform was to unite Japanese Buddhists under a single code of dress and behavior, by the mid-eighteenth century internal and external pressures increased sectarianism and shifted the goals of the movement.[3] Nevertheless studies of Buddhist vestments were still active, and pressure from the government for schools to define their code of dress would not occur until the beginning of the nineteenth century. Sōtō Zen writers therefore could benefit from the scholarship of the preceding century and a half and explore issues pertinent to Zen and its teachings about the robe.

In the Tokugawa period, reform of Buddhist vestments focused on the rectangular robe, referred to as *kesa*, which is worn wrapped around the body so that it passes under the right arm and covers the left shoulder.[4] Japanese robe practice follows customs begun in China, where the Indian practice of wearing three rectangular garments wrapped around the body, each with its own function, was replaced by the practice of wearing one of these robes (usually of five or seven panels) over garments that satisfied Chinese modesty.[5] In practice, therefore, only the *kesa* resembled robes worn in India. In the Tokugawa period, when studies of the Vinaya made people more aware of the discrepancies between the texts and Japanese robe practice, reformers were not so extreme as to reject the Chinese-style clothing. Instead the energy for reform was almost entirely focused on the *kesa* as the only garment that remained of the original Indian monastic outfit, and therefore the only opportunity for approaching the form of garments worn by the Buddha.

In the Vinaya descriptions of the three-robe set, the great robe (*sanghati*) of nine to twenty-five panels is used to cover the body more fully when interacting with the laity. It is honored as the robe that the Buddha wore when giving sermons, and it appears in stories of exchanges between Sakyamuni Buddha and his disciple Mahakasyapa. These exchange stories reveal a fundamental tension in the Buddhist tradition between the rag robe and the golden robe of the Buddha. Vinaya rules about materials suitable for the rag robe focus on the circumstances that caused it to be discarded as unsuitable for ordinary garments. These circumstances include, for example, cloth that was chewed by animals or cloth used to wrap a corpse. The Buddhist ascetic who gathers, washes, and sews the cloth into robes transforms it through the power of his ascetic practice.[6] In one of these narratives Sakyamuni offers to exchange his rag robe for Mahakasyapa's patchwork robe made of fine materials in recognition of Mahakasyapa's ascetic practice. In the other story Sakyamuni bestows a "golden robe" on Mahakasyapa, to be kept in trust for the future Buddha, Maitreya. This type of narrative begins with an account of Mahaprajapati's gift of a golden robe to Sakyamuni Buddha, which was subsequently rejected by both the Buddha and his community.

In one version of the story popularized in Xuanzang's seventh-century record of his travels to India, *Record of Western Lands in the Great Tang* (*Da Tang xiyu zhi*), the problem is resolved when Sakyamuni gives the robe to Mahakasyapa to be held in trust for Maitreya.[7] In both types of narratives, the exchange or gift robe is designated as a "great robe," but it takes one of two forms: the rag robe, which is evidence of the merit of the Buddha's ascetic practice, or the golden robe, which is evidence of the continuation of his teaching. In these narratives the great robe is not presented as one of the three monastic robes; it is associated with the spiritual power of the Buddha.

More pertinent to the debate between Menzan and Tōryū is the fact that these narratives of exchange form the basis of the Zen tradition of the master bestowing a robe on his disciple in dharma transmission. Such robes are referred to as "transmission robes" or, more strictly, a "transmit-dharma robe" (*denbō e*).[8] Xuanzang's account of Mahakasyapa preserving Sakyamuni's robe for Maitreya was recorded in fascicle 1 of the Zen text *Jingde Record of the Transmission of the Lamp* (*Jingde Chuandenglu*).[9] The robe of golden threads to be held in trust for Maitreya thus becomes fused with the Zen school's account of their lineage. It was not clear to Sōtō Zen reformers, however, whether the robe given in Zen transmission reenacted the narrative of the rag robe or the golden robe. Yōson asked in his 1703 essay, "Thoughts on the *Kesa* of the Buddhas and Ancestors" ("Busso kesa kō"), "Was the robe that Sakyamuni gave to Mahakasyapa the golden robe or a rag robe?"[10] Fifty years later Tōryū's arguments in favor of the golden robe supported the use of gold brocade in Sōtō Zen *kesa*, whereas Menzan, following scripture and Dōgen's view more closely, characterized the Zen transmission robe as the rag robe. Neither Tōryū nor Menzan, however, disputed that the great robe carries the significance of the Buddha's teaching.

These two images, the rag robe and the golden robe of the Buddha, were expressed in the material culture of Japanese Buddhism. Beginning in the eighth century the image of the rag robe in the form of a multicolor pieced *kesa* was reproduced in *kesa* textiles and portraits of statesmen and high-ranking clerics. In the twelfth century, however, when Myōan Eisai (1114–1215) returned from the continent wearing Zen robes from Song China, the golden robe, with its lore of mind-to-mind transmission, added new challenges. By the Tokugawa period both versions of the Buddha's robe had developed accepted traditions in art and textile.

For the rag robe, perhaps the most influential image is the eighth-century portrait statue of the Chinese Vinaya master Ganjin (Ch. Jianzhen; 688–763).[11] Ganjin, who introduced proper ordination ritual to Japan, resolved to make the journey in part because of the gift of one thousand *kesa* that Nagaya-Ō (684–729) had sent to Tang China.[12] In the last year of his life Ganjin, who had been deeply impressed by the "true image" of the mummy statue of the Zen patriarch, Huineng (638–713), carefully instructed his disciple Sitou (fl. 750) how to make his portrait statue be an accurate representation.[13] In the absence of Ganjin's written instructions, the statue becomes his teaching on the *kesa*. The portrait statue depicts a multicolor pieced *kesa* worn over Chinese garments, with the surplus fabric flung over the left shoulder to the back. The form of the *kesa* on Ganjin's statue was reproduced in Japanese art, most notably in Kaikei's (fl. 1189–1236) 1201 statue of the bodhisattva Hachiman. In addition the Hachiman statue meticulously depicted precise construction details of the multicolor stitched and pieced robe, including the running stitch that covers the surface of the cloth. These details of color and stitching also appear on Kamakura-era portraits of Prince Shōtoku Taishi (574–622).[14]

Many other images of high-ranking Buddhist clerics and statesmen are also depicted wearing multicolor *kesa*, some of which border on brocade-like designs.[15] The image of the multicolor pieced "rag robe" was therefore an important feature of artistic depictions of *kesa* in premodern Japan. The fact that at least some of these images were regarded as true likenesses suggests an identification forged in Japanese art between the rag robe that represents the merit of the Buddha's ascetic practice and the spiritual and worldly power of statesmen and clerics. The Japanese tradition of statues and portraits providing a "true likeness," or even the idea that certain statues such as of the Seiryōji Sakyamuni are "living Buddhas," was the premise for Tōryū's argument that the Buddha wore an elephant trunk robe. For Menzan, however, this evidence lends support to Dōgen's arguments in "Merit of the *Kesa*" ("Kesa Kudoku") about the preeminence of the rag robe as the true transmission robe of the Buddha.

Ganjin also brought gifts of *kesa* to Emperor Shōmu (701–56), including a number of multicolor pieced robes and one *kesa* using a technically advanced weaving technique to imitate the different colors of sewn patches.[16] These robes were preserved at the Shōsōin as Emperor Shōmu's personal possessions. A multicolor pieced "rag robe" *kesa* preserved at Hōryūji, the temple founded by Prince Shōtoku, was periodically shown to select groups throughout the medieval period as an opportunity to come in personal contact with Shōtoku's merit.[17] In the nineteenth century Hōryūji realized the commercial potential of displaying to the public these *kesa* and other objects attributed to Prince Shōtoku. Even though the *kesa* was displayed folded up in a box, the numerous images of Shōtoku wearing *kesa* would reinforce his connection with the multicolor pieced rag robe. Thus an important feature of Dōgen's essay "Merit of the *Kesa*" includes the notion that lay men wore *kesa* and kings throughout history gave homage to important *kesa* artifacts. This high regard for the authority of historical exemplar in Dōgen's writings must have left a deep impression on Tōryū, for it forms the basis of his approach to the *kesa*.

The brocade Zen transmission robes first imported to Japan during the Kamakura period and the increasingly lavish brocade robes of the early modern and modern periods of Sōtō Zen derived a portion of their significance and legitimacy from the narrative in which Sakyamuni bestows a "golden robe" on Mahakasyapa to be kept in trust for the future Buddha Maitreya. These robes were regarded as providing evidence of the transcendent mind-to-mind transmission of the dharma from master to disciple in the Zen school, but the physical garments themselves represented the internationalization of Zen material culture in the twelfth to fifteenth centuries.[18] These *kesa* attributed to founders and important clerics in the Rinzai, Ōbaku, and Sōtō Zen schools are the most important material evidence for Tōryū's claim that the true form of the transmission *kesa* must be the so-called elephant trunk robe.

Eisai, who founded the Zen temple Kenninji in Kyoto, is traditionally credited with introducing a new style of robes to Japan on his return from China in 1191. The long sleeves on his Song-style underrobe (*jikitotsu*) were shocking enough, but Eisai also brought an unusually widened style of *kesa* that dwarfed the five- or seven-panel *kesa* commonly worn by Japanese monks at the time. Over a hundred years later, in 1322, the Rinzai cleric Kokan Shiren (1278–1346) comments wryly on these garments in his *Record of Buddhism through the Genkō Era* (*Genkō Shakusho*):

> In the third month of 1204 there was a typhoon in central Kyoto. The townspeople said, "Recently, Eisai has been proclaiming a new teaching of the essentials of Zen. His disciples' robes are of an unusual construction with increased dimensions and the *jikitotsu* has great sleeves. When he walks along the street, great winds swirl within the bellowing [garments]." Now, accordingly, this is the basis of the fear that Eisai will cause a fire.[19]

In addition to their unusually large size, the transmission robes introduced in the Kamakura period used gold brocade, or *kinran* cloth.[20] During the seventeenth century the Ōbaku Zen school's use of elaborate gold brocade *kesa* affected both Rinzai and Sōtō Zen monks, many of whom had trained with the Ōbaku masters.[21] One of Tōryū's strongest arguments is that he personally viewed some of the most significant of the Gozan temple transmission robes. He mentions a *kesa* attributed to Wuzhun Shifan (1178–1249), teacher of Enni Ben'en (1202–80), founder of Tōfukuji, and Eisai's *kesa* at Kenninji. Until the Tokugawa period, when Japanese weaving techniques improved and the Nishijin weaving industry began to produce a better grade of gold brocade, such *kesa* were fairly rare. As the Japanese became less dependent on Chinese imports, however, these fabrics were adopted by many of the Buddhist schools.[22]

When Tokugawa-era Vinaya enthusiasts set out to reform the *kesa*, their material culture was very much at odds with the textual materials they studied.

It appeared to them that Japan had indeed strayed from the narrow path of Buddhist robe practice. Their commentaries include criticism of current practices, including the use of tassels, gold brocade, silk, and other customs that did not follow Daoxuan's interpretations. The brocade fabrics that first appeared in Zen transmission robes had spread to other schools of Japanese Buddhism, driven in part by improvements in Japanese textile production but also supported by the East Asian tradition in which robes of valuable fabrics were awarded by the ruler to honor clerics.[23]

For the Sōtō Zen school, however, the issue of whether and how to use Vinaya teachings and how to define the proper robe became increasingly an issue of determining Dōgen's approach to the Buddhist robe based on his writings. In contrast to their peers in other schools, Sōtō Zen scholar-monks were concerned with the robe as an emblem of transmission and awakening deeply connected with Zen lineage mythology as interpreted by Dōgen. The Sōtō lineage produced approximately seventeen works from 1703 to 1825 about the significance of the robe as a sign of transmission in Zen sources, placing Dōgen's writings on the *kesa* at the center of their arguments. Sōtō Zen writers were thus in a better position than other schools to fuse studies of the *kesa* with a study of the founder's teachings.

Same Evidence, Different Conclusions in Tōryū's and Menzan's Studies

Tōryū and Menzan have serious differences concerning three major questions. First, is the Vinaya relevant to Sōtō Zen studies of the robe? Second, what is the significance of the "elephant trunk" form of the robe in Sōtō Zen? Third, how should the narrative of the golden robe given to Mahakasyapa be interpreted? For both of them, the basis is Dōgen's *Treasury of the Eye of the True Dharma* (*Shōbōgenzō*), which contains two sections that deal with the robe: "Merit of the *Kesa*" and "Transmit the Robe" ("Den'e").

This focus is, however, something of a departure for Sōtō writings on the robe. Yōson's groundbreaking 1703 essay does cite Dōgen, but he also uses a wide range of sources to discuss the form and meaning of the *kesa* in Zen.[24] Yōson asks whether the robe that Sakyamuni gave to Mahakasyapa was the golden robe or a rag robe. Would the human-size robe of Sakyamuni fit the larger frame of Maitreya?[25] Yōson discusses Zen kōan and the chronology of transmission stories about the robe, including, for example, the story of Huineng's "heavy" robe that cannot be lifted by those without understanding. He also writes at some length about lay people wearing *kesa*, an issue that Dōgen raises in his essays.[26] Finally, Yōson presents an account of the thousand robes that Nagaya-Ō sent to China in his capacity as minister of the left and the effect of this gift on Ganjin's decision to travel to Japan. He then reveals that in 1702 Tanshin (fl. 1660) bestowed on him one of a thousand great robes (*fu sōgyari kesa*) that Ganjin had brought with him to Japan and that had been preserved at Tōshōdaiji after Ganjin's death.[27] Yōson seems thrilled to have received this historical artifact, but there is no indication that he views it as a transmission robe. Yōson's essay brought Zen perspectives to *kesa* studies, but his goal is not limited to interpreting Dōgen. Fifty years later Sōtō writings on the *kesa* had shifted to emphasize Dōgen's thought.

The change of emphasis was due to the context of the mid-eighteenth-century reforms called "return to the old ways." The reforms, initiated by Gesshū Sōko (1618–96) and Manzan Dōhaku (1636–1715), established a monastic code that combined the writings of Dōgen and Keizan, founders of Sōtō Zen lineages, with regulations of the Ōbaku Zen sect (Ōbaku Shingi). This combined code was to be implemented at Daijōji and its affiliated temples.[28] Tōryū, who became abbot at Daijōji in 1750, was committed to establishing these reforms.

These monastic rules were criticized by Sonnō Sōeki (1557–1620), Menzan's teacher, for incorporating Ōbaku influence. Menzan continued his teacher's stand against Ōbaku, but because he never became abbot of a major Sōtō Zen temple, he was able to carry out reforms only in his own temple. In the late eighteenth century, however, Sonnō's and Menzan's intentions were bolstered by Gentō Sokuchū (1729–1807), who actively sought to excise the Ōbaku influence from the "return to the old ways" movement when he became abbot of Eiheiji in 1795. He also supported Sōtō scholarship that used Vinaya and other Buddhist sources to interpret Dōgen's teachings on the robe.[29] Through lineage and perhaps disposition Tōryū and Menzan were therefore at odds over the monastic codes that were to shape Sōtō Zen practice for the future. Their writings on the *kesa* express aspects of these differences. The following section discusses the most important of these three areas of contention.

Is the Vinaya Relevant for Sōtō Zen Robes?

In 1759 Tōryū published his first work on the *kesa*, "Chapter on Elephant Trunk Transmission Robe" ("Den'e Zōbi shōkō"; hereafter "Elephant Trunk Robe").[30] Tōryū was insistent that Vinaya teachings are not suitable for Sōtō Zen, in using, for example, the following passage from "Merit of the *Kesa*," where

Dōgen argues that *kesa* made by Vinaya lineages were unduly influenced by Daoxuan and his innovations:

> Therefore, those who have aroused the mind of awakening, if they receive and wear *kesa*, then it must be a properly transmitted *kesa*, and one must not receive and wear a robe that is made in a new way according to a single individual's conception. The properly transmitted *kesa* is the lineage of transmission from Bodhidharma and Huineng, the face to face transmission of the Tathagata, without a break in the succession of generations. It was worn by their dharma heirs and it is the properly transmitted *kesa*. The new way of making it from Tang [China] is not the proper transmission. Now, as of old, the *kesa* worn by monks and their followers from India are all worn according to the proper transmission of the Buddhas and ancestors. Not one of them wears a *kesa* that is made according to the new Chinese way. They are the ones in the dark, those who believe in the *kesa* of the Vinaya scholars. Those who have come into the light abandon it.

> しかあればすなはちいま發心のともがら、袈裟を受持すべくば、正傳の袈裟を受持すべし、今案の新作袈裟を受持すべからず。正傳の袈裟といふは、少林.曹溪正傳しきたれる、如來の嫡嫡相承なり、一代も虧闕なし。それ法子法孫の著しきたれる、これ正傳袈裟な り、唐土の新作は正傳にあらず。いま古今に、西天よりきたれる僧徒の所着の袈裟、みな佛祖正傳の袈裟のごとく著せり。一人としても、いま震旦新作の律學のともがらの所製の袈裟のごとくなるなし。くらきともがら、律學の袈裟を信ず、あきらかならものは拋却するなり.³¹

In this passage the phrases "single individual's conception," "new way of making it from Tang," and *"kesa* of the Vinaya scholars" refers to Daoxuan, particularly his independent works on Buddhist robes, *Vinaya Characteristics Revelation (Luxiang Gantong)* and *Chapter on Buddhist Vestments (Shimen Zhang Fuyi).*³² In these works Daoxuan improvises on Vinaya teachings by attributing his ideas to visions granted to him by the gods. These two works contain some of Daoxuan's most controversial teachings about the robe, such as his prohibition of silk and the manner of lining the great robe, that were later criticized for their self-confessed visionary source. Here Dōgen is not critical of the Vinaya per se, as he praises both Indian monks and the Zen lineage as a source of orthodoxy. The problem, he argues, is the intervention of Chinese styles based on idiosyncratic rules. In his view the Zen lineage through Bodhidharma allows Japanese Zen monks to return to the original teaching of Sakyamuni and avoid the pitfalls of "Vinaya scholars."

Clearly this passage could support the view that Dōgen opposes Vinaya teachings as a whole, an argument that Tōryū makes after citing it. Tōryū then intensifies the criticism in arguing that Daoxuan, by following the guidance of divine beings, has slandered the elephant trunk dharma robe transmitted by the Buddha and ancestors.[33] He asserts, "From the lineage of Shaolin [Bodhidharma] passed down from old, the transmitted great robe is properly called the elephant trunk [robe]" 少林門下從往古自伝大衣正象鼻称.[34] Why does Tōryū insist at this point on the form of the elephant trunk robe while admitting that the term does not appear in Dōgen's works? Tōryū has seen these robes in Zen temples. Tōryū's assertion therefore is actually an affirmation of Japanese Buddhist artifacts, saying, in effect, we have the Buddha dharma right here in Japan. All we need to do to understand the true *kesa* is to examine the robes that have been transmitted from teacher to disciple in Zen lineages.

In another passage Dōgen develops his idea about the relationship between the Vinaya and the Zen lineage that provides further support for Tōryū's position. In this passage Dōgen asserts that Sakyamuni gave Mahakasyapa the robe that he himself had received from Kasapa Buddha.[35] Dōgen then claims that this is the robe that was subsequently transmitted through the Zen lineage (not the robe that Mahakasyapa held in trust for the future Buddha Maitreya) and that the correct instructions for material, color, form, and care of Sakyamuni's *kesa* were transmitted from generation to generation to the present.[36] Dōgen appears to be setting up transmission in the Zen lineage as a parallel Vinaya lineage that preserves and transmits knowledge of the physical robe. To understand Dōgen's text, Tōryū believes, one must turn to the physical robes properly made and used in Zen lineages.

Dōgen also recounts the following dialogue between his teacher Rujing (1169–1228) and a disciple. In the dialogue Rujing is referred to as "the old Buddha":

Long ago a monk asked the old Buddha, "Was the transmitted robe [given] on Plum Mountain in the middle of the night cotton or silk, or was it, after all, any kind of thing?" The old Buddha said, "It is not cotton, it is not silk." You should know that the *kesa* is neither silk nor cotton. This is the essential training of the Buddha's way.

ある僧かつて古佛にとふ黄梅夜半の傳衣これ布
なりよやせん絹なりとやせん、畢竟じてなにものなりとかせん。
古佛いはく、これ布にあらず、これ絹にあらず。しるべし袈裟
は絹布にあらざる、これ佛道の玄訓なり.³⁷

For Dōgen any physical feature that one can posit is not the true *kesa*, an argument that he also uses to solve the problem of whether Sakyamuni's *kesa* that is held in trust by Mahakasyapa will fit the larger frame of the future Buddha Maitreya.³⁸

Tōryū utilizes this rhetoric when he argues in favor of wearing gold brocade robes. In "Elephant Trunk Robe," Tōryū reinterprets the term "gold brocade" (*kinran*) as a generic term for *kesa* in which any color can be used, and "rag robe" as a generic term for *kesa* in which any fabric is good, whether it is gold brocade, silk, or cotton. He dissolves the boundaries between rag robes and gold brocade robes by arguing that this Zen teaching transcends the biased grasping of the inferior teachings of the Vinaya.³⁹ However, this is only one side of Dōgen. Tōryū seems to ignore passages that display Dōgen's understanding and respect for Vinaya teachings.

If the only authentic transmission of the robe is in the Zen lineage of Bodhidharma, did Dōgen ignore Vinaya teachings about the robe? In his "Merit of the *Kesa*" there are many passages in which he discusses robe-making in great detail by describing the set of three robes, the ten kinds of cloth used in rag robes, the nine types of great robes according to the number of panels, and even the methods of cutting and sewing the cloth.⁴⁰ This evidence suggests that Dōgen used his knowledge of Vinaya teachings in "Merit of the *Kesa*." For Tōryū to maintain his position that Vinaya teachings are inappropriate for Sōtō Zen monks who have "come into the light," he would have to ignore or reinterpret such passages.

Menzan disputes Tōryū's evidence and puts his methods into question in his 1763 work, "Questions about Ordination" ("Tokudo Wakumon").⁴¹ Unlike Tōryū's condemnation of Vinaya scholars, Menzan distinguishes between Vinaya texts and Daoxuan's interpretations. Various Vinaya texts indicate that there are rag robes, cut-and-sewn robes, strip-seam robes, and so on, he explains, each having its own origin and purpose. Furthermore the Buddha encouraged his monks to sew their own robes. In sum, since all these types of robes are described in the Vinaya they are by definition in accord with the Buddha's teaching.⁴² Menzan interprets Dōgen's criticism as directed only at Daoxuan's visionary commentaries, not the Vinaya itself, and perhaps not in other works in which Daoxuan stays closer to the text of the *Four Part Vinaya*.

Menzan argues that while some of Daoxuan's teachings went beyond the Vinaya, Zen monks did not accept these deviations. He cites the four sources of authority: the word of the Buddha, the word of the teacher, the teachings of the assembly, and the teachings of a single monk. Menzan comments that if one hears a teaching that is not appropriate to the dharma, then one must reject it, citing the example of Yijing, who rejected Daoxuan's prohibition of silk based on his reading of the Vinaya and his observations of monks he saw in his travels to India.[43] By appealing to the precedent of Yijing's criticism of Daoxuan, Menzan demonstrates his awareness of the larger context of Tokugawa Vinaya studies in which this historic dispute about silk was well known.[44] The real problem, Menzan emphasizes, is that disrespect for the Vinaya is disrespect for the Buddha's teachings, thus implicating both Daoxuan and Tōryū in his criticism. Unlike Tōryū, Menzan reads Dōgen's "Merit of the *Kesa*" as a call to encompass all of Sakyamuni's teachings on the *kesa*, including the Vinaya.

What Is the Elephant Trunk Robe, and Is It Appropriate for Sōtō Zen?

In his treatise "Elephant Trunk Robe" Tōryū claims that the "elephant trunk" robe is the authentic form of transmitted robes in the Zen school, even though Dōgen does not use this term. Tōryū, however, uses the term with confidence, claiming that there are full and half-size elephant trunk robes. Kawaguchi Kōfū, the author of several books on Sōtō Zen vestments, calculates that Tōryū's description of the full-size elephant trunk robe would be 1.5 meters vertical by 3 meters horizontal.[45] Compared to directions for robes in the *Four Part Vinaya* that produce an average robe of 1.25 meters vertical by 2 meters horizontal, the elephant trunk robe is somewhat longer vertically and a full 50 percent wider horizontally.[46] How can Tōryū be so confident about the physical characteristics of the elephant trunk robe when the term never appears in Dōgen's works?

For evidence Tōryū first discusses the statue of Sakyamuni Buddha at Seiryōji in Sagano, which is traditionally regarded as Sakyamuni's living presence. Imported from China in the tenth century, it was revered as a "three-country transmission," having been created in India, copied for China, and then exported to Japan.[47] In Dōgen's time copies of the Seiryōji Sakyamuni image were used in the cult of Sakyamuni worship, which focused on the merit of five hundred vows taken by Sakyamuni during his life as a bodhisattva detailed in the *Compassionate Lotus Scripture (Karunapundarika Sutra)*.[48] The last five vows describe the merit of Sakyamuni's *kesa* in his future Buddha land. When Dōgen cites this passage in "Merit of the *Kesa*," he comments that the merit of the entire five hundred vows is concentrated in the Buddha's *kesa*, thus making it superior to the *kesa* of other Buddhas.[49] This statue therefore is a focus for worship of Sakyamuni in Japan and also has significance for Sōtō Zen.[50] Tōryū also used the statue as an example of how the Buddha wears the *kesa*, but he asserts that its *kesa* is the elephant trunk robe. His comments appear more ideological than analytic:

> I, an old patched [monk], have seen in person the Saga [Seiryōji] Sakyamuni statue and other Buddha and bodhisattva statues in present day Japan. They all wear the *kesa* on both shoulders. The top corners of the *kesa* hang down in front and back, covering the left and right underarm and shoulders and encircling the whole body. It is, therefore, the construction of the Buddha's *kesa*. These all correspond to the full elephant trunk once-received robes. One must wear the *kesa* with the deportment of the Buddhas and Bodhisattvas.

> 老衲會見嵯峨釋迦尊像並扶桑國中現在佛菩薩像觀。皆同在通肩披。前頭後頭袈裟角。左右臂肩繞全身圍。然則佛袈裟之製樣。皆全象鼻一頂衣當。然佛菩薩搭袈裟威儀可.[51]

Tōryū uses the Seiryōji Buddha statue as evidence that Sakyamuni Buddha wore an "elephant trunk robe" but does not clarify what the physical characteristics of such a robe might be. In addition he refers to the robe as a "once-received" or "singular" robe, an issue discussed below. He is more interested in promoting the statue as an example of the authentic *kesa* of Sakyamuni Buddha and as a model for how to wear the *kesa* as a Buddha, namely, with the robe draping over both shoulders. In Tōryū's view, if one is a disciple, one must wear the robe exactly as the Buddha. His premise, however, collapses the difference in robe practice between Sakyamuni and his disciples, with the implication that if Buddha wears a golden robe, so might his disciples.

The key to Tōryū's confidence is the *kesa* that he believes represent the true Zen transmission robe. Among these, the most significant is a nine-panel robe that he believes Furong Daokai (1043–1118) gave to Dōgen's teacher Rujing and that must have been transmitted to Dōgen, or so Tōryū believes. He writes that this *kesa*, which is kept in a hidden room at Eiheiji, is a nine-panel full elephant trunk robe made of black cloth with a fastening ring made of black wood. He explains that there are twelve temples in Japan that claim to have Furong's robe, but they are all made differently from the great robe kept in the secret room at Eiheiji. Tōryū also investigated transmission robes at Rinzai temples, including a nine-panel robe at Tōfukuji that was believed to have belonged to the Chinese patriarch Wuzhun Shifan, teacher of Enni Ben'en, founder of Tōfukuji, as well as one at Kenninji that belonged to Eisai.

Tōryū explains that the robes at these temples are all the same type of nine-panel robe, which is meant to hang down in the back and the front as on the statue of Sakyamuni at Seiryōji—hence an elephant trunk robe, according to his definition. He also claims that when Ōbaku monks came to Japan they brought robes made according to the Vinaya school, but over time they converted to wearing robes using the nine-panel elephant trunk robe construction.[52] Tōryū's point is that when Ōbaku monks came in contact with the authentic manner of wearing the *kesa* according to the elephant trunk style preserved in Japan, they abandoned their false dependence on the Vinaya as the authority of their robe practice. It is the material evidence of Zen robes dating from the Kamakura period that Tōryū uses to emphasize Dōgen's estrangement from the Vinaya.

In summary, the nine-panel *kesa* attributed to Furong, which Tōryū viewed at Eiheiji, provides him with convincing evidence that Dōgen wore an elephant trunk robe. It is this artifact that allows him to argue that the elephant trunk robe is appropriate for Sōtō Zen monks. Believing in the inseparability of the transmission of the dharma and receiving the robe from one's teacher, Tōryū concludes that since Dōgen must have received transmission from Rujing, there must be a robe as well. Furong's *kesa* must therefore be in Japan. But which of the many robes that claim to be Furong's robe is it? Tōryū does not make comparative judgments. Having been shown the black nine-panel robe in the hidden room at Eiheiji that has the characteristically elongated shape of his idea of the full elephant trunk, Tōryū recognizes this robe as the true robe of transmission from Furong via Rujing. Step by step the logic of belief leads Tōryū to the conclusion that Dōgen's conception of the physical characteristics of the true robe of transmission would be based on this particular robe, which he characterizes as a full elephant trunk robe.

Menzan, however, questions the idea that the robe transmitted from the Buddha to Mahakasyapa was an elephant trunk robe. He discusses the use of the term "elephant trunk" in fascicle 19 of the *Four Part Vinaya*, in which the Buddha criticizes a group of six monks for various infractions of the robe, including wearing them high or low, wearing them so that one corner hangs in front like an "elephant trunk" or with two corners hanging down in front, like a leaf of the tala tree, or making small pleats.[53] The term "elephant trunk," Menzan argues, appears in Buddhist literature only as a criticism of decorum, and Dōgen does not mention it in any of his house rules.[54] Menzan therefore challenges Tōryū's claim that Dōgen recognized the elephant trunk robe as the true form of the transmission robe.

A key area of dispute involves an elliptical sentence in Dōgen's "Transmit the Robe" that Menzan and Tōryū interpret quite differently:

> Now the once-received robe, the nine-type robe, must be properly transmitted based on the Buddha dharma.
>
> いま一頂衣・九品衣、まさしく佛法より正伝せり
>
> *ima itchō e, kuhon e, masashiku buppō yori shōden seri.*[55]

Dōgen's use of the phrase *itchō e*, 一頂衣, is idiosyncratic, as the standard counting word for *kesa* is ryō 領. The glyph 頂 (*chō*) appears in the compound used to translate the Sanskrit word *abhiseka* (Jp. *kanjō*), where it indicates the aspersion of water on the head in the ritual of esoteric initiation or consecration. Perhaps by using *chō*, Dōgen meant the ritual act of receiving the robe as in ordination and transmission. The earliest use of this expression outside of this passage that I was able to find is after Dōgen's lifetime, when it appears in the section on transmission in the collected verses of Kurin Seimo (1262–1329) of the Rinzai lineage. Based on this evidence, *itchō e* in this context refers to the robe that a master gives to a disciple in recognition of dharma transmission.[56] For Menzan and Tōryū the critical point of dispute is the relationship between the two terms "once-received robe" and "nine-type robe."

Tōryū's interpretation of Dōgen is strongly influenced by the authority he grants to Zen transmission *kesa* he has seen. Having designated the true transmission robe as an elephant trunk robe, he uses this appellation as a wedge to divide Dōgen's use of Vinaya teachings in "Merit of the *Kesa*" from Dōgen's claim to be the bearer of the knowledge of the true transmission *kesa*. This is most apparent in Tōryū's interpretation of the sentence above. Tōryū argues that "nine-type robe" means a single nine-panel robe, maintaining that the iconic Zen transmission *kesa* of Bodhidharma included all nine types of great robe.[57] In spite of Dōgen's meticulous reproduction of the Vinaya descriptions in "Merit of the *Kesa*" of nine types of great robe based on the number of panels (i.e., 9–11–13–15–17–19–21–23–25), Tōryū subsumes them all within Bodhidharma's robe, thereby rendering Vinaya teachings on the robe irrelevant to Sōtō Zen. The delicate balance proposed by Dōgen in which the Zen lineage preserves these Vinaya teachings is lost in Tōryū's interpretation. His method of interpreting Dōgen is based on his study of statues and extant transmission *kesa* attributed to early Kamakura-era Zen founders. The authority he grants these artifacts directs his reading of Dōgen's text.

Menzan, on the other hand, analyzes Dōgen's meaning in the sentence using texts, not artifacts. He comments that the two terms "once-received robe" and "nine-type robe" appear in the sentence together, but this does not mean that Dōgen equated them. Rather, Menzan argues, this sentence refers to the Buddha's teachings of the four supports: wearing rag robes, eating once a day, sleeping under a tree, and using fermented urine for medicine.[58] Menzan explains that the rag robe, as the first support, is distinguished from all types of robes made from donated fabric, including the nine types of great robe. Thus the two terms refer to different manifestations of the Buddhist robe: first, the singular robe of the Buddha, that is, the rag robe; and second, the nine types of great robe made of donated cloth as described in the Vinaya. Here Menzan uses Buddhist texts to analyze Dōgen's terse and elliptical sentence rather than relying on material evidence of *kesa* in Japanese temples. Menzan interprets "once-received robe" as the singular rag robe (of the Buddha), which is not divided into types.[59] Strictly speaking, in Menzan's interpretation "once-received" does not refer to transmission robes in general. His interpretation is more in line with the dominant theme in "Merit of the *Kesa*" that the rag robe is the highest, most pure form of the Buddhist robe, a perspective that Tōryū appears to ignore in his essay.

Having shown that the term "elephant trunk" in the Vinaya is limited to a criticism of wearing styles, Menzan introduces historical and sociological evidence. He states that "elephant trunk robe" is a Japanese term that identifies a particular type of robe construction introduced by Zen monks returning from China during the Kamakura period. There are those during the time of *mappō*, he explains, who deprecate the Vinaya in changing the robes according to their own preference. Wearing secular clothing underneath the *kesa* causes the fabric to bunch up and spoil the smooth appearance of the robes, so they secretly scoop out the upper part of the garment that wraps around the body underneath the sleeve, thus breaking the rules about the dimensions of the *kesa*:

> In recent times, robe makers have come to call this technique the "elephant trunk." Ignorant Zen monks hear this term and spread it around so that now there is such a thing called the "elephant trunk *kesa*." Thinking that it is something that comes from the Buddha's time, they say things like, "there are full elephant trunks and half elephant trunks." To secretly scoop out even a small amount of the *kesa* described by the Buddha changes the length and width of the panels and it is a violation. It is sad when such self-centered ideas appear in the writings of Zen monks; such a waste.

近世ノ衣屋ガ、コレヲ象鼻ト稱ス、ソレヲ文妄ナ禪僧ガ
聞テ展轉シテ、今此ハ實ニ、象鼻袈裟ト稱リ、佛
世ヨリアルコトト思テ、全象鼻、半象鼻ナド
云様ニナレリ、佛説ノ法袍ヲ、少シモ和ニエグテハ、
壇隔ノ長短ガ違郤ス、非法ハ云フニヲヨバズ、禪僧ノ經
論ニウトキ私案、カナシムベシ、穴賢。60

In direct criticism of Tōryū's argument, Menzan put the issue of elephant
trunk robes versus Vinaya robes in a different light. It is not that the elephant
trunk robe is the Zen answer to Daoxuan's deviations. Rather, Menzan argued,
this form of robe, produced from vanity, shows a lack of respect for the teachings of the Buddha. The scooped-out portion warps the overall rectangular
form of the kesa as well as the individual panels. These alterations originate
with robe makers who copied robes imported from China for their clients. In
his 1768 essay, "Guidelines for Dharma Robes of Buddhist Monks" ("Shakushi
Hōekun"), Menzan described the social origins of this garment more fully.61
He suggested that the practice of gouging out the top edge of the kesa into a
bow shape was prevalent among Song-period clerics who attended court functions wearing purple and gold brocade robes given to them by the ruler. He
explained that because these outfits included secular clothing worn over the
Chinese sleeved and collared garments, the voluminous kesa would bunch
up under the right arm. The practice of altering the top edge of the kesa
decreased the thickness.

Menzan asserted that Japanese clerics who visited Song China imitated
this style, and it has continued to this day in Kyoto and Kamakura, especially among the Rinzai (Gozan) temples. The colloquial term "elephant
trunk robe," which in the Vinaya (as "elephant trunk") refers to the way the
corner of kesa may droop, developed among robe makers to distinguish
this form from robes made according to the instructions of monks knowledgeable in the Vinaya. Menzan argues that it was in fact a pejorative nickname and does not reflect the Buddha's teaching.62 According to Menzan,
the elephant trunk robe is a commercial expedient, not the hallowed form
of the Buddha's robe.

In response to Menzan's criticisms, Tōryū vigorously defended his position on the elephant trunk robe in his 1764 "Critique of 'Questions about
Ordination'" ("Tokudo Wakumon bengishō").63 Tōryū gave detailed instructions on how to wear the elephant trunk robe and continued the argument in
"Clear Mirror of Daijōji's Defense of the Dharma" ("Daijōji Gohō Myōkan"),
published posthumously in 1766.64 Forty years later Daisen's 1808 commentary gave Tōryū's "Elephant Trunk Robe" new life. Menzan's approach, on the

other hand, was developed in the early nineteenth century by Mokushitsu Ryōyō's work, *Hōbuku Kakushō.*

Should Sōtō Zen Monks Wear
Gold Brocade Robes?

Tōryū and Daisen also justified the use of the gold brocade robes in Sōtō Zen. As mentioned earlier, in "Elephant Trunk Robe" Tōryū explained that the term "gold brocade" is a common name for *kesa* in which any color can be used, and "rag robe" is a common name for *kesa* in which any fabric is good, whether it is gold brocade, silk, or cotton. This Zen teaching, he argued, transcends the biased grasping of the inferior Vinaya.[65] Daisen affirmed this position by adding that since the robe that Sakyamuni gave to Mahakasyapa was gold brocade it would be acceptable for the Zen school. Daisen's interpretation conflates the narrative of the robe given in trust for Maitreya with the narrative of the robe given in recognition of Mahakasyapa's ascetic practice. Daisen also suggested that the Sōtō Zen school balances the two extremes, as seen in the robes of its two most influential teachers, Dōgen and Keizan. He comments that although Dōgen wore a black robe all his life, Keizan received a colored robe by the ruler's command, and he wore it. Dōgen, subdued on the outside, was highly decorated on the inside, whereas Keizan was decorated on the outside. The most important thing, Daisen concludes, is to ask whether the person has a way-seeking mind. According to the mind of the way, either gold brocade or ragged clothes are appropriate.[66] Tōryū's and Daisen's arguments proposed a justification for Sōtō Zen clerics to don decorative gold brocade *kesa*, but they garbled the scriptural narratives of these two iconic great robes by arguing that the golden robe and the rag robe refer to *kesa* regardless of color or fabric.

Tōryū's argument explicitly dissolves the boundaries between the rag robe and the golden robe of the Buddha. He reduces the narratives of these two types of "great robe" to a material level, and then further reduces the distinction between materials by arguing that both rags and brocade may have "all colors." Here he uses Dōgen's observations in "Merit of the *Kesa*" that the *kesa* is neither silk nor cotton and that any fabric can be considered rags. Dōgen's remarks open up the possibility of an "anything goes" approach that Tōryū and Daisen seized on.

Menzan firmly rejects Tōryū's merging of the narratives of rag robe and golden robe. He argues from scriptural passages that the gold brocade robe given to Mahakasyapa by Sakyamuni was given in trust for Maitreya Buddha and was not to be worn. Mahakasyapa, he comments, was renowned for wearing rag robes and was never referred to in scripture as wearing a gold brocade robe. Furthermore, Menzan argues, all fabrics with a design of colors (*madara*) or glittering fabric (*ran*) are also to be rejected.[67] Menzan critiques Tōryū's position on the gold brocade robe based on his knowledge of Buddhist scripture and of Dōgen, but Menzan is the only voice in Sōtō that opposes the adoption of gold brocade robes.[68] Tōryū's influence as abbot of Daijōji gave weight to his interpretation, which was preserved and later promoted by Daisen in the beginning of the nineteenth century.

Conclusion

The debates between Menzan and Tōryū set the stage for the mid-nineteenth-century "three-robe controversy" that resulted in an atmosphere of conflict about the *kesa* that continued into the modern era. Remarkably the controversy revolved around the physical construction and manner of wearing the *kesa*, which had become a kind of straw man for power struggles between Sōjiji and Eiheiji. The various elements of these disputes, however, cannot be reduced to conflict between these two head temples. Sōtō clerics had convinced themselves that the writings of Dōgen and/or Keizan were sufficient to establish rules concerning *kesa*. To resolve the inevitable inconsistencies and lacunae of these texts, clerics either turned to the *kesa* artifacts and art to answer their questions, as did Tōryū, or relied on the Vinaya and Zen sources, as did Menzan.

The problem of relying solely on the founding figures of Dōgen and Keizan was that disagreements over form and practice could threaten the integrity of the whole school. In comparison, Vinaya enthusiasts in other schools could occupy a specialist niche without challenging the institutional structure of their school. This might have occurred in Sōtō as well, but the insistence of reformers on establishing an institutional reform that directly challenged long-held customs of dress and practice led the Sōtō school to the brink of schism. The hard-won compromise achieved during the Meiji period meant that the definition of Sōtō Zen robes would now be firmly held by the Sōtō corporation, and decisions about dress would be based on compromise rather than an effort to establish a coherent and encompassing vision of the Sōtō Zen robe.

NOTES

1. Yōson's essay is titled "Thoughts on the *Kesa* of the Buddhas and Ancestors" ("Busso kesa kō").

2. See fascicle 1 of *Ranks of All Buddhists (Shoshū Kaikyū)*, in *Zokuzoku Gunsho Ruijū*, 17 vols., ed. Zoku Gunsho Ruiju Kanseikai (Tokyo, 1969–70 (an earlier edition was published by Kokusho kankōkai, 1906–9) [hereafter ZGR] 12, 365b, 389a, 369b, respectively.

3. Government demands that Buddhist schools define their principles and regulations promoted sectarian divisions. The government viewed Vinaya studies as a way to regulate the schools; see Tamamuro Fumio, *Zusetsu Nihon Bukkyō no Rekishi: Edo Jidai* (Tokyo: Hyōronsha, 1996), 7–9. For a discussion of growing sectarianism, see Ueda Tenzui, *Kairitsu no Shisō to Rekishi* (Wakayama Prefecture: Mikkyō bunka kenkyūjo, 1976), 38.

4. An alternative method, often seen in Buddha images, drapes the *kesa* over both shoulders.

5. The set of three robes includes a lower robe of five panels worn around the waist while working; an upper robe worn over the left shoulder and under the right arm when attending monastic events; and the great robe, of nine to twenty-five panels, worn over the other two robes when interacting with the laity. See Izutsu Gafu, *Kesashi* (Kyoto: Bunka jihosha, 1965).

6. For an extensive description of these stories, see Jonathan A. Silk, "Dressed for Success: The Monk Kasyapa and Strategies of Legitimation in Earlier Mahayana Buddhist Scriptures," *Journal Asiatique* 291.1–2 (2003): 173–219. For a discussion of the symbolism of the *kesa*, including medieval Sōtō Zen esoteric writings, see Bernard Faure, "Quand l'habit fait le moine: The Symbolism of the kasaya in Chan/Zen Buddhism," *Cahiers d'Extreme Asie* 8 (1995): 335–69.

7. T 51.902a.

8. For the use of the term "transmission robes" in a modern English-language context, see Yamakawa Aki, *Transmitting Robes, Linking Mind: The World of Buddhist Kasaya* (Kyoto: Kyoto National Museum, 2010), vi. In addition to *kesa*, portraits, bowls, and other objects were also used as verification in Zen; see T. Griffith Foulk and Robert H. Sharf, "On the Ritual Use of Ch'an Portraiture in Medieval China," *Cahiers d'Extrême-Asia* 7 (1993–94): 149–220.

9. T 51.364b.

10. ZS 2:523–547.

11. I am using the Japanese pronunciation, Ganjin, in order to highlight his role in Japanese Buddhism.

12. The conviction that Nagaya-Ō's gift to Chinese monks influenced Ganjin's decision to come to Japan was an important factor in Jiun's decision to replicate the making of one thousand robes; see Hase Hōshū and Okumura Keishin, *Jiun Sonja: Jiun Sonja Nihyaku Nen Onki Kinen* (Nara: Kokiji, 2004); Andō Kōsei, *Ganjin Wajō* (Tokyo: Yoshikawa kōbun kan, 1971).

13. For information on Huineng's mummy statue, see Robert H. Sharf, "The Idolization of Enlightenment: On the Mummification of Ch'an Masters in Medieval China," *History of Religions* 32.1 (1992): 1–31. For the concept of the

true image and its effect on art by valuing realistic representation over idealization, see Inoue Tadashi, "Ganjin wajō zō josetsu," *Museum* 314 (1977): 17–26.

14. Hachiman was considered a bodhisattva for his role in building the Great Eastern Temple (Tōdaiji). For details on this statue, see Christine Guth Kanda, "Kaikei's Statue of Hachiman in Tōdaiji," *Artibus Asiae* 43.3 (1981): 190–208. For details on artworks that reproduce the image of the *kesa* on the portrait statue of Ganjin, see chapter 2 of Diane E. Riggs, "The Cultural and Religious Significance of Japanese Buddhist Vestments," Ph.D. diss., University of California, 2010.

15. See Andrew Goble, "Visions of an Emperor," in Jeffrey P. Mass, ed., *The Origins of Japan's Medieval World* (Stanford: Stanford University Press, 1997); Kuroda Hideo, "Shōzōga toshite no Go-Daigo tennō," in *Ō no Shintai, Ō no Shōzō* (Tokyo: Heibonsha, 1993).

16. Ganjin is recorded as having brought one thousand sewn, pieced *kesa* and two thousand cotton *kesa* (*fugesa*). T 51.992a; see also Andō, *Ganjin Wajō*.

17. Jiun Onkō (1718–1804), the founder of the "True Dharma Vinaya" (*Shōbōritsu*) reform movement, was invited to view the Shōtoku robe. His account includes the prayers and homage that he paid to the *kesa* as well as recording their dimensions and sewing styles. See Riggs, "The Cultural and Religious Significance of Japanese Buddhist Vestments," chapter 4.

18. For more information and color reproductions of these *kesa*, see Yamakawa, *Transmitting Robes, Linking Mind*.

19. Michel Mohr, "Electronic Text of the Genkō Shakusho by Kokan Shiren," accessed September 2013, http://iriz.hanazono.ac.jp/frame/data_food.en.html, 26b; DNB 101.26b.

20. See Izutsu Gafu, *Kesashi* (Kyoto: Bunka jihosha, 1965).

21. The influence of Ōbaku-style robes on Sōtō Zen vestments is a topic for future research.

22. Kawaguchi Kōfū, *Hōbuku Kakusho no Kenkyū* (Tokyo: Daiichi shobō, 1976), 372.

23. Adopted from China, the custom of the emperor's awarding of the "purple robe" to clerics was especially important to Japanese Rinzai lineages, which were closely associated with the court. The Tokugawa government attempted to curtail this long-standing religious and political custom; see Duncan Williams, "The Purple Robe Incident and the Formation of the Early Modern Sōtō Zen Institution," *Japanese Journal of Religious Studies* 36.1 (2009): 27–43.

24. Yōson received dharma transmission from Tetsuzan Shinyō (fl. 1660), the thirteenth abbot of Kenshōji. Kawaguchi identifies Yōson as a Sōtō cleric, although Yōson's writings on various scriptures led others to believe that he was affiliated with Tendai or Rinzai lineages; see Kawaguchi, *Hōbuku Kakusho no Kenkyū*, 363–64.

25. ZS 2:523–547.

26. ZS 2:539a, 541a.

27. ZS 2:545–46. The prefix *fu* indicates that the robes were made of cotton or linen. More research must be done to determine the provenance of Tanshin's gift to Yōson.

28. For a discussion of the movement to "return to the old ways" in Sōtō Zen, see Kagamishima Genryū, *Dōgen Zenji to Sono Shūhen* (Tokyo: Daitō Shuppansha, 1985), 155–68. For an English-language discussion, see David E. Riggs, "The Rekindling of a Tradition: Menzan Zuihō and the Reform of Japanese Sōtō Zen in the Tokugawa Era," Ph.D. diss., University of California, 2002, 84–130. For a history of Daijōji in the early period of the Sōtō Zen school, see William M. Bodiford, *Sōtō Zen in Medieval Japan* (Honolulu: University of Hawaii Press, 1993).

29. The most important work was *Hōbuku Kakushō*, completed in 1821 by Mokushitsu Ryōyō.

30. ZS Shingi, vol. 2. The original manuscript of "Elephant Trunk Robe" is no longer extant, but its content was preserved by Daisen Tamashū (1739–1814) in his 1808 *Easy Teachings from the Chapter on the Elephant Trunk Transmission Robe (Den'e Zōbi Shōkō Haka)*, ZS 2:600–637. Daisen was the fourth generation from Tōryū. In the modern edition of his commentary, quotations from Tōryū's original text in indented passages alternate with Daisen's comments. Daisen also wrote his own commentary on the robe, "Questions and Answers on the Secret Explanation of 'Transmitting the Robe' and 'Merit (of the *Kesa*)' in the *Shōbōgenzō*" ("Shōbōgenzō Den'e Kudoku Setsukai Mondō"), but this work may not be extant; see Kawaguchi, *Hōbuku Kakusho no Kenkyū*, 367.

31. DZZ-1 1:627.

32. T 45.1898 and T 45.1894, respectively.

33. ZS 2:614b–615a.

34. ZS 2:605b.

35. DZZ-1 1:625.

36. DZZ-1 1:625–26.

37. DZZ-1 1:629.

38. DZZ-1 1:636.

39. ZS 2:607a.

40. DZZ-1 1:626, 629, 635, 637, respectively.

41. SZ 2:199–204.

42. SZ 2:201a–b.

43. SZ 2:202b–203a.

44. For information on Tokugawa studies of Yijing's work on the Mulasarvastivada Vinaya, see Shayne Clarke, "Miscellaneous Musings on Mulasarvastivada Monks: The 'Mulasarvastivada Vinaya' Revival in Tokugawa Japan," *Japanese Journal of Religious Studies* 33.1 (2006): 1–49.

45. Kawaguchi, *Hōbuku Kakusho no Kenkyū*, 371.

46. T 22.863a.

47. For the idea of statues as living buddhas, see Donald F. McCallum, *Zenkōji and Its Icon* (Princeton, NJ: Princeton University Press, 1994), 170. For information on the Seiryōji Sakyamuni Buddha, see Gregory Henderson and Leon Hurvitz, "The Buddha of Seiryōji: New Finds and New Theory," *Artibus Asiae* 19.1 (1956): 5–55.

48. T 2.157. For the role of this sutra in Sōtō Zen, see Ishikawa Rikizan, "Shaka Shinkō to Dōgen Zen," *Indo Bukkyōgaku Kenkyū* 44.1 (1995): 229–34, 232a–b.

49. DZZ-1 1:631–33.

50. Eight years before Tōryū's "Elephant Trunk Robe," Jiun discussed this statue in his 1751 work, *Illustrated Garments of the Way* (*Hōbuku zugi*), in order to illustrate the manner in which buddhas wear *kesa* over both shoulders. It is possible that Tōryū was aware of this work. Jiun Onkō, *Jiun Sonja Zenshu* (Osaka: Kokiji, 1922–26). See also Riggs, "The Cultural and Religious Significance of Japanese Buddhist Vestments," chapter 4.

51. ZSSZ 2:612b.

52. ZSSZ 2:616b.

53. T 22.698b.

54. SZ 2:200a–b.

55. DZZ-1 1:287.

56. Although Seimo's five-volume record was published in 1325, shorter works were published as early as 1309, including a selection of his verses, *shuigeju*. See *Zoku zōkyō* (Kyoto: Zōkyō shoin, 1905–12), 2.28.3; "Kurin mo zenji goroku" in Komazawa Daigakunai Zengaku Dai Jiten Hensanjo, *Zengaku Daijiten* (Tokyo: Taishukan shoten, 1985), 254c. Modern scholars have interpreted the phrase in various ways that reflect the two rituals of ordination and transmission. The entry for *itchō e* in Komazawa, "Zengaku daijiten," 47a, defines this term as the *kesa* that is properly transmitted. It adds that this *kesa* is also referred to as the gold brocade robe, *kinran e*, and as Bodhidharma's blue-black cotton robe, *kutsujun*. Which of these types of *kesa* should be the sole model for the transmission robe, however, was a matter of dispute during this period. The entry for *itchō e* in Nakamura Hajime, *Bukkyō go Daijiten* (Tokyo: Tokyo shoboku, 1981), 65a, states that *itchō* is a counter word used when one is wearing a hat (i.e., ceremonial dress). This definition, however, cites Dōgen's "Transmission of the Robe," so it is inconclusive.

57. ZSSZ 2:608a, 609a.

58. The practice of wearing the rag robe is also idealized in Vinaya literature as one of the four supports of practice: wearing rag robes, taking frugal meals, residing under a tree, and using only medications made from fermented urine. See Charles S. Prebish, *Buddhism: A Modern Perspective* (University Park: Pennsylvania State University Press, 1975), 4.

59. SZ 2:200a.

60. SZ 2:203a–b.
61. ZS Shingi, vol. 2. This work retained its popularity through the Meiji period and claimed a readership outside of Sōtō Zen circles.
62. ZS 2:568b–569a.
63. ZS 1:149–200.
64. I have not been able to obtain a copy of this work; see Kawaguchi, *Hōbuku Kakusho no Kenkyū*, 371.
65. ZS 2:607a.
66. ZS 2:607b.
67. ZS 2:558.
68. See Kawaguchi, *Hōbuku Kakusho no Kenkyū*, 382.

10

Embodying Sōtō Zen

INSTITUTIONAL IDENTITY AND IDEAL BODY
IMAGE AT DAIHONZAN EIHEIJI

Pamela D. Winfield

SINCE 1894 SŌTŌ Zen sectarian identity has been premised upon the distinctive notion that "both of its head temples are one essential body, not two" (*ryōzan ittai funi*).[1] This unique institutional axiom, which obliquely anthropomorphizes the two powerful monastic bodies of Eiheiji and Sōjiji temples, brought both institutions together after centuries of rivalry and competition to share in the joint governance and training of Sōtō's priesthood. Their extraordinary government-brokered accord further established the dharma equality of the sect's two founding figures, Dōgen Kigen (1200–1253) and his fourth-generation dharma heir Keizan Jōkin (1268–1325). The sect's corollary maxim of "one Buddha, both patriarchs" (*ichibutsu ryōso*) subsequently has been visually reinforced by placing the bodies of the two founders alongside Sakyamuni Buddha himself. This unprecedented iconography of affiliation developed during a temporary détente in Eiheiji-Sōjiji relations between 1872 and 1892. The figures in the *ichibutsu ryōso* triad in Figure 10.1, for example, were donated to the sect's new *senmongakkō* in Tokyo (later to become Komazawa University) on its opening day, October 10, 1882. Kitayama Zessan, chief priest of Osaka's Taiheiji temple, offered the "one Buddha" Sakyamuni in the center, while an inscription on the back of the Dōgen sculpture to the spectator's right credits Itokawa Ryūtatsu's gift of "both patriarchs" in memory of his mother.[2] Keizan sits to the spectator's left on the same plane of the Mount Sumeru platform.

木魚　花瓶　燭台　香炉　鏧子

FIGURE 10.1 "One Buddha, Both Patriarchs" triad, Komazawa University Museum of Zen History and Culture, ca. 1882. Komazawa University Museum Catalogue, (Tokyo, n.d.), 14. Used with permission.

In written and visual texts such as these, Dōgen is identified as the so-called highest patriarch (*kōso*) and founding "father" figure of the Sōtō Zen sect, since he planted the seed of Sōtō's original teaching when he first established Eiheiji temple in 1243. Keizan, for his part, is known as the broadest patriarch (*taiso*) and founding "mother" figure of the denomination. He is said to have nurtured Sōtō's institutional growth and development by propagating Dōgen's Zen and placing Sōtō's subtemples (*matsuji*) under the administrative control of Sōjiji temple, which he established in 1321. A certain priority may be accorded to Dōgen due to Japanese reading convention, which starts from right to left, but the overall iconographic message of this now-standard Sōtō arrangement of figural bodies indicates that the vertical reach and the horizontal expanse of Sōtō's original founders infinitely extends the Buddha's teaching throughout time and space.[3] In addition, the gendered associations and powerful biological metaphors that the sect promotes to construct Sōtō Zen's institutional birth and growth narrative reflect the corporeal focus of this study.[4]

Eiheiji's visual and textual discourse of harmony, cooperation, and even familial ties with Sōjiji thus promotes a family-friendly vision of institutional equality, parental cooperation, and dharmic parity with Sakyamuni Buddha that continues to this day. At the same time, however, given the virtual absence of income from subtemples, Eiheiji today must leverage its reputation for authenticity and "tradition" in order to attract tourism, income from temporary retreatants (sanrōsha), memorial service fees, and morning ceremony donations.[5] Eiheiji thus concurrently—and successfully—has had to compete for institutional survival in the face of Sōjiji's financial and administrative predominance.[6] As a result, in this chapter I investigate Eiheiji's material and visual strategies for identity-construction and self-promotion as the de facto point of origin of Sōtō Zen in Japan.

William Bodiford has demonstrated that Eiheiji consistently sold titles, solicited imperial patronage, and mounted memorial rituals for Dōgen in order to finance its ambitious building programs and assert itself as *the* principal locus of Dōgen's lineage and legacy over and above Sōjiji.[7] I use Bodiford's argument as my point of departure in order to investigate further the nature and function of Eiheiji's physical and figural constructions. I also borrow from Henri Lefebvre's spatial theories grounded in the body. Accordingly I analyze Eiheiji's visual displays of authenticity and tradition in terms of its material and visual "temple bodies":

1. The architectural body: Eiheiji's anthropomorphic seven-hall layout as opposed to Sōjiji's somewhat idiosyncratic temple layout.
2. The figural body: Eiheiji's sculpted buddha bodies that signal the eternity of practice as opposed to Sōjiji's more historic emphasis on dharma heirs and specific temple founders.

Taken as a whole, therefore, I argue that Eiheiji has consistently constructed concrete material and visual markers to physically embody the dharma in Japan and that its anthropomorphic structures, sculptures, and other embodied displays of authority and authenticity have been instrumental to its institutional survival and success.

Analyzing Eiheiji's ideal body types in this way offers a novel approach for understanding Sōtō's institutional identity issues and further helps to cement the vital connection between the visibility and the viability of Eiheiji's self-consciously constructed "tradition." Investigating the various layers of temple bodies at Eiheiji may provide a model for analyzing other sites as well, but here it is significant because it is the first survey of the temple's material and visual history over the *longue durée* in order to speak to the continuity and change in institutional strategies for self-promotion. To be clear, I primarily focus on Eiheiji's contemporary self-promotional strategies but make substantial reference to historical precedents and Sōjiji's counterexamples to bring the former into high relief. I consider poetic, calligraphic, architectural, art historical, and contemporary sources in an attempt to acknowledge the ongoing and vital role of visual display and body imagery in establishing, sustaining, and promoting the temple's reputation. Finally, this analysis of the "figure and place of the sacred" (to borrow Yoritomi Motohiro's phrase, *seinarumono katachi to ba*) helps to relativize any stereotyped misperceptions of Zen as a solely meditative, minimalistic, or disembodied tradition that somehow lacks the physical forms of other iconic traditions.

Theorizing the Temple Body

As Joshua Irizarry points out, Sōtō's sectarian motto quite deliberately uses the term *ittai*, or "one body," to describe the unity of its dual institutional headquarters, which, he argues, are designed to both "cultivate and discipline" the novice body-in-training.[8] Irizarry's reliance on Foucault and other leading theorists speaks to the voluminous scholarly literature dedicated to the importance of the body in religious studies. Accordingly, the theoretical importance of the body in constructing Sōtō's physical and conceptual landscapes needs to be briefly outlined here. This analysis will rely primarily on the seminal spatial theories of Henri Lefebvre (1910–91).

In his 1974 treatise on spatial theory, *The Production of Space*, Lefebvre grounds all socially-constructed spaces in the human body. He first posits, "The whole of space proceeds from the body.. . . The genesis of a far-away order [i.e., social space] can be accounted for only on the basis of the order that is nearest to us—namely the order of the body."[9] He then describes how any given corporeally produced space in history (e.g., a Zen monastery) can in turn operate on three levels: *l'espace perçu, conçu, et vecu.* "Perceived space" (*l'espace perçu*) can be readily seen in everyday embodied practices in situ, such as zazen, chanting before icons, and communal eating, while "conceived space" (*l'espace conçu*) maps out theoretical, ideological, or conceptual tropes, such as Eiheiji's seven-hall compound as a living dharma body. The fully human total man (*l'homme total*), however, resides in the "lived space" (*l'espace vecu*) of the social imaginaire, which is embodied and enlivened by art and literature, such as the imagery and poetry of Eiheiji that will be discussed presently. According to Lefebvre, this third imagined space transcends real and ideal spaces, and also occasionally is able to recalibrate previously held assumptions about self-location (e.g., the unifying *ichibutsu ryōso* triad, which fundamentally reoriented Eiheiji and Sōjiji's institutional positions).[10]

Lefebvre's theoretical speculations were originally formulated to trace the production of modern urban space, but when applied to the specifics of Eiheiji's architectural and sculptural bodies, his categories can also help to strengthen the analysis of Eiheiji's material and visual culture as it relates to its institutional identity issues.

Underlying these theoretical remarks is the presupposition that material and sculptural bodies are important visual texts that need to be "read" and analyzed like any other text, for they communicate meanings and convey doctrinal messages as clearly as, and sometimes even more immediately or intuitively than, the written word. I further presuppose that visible art and architecture certainly express—but also actively shape—invisible religious thought. For example, Dōgen's viewing of circular *shisho* transmission certificates and of Mount Tiantong's three buddhas of past, present, and future may have been influential in shaping his unique understanding of being-time and time's ranging, as I argue below. It is therefore important to cultivate a kind of scholarly visual literacy that is able to read Eiheiji's built environments and visual worlds so as to gain a deeper understanding of the variegated temple bodies which have been so instrumental to contouring its identity and reputation up to the present day.

The Architectural Body

In spite of the numerous fires and other disasters that have plagued Eiheiji,[11] the monastery has consistently rebuilt its structures according to the Southern Song Chan model of the seven-hall compound (*shichidō garan*). It is this architectural body with discrete structures associated with distinct human body parts that Eiheiji continues to highlight today as a key component of its traditional identity. Sōjiji, I argue, historically did not and still today does not, strictly speaking, possess a truly axial *shichidō garan*, even though it idealistically invokes this traditional layout in its literature and liturgy. As a result, to invoke Lefebvre's spatial theory, both Eiheiji and Sōjiji may participate in the *shichidō garan*'s "conceived space" of tradition and authenticity, but it can only truly be embodied, and considered "perceived space," at Eiheiji.

The physical siting of Eiheiji temple dates to 1243, when Hatano Yoshishige donated to Dōgen a small portion of his *Shibinoshō* estate in Echizen Province (present-day Fukui Prefecture). Many scholars point out that this was just when Dōgen's *Gokokushōbōgi* petition was rejected by the court in Heian (present-day Kyoto) and when Enni Bennen's rival Zen community at nearby Tōfukuji (est. 1239) in addition to other Buddhist sects were challenging

Dōgen's young Zen community at Kōshōji, located in the suburbs of the old capital. Therefore, Dōgen's decision to accept Hatano's land grant and move after sixteen years in the city was quite conceivably motivated by pragmatic considerations, although one must recognize that these are but circumstantial speculations. Regardless, once Dōgen arrived in Echizen in 1243, he and his followers stayed at Kippōji and Yamashibu temples until the first buildings were completed. According to the Dōgen translator Kazuaki Tanahashi, construction began in the seventh month of 1244, with the dharma hall (*hattō*) completed in the ninth month and the monks' hall (*sōdō*) completed in the tenth.[12] Dōgen first named this single edifice temple Sanshōhō Daibutsuji and consecrated its main image (*honzon*) of the Buddha in 1244. More on this first Buddha statue follows in the section "The Figural Body." Dōgen renamed the temple Kichijōzan Eiheiji in 1246 in honor of the pure (*kichijō*) Buddhadharma that was believed to have entered into China in 67 CE, during the tenth year of the Eihei period of "Eternal Peace" (Ch. Yongping, 58–76 CE). In this same year of 1246, temple publications are keen to point out, Eiheiji was granted the title "Japan's first Sōtōshū training temple."[13]

Eiheiji's impressive architectural imprint on the mountain began only with the third patriarch, Tettsū Gikai (1219–1309). Gikai had occupied the important office of head cook, was appointed head abbot of Eiheiji during Dōgen's final absence, and studied Chan monastic architecture and ritual codes from 1259 to 1262, reportedly at the request of the second patriarch, Ejō.[14] William Bodiford questions whether Gikai ever went to China, stating, "There is no hard proof that he ever journeyed outside of Japan,"[15] but among other Sōtō Zen historians and architectural historians of China and Japan, Gikai's travels and importation of Southern Song architectural models to Japan remains unquestioned. They credit him with returning with *The Illustrated Record of Mountain Monasteries of the Great Song* (*Daisō Shozanzu*), which is stored at Tōfukuji in Kyoto and is classified as an Important Cultural Property.[16] This text includes architectural diagrams of three of the ten most important Chan monasteries in the Jiangnan region, namely, Lingyinsi, Tiantongsi, and Wanniansi.[17] All three illustrations are characterized by their orientation to the south and by a strict north-south central axis along which the larger and/or successively more important halls are aligned.

The blueprint in Figure 10.2 for Jingdesi (Bright Virtue) monastery at Mount Tiantong, where Dōgen achieved awakening under his mentor Rujing and where Gikai ostensibly studied, shows a bird's-eye view of the temple buildings. Its wooden pillar supports, stairways, and over forty-five structures are clearly indicated. Moving from the bottom of the plan upward (i.e., from south to north), one observes six main buildings that successively make up the

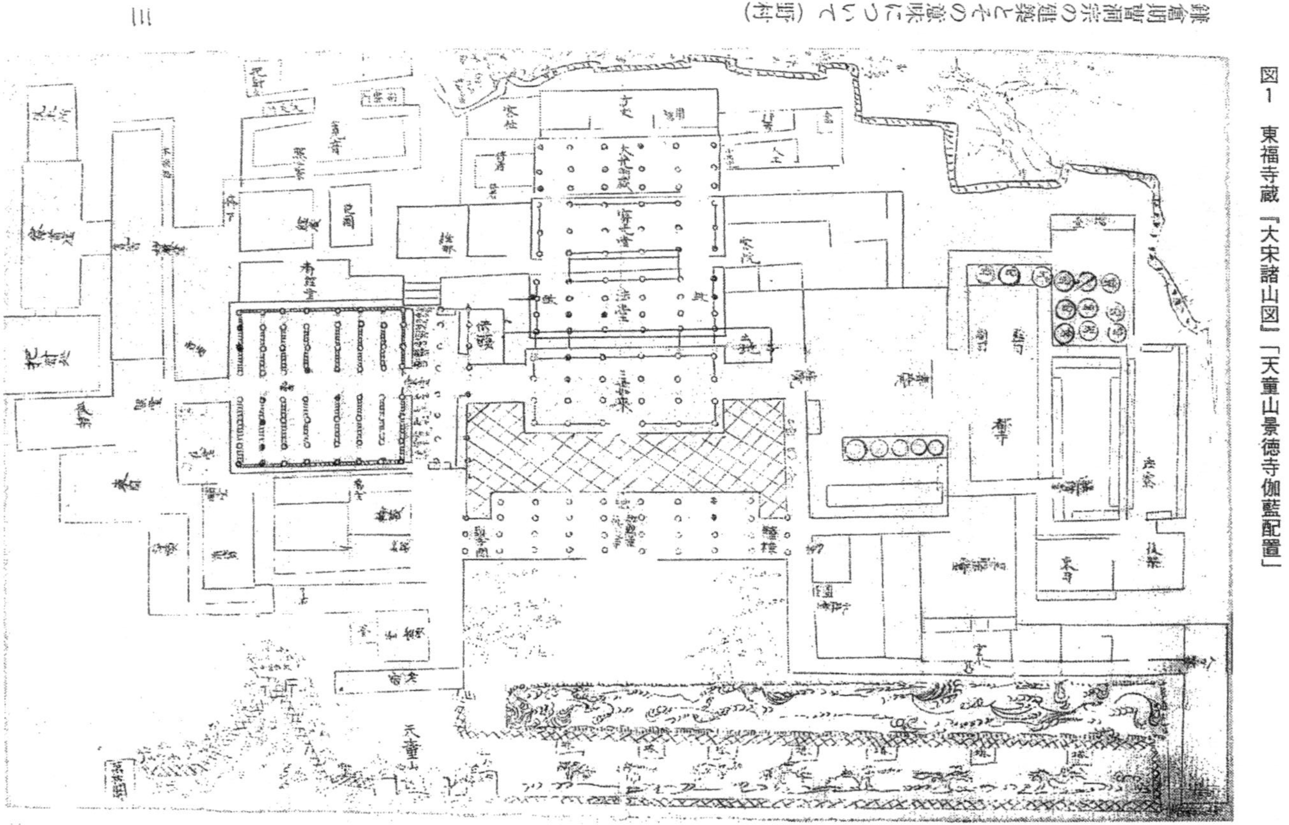
鎌倉期曹洞宗の建築とその意味について（野村）
三
図1　東福寺蔵『大宋諸山図』「天童山景徳寺伽藍配置」
天童山

FIGURE 10.2 Gikai's architectural rendering of Jingdesi temple, Mount Tiantong, China. Dated 1259–62. Tōfukuj Important National Property. Reproduced from Nomura Shunichi, "Kamakura dai sōtōshū no kenchiku" (Kyoto, n.d.), 3 (Figure 1).

central core of the compound: a *sanmon* gate; a *butsuden* (buddha hall), which
is clearly labeled *sanze nyorai* (indicating the three enshrined buddhas within);
a *hattō* (dharma hall); a *jakkōdō* (memorial hall); a *daikōmyōzō* (sutra repository); and the *hōjō* (abbot's quarters) crowning the complex.[18] Most noticeable
among the other buildings is the detailed *sōdō* (monks' hall) to the west of center, with a dozen meditation platforms clearly delineated, as well as the large
kuin (refectory) to the east of center, with five large circles perhaps indicating
large cooking pots for making gruel. Storage vats in the upper right-hand corner are labeled with the character for soybean paste (*jiang*). Other traditional
characters for salt (*yan*) and black bean paste (*chi*) in the upper register also
indicate other condiments for the monks' rudimentary monastic diet.[19] The
tōsu (latrine) to the southwest and *yokushitsu* (bathing facilities) to the southeast appear as smaller subsidiary buildings in the complex.

This axial arrangement does not depart significantly from other large-scale
architectural antecedents in China, such as religious and imperial palace compounds of Northern Wei Luoyang, Tang dynasty Chang'an, and Northern Song
Dongjing (Kaifeng).[20] Certainly not all Chan temple compounds in China
were laid out according to the ideal axial plan, but as Daiheng Guo points out,
Chan monasteries of the Southern Song did diverge from their precursors
by arranging subsidiary halls for the monks along an auxiliary east-west axis,
for "in earlier Chan monasteries, residential space for monks was scattered
throughout the monastery."[21]

Gikai's *Illustrated Record* of Mount Tiantong and other Chan monasteries
is thus considered to be the principal source text providing the basic blueprint
for Eiheiji's biaxial organization of structures. After his return to Japan in 1262,
Gikai served as the third abbot of Eiheiji, from 1267 to 1272, but continued to
remain in the Eiheiji environs caring for his mother until 1287, when he supposedly left the area due to the *sandai sōron* succession controversy. While
at Eiheiji, Gikai is credited with building a two-story *sanmon* gate in front of
Dōgen's preexisting *hattō* and connecting the structures with corridors.[22] The
fifth abbot, Giun (1253–1333), completed the rest of the seven halls, ostensibly
based on Gikai's illustrated record or personal accounts of his travels.

No extant records illustrate what Gikai's or Giun's temples looked like
before the fire of 1340 completely destroyed the entire compound. However,
the oldest extant map of Eiheiji's architectural body within the larger environmental body of Echizen in Figure 10.3 dated to 1676–81 does still clearly
embody the biaxial model of its continental prototypes, though on a much
more simplified scale. It features a *sanmon* gate, a *butsuden*, and a *hattō* along
the north-south axis; a *kuin* and *yokushitsu* to the right of center; and a *sōdō*
and *tōsu* to the left of the core. This same layout characterizes the compound

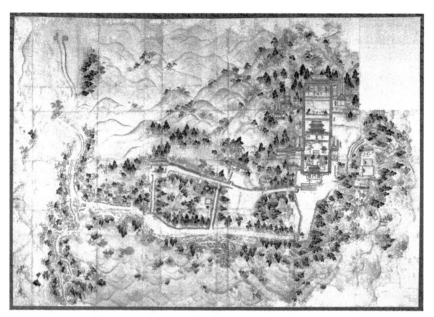

FIGURE 10.3 Oldest extant map of Eiheiji, mountain monastery, ca. 1676–81. Courtesy of Eiheiji Temple, Fukui Prefecture. Used with permission.

to this day, though naturally the actual structures and the noticeably different roofing materials have changed over the numerous rebuilds.[23]

Eiheiji's seventeenth-century appearance thus seems to accurately reflect and reproduce Mount Tiantong's organizing layout, though on a much simplified scale. According to the Zen art and architectural historian Helmut Brinker, the typical Zen *shichidō garan* layout was standardized in Japan only in the fifteenth century. In a text entitled *Corresponding Measuring Units* (*Sekisō Ōrai*) by the court official Ichijō Kaneyoshi (also read as Kanera; 1401–81), Ichijō stipulates only the above-mentioned seven halls and omits the architectural conventions of the crowning abbot's quarters, bell tower, sutra repository, and other subsidiary structures that typically existed in Chinese Chan monasteries. Brinker further observes that the *shichidō garan*'s now famous anthropomorphic associations were grafted onto the axial Zen temple layout only during the early Edo period by the great Mujaku Dōchū (1653–1744).[24] His text *Basket of Articles from the Zen Tradition* (*Zenrin Shōkisen*) graphically maps out the seven halls onto the figure of a male body and explicitly equates the *sanmon* gate with the genitals, the *butsuden* with the heart, the *hattō* with the head, the monks' hall and kitchen with the arms, and the lavatory and bathhouse with the feet. Other accounts liken the *shichidō garan* to the contours of a meditating monk seated in full lotus position, as the location of his symbolic feet (the bath and latrine buildings) roughly line up along the same latitude as his metaphorical groin (the *sanmon* gate).

Although the *shichidō garan*'s correlation of body and building in Japan can be directly traced only to the early Edo period, this source of authenticity and tradition is still invoked today at all levels, from elite scholarship to tourist literature and media products. For example, Yokoyama Hideya's seminal scholarly study of Zen architecture opens with Eiheiji's seventeenth-century map as its first prototypical exemplar, and the voice-over of one promotional YouTube video explicitly explains, "If we think of the temple as a human body, this [the *hattō*] is the head. . . [and] an image of the Buddha enshrined in the [*butsuden*] building corresponds to the heart."[25] Most significantly, today Mujaku's same body-building discourse is still invoked at Eiheiji almost immediately upon the visitors' arrival. Once visitors pay their entrance fee, enter into the *sanshō* (reception hall), remove their shoes, and receive glossy Japanese- or English-language tourist booklets, they are invited to sit and wait in formal *seiza* position on the tatami mat floor of an orientation room. There, every ten minutes or so, a young robed novice stands before a floor-to-ceiling color-coded map of the temple grounds and delivers an *etoki*-like explanation of the highlighted seven halls of the main compound. When explaining the sites and rites of the *shichidō garan* with a long pointer, he uses words like *shinzō* (heart organ), *nō* (brain), and other physical organs and body parts of the architectural corpus.[26]

The monk is also keen to mention the building dates of all the structures and to emphasize the history and sense of long-standing tradition at the site. He notes that the *sanmon* gate dating from 1749 is the oldest extant building in the complex, followed by the *hattō* (1843) and *butsuden* (1902). He also makes special mention of the *joyōden* (founder's hall) for Dōgen and the *kounkaku* (hall for the second abbot, Koun Ejō), both rebuilt in 1881. He omits other subsidiary structures that are not strictly part of the standard *shichidō garan* in Japan, however. These include the abbot's quarters to the north of the kitchen (1852), a reception room for important visitors to the west of the abbot's quarters (the platform of mysterious light, *Myōkōdai*, 1844), the monks' quarters (1901), the brilliant treasury library (*Daikō Myōzō*, 1930) to the southwest of the abbot's quarters, and a reading hall for scripture study on the western side of the compound (1951).[27]

In contradistinction to Eiheiji's strong ties to the continent, its clearly discerned axes, and its perpetuation of the traditional anthropomorphic metaphor throughout history, Sōjiji's architectural body in Figure 10.4 is less clearly discerned. A late Edo period map of Sōjiji in its original Noto peninsula

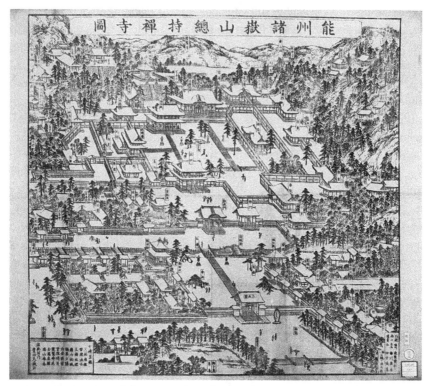

FIGURE 10.4 Map of the original Sōjiji temple in Noto, latter half of the Edo period. Courtesy of Komazawa University Library.

location (roughly contemporary with the Eiheiji map in Figure 10.3) reveals that Sōjiji's architectural compound had by then metasticized into a sprawling amalgamation of buildings, gates, subtemples, and mausoleums. These are all loosely knit together by a labyrinth of open-air pathways, in sharp contradistinction to Eiheiji's famous grid of covered corridors (*kairō*), which serve as the connective tissue to the architectural organs of the site. The Noto Sōjiji map features a double entrance gate (the ornate left-hand gate exclusively reserved for the emperor's carriage), a *sanmon* gate, and a *butsuden* on a somewhat axial line. However, due to the topographical features of the site, the *hattō* lies to the northeast of center. It is pushed diagonally up and over to the right of the invisible axis by what appears to be a hill, with a steep staircase leading up to a memorial hall. If the ideal seven-hall layout is supposed to mimic the body of a Zen practitioner meditating, then it seems that at Noto Sōjiji the meditator's head has definitely nodded off to the right and needs a compassionate smack with the *kyōsaku* staff to get back on track.

It must be noted that at Eiheiji Gikai had directly imported the blueprints to construct a new Chinese-style Chan monastery from the ground up, whereas at Noto Sōjiji Keizan and his dharma heirs had inherited a Shingon sanctuary that was incrementally added to over time. In addition, it must be recognized that not all Zen temple compounds in Japan always translated architecturally according to plan. The Rinzai temple Nanzenji in Kyoto, for example, is oriented to the west, Kenchōji's layout in Kamakura curves faintly to the right, and Yokoyama Hideya's authoritative appendix of Zen temple plans reveals a surprising variation of layouts throughout history. As mentioned previously, the axial arrangement of seven halls was standardized in Japan only in the fifteenth century.

Yet even when presented with the opportunity to rebuild the temple in 1911 according to ideal Sino-Japanese axial standards, Sōjiji temple in Tsurumi outside of Yokohama today still replicates this same off-kilter location of the *hattō* (referred to as the *daisodō*). The *daisodō* today stands to the northeast of the *butsuden*, even though there is no topographical obstacle behind it to prevent a crowning *hattō* atop the temple body's (nonexistent) spine. In addition, the visitor first entering the compound from below must first pass through Sōjiji's magnificent *sanmon* gate, completed in 1969, but must immediately turn right to enter into the complex. This already breaks the axis. Ahead, past the monumental *sanshōkaku* hall built in 1990 for lay instruction, past the 1920 *kōshakudai* (main reception building) on the right, and behind the east-west corridor bifurcating the temple compound as a whole, the visitor can discern Sōjiji's imposing 1965 concrete *daisodō* with its oxidized copper-green roof lines rising slightly to the right above the treetops.[28]

The diminutive but graceful hip-gable rooflines of the wooden *butsuden* stand far to the left in the western quadrant of the compound. Thus if one were to attempt to experience the ideal axial progression of buildings at Sōjiji today, one would have to enter through the *sanmon* gate, turn right heading north, go straight past the reception hall, turn left and walk west along the corridor, turn right and pass up through the middle *chūjakumon* gate, go straight north again to visit the *butsuden*, and then make one's way diagonally up and over to the right to finally arrive at the *daisodō* in the northeast. This does not adhere to the long-standing *shichidō garan* ideal sequence of buildings that line up single file directly behind one another along an invisible but clearly discerned spinal column.

One young novice monk in the summer of 2013 showed a moment of cognitive dissonance when questioned about Sōjiji's somewhat haphazard arrangement of buildings versus the ideal axial positioning of the ideal temple body's architectural anatomy. However, he quickly recovered and laughingly noted that the actual locations of the seven halls do not matter much. "Even the *tōsu* toilets" (written with the character for "east"), he joked, "are in the wrong place. They should be called *seisu*" (written with the character for "west," as the latrine typically is located on the western side of the core). On the one hand, his comments clearly demonstrate that, at Sōjiji, simply having seven core buildings in any location legitimately qualifies it as a *shichidō garan*. On the other hand, it could demonstrate that this young monk at least was willing to overlook what Lefebvre calls the real "perceived space" of the buildings before him and instead imagine only the "conceived space" of the ideal *shichidō garan* architectural body, which, it has been shown, still persists at Eiheiji.

The Figural Body

Eiheiji prides itself on tracing its architectural body directly back to its founder's home temple in China via Gikai and replicating Dōgen's experience in China by duplicating Mount Tiantong's material architecture. It also prides itself on faithfully reproducing the visual culture that Dōgen himself encountered within its halls. I argue that Eiheiji's interior imagery symbolically indicates the eternity and permanence of enlightened buddhahood, as opposed to Sōjiji's concern with historically specific dharma heirs and temple founders. Both iconographic programs, however, serve to legitimate and promote the temples' respective reputations.

The Sanmon

Taken as a whole, the key imagery of Eiheiji's three main axial buildings embodies and manifests the universal yet local, eternal yet ever-present body of buddhahood (*dharmakaya*). Beginning with Eiheiji's *sanmon* gate, Gikai is known to have first enshrined images on the second floor of the structure when he constructed it between 1267 and 1272. This standard practice for Chan/Zen monasteries continued through the most recent rebuild in 1749, which, as noted earlier, makes it the oldest extant structure in the compound. Today the lower story of the *sanmon* exhibits newly painted and gilded *shitennō* (guardians), and its second story houses a colorfully painted set of sixteen larger and five hundred smaller arhats (*rakan*).[29]

These images are not usually accessible to visitors due to the *sanmon*'s perilously steep ladder, but I was given brief access to the second story in

September 2001. These wooden statues date from the Edo period and are arranged behind and around Sakyamuni Buddha five rows deep. The mise-en-scène above depicts the episode in which Sakyamuni Buddha preaches the *Kegonkyō* (*Avatamsaka Sutra*) not only to the pilgrim youth Sudhana but also to all assembled past and future enlightened beings, such as the *rakan*. Given the sutra's mythopoetic vision of holographic buddha-worlds iterating throughout space and time, the visual message of the *sanmon*'s second-floor scene simulates and condenses the eternity and infinity of everyone's enlightenment potential into the present place and moment. The symbolism of the scene is not lost on the newly arrived *unsui* (novices), who perform rituals above here after having passed directly below upon their admittance to the monastery, the place-time where they ostensibly train to become enlightened like the arhats.

Sōjiji also houses *rakan* in the second story of its monumental concrete 1969 *sanmon*, but I have never seen the second floor at Sōjiji and cannot comment on the arrangement, and the weight of history and the automatic aura of legitimacy that time-honored structures and rituals carry over the generations lend Eiheiji's *sanmon* a certain cachet that probably cannot be matched at Sōjiji. Simply appealing to history is, admittedly, a blunt and unsophisticated argument, but the combination of nostalgia and continued practice is how Eiheiji constructs its own importance, as evidenced in the New Year's poem by the current abbot, Fukuyama Taihō, published in Eiheiji's bimonthly temple journal *Sanshō*:

For over seven hundred seasons the beloved old plum

Year by year, age by age, still opens here;[30]

There is nothing beyond the Buddha dharma of this new spring,

So we just sit silently, obeying the command that has come down to us.[31]

The Butsuden

The eternity yet immediacy of practice within Eiheiji's "fences and walls, tiles and pebbles," to quote Dōgen's "Bendōwa," is further reinforced visually in the main buddha hall.[32] Here, at the physical and metaphorical heart of the monastery, there are enshrined three main images (*honzon*) representing the buddhas of the past, present, and future.

This triple *honzon* group was not original to Dōgen's first Daibutsuji temple; as mentioned earlier, Dōgen consecrated only a single buddha image there during his lifetime.[33] According to the 1743 edition of the *Kenzeiki*, a fifteenth-century biography of Dōgen attributed to the abbot Kenzei (1417–74), Dōgen supposedly said during the construction process of Daibutsuji in the summer of 1244:

> It is auspicious that today the work of laying out the site for the Buddha hall has been completed. The officer of the local government supervised the work. Now that the layout is finished I want to have a temporary building constructed on this site and have a purification ceremony for the Buddha. After this we will gradually build the Buddha hall. As a vow of my lifetime, I am determined to carve a statue of Sakyamuni Buddha with my own hands. I am not certain how long I will live, but this is my intention. It might not be exquisitely crafted but my intention is to carve it with my own hands, even if it takes many years.
>
> In reverence, Dōgen
>
> The fourteenth day, the eighth month, the second year of the Kangen era (1244).[34]

Tanahashi notes that Dōgen's hand-carved single buddha statue was indeed completed but did not survive the fire of 1473, whereas Asami Ryūsuke maintains that all of Eiheiji's statuary perished in the fire of 1340.[35]

The triple buddha *honzon* in the *butsuden* of Eiheiji therefore does not date to Dōgen's lifetime, but rather to Gikai's tenure as third abbot (1267–72).[36] They replicate exactly the *sanze nyorai* (three main Buddha images) in the *butsuden* of Mount Tiantong monastery in China, where Dōgen achieved enlightenment under Rujing in 1227 and where Gikai studied from 1259 to 1262. It is not certain whether Dōgen's first hand-carved single figure (ostensibly of Sakyamuni Buddha) served as the anchor to Gikai's triple *honzon* or if Gikai commissioned a new set. Regardless, Mount Tiantong's model of past, present, and future buddhas, and its exact replication at Eiheiji ("Mt. Tien-t'ung East," to borrow Steven Heine's phrase),[37] has linked the two temples iconographically from Gikai's tenure from the mid-thirteenth century onward. According to Asami, the actual sculptures on display today are believed to date from the mid-fourteenth-century rebuild after the 1340 fire destroyed the fourth patriarch Giun's completed *shichidō garan*.[38] The only surviving sculptures dating from the thirteenth century are two sculptures of the *garan*'s local protective deities, Kanseishisha (or Kansaishisha) and Shōbō Shichirō Daigenshuri Bosatsu.[39] Other medieval Buddhist sculptures at Eiheiji also date from the mid-fourteenth century onward.

Reading the partially obstructed *honzon* triad from right to left is Amida Buddha of the past, Sakyamuni Buddha of the present world age, and Miroku (Skt. Maitreya) Buddha of the future. Known as the Buddhas of the Three Ages (*sanzebutsu*) or Buddhas of the Three Ages and Ten Directions (*sanze jippō shobutsu*), these three eternal yet ever-present embodiments of buddhahood are said to span the past (*shōgon*), present (*ken*), and future (*shōshuku*) kalpa ages.[40] It is not insignificant that Dōgen, once exposed to this timeless yet timely imagery in China, returned to Japan and formulated his unique theory of being-time (*uji*) in 1240.[41] In his *Uji* fascicle, Dōgen articulates a nonlinear vision of ranging time (*kyōryaku*) in which past, present, and future mutually (and in this sculptural context, physically) interface.

Elsewhere I have argued that Dōgen's *shisho* (transmission certificate) was instrumental in helping him to formulate his eclectic notion of being-time, for in the *shisho* lineage chart, all the historic names of Zen Buddhist patriarchs are written out in a circle, without beginning or end, like the spokes of a time-less wheel radiating out from Buddha's enlightened mind in the center. The patriarchs' ideal physical bodies are invoked both discursively in the *Shisho* fascicle and calligraphically in the scroll. A thin red bloodline traced in vermillion ink weaves in and out of the radiating name-bodies of all the lineage holders, who graphically stand "shoulder to shoulder" (*shobutsu seiken*) with one another but can "see" one another (in the sense of meeting buddha-eye to buddha-eye) across the wheel of compressed eternity-time. This is one way of envisioning the self-legitimating figural body of enlightenment at Eiheiji, for the temple continues to claim that it holds the original *shisho* scroll that Dōgen brought back from Japan in 1227 (though other scholars maintain it is a medieval copy).[42]

However, one must also consider the possibility that other images, such as Mount Tiantong's triple *honzon*, may have also influenced Dōgen's unique notion that time can range back and forth across past, present, and future, and that all realized beings therefore are united in the eternal present of their shared dharma transmission. By extension, when Gikai sculpturally replicated Mount Tiantong's symbolic message at Eiheiji three generations later, he signaled the eternity and unity of all past, present, and future realized beings throughout the known world at the time (i.e., both in China and in Japan). This eternal message "comes down to us today," to paraphrase Eiheiji's current abbot's poem.

By contrast, the iconographic message of modern-day Sōjiji's *butsuden* emphasizes the historic specificity and legitimacy of Buddha's dharma heirs, not any transtemporal or transgeographic message of eternal buddhahood linking China and Japan. Sōjiji's main images of veneration are a central Sakyamuni Buddha flanked by his two favorite disciples, Mahakasyapa and Ananda, two historic figures who loom large in Zen legend and lore. Mahakasyapa was the sole mind-to-mind recipient of Buddha's famous silent flower sermon, and Ananda is famous for inquiring what Mahakasyapa received from Buddha and for later promulgating the Buddha's teachings in the sutras.[43] Given Sōjiji's preoccupation with legitimating its own institutional power (especially since Keizan never actually held the abbacy at Eiheiji), this triad at Sōjiji can be read to suggest that Dōgen, like Mahakasyapa, mystically received the dharma transmission from the Buddha, and that Keizan, like Ananda, promulgated his teachings thereafter. The *butsuden*'s triad of enlightened bodies thus emphasizes the importance of the dharma lineage that gets transmitted at specific times in history, as opposed to the timeless nature of buddahood. By extension, this highly contextualized reading of Sōjiji's visual texts suggests that Keizan is the principal inheritor, steward, and promulgator of Buddha's teachings via Dōgen Zen. This same impulse to legitimate Sōjiji's historic lineage extends into its *daisodō* (dharma hall) as well, as discussed below.

The *Hattō*

In addition to the *butsuden*, the *hattō* at Eiheiji enshrines a seated image of Shokanzeon bosatsu holding a lotus flower and sporting an elaborate crown with streamers dangling around the ears. Popularly known as Kannon, this bodhisattva of compassion hears the cries of the entire world and employs expedient means to relieve suffering universally. It is not known when exactly this Kamakura-period image entered into the monastery's pantheon, or when or how it made its way into the *hattō*, but for centuries the *Invocation of Great Compassion* (*Daihishin Darani*) has been chanted daily in this hall before the Kannon image during morning ceremonies.[44]

In Figure 10.5, Kannon's exquisitely wood-carved body of enlightened compassion is not the only body in the hall. In addition, the Mount Sumeru altar is flanked by four mythological *shishi* (alt. *komainu*; guardian lions), who look across and beyond the dharma seat placed between them. These animal bodies are painted white, just as they were at Mount Tiantong, and their mouths are fixed perpetually in the distinctive open *A* or closed *Un* positions, symbolizing the alpha and omega of the Sanskrit alphabet. They thus signal the message that Buddhist compassion extends through everything from A to Z, unifying all under the ubiquity and eternity of their wrathful yet compassionate protective gazes. According to Dōgen's diary of his years in China, the *Hōkyōki*, Mount Tiantong also featured *shishi* lions in its dharma lecture hall.

FIGURE 10.5 Dharma hall at Eiheiji with enshrined Kannon (not visible), four guardian lions, and lotus canopy bells. Photograph by Pamela D. Winfield.

Dōgen notes (in entry 37, according to Kodera's translation), "The Lecture Hall has images of lions on the east and west side of the floor to the south of the Dharma Seat. The lions face one another, looking slightly toward the south. Their color is white throughout the whole body from the mane down to the tail."[45] Dōgen then quotes Rujing metaphorically distinguishing between realized and unrealized lion-monks by virtue of the color of their mane (i.e., the purity of their mind): "Lately, although the lions are colored white, the manes are still blue; this shows that they have not inherited the transmission of the masters. A lion must be entirely white from the mane all the way down to the tail."[46]

Dōgen notes that Rujing immediately abrogates this dualism in the following lines, however, and unifies both realized white-maned lion-monks and unrealized blue-maned lion-monks throughout the world under the all-embracing lotus canopy of Kannon's compassion (the eight corners of the canopy symbolize the earth's cardinal and ordinal directions):

The canopy that hangs above the Dharma Seat is the Lotus Canopy. It looks as if a lotus flower covers the earth. That is why it is called the

Lotus Canopy. It has eight corners with eight mirrors and streamers. The streamers are attached to [the clapper of] the eight bells, one on each corner. The lotus leaves are five-layered with a bell suspended on each. They constitute the One Suchness of the [Lotus] Canopy above the Dharma Seat of this monastery.[47]

This detailed description of the lotus canopy of compassion suspended over the dharma seat of wisdom is not a mere art historical observation of the adornment of the sanctuary (shōgon). Rather Dōgen's careful notation of the canopy's hanging bells is a deliberate allusion to a stock image he favors from a poem by his master about a windbell, whose "whole body, hanging in emptiness," jingles out enlightenment with an onomatopoetic ring-a-ting-ting.[48] Elsewhere, in his fascicle Space (Kokū), written ca. 1245, Dōgen even anthropomorphizes this bell, commenting, "Thus the whole body of skin, flesh, bones, and marrow, hangs in empty space."[49]

In this case, therefore, the temple bodies in Eiheiji's hattō include not only the sculpted wood bodies of the anthropomorphic Kannon and zoomorphic lions, but also the gilt bronze cast object-bodies of the lotus canopy and the sonorific bell-bodies that ring out prajna throughout all the corners of the earth. These material object bodies, like other inanimate ritual bodies in the hattō (e.g., the wooden fish-drum, bell bowl, and other ritual accoutrements), individually and collectively embody Dōgen's signature teaching regarding the preaching of the insentient (mujō seppō). This in turn is Dōgen's own spin on the Buddhist doctrine of hosshin seppō, the preaching of the world-body of buddhahood, which includes all such forms and physiques. This larger consideration of all worldly forms embodying and thereby communicating the true dharma in concrete form adds yet another overarching layer of ideal body imagery to the discussion of Eiheiji's variegated temple bodies.[50]

The daisodō at Sōjiji, which functionally corresponds to Eiheiji's hattō, also enshrines great bodies of Buddhist wisdom, but in a way that emphasizes the pivotal figures in Sōjiji's illustrious institutional history. Its altar enshrines sixty-two memorial tablets (ihai) for Sōjiji's earliest patriarchs, and secreted away behind the altar are master portraits of some of Sōjiji's great institutional leaders. These images have not been published and are not visible to the public, but according to the oral description of a novice in June 2013, Keizan occupies pride of place in the center, flanked by his dharma predecessor Dōgen on the right, and his dharma heir Gasan Jōseki (1275–1365/6) on the left. Especially when compared with the "one Buddha, two patriarchs" triad, this site-specific arrangement makes a clear ideological statement about the importance of Keizan to the sect as a whole. The triad is also joined by five other major temple founders, the so-called *goin kaiki*. According to the Sōjiji researcher Joshua Irizarry, to the left of Gasan are Daitetsu Sōryō (1333–1438), who opened Denpō-an, and Jippō Ryoshū (1318–1405), who established Nyoi-an. To the right of Dōgen are Tsūgen Jakurei (1322–91), who established Myōkō-an, Taigen Sōshin (d. 1371), who opened Fuzō-in, and Mutan Sokan (dates unknown), who opened Tōsen-an.[51] These temple bodies again reiterate Sōjiji's overwhelming historical interest in institution-building.

Sōjiji's iconographic message therefore is quite clear. Instead of gaining legitimacy by replicating continental prototypes, Sōjiji marks out its own legitimacy by charismatic autonomy. Instead of reinforcing long-standing figures for eternal yet ever-present Buddhist wisdom and compassion, it reconfigures the body of enlightenment to inhabit its historical institution-building lineage figures. Instead of emphasizing linkages to China and the source of Dōgen's enlightenment, Sōjiji venerates its own institutional founders as model disciples par excellence, just like Mahakasyapa and Ananda. Instead of embodying buddhahood in terms of Dōgen's ranging time, it embodies it in terms of what Lefebvre calls "lived time" (*temps vecu*), which reconfigures and recontours one's sociopolitical self-location through art.

Conclusion

I have focused primarily on Eiheiji's material and visual temple bodies, but one should not forget all the other kinds of temple bodies present at Eiheiji. There are animal bodies like Manjusri's lion mount in the *sōdō*, as well as Samantabhadra's elephant mount and another lion-mounted Manjusri flanking Buddha in the *kichijōkaku* (main reception hall). In addition, 230 bird and flower bodies illustrate each roundel in the coffered ceiling of the *sanshōkaku* (lay reception hall), while numerous other phoenix bodies, crane bodies, turtle bodies, and other creatures are carved or brushed into the very walls of the temple itself. Carved bas-relief bodies in Confucian-style dress are exquisitely carved into wooden panels above eye level, while carved Daoist bodies like the Seven Sages of the Bamboo Grove in other panels frolic in a state of perpetual animation. "Bodies of emptiness" show their presence by their very absence, as with an unusually long thin gourd in the *tokonoma* (alcove) of the abbot's private reception room. Subsidiary deity bodies such as Benzai sonten and Sanbōdai kōjin are enshrined in the middle courtyard between the *sanmon* and *chūjakumon* middle gates, while the *goshintai* (bodies of kami) reside in Shintō shrines across the river.

If we take seriously Dōgen's teaching about the preaching of the insentient, we also need to consider the body of the Kuzuryū River itself, which appropriately has been given the theriomorphic body of a moss-covered dragon spouting water from the rocks. So too must we consider the cypress-bodies, flower-bodies, and even rock-bodies, such as the one in front of the *jōyōden* where Dōgen is said to have sat in meditation. In keeping with Fabio Rambelli's scholarship on material Buddhism, furthermore, we must also recognize the performance bodies of the Buddhist sutras themselves, which are fanned out and "read" accordion-style during metonymic morning services in the *hattō*. Eiheiji's bodies of ritual memory include both the departed who are memorialized and the living who remember them and therefore commission the ritual bodies of monks-in-training, who in turn have memorized and internalized rituals through a kind of deep muscle memory. These ritual bodies, which have already been highly mediated through bells and gongs, robes and staffs, strict diets and lack of sleep, are mediated even further and extended beyond Eiheiji's temple walls through mass-media vehicles, such as CD recordings, commercial documentaries by NHK and Fukui TV, or internally generated websites and sectarian publications. Noticeably absent among all these temple bodies are women's bodies, which have been allowed to visit the mountain enclave only since Japan's *nyonin kekkai* ban was lifted in 1869.

When Sōjiji sought independence from Eiheiji in 1892, it could have eclipsed Eiheiji and propelled it into another prolonged period of being overshadowed by Sōjiji's administrative and financial superiority. However, since the reconciliation accord of 1894, Eiheiji has continued to capitalize effectively on its history and cultural assets for institutional flourishing in the modern period. Sōjiji today technically controls thousands more subsidiary subtemples than Eiheiji, but this de jure distinction holds little sway in the hearts and minds of many contemporary Sōtō Zen followers, who still consider Eiheiji to be the de facto *honzan* of the Sōtō Zen sect. This is particularly true of foreign Zen adherents, who tend to romanticize Eiheiji's place in Sōtōshū history.

Yet the reason they do so, I have argued, is precisely because its discursive, architectural, and visual strategies for identity-construction and self-promotion have been so effective over time. One promotional YouTube video in English, for example, features a single female visitor peacefully ambling through the temple structures as it highlights a series of statistics that appeal to tradition and authenticity in nature; it notes its establishment by Dōgen over 750 years ago among its six-hundred-year-old cedars, where today 150 monks practice daily within its seventy buildings arranged over thirty thousand square meters.[52] Popular magazines like the glossy *Zen no Kaze* profiled Eiheiji first above Sōjiji in its 1981 inaugural issue, and its section "Heart to Heart Zen"

("Zen wa kokoro kara kokoro e") prominently features and illustrates Eiheiji's anthropomorphic architectural analogy.[53]

Important architectural and iconographic connections have accorded Eiheiji a long-standing legitimacy by visual association with Mount Tiantong that does not exist at Sōjiji today. Eiheiji still embodies the ideal architectural anatomy of its thirteenth-century Chinese prototype as relayed by Gikai, and this larger temple body still enshrines Mount Tiantong's model for personifying the eternal world-body of buddhahood, with statues of the arhats, the three buddhas, and other sentient and insentient enlightened entities. By contrast, Sōjiji's somewhat haphazard layout of seven halls effectively dismembers the *shichidō garan* body type metaphor, and its main halls are filled with its own dharma heirs and temple founders. Eiheiji's fourteenth-century sculpted bodies carry the weight and authenticity of history and tradition, for it is assumed that they are older, closer to the founder, and therefore of more reliable provenance, theoretically speaking at least (viz. Dōgen's contested *shisho* certificate).

Similarly Sōjiji's twentieth-century sculpted and painted images are equally powerful messaging agents for its institutional identity, but its reputation is instead intimately bound up with the sustained importance of its subtemples. Eiheiji's visual markers of authenticity and "tradition," I have argued, have been instrumental in constructing the temple's reputation that, by extension, has successfully been leveraged for financial gain in the modern period. Its institutional identity rests on these variegated temple bodies, and it can be assumed that it will continue to sustain and promote these ideal body types in the centuries to come.[54] At the very least, this investigation into Eiheiji's material and visual temple bodies has dispelled any stereotypical assumptions about Zen minimalism, iconoclasm, or supposed lack of iconicity that purportedly characterizes other Buddhist sects in Japan.

Acknowledgment

This research was facilitated by grants from the Elon University Faculty Research and Development Fund and from the North East Asian Council of the Association of Asian Studies (NEAC-AAS) in the summer of 2013. I would also like to thank Professors Ishii Seijun and Tsunoda Tairyu of Komazawa University, Rev. Takayama Koten of Eiheiji Sanshōkai, Tsukada Hiroshi, Iwamoto Akemi, Yonehara Yoshio, Patricia Fister, Michaela Mross, Joshua Irizarry, Grace Lin, Nancy Steinhardt, Kristina Troost, and Steven Heine for their many kindnesses and helpful suggestions.

NOTES

1. Joshua Aaron Irizarry, "A Forest for a Thousand Years: Cultivating Life and Disciplining Death at Sōjiji, A Japanese Sōtō Zen Temple," Ph.D. diss., University of Michigan, 2011, 29, quoting Nodomi Jōten, "Sōjiji no Konjaku: Tsurumi Goiten Zengo wo Chūshin ni," *Kyōdo Tsurumi* (2007): 15. The term *ittai* can be translated as "essence" or "substance" in a technical philosophical sense, but it can also be translated as "one body" in the literal sense. Given my stated focus on Eiheiji's temple bodies, I have chosen to render this term as "essential body" in order to highlight both its ideological and its anthropomorphic valences.

2. Komazawa daigaku zen bunka rekishi hōmotsukan, ed., *"Kigakuten 'Sōtōshū no Kyōiku to Shuppan' Zuroku"* (Tokyo: Komazawa Daigaku, 2012), 19. Many thanks to Tsukada Hiroshi for providing this helpful resource.

3. In ancient Sino-Japanese Buddhist parlance, verticality indicated temporality and horizontality indicated spatiality. Pamela Winfield, *Icons and Iconoclasm in Japanese Buddhism: Kūkai and Dōgen on the Art of Enlightenment* (New York: Oxford University Press, 2013).

4. Alternately one may interpret the metaphor of Dōgen planting the seed and Keizan nurturing it in purely botanical terms. One may find a contemporary echo of this sentiment in Eiheiji and Sōjiji's collaborative project to germinate and eventually donate cherry trees to temples affected by the 2011 Great Eastern Japan earthquake and tsunami disaster. This Joint Honzan Collaboration: Renewed Prayer Sakura Project has been well publicized in both Eiheiji's temple magazine *Sanshō* and in Sōjiji's temple magazine *Chōryū*. See, for example, Daihonzan Eiheiji, *Sanshō* 832 (January 2013): 63–64.

5. Temple official's verbal communication with the author, June 14, 2013.

6. At the time of Japan's first official census in 1745, only 1,370 of Sōtō's 17,500 temples affiliated with Eiheiji. Irizarry, "A Forest for a Thousand Years," 23, citing Nodomi, "Sōjiji no Konjaku," 8. As of 1980, only 148 of Sōtō's fourteen thousand temples officially affiliated with Eiheiji. William Bodiford, "Remembering Dōgen: Eiheiji and Dōgen Hagiography," *Journal of Japanese Studies* 32.1 (2006): 2.

7. Bodiford, "Remembering Dōgen," 1–21.

8. Irizarry's notion that the monastery is a place that "cultivates and disciplines" bodies infuses his dissertation but is first introduced in Irizarry, "A Forest for a Thousand Years," 13–15.

9. Henri Lefebvre, *The Production of Space*, trans. Donald Nicholson-Smith (1974; Oxford: Blackwell, 1991), 405. Earlier in this same passage Lefebvre observes, "The whole of space proceeds from the body, even though it so metamorphoses the body that it may forget it altogether" (405). This observation takes on deeper significance if one loosely paraphrases this passage to mean that "the whole of [the socially constructed] space [of the monastery] proceeds from the body, even

though it so metamorphoses [or cultivates and disciplines] the body [and mind] that it may forget [them or drop them off altogether in *shinjin datsuraku*]."

10. Henri Lefebvre, "Introduction," *The Production of Space* (Malden, MA: Blackwell Publishers, 1991).

11. In 1340, 1473, 1574–75 (the result of *Ikkō ikki* riots), 1641, 1714, 1786, 1833, 1879. Asami Ryūsuke, "Chōsa Hōkoku: Eiheiji no Chūsei Chōkoku," *Myuzeamu: Kokuritsu Hakubutsukan Bijutsushi* 629 (2010): 7.

12. Dōgen, *Enlightenment Unfolds: The Essential Teachings of Zen Master Dōgen*, ed. Kazuaki Tanahashi (Boston: Shambhala, 1999), xxiv.

13. Daihonzan Eiheiji, ed., *Eiheiji* [temple publication] (Fukui ken: Daihonzan Eiheiji, 1999), n.p.

14. William Bodiford, *Sōtō Zen in Medieval Japan* (Honolulu: University of Hawaii Press, 1993), 59, referencing Eiheiji's *Sanso Gyōgōki* (commonly referred to as the *Sandaison gyōjōki*), a reliable anonymous history of Dōgen, Ejō, and Gikai written in Chinese and dated to 1394–1428. See Takashi James Kodera, *Dogen's Formative Years in China: An Historical Study and Annotated Translation of the Hōkyōki* (Boulder, CO: Prajna Press, 1970), 10.

15. Bodiford, *Sōtō Zen in Medieval Japan*, 60.

16. *The Illustrated Record* is listed on Tōfukuji's Cultural Properties / Texts and Volumes tab as "Diagrams of Chinese Zen Temples: Illustrated Temple Traditions of the Song's Various Mountain Monasteries" (*Shina Zensetsu Zushiki–Jiden Sōshozanzu*), accessed July 18, 2013, http://www.tofukuji.jp/cultural_properties/brush_nationality.html. According to the Chinese architectural historian Zhang Shiqing, the source text "Five Mountains and Ten Temple Plans" ("Gozan Jūsetsuzu"), including the Tiantongsi plan, dates to 1247–48, and Guo dates it to 1247–56. Zhang Shiqing, *Wushan Shi Cha Tu: Yu Nan Song Jiangnan Chansi* (Nanjing: Dong nan da xue chubanshe, 2000). Robert Treat Paine and Alexander Coburn Soper, *The Art and Architecture of Japan* (Baltimore: Penguin Books, 1955), 383, note that "three manuscript versions of his [Gikai's] notes have survived, with a large number of drawings carefully recording the buildings and ritual furnishings of the Chan houses in Zhejiang, Jiangsu, and Fujian." It is unclear whether Gikai just saw this 1247–48 text, copied it, or directly imported one version of it into Japan when he returned in 1262.

17. Guo Daiheng, "The Liao, Song, Xi Xia, and Jin Dynasty," in Nancy Steinhardt, ed., *Chinese Architecture* (New Haven, CT: Yale University Press, 2002), 168.

18. Nomura Shunichi, "Kamakuraki Sōtōshū no Kenchiku to sono Imi ni tsuite: Dōgen, Gikai, Keizan no kenchiku sōei o megutte," *Komazawa Daigaku Zen Kenkyūjō Nenpō* 19 (2008): 2. Guo notes, "With time. . . the abbot's quarters came to be located on the same line as the halls that housed Buddhist images, thereby revealing the elevation of the monks' status at the time" ("The Liao, Song, Xi Xia, and Jin Dynasties," 169). However, this feature of Chinese monasteries was not always replicated in Japanese Zen monasteries such as Eiheiji.

19. Many thanks to Grace Lin of Elon University for her help in reading and explaining these characters.

20. See, for example, Steinhardt, *Chinese Architecture*, 73, 99, 147, respectively. Also see Johannes Prip-Møller, *Chinese Buddhist Monasteries: Their Plan and Its Function as a Setting for Buddhist Monastic Life*, 2nd ed. (Hong Kong: Hong Kong University Press, 1967), 2.

21. Guo, "The Liao, Song, Xi Xia, and Jin Dynasties," 169.

22. Yokoyama Hideya, *Zen no Kenchiku* (Tokyo: Shōkokusha, 1967), 128.

23. According to Tsukada Hiroshi's study of this seventeenth-century map, Eiheiji's *hattō* and *sōdō* originally had thatch roofs held in place by large rocks along the eaves. Tsukada, "Bunken kara mita Edo Jidai Sōtōshū Jiin no yane—Daihonzan Eiheiji no Kozu kara," in *Kōko Shiryō 1 "Nihon, Chugoku no Koga" Zuroku* (Tokyo: Komazawa Daigaku, 2006).

24. Helmut Brinker and Hiroshi Kanazawa, *Zen: Masters of Meditation in Images and Writing*, trans. Andreas Leisinger (Zurich: Artibus Asiae, 1996).

25. Yokoyama, *Zen no Kenchiku*, frontispiece; see "Eiheiji Temple," YouTube, April 30, 2007, accessed January 1, 2013, http://www.youtube.com/watch?v= HDuePyaEBFc.

26. Author's visit to Eiheiji, June 14–18, 2013.

27. "Eiheiji," Oxford Art Online, accessed July 16, 2013, http://www.oxfordartonline.com/public/.

28. For more on Itō Chūta's Buddhist architecture, see Richard Jaffe, "Buddhist Material Culture, 'Indianism,' and the Construction of Pan-Asian Buddhism in Prewar Japan," *Material Religion: The Journal of Religion Art and Objects* 2 (2006): 266–92.

29. Before the *sanmon* was built by Gikai, painted and sculpted images of the sixteen arhats were venerated in the abbot's quarters of Eiheiji. One short text in Dōgen's collected works entitled *Omens of the Sixteen Arhats* records a miraculous apparition of auspicious flowers before images of the Buddha and the sixteen arhats during a ceremony there around 11 a.m. on the first day of the first month of Hoji 3 (1249); see Dōgen, *Enlightenment Unfolds*, 259.

30. Here the plum can indicate either the flower of practice or the mountain monastery itself, which "opens" year after year. As Jiren Feng, *Chinese Architecture and Metaphor: Song Culture in the Yingzao Fashi Building Manual* (Honolulu: University of Hawaii Press, 2012), demonstrates, botanical names and floral metaphors were used by Sino-Japanese architects to refer to their rafter, beam, post and lintel constructions, so the "beloved old plum" can refer to the temple complex itself. Furthermore, in standard Buddhist parlance, Zen temples are "opened" when they are first established, so use of this verb instead of "to blossom" or "to bloom" expresses the continued renewal of the site each year.

31. Daihonzan Eiheiji, ed., *Sanshō* (2013), 1.

32. Dōgen Kigen, *Zen Master Dōgen's Shōbōgenzō*, trans. Nishijima Gudo and Chodo Cross (London: Windbell, 1994), 1: 5. In the *Bendōwa* and other fascicles Dōgen metonymically uses these architectural objects to stand for the entirety of Zen practice-realization.

33. Dōgen, *Enlightenment Unfolds*, xlix, 200; DZZ-1 2:405.

34. Dōgen, *Enlightenment Unfolds*, 200.

35. Dōgen, *Enlightenment Unfolds*, xlix; Asami, "Chōsa Hōkoku," ii.

36. Nomura, "Kamakuraki Sōtōshū no Kenchiku to sono Imi ni tsuite," 9.

37. Steven Heine, "Is Dōgen's Eiheiji Temple Mt. Tien-t'ung East? Geo-Ritual Perspectives on the Transition from Chinese Ch'an to Japanese Zen," in *Zen Ritual: Studies of Zen Buddhist Theory in Practice* (New York: Oxford University Press, 2008), 139–65.

38. Asami, "Chōsa Hōkoku," ii.

39. Originally local kami of the Sōtō Zen *garan* were grouped into sets of five, but over time they became consolidated into these two dharma protector bodhisattvas (wall copy, Eiheiji treasure house). For more on these figures, see Nakaseno Shōdō, "Shōbōshichirō daigenshuri bosatsu ni tsuite," *Shūgaku Kenkyū* 35 (1993): 232–37; Ryūkai, "Eiheiji no Chūsei Chōkoku," 12–17.

40. "Buddha Menu," Japanese Buddhist Statuary, accessed August 21, 2013, http://www.onmarkproductions.com/html/nyorai.shtml#.UetPc6xACkw.

41. Steven Heine, *Did Dōgen Go to China?* (New York: Oxford University Press, 2006), 236.

42. Winfield, *Icons and Iconoclasm in Japanese Buddhism*, 49–55.

43. See, for example, Dōgen's inscription for Ananda's portrait (no. 4, note 6) in Dan Leighton and Shohaku Okumura, *Dōgen's Extensive Record: A Translation of the Eihei Kōroku* (Somerville, MA: Wisdom, 2004), 600–601.

44. Eiheiji email to the author, August 2011. The image of the seated Shōkanzeon Bosatsu has been best reproduced in Sakurai Shūyū, *Eiheiji* (Tokyo: Sōtōshū shūmucho, 1987), 52, though it is also reproduced in Eiheiji's main temple publication and in Winfield, *Icons and Iconoclasm in Japanese Buddhism*, 132, fig. 4.7.

45. Kodera, *Dogen's Formative Years in China*, 135.

46. Kodera, *Dogen's Formative Years in China*, 135.

47. Kodera, *Dogen's Formative Years in China*, 135.

48. DZZ-1 1:12.

49. Dōgen, *Enlightenment Unfolds*, 201; DZZ-1 1:561.

50. For more on the animate/inanimate divide and the ability of worldly objects to preach the dharma in the esoteric context (*hosshin seppō*), see Fabio Rambelli, *Buddhist Materiality: A Cultural History of Objects in Japanese Buddhism* (Stanford: Stanford University Press, 2007).

51. To my knowledge, these images have not been published and are not accessible to the average lay person. I am deeply indebted to the anthropologist

Joshua Irizarry, who has seen the figures and who has here corrected and amplified the rudimentary information I received from my informant at Sōjiji on June 11, 2013.

52. "Eiheiji Temple," YouTube.

53. *Zen no Kaze* 1 (1981): 96.

54. As of June 2013, a ten- to fifteen-year architectural conservation project has commenced.

Sino-Japanese Glossary

"Bendōwa"	辨道話
buppō	佛法
busshō/foxing	佛性
Daie Sōkō/Dahui Zonggao	大慧宗杲
Denkōroku	傳光錄
Dōgen	道元
Echizen	越前
Eihei Kōroku	永平廣録
Eiheiji	永平寺
Ejō	懷奘
Enni Ben'en	圓爾辯圓
Fukakusa	深草
geju/jisong	偈頌
Giun	義雲
Hakuin Ekaku	白隱慧鶴
hattō/fatang	法堂
hōgo/fayu	法語
Hōkyōki	寶慶記
Huineng	慧能
jakugo/zhuoyu	箸語
jōdō/shangtang	上堂
juko/songgu	頌古
kanbun	漢文
kanhua/kanna	看話
Keitoku Dentōroku/Jingde Chuandenglu	景德傳燈録
Keizan Jōkin	瑩山紹瑾
Kenchōji	建長寺

Kenninji	建仁寺
Kenzeiki	建撕記
kōan/gongan	公案
Linji/Rinzai/Imje	臨濟
Manzan Dōhaku	卍山道白
Menzan Zuihō	面山瑞方
Mujaku Dōchū	無著道忠
Myōan Eisai	明庵榮西
nianfo/nenbutsu	念佛
Ōbaku Zen	黄檗禅
qiguan dazuo/shikan taza	衹管打坐 or 只管打坐
satori	悟り
Shingon	真言
Shinran	親鸞
Shōbōgenzō	正法眼藏
Shōbōgenzō Zuimonki	正法眼蔵随聞記
shōji	生死
Shōyōroku/Congronglu	從容録
sōdō	僧堂
Sōjiji	總持寺
Sōtō/Caodong	曹洞
Sōtōshū	曹洞宗
taiso	太祖
Tendai	天台
Tendō Nyojō/Tiantong Rujing	天童如淨
Tettsū Gikai	徹通儀介
tōroku	燈録
Uji	有時
Wanshi Shōgaku/Hongzhi Zhengjue	宏智正覺
watō/huatou	話頭
zazen	坐禪
Zen/Chan	禪

INTRODUCTION

Abe Masao	阿部正雄
Azuma Ryūshin	東隆眞
Budda kara Dōgen e	ブッダから道元へ
Busshū Sen'ei	佛洲仙英
daihonzan	大本山
Daijōji	大乗寺
Daoxuan	道宣

Dōgen to Sōtō-shū	道元と曹洞宗
Eihei Shingi	永平清規
Eiheiji	永平寺
Etō Sokuō	衛藤即応
gozan bungaku	五山文學
Gyakusui Tōryū	逆水洞流
Hihan Bukkyō	批判仏教
Hōjō Tokiyori	北条時頼
Hōnen	法然
hōon kōshiki	報恩講式
Ishikawa Rikizan	石川力山.
Jisan	自賛
kanhua chan/kanna zen	看話禪
kanshi	漢詩
Kaimyō	戒名
Kawamura Kōdō	河村孝道.
kechimyaku	血脈
Keizan Oshō Denkōroku	瑩山和尚傳光録
Keizan Shingi	瑩山清規
kesa	袈裟
kikigaki	聞書
Kimura Uno	木村卯之
kirigami	切り紙
Komazawa Daigaku	駒澤大学
kōso	高祖
kūshu genkyō	空手還郷
Mana Shōbōgenzō	真字正法眼蔵
Nanzenji	南禅寺
Nichiren	日蓮
Nishitani Keiji	西谷啓示
"Raihaitokuzui"	礼拝得髄
Sanshōdōei	傘松道詠
Shamon Dōgen	沙門道元
Shinsan	真賛
shō	證
Shūmūchō	曹洞宗宗務庁
Shushōgi	修証義
Shūso toshite no Dōgen	宗祖としての道元
Sōtōshū Daigaku	曹洞宗大学
Sōtōshū Shūmuchō	曹洞宗宗務庁
Teiho Kenzeiki	訂補建撕記
Tenkei Denson	天桂傳尊

tōshi	燈史
waka	和歌
Watsuji Tetsurō	和辻哲郎
Yoshizu Yoshihide	吉津宜英
Zazenyōjinki	坐禅用心記

CHAPTER 1—FOULK

agyo	下語
ango	安居
anraku no hōmon	安樂の法門
An Shigao	安世高
bendō	辨道
Bendōhō	辨道法
biandao gongfu/bendō kufū	辨道功夫
bosatsudō	菩薩道
buji zen	無事禪
Bukkyō	佛經
busso	佛祖
Butsudō	佛道
butsugyō	佛行
butsu shōbō wo akirame	佛正法をあきらめ
Chanyuan Qingui	禪苑清規
chanzong/zenshū	禪宗
Daibiku Sanzen Iigi Kyō/Dabiqiu Sanqian Weii Jing	大比丘三千威儀經
Dahui Pujue Chanshi Yulu	大慧普覺禪師語録
Daigo	大悟
Daoxuan	道宣
dazuo/taza	打坐
de/toku	得
dō	道
dodatsu	度脱
dokusan	獨參
e	慧
Eka	慧可
ekō	廻向
eru	得る
eyo	得よ
Fenyang Heshang Yulu	汾陽和尚語録
Fori Qisong	佛日契崇
fugin	諷經

Fukanzazengi	普勸坐禪儀
fukyō	布教
fuzenna	不染汚
ganzei kyō	眼睛經
gedō no ken	外道の見
go	悟
godō	悟道
go yaku nyoze, jo yaku nyoze	吾亦如是,汝亦如是
gugen	具眼
Guifeng Zongmi	圭峰宗密
gyōbutsu	行佛
hashigo zen	梯子禪
hayaku iu	速道
hi	皮
hi niku kotsu zui	皮肉骨髓
Hokkekyō	法華經
hongo	本期
Hongzhi Chanshi Guanglu	宏智禪師廣錄
honrai mu ichi motsu	本來無一物
honshō no zentai	本證の全體
hōyaku	法益
itazura no taigo su	いたづらの待悟す
jō (concentration)	定
jō (becoming)	成
jōbutsu saso	成佛作祖
jōdō (attaining the way)	成道
Jōshū Kannon 'in Shinsai Daishi	趙州觀音院眞際大師
Jōshū kushi	趙州狗子
Juefan Huihong	覺範慧洪
jūji	住持
kai	戒
kaigo	開悟
kan	看
kan huatou/kan watō/gan hwadu	看話頭
kanjing/kankin	看經
Kankin	看經
kanna zen	看話禪
Keitokuji	景德寺
Kenbutsu	見佛
kien mondō	機縁問答
kinhin	經行
kokoro no taza	心の打坐

kosoku	古則
kotsu	骨
kyo	舉
kyō	教
kyōge betsuden	教外別傳
libai/raihai	禮拜
Mazu Daoyi	馬祖道一
migugen	未具眼
mi no taza	身の打坐
mondō	問答
mozhao/mokushō/mukjo	默照
mu	無
mui	無爲
muichi motsu	無一物
mui zen	無爲禪
mushotoku	無所得
myōjutsu	妙術
Nanyue Huairang	南嶽懷讓
niku	肉
niso	二祖
nisshitsu	入室
qiguan/shikan	祇管
qiguan dazuo er yi	祇管打坐而已
qiguan dazuo shide	祇管打坐始得
qiguan zuochan	祇管坐禪
randa	懶墮
rarō taha	羅篭打破
Rinzai bushi Sōtō hyakushō	臨済武士 曹洞百姓
rokuso Enō	六祖慧能
rōshi	老師
ryōso	兩祖
sa	作
sabutsu	作佛
sabutsu wo motomezaru	作仏をもとめざる
sabutsu wo zu su	作仏を圖す
sabutsu wo zu suru koto nakare	作仏を圖することなかれ
sahō	作法
samu	作務
sanchan zhe shenxin tuoluo ye	參禪者身心脱落也
sangaku (rigorous investigation)	參學
sangaku (three modes of practice)	三學

sankyū	參究
sanshu	參取
satoru	悟る
Senjō	洗淨
shagan	遮眼
shaka	蹉過
shaoxiang/shōkō	燒香
shenxin tuoluo/shinjin datsuraku	身心脱落
shike	師家
Shimen	石門
Shimen Linjianlu	石門林間録
shinbutsu	身佛
shingi	清規
shingon	親近
shingon hosshi	親近法師
shinji	心地
shinjin datsuraku no taza	身心脱落の打坐
shinjin datsuraku suru koto	身心脱落すること
shinjin datsuraku suru koto wo eyo	身心脱落することを得よ
Shinjin Gakudō	身心學道
Shinji Shōbōgenzō	眞字正法眼藏
Shōbōgenzō Sanbyakusoku	正法眼藏三百則
Shōhōjissō	諸法實相
shoshin no bendō	初心の辨道
shō wo toru	證をとる
shugyō	修行
shukke	出家
shushō	修證
shushō ittō	修證一等
shushō kore ittō	修證これ一等
shūzen/xichan	習禪
soshi	祖師
tadashi	ただし
tadashi taza shite	ただし打坐して
taigo	待悟
taigo zen	待悟禪
tan	單
taza shite	打坐して
Tendōzan	天童山
tenzō	轉藏
Tenzokyōkun	典座教訓

Tōinshōso	東印請祖
tokuzui	得隨
tongo	頓悟
unsui	雲水
wa	話
Weishan Lingyou	溈山靈祐
wo	を
xiuchan/shusan	修懺
Xutang Heshang Yulu	虛堂和尚語錄
Xutang Zhiyu	虛堂智愚
Yakusan Shinza	藥山陞座
Yangshan Huiji	仰山慧寂
Yongming Yanshou	永明延壽
Yunmen Guanglu	雲門廣錄
zabutsu	坐佛
zabutsu sara ni sabutsu wo saezu	坐佛さらに作佛をさへず
Zanmai Ō Zanmai	三昧王三昧
zazen bendō	坐禪辨道
Zazengi	坐禪儀
Zazenhō	坐禪法
Zazenshin	坐禪箴
zengo	漸悟
zenhi	全臂
Zhengfayanzang	正法眼藏
Zhenxie Qingliao	眞歇清了
Zongmen Liandeng Huiyao	宗門聯燈會要
zui wo uru	髓をうる
zuochan/zazen	坐禪
zu sabutsu	圖作佛
zu su	圖す
Zutangji	祖堂集

CHAPTER 2—LEVERING

ama	尼
busso shōden	佛祖正伝
byakue	白衣
Dahui Pujue Chanshi Pushuo	大慧普覺禪師普説
dajangfu/daijōbu	大丈夫
Daofu	道副
Daoyu	道育

Daruma-shū	達磨宗
Dōgen no "Nyoshin fujobutsu ron"	道元の女身不成仏論
Egi Bikuni	懐義比丘尼
Eison	叡尊
Enryakuji	延暦寺
gokai	五戒
Go-Toba-Tennō	後鳥羽天皇
Guanqi Zhixian	灌谿志閑
Himitsu Shōbōgenzō	秘密正法眼蔵
hōben	方便
Hongzhi Chanshi Guanglu	宏智禪師廣錄
honzan	本山
Huike	慧可
immo	恁麼
Ishii Shūdō	石井修道
Ishikawa Rikizan	石川力山
jangfu	丈夫
Jingde Era	景德
Jisshū Yōdōki	十宗要道記
Jūnikanbon Shōbōgenzō	十二巻本正法眼蔵
kana	カナ
kansō	官僧
Kattō	葛藤
kōan	公案
Kōshōji	興正寺
Kōyasan	高野山
kudoku muryō	功徳無量
Liaoran	了然
Linji Yixuan/Rinzai Gigen	臨濟義玄
Miaoxin	妙信
Miaoxin Huaizi	妙信 淮子
Minamoto no Michichika	源通親
Moshan Liaoran	末山了然
Mount Hiei	比叡山
Myōzen	明全
naidaijin	内大臣
nanzi	男子
ni (bikuni)	尼（比丘尼）
nyoshin fujobutsu ron	女身不成仏佛
nyoshin jōbutsu	女身 成仏
"Raihaitokuzui"	礼拝得髄

Raihaitokuzui kō	礼拝得髄考
"Rulaixing"	如來性
Ryōnen	了然
shiki	志気
Shitou	石頭
Shōgaku	正覺
shukke	出家
shukke jōbutsu	出家 成仏
"Shukke Kudoku"	出家功德
Song	宋
tonseisō	遁世僧
Wuzhun Shifan	無準師範
xiang	相
Yangshan Huiji	仰山慧寂
Yuanwu Keqin	圜悟克勤
Zengaku Daijiten	禪學大辭典
Zongchi	總持

CHAPTER 3—HEINE

Baika	梅花
Biyanlu/Hekiganroku	碧巖錄
cheng	承
Daijōji	大乘寺
Dōgen kenkyū	道元研究
Eihei Dōgen	永平道元
Fujiwara Teika	藤原定家
Fukanzazengi	普勧坐禅儀
Gakudōyōjinshū	学道用心集
Genji Monogatari	源氏物語
Gien	義演
Gozan bungaku	五山文學
Hakujushi	柏樹子
he (jie)	合 (結)
Heike Monogatari	平家物語
Hōjōki	方丈記
hongaku shisō	本覺思想
Hongzhilu	宏智錄
jiaowai biechuan buli wenzi/kyōge betsuden furyū monji	教外別傳不立文字
jisan/zizan	自賛
jue	覺

jueju	絶句
kanshi	漢詩
Kawabata Yasunari	川端康成
keijijōgaku no mujō	形而上学の無常
Keisei sanshoku/Xisheng shanse	谿聲山色
Kenbutsu	見仏
Kokin Wakashū	古今和歌集
kong/kū	空
Kūge	空華
kūshu genkyō	空手還郷
Mana Shōbōgenzō	真字正法眼蔵
mengzhong	夢中
mi	迷
Mujō no shisō	無常の思想
Mujō seppō	無情説法
Mu Kōan/Wu Gongan	無公案
Nihon no Koten Bungaku	日本の古典文学
qi	起
qi cheng zhuan he [jie]	起承轉合[結]
Rankei Dōryū/Lanxi Daolong	兰溪道隆
Sanbyakusoku Shōbōgenzō	三百則正法眼蔵
Seishōji	青松寺
she (living)	舍
she (renouncing)	捨
shichidō garan	七堂伽藍
Shinkokin Wakashū	新古今和歌集
shinsan/zhenzan	真賛
shizhong/jishu	示衆
shōsan/xiaocan	小參
Su Shi	蘇軾
Tendō/Tiantong	天童
Touzi Yiqing	投子義青
Tsurezuregusa	徒然草
u/you	有
uta-awase	歌あわせ
Utsukushii Nihon to Watakushi	美しい日本と私
waka	和歌
Wang Wei	王維
Wansong/Banshō	萬松
wenzi Chan/monji Zen	文字禅
wu/mu	無

xing	行
Yang Yi	楊億
yuige	遺偈
Zhaozhou	趙州
zhuan	轉
Zongmen Tongyaoji/Shūmon Tōyōshū	宗門統要集

CHAPTER 4—MARALDO

daiga	大我
Eihei shingi	永平清規
fumetsu	不滅
fushō	不生
Gaijashō	改邪鈔
Gakudōyōjinshū	学道用心集
geke shujō	下化衆生
Genjōkōan	現成公案
Genshin	源信
Hisamatsu Shin'ichi	久松真一
hō-i	法位
Hōnen	法然
ide	遺弟
izoku	遺族
jiko	自己
jisei	自性
jisetsu	時節
Jōdoshū Ryakushō	浄土宗略抄
jōgu-bodai	上求菩提
Kakunyo	覚如
Kiyozawa Manshi	清沢満之
Kūkai	空海
mushōnin	無生忍
nen	念
nikon	而今
Orategama Zokushū	遠羅天釜続集
rin-ne	輪廻
Shari Raimon	舎利礼文
shinjin	身心
soregashi	それがし
takai	他界
ware	われ
yo	予

yuige	遺偈
Zenki	全機
zettai	絶対
zettai tariki no daidō	絶対他力の大道

CHAPTER 5—KOPF

Abe Masao	阿部正雄
basho no ronri	場所の論理
busshōkū	佛性空
butsudō	仏道
butsuriteki sekai	物理的世界
Chanyulu	禪語録
Daitō Kokushi	大燈国師
dōtoku	道得
dōtokufudōtoku	道得不道得
fushiryō	不思量
gabyō	畫餅
genjō	現成
Genjōkōan	現成公案
Guoan	廓庵
gyōji	行持
Hakamaya Noriaki	袴谷憲昭
hanshinron	汎神論
Hihan Bukkyō	批判仏教
hishiryō	非思量
hitei soku kōtei	否定即肯定
hitotsu no sekai	一つの世界
hongaku	本覺
hongakushisō	本覺思想
Huayan	華厳
hyōgen	表現
itsu	一
jiko	自己
jiritsuteki rinrigakusetsu	自律的倫理学説
jita ichinyo	自他一如
jitari	自他利
katsudōsetsu	活動説
kattō	葛藤
Kimura Uno	木村卯之
koji kyūmei	己事究明
kūbusshō	空佛性

kyakkan shugi	客観主義
manbō	萬法
Matsumoto Shirō	松本史朗
mayoi	迷
meigo	迷悟
monji	文字
mubusshō	無佛性
muga	無我
mujōbusshō	無常佛性
muniutou	牧牛図
Mutai Risaku	務台理作
Nishida Kitarō	西田幾多郎
Nishitani Keiji	西谷啓治
Ōkubo Dōshū	大久保道舟
panjiao	判教
rekishiteki sekai	歴史的世界
sadō	茶道
sanmoti	三摩提
seibutsuteki sekai	生物的世界
seishin	精神
seishinteki tōitsu	精神的統一
senni gedō	先尼外道
shi	死
shigaku	始覺
shin	心
shin	身
shinjin datsuraku	身心脱落
shiryō	思量
shizen	自然
shō	生
Shoakumakusa	諸惡莫作
shōbutsu (sentient beings-and-buddhas)	生佛
shobutsu (all buddhas)	諸佛
shōbutsu (actualizing Buddha)	證仏
shobutsu shoso	諸佛諸祖
shodō	書道
shōken	證驗
shōkyū	證究
shōsekai	小世界
shō suru	證する
shu	種

shugyō	修行
shujō	衆生
shukan shugi	主観主義
shushō kore ittō nari	修證これ一等なり
siniutou	十牛図
Sokushin Zebutsu	即心是佛
ta	多
tako	他己
taritsuteki rinrigakusetsu	他律的倫理学説
tetsugakuteki zen	哲学的禅
Tiantai	天台
tōitsu chikara	統一力
tokushuteki hōkō	特殊的方向
tokushuteki zentai	特殊的全体
Ueda Shizuteru	上田閑照
wasureru	忘れる
Watsuji Tetsujirō	和辻哲郎
Wumenguan	無門關
xianzheng	現證
xuizheng	修證
Yanagida Seizan	柳田聖山
yūbusshō	有佛性
yūshinron	有神論
Zazengi	坐禪儀
zettai mujunteki jiko dōitsu	絶対矛盾的自己同一
zheng	證
zhengde	證得

CHAPTER 6—BODIFORD

Arai Sekizen	新井石禪
Arai Shōryū	新井勝龍
Azuma Ryūshin	東隆眞
Biyanji/Hekiganshū	碧巖集
Busshū Sen'ei	佛洲仙英
Chōenji	長圓寺
chūkyaku	注脚
daigo	代語
Daijōji	大乘寺
Daijōji Hihon Tōkokuki	大乘寺秘本 洞谷記
Daikū Genko	大空玄虎

Danxia Zichun	丹霞子淳
denchi	田地
denpō ge	傳法偈
dentō	傳燈
Dongshan Liangjie/Tōzan Ryōkai	洞山良价
e	惠
Eihei Gen zenji goroku	永平元禪師語録
Eishōin	永昌院
Eishū	英就
Foguo Biyan Poguan Jijie/Bukka Hekigan Hakan Kyakusetsu	佛果碧巖破關擊節
Furuta Shōkin	古田紹欽
Fusai Zenkyū	普濟善救
ge	偈
Gesshū Sōko	月舟宗胡
Giun Oshō Goroku	義雲和尚語録
goroku	語録
Gozan	五山
Gyōji Jijo	行事次序
Hekigan Daikūshō	碧巖大空抄
Hōkyōji	寶慶寺
honsoku	本則
Hōonroku	報恩録
hyōshō	評唱
ichiya	一夜
Iriya Yoshitaka	入矢義高
Ishikawa Sodō	石川素童
Itō Tōshin	伊藤東慎
Jiatai Pudenglu/Katai Futōroku	嘉泰普燈録
jishu	示衆
jō	定
Kagamishima Genryū	鏡島元隆
kaidō	開堂
Kanhwa Son/Kanhua Chan/Kanna Zen	看話禪
ke	家
Keizan Oshō Denkōroku	瑩山和尚傳光録
Keizan Oshō Goroku	瑩山和尚語録
Keizan Oshō Shingi	瑩山和尚清規
kengō	賢劫
Kenkon'in (a.k.a. Kenkōin)	乾坤院
Kidō Sōe	暉堂宗惠

kien	機縁
kikigaki	聞書
Kikudō Soei	菊堂祖英
kō	光
Kōchi Eigaku	光地英學
Kohō Chisan	孤峰智燦
Kōhō Tōshun	高峯東晙
Kongguji/Kūkokushū	空谷集
Kōshōji	興聖寺
Linquan Conglun/Rinsen Jūrin	林泉從倫
Matsuda Fumio	松田文雄
monji Zen	文字禪
naidai	内題
Nan'ei Kenshū	南英謙宗
nentei	拈提
Ōkubo Dōshū	大久保道舟
Ōtani Teppu	大谷哲夫
Ōuchi Seiran	大内青巒
Rozan Bunko	魯山文庫
Ryūmonji	龍門寺
Ryūsenji	龍泉寺
san	贊
sanbō	三寶
sangō	三業
Seiboku Gitai	聖僕義諦
shichibutsu	七佛
shichigon niku	七言二句
Sijia Pingchanglu/Shike Hyōshōroku	四家評唱録
Shikō Sōden	芝岡宗田
shō	證
shōbutsuji	小佛事
shōgon kō	莊嚴劫
shōsan	小參
Shōzanji	松山寺
Shūgen	宗源
sō	宗
soshi	祖師
suiji	垂示
tai	體
Tajima Hakudō	田島柏堂
Takeuchi Kōdō	竹内弘道

Tamamura Takeji	玉村竹二
tanden	單傳
teishō	提唱
Tessō Hōken	喆叟芳賢
tō	燈
Tōkokuki	洞谷記
Touzi Yiqing/Tōsu Gisei	投子義青
Tsūgen Jakurei	通幻寂靈
Tsūgenroku	通幻録
Tsūgen Zenji Goroku	通幻禪師語録
Wansong Xingxiu/Banshō Gyōshū	萬松行秀
Wudeng Huiyuan/Gotō Egen	五燈會元
Wuwai Yiyuan	無外義遠
Xuedou Chongxian/Setchō Jūken	雪竇重顯
Xutangji/Kidōshū	虛堂集
Yamauchi Shun'yū	山内舜雄
Yasutani Hakuun	安谷白雲
Yōkokuji	永谷寺
Yokoseki Ryōin	橫關了胤
yū	用
Yuanwu Keqin/Engo Kokugon	圜悟克勤
Yunyan Tancheng/Ungan Donjō	雲巖曇晟
Yūzan Senshuku	融山泉祝
Zenrin Shōkisen	禪林象器箋
Zenrinji	禪林寺
Zenseki Shi	禪籍志

CHAPTER 7—DAVID RIGGS

baika ryūei sanka	梅花流詠讚歌
Banjin Dōtan	萬仞道坦
Bonmōkyōryakushō	梵網經略抄
Busso Shōden Bosatsukai kyōju kaimon	佛祖正傳菩薩戒教授戒文
Busso Shōden Bosatsukai sahō	佛祖正傳菩薩戒作法
Busso Shōden Daikaiketsu	佛祖正傳大戒訣
Busso Shōden Zenkaishō	佛祖正傳禪戒鈔
daishū	大衆
Daozhe Zhaoyuan	道者超元
denkai	傳戒
Dokuan Genkō	獨菴玄光
Eihei Soshi Tokudo Ryaku Sahō	永平祖師得度略作法

endonkai	圓頓戒
Genrō Ōryū	玄樓奧龍
Gesshū Sōko	月舟宗胡
Gukaihōgi	弘戒法儀
Gyakusui Tōryū	逆水洞流
ichijōkai	一乘戒
isshinkai	一心戒
Jakushū Eifuku Oshō Sekkai	若州永福和 尚説
jissōshin	實相心
jōbutsu	成仏
jukai	授戒
jukaie	授戒會
kaimyō	戒名
kaishi	戒弟
kechimyaku	血脈
kechimyaku kaidan	血脈戒壇
Kokan Shiren	虎關師錬
mōkai	亡戒
Mokugen Genjaku	黙玄元寂
Muan Xingdao	木菴性牝
namu honshi shakamuni butsu	南無本師釋迦牟尼佛
namu honshi shaka nyorai	南無本師釈迦如來
Ōjukai Gowasan	御受戒御和讚
rinzai shōshū	臨濟正宗
ryakusu	絡子
sangemon	懺悔文
sangeshiki	懺悔式
Sekiun Yūsen	石雲融仙
sekkaishi	説戒師
shamikai	沙彌戒
shingi	清規
Shōe Dōjō	性慧道定
shōzai muryō	小罪無量
Shukke Ryaku Sahōmon	出家略作法文
Taikaku Kanwa	對客閑話
Tenkei Denson	天桂傳尊
Tokudo Wakumon	得度或問
Tokudo Wakumon Bengishō	得度或問辨儀章
Yinyuan Longqi/Ingen Ryūki	隠元隆琦
Zenji sama	禪師樣
zenkai	禪戒
zenkaie	禪戒會

zenkai itchi	禪戒一致
Zenkaiki	禪戒規
zheng	證

CHAPTER 8—MROSS

Bonnon no Ge	梵音偈
Bukkan Bonjō	仏鑑梵成
Buppō Zenji Kōshiki Ryaku	仏法禅師講式略
burakumin	部落民
Busshōe Kōshiki	仏生会講式
Butsuji Kōshiki	仏慈講式
chō	帳
Chōkokuji	長谷寺
Daifusatsu Bosatsu Shiki	大布薩菩薩式
daishū	大衆
dan	段
Daruma Kōshiki	達磨講式
Dōgen Kōshiki	道元講式
Dōgen Zenji Kōshiki	道元禅師講式
Eichizen	越前
Eihei Dōgen Zenji Kōshiki	永平道元禅師講式
Eiheiji Betsuin	永平寺別院
Eiheiji Kaisan Kigyō Hokke Kōshiki	永平開山忌行法華講式
Eihei Kaisan Hōon Kōshiki	永平開山報恩講式
Eihei Kōshiki	永平講式
Eihei Kōso Dōgen Zenji Kōshiki	永平高祖道元禅師講式
Engetsu Kōjaku	円月江寂
Ennin	円仁
Fuekō	普回向
Fukanzazengi	普勧坐禅儀
Furong Daokai	芙蓉道楷
Gasan Jōseki	峨山韶碩
Genshin	源信
Goyuigon Kiroku	御遺言記録
hachi	鈸
Hachidainingaku	八大人覚
hakase	博士
Hashimoto Yūji	橋本雄二
hatsu	鈸
Hieizan	比叡山
Hokke Kōshiki	法華講式

Hongren	弘忍
hōon	報恩
Hōon Kōshiki	報恩講式
Hōshōji	法祥寺
Hossō	法相
Huike	慧可
hyōbyaku	表白
Imamura Genshū	今村源宗
inkin	引磬
ino	維那
Jōdo-shin	浄土真
Jōgyō Sanmaidō Gyōhō	常行三昧堂行法
Jōkei	貞慶
Jōten Sokuchi	承天則地
kada	伽陀
Kakua	覚阿
Kakunyo	覚如
Kannon Kōshiki	観音講式
Kannon Senbō	観音懺法
Kegon	華厳
keisu	磬子
Kichijōzan Eiheiji Nenchū Teiki	吉祥山永平寺年中定規
Koga Michichika	久我通親
Koga Michitomo	久我通具
Kōin	公胤
kōshiki	講式
Kōso	高祖
kundoku	訓読
Machida Muneo	町田宗夫
Meiken	明賢
Meishūbon	明州本
Miidera	三井寺
Myōe	明恵
Nijūgo Zanmai E	二十五三昧会
Nijūgo Zanmai Shiki	二十五三昧式
Nomura Yoshio	野村良雄
nyo	鼓
Nyoraibai	如来唄
Nyoraibaimon	如来唄文
Ōjō Kōshiki	往生講式
Ōjō Yōshū	往生要集
on	恩

Ōuchi Seiran	大内青巒
Raihai no Ge	礼拝偈
Rakan Kōshiki	羅漢講式
Rokudō Kōshiki	六道講式
sabetsu kaimyō	差別戒名
saimon	祭文
Sange no Ge	散華偈
Sanron	三論
Sanso Gyōgōki	三祖行業記
Seigan Kōshiki	誓願講式
shakujō	錫杖
Shakujō no Ge	錫杖偈
Shichisan	四智讃
Shika hōyō	四箇法要
shikimon	式文
shikishi	式師
Shinpen Hōon Kōshiki	新編報恩講式
shōmyō	声明
Shōzen	性泉
shūtō fukko undō	宗統復古運動
sōrai no ge	総礼の偈
Tanbutsue	歎仏会
tantō rōshi	担当老師
tenshō	殿鐘
Tōdaiji	東大寺
Tōjō Dentō Kōshiki	洞上伝灯講式
Yōkan	永観
Zuichōbon	瑞長本
Zuihō Daiki	瑞峰大奇

CHAPTER 9—DIANE RIGGS

Busso kesa kō	佛祖袈裟考
Daisen Tamashū	大泉玉州
Da Tang xiyu zhi	大唐西域記
denbō e	傳法衣
Den'e	傳衣
Den'e Zōbi shōkō haka	傳衣象鼻章稿巴歌
fugesa	布袈裟
Furong Daokai	芙蓉道楷
fu sōgyari kesa	布僧伽梨袈裟
Ganjin/Jianzhen	鑑真

Genkō Shakusho	元亨釋書
Gentō Sokuchū	玄透即中
Gozan	五山
Hachiman	八幡
Hōbuku Kakushō	法服格正
jikitotsu	直綴
Jingde Chuandenglu	景徳傳燈録
Kaikei	快慶
Kanjō	灌頂
kesa	袈裟
Kesa Kudoku	袈裟功徳
kinran	金襴
kinran e	金襴衣
Kokan Shiren	虎關師錬
Kurin Seimo	古林清茂
Luxiang Gantong	律相感通
madara	斑
Mokushitsu Ryōyō	黙室良要
Nagaya-Ō	長屋王
Ōbaku Shingi	黄檗清規
ran	爛
Seiryōji	清凉寺
Shakushi Hōekun	釋氏法衣訓
Shōbōgenzō Den 'e Kudoku Setsukai Mondō	正法眼藏傳衣功徳竊解問答
Shōbōritsu	正法律
Shōmu	聖武
Shōtoku Taishi	聖徳太子
shuigeju	拾遺偈頌
Sitou	思託
Sonnō Sōeki	損翁宗益
Tanshin	丹心
Tetsuzan Shinyō	鉄山心養
Tōfukuji	東福寺
Tokudo Wakumon	得度或問
Tokudo Wakumon bengishō	得度或門辨儀章
Tokugon Yōson	徳厳養存
Wuzhun Shifan	無準師範

CHAPTER 10—WINFIELD

Amida	阿弥陀
Benzai (shinzai) sonten	弁財(新財)尊天

butsuden	仏殿
Chang'an	長安
chi	豉
Chōryū	跳龍
chūjakumon	中雀門
Daihishin darani	大悲心陀羅尼
daihonzan	大本山
Daikō Myōzō	大光明蔵
daisodō	大祖堂
Daisō Shozanzu	大宋諸山図
Daitetsu Sōryō	大徹宗令
Denpō-an	伝法庵
Dongjing	東京
Eihei/Yongping	永平
Ejō	懐奘
etoki	絵解き
Fukui	福井
Fukuyama Taihō	福山諦法
Fuzō-in	普蔵院
garan	伽藍
Gasan Jōseki	峨山韶碩
goin kaiki	五院開基
Gokokushōbōgi	護国正法義
goshintai	御神体
Gozan Jūsetsuzu	五山十刹図
Hatano Yoshishige	波多野義重
Heian	平安
hōjō	方丈
honzan	本山
honzon	本尊
hosshin seppō	法身説法
ichibutsu ryōso	一仏両祖
Ichijō Kaneyoshi/Kanera	一条兼良
ihai	位牌
ikkō ikki	一向一揆
Itō Chūta	伊東忠太
Itokawa Ryūtatsu	糸川立達
ittai	一体
jakkōdō	寂光堂
jiang	醬
Jiangnan	江南

Jingdesi	景徳寺
Jippō Ryoshū	実峰良秀
jōyōden	承陽殿
Kaifeng	開封
kairō	回廊
Kamakura	鎌倉
kami	神
Kannon	観音
kanseishisha	監斎使者
Kegonkyō	華厳経
ken	賢
Kenzei	建撕
kichijō	吉祥
kichijōkaku	吉祥閣
Kichijōzan Eiheiji	吉祥山永平寺
Kippōji	吉峰寺
Kitayama Zessan	北山絶三
Kokū	虚空
komainu	狛犬・胡麻犬
Komazawa Daigaku	駒澤大学
kōshakudai	香積台
Kōshōji	興聖寺
kōso	高祖
kounkaku	孤雲閣
kuin	庫院
Kuzuryū	九頭竜
kyōryaku	経歴・交絡
kyōsaku	警策
Kyōto	京都
Lingyinsi	靈隠寺
Luoyang	洛陽
matsuji	末寺
Miroku	弥勒
mujō seppō	無情説法
Mutan Sokan	無端祖環
Myōkō-an	妙高庵
Myōkōdai	明光台
Nanzenji	南禅寺
nō	脳
Noto	能登
Nyoi-an	如意庵

nyonin kekkai	女人結界
rakan	羅漢
ryōzan ittai funi	両山一体不二
sanbōdai kōjin	三寶荒神
sandaison gyōjōki	三大尊行状記
sandai sōron	三代相論
sanmon	山門
sanrōsha	参籠者
sanshō	傘松
Sanshōhō Daibutsuji	傘松峰大仏寺
sanshōkaku	傘松閣
Sanso Gyōgōki	三祖行業記
sanze jippō shobutsu	三世十方諸仏
sanze nyorai	三世如来
seinarumono katachi to ba	聖なるもの形と場
seisu	西司
seiza	正座
sekisō ōrai	尺素往來
senmongakkō	専門学校
Shibinoshō	志比荘
shichidō garan	七堂伽藍
shina zensetsu zushiki (jiden sōshozanzu)	支那禅刹図式 (寺伝宋諸山図)
Shintō	神道
shinzō	心臓
shishi	石獅
shisho	嗣書
shitennō	四天王
Shōbō Shichirō Daigenshuri Bosatsu	招宝七郎大権修理菩薩
shobutsu seiken	諸仏斉肩
shōgon (past)	莊嚴
shōgon (adornment)	莊厳
Shōkanzeon bosatsu	聖観世音菩薩
shōshuku	星宿
Song	宋
Sumeru	須弥
Taigen Sōshin	太源宗真
Taiheiji	太平寺
tatami	畳
Tiantong	天童
Tiantongsi	天童寺
Tōfukuji	東福寺

tokonoma	床の間
Tōkyō	東京
Tōsen-an	洞川庵
tōsu	東司
Tsūgen Jakurei	通幻寂霊
unsui	雲水
Wanniansi	万年寺
Yamashibu	山師峰
yan	鹽
Yokohama	横浜
yokushitsu	浴室
Zen no Kaze	禅の風
Zenrin Shōkisen	禅林象器箋
Zen wa kokoro kara kokoro e	禅は心から心へ

Index

Banjin Dōtan, 200–201, 205
Biyanlu (*Blue Cliff Record*, also known as *Blue Cliff Collection*)
  history of, 174–178
  issues on title of, 183n22
Brahma's Net Sutra, 191–193, 196, 201
Busshū Sen'ei, 14, 167–170, 172

Caodong. *See* Sōtō Zen
Chan. *See* Zen
Chanyuan Qingui (*Rules of Purity for Chan Monasteries*), 30, 198–199
Chōkokuji, 16, 210
Congronglu (*Record of Serenity*), 31–33, 97–100, 108n40, 175–176

Dahui Zonggao
  and criticism of silent illumination, 23–25, 27, 34–35 (*See also* Kanna Zen)
Daijōji, 184n24, 243
Danxia Zichun, 176
Daoxuan, 16, 235, 242–247, 252
Death
  Buddhist philosophy of, 12–13, 110–113, 130n10, 137n56
  of Dōgen, 120–122, 133n32
from the perspective of three grammatical persons, 113–120
Denkōroku (*Record of the Transmission of the Light*)
  comparison with *Blue Cliff Record*, 174–178
  content and style of, 178–181
  format of, 170–178
  textual history of, 168–170
Dōgen
  750th death anniversary, 3, 214–217, 221–223
  approaches to reading of, 138–142
  commentary on Su Shi's Buddhist verse, 95–97
  in comparative philosophy, 138–142, 144–147, 155–157
  and doctrinal poems, 97–104
  and impact of poetic composition
    and autobiographical poems, 89–92
    and Chinese poetry collection, 74–81,
    and Japanese poetry collection, 78–79, 79 fig. 3.1, 83–85
  and kōshiki
    with biographical accounts of, 213–222 (*See also* kōshiki)

Dōgen (*Cont.*)
  and language theory, 77–78, 86–89, 149–156
  and literature and spiritual development, 86–89, 93–95
  and Mahayana sutras, 29–30, 35, 61–62
  modern studies of, 7–8, 34–35, 38–42
  and naturalism or affirmation of phenomenal reality, 77–82, 87–89, 93–97, 103–104
  as a philosopher, 13, 138–142
  and shikantaza
    and just sitting, 24–28, 38–43, 91–92, 181, 226
    as a kōan, 27–28, 36–38, 42
    shikan taza, 4 fig. 0.1, 43n2
  and studying the self, 146–147, 152–153
  and teachings on women
    and awakening, 49–50, 56
    in *Bendōwa*, 48–51
    in *Eihei Kōroku*, 52
    in *Raihaitokuzui*, 50–54
    as teachers, 47, 50–54
    and the wild fox and Indra, 57–58
  translations of, 5–6, 54–55
  and usage of kōans, 23–24, 28–35, 76–80 (*See also* kōan)
Dōgen's writings
  Bendōwa (*A Talk on Cultivating the Way*), 27–28, 38–40, 47–51, 69
  Eihei Kōroku (*Extensive Record of Eihei Dōgen*), 11–12, 76–79, 79 fig. 3.1
  Eihei Shingi (*Dōgen's Pure Standards for the Zen Community*), 120
  Fukanzazengi (*Universally Recommended Instructions for Zazen*), 27, 82, 85 fig. 3.4
  Hōkyōki (*Record of Hōkyō Era*), 35, 276–278
  Mana Shōbōgenzō (*Dōgen's Chinese Kōan Collection*), 78, 97–98, 102

  Shōbōgenzō Zuimonki (*Record of Dōgen's Talks*), 53, 87, 132–133n30
  Tenzokyōkun (*Admonitions for the Cook*), 30–31
  See also *Shōbōgenzō*

Echizen, 9, 52–53, 76–77, 92–93, 264–268, 268 fig. 10.3
Egi, 52–53, 63
Eiheiji
  architectural body of, 264–269, 268 fig. 10.3
  in comparison with Sōjiji, 262–264, 269–273, 280–281
  and Dharma hall, 202–203, 265, 277 fig. 10.5
  establishment of, 264–265
  figural body of, 272–278, 277 fig. 10.5
  and Kannon, 276–278, 277 fig. 10.5
Eiheiji Betsuin. *See* Chōkokuji
Enni Ben'en, 72n35, 241, 249, 264–265

Four Part Vinaya, 191–193, 246–247, 249
Furong Daokai, 220, 248–249

Gadamer, Hans-Georg, 140, 156, 161n49
Ganjin, 239–240, 243, 256n16
Gasan Jōseki, 212, 278–279
Genshin, 110, 112, 211
Gesshū Sōkō, 184n24, 195, 196, 243
Giun, 171, 213, 267, 274
Gozan bungaku (Five Mountains literature), 14, 75, 83–84, 241, 252
Guanqi Zhixian, 55–57, 60, 72n34
Gyakusui Tōryū, 16–17, 199, 235–237, 239–254

Hakuin Ekaku, 24, 110, 138, 180
Heart Sutra, 124–125, 225–226
Hōkyōji, 171
home-leaver (Jp. *shukke*), 31, 63–64, 66–69

Hongzhi Chanshi Guanglu
    (*Extensive Record of Chan Master*
    Hongzhi), 31
Hongzhi Zhengjue (Jp. Wanshi
    Zenji), 31, 49–51, 74, 97–100,
    175–176
huatou. *See* Zen of contemplating
    sayings *under* Rinzai
Huike, 29, 43n7, 55, 57, 220–221
Huineng, 25, 29, 31–32, 173, 239, 242
Imamura Genshū, 210, 214–218,
    220–223, 230

Jingde Chuandenglu (*Jingde Record of the*
    Transmission of the Lamp), 55, 60,
    76, 172–173, 239
Jogye Order, 23–24
Juefan Huihong, 35–36

Kanna Zen (Ch. *Kanhua Chan*). *See* Zen
    of contemplating sayings *under*
    Rinzai
Keizan Jōkin
    and influence on robes, 236 fig. 9.2,
        253
    studies of, 7, 14, 24–26, 167–173,
        184n24
    veneration of, 260–261, 278, 282n4
    See also *Denkōroku*
Kenchōji, 4, 90–92, 271
Kenkon'in (Kenkōin), 169–171
Kenninji, 48, 51, 74, 218–220, 241, 249
kōan
    and capping phrases, 80, 98–100,
        102–104, 106n12
    and Mu Kōan, 97–102
    See also shikantaza *under* Dōgen
Kōjō
    and Zen precepts, 196–197, 199
Kokan Shiren, 199, 241
Komazawa University, 1, 8, 260, 261
    fig. 10.1

Kongguji (*Empty Valley Collection*), 176,
    184n25
kōshiki
    central text of the ceremony, 212
    history of, 211–214
    modern studies of, 214–216
    and musical tradition, 225–230
    Shinpen Hōon Kōshiki
        compared with the *Eihei Kaisan*
            Hōon Kōshiki, 214–222, 224 figs. 8.1
            and 8.2, 227 fig. 8.3, 229 fig. 8.4
Kōshōji, 52–53, 171, 264–265
Kōzen Gokokuron (*On Protecting the*
    Country by the Revival of Zen), 192
Kūkai, 110, 112–113, 119
Kyōto School, 13, 110, 138

Lefebvre, Henri
    spatial theories of, 262–264, 272,
        282n9
Linji Huizhao. *See* Rinzai
Linquan Conglun, 176
Literary Zen, 86–87, 173
Lotus Sutra
    quotations in the *Eihei Kaisan Hōon*
        Kōshiki, 218–221
    and the story of the dragon girl, 62,
        65–66, 69

Mahakasyapa
    in Buddhist literature, 179, 275–276
    and robe transmission, 238–239,
        245–246, 253–254
Manpukuji, 194–195
Manzan Dōhaku, 43, 195–197,
    200, 243
Mazu Daoyi, 40–41
Menzan Zuihō
    and influence on Sōtō Zen, 15, 43,
        198–200
    and koshiki, 213–215
    and robes, 239–240, 247

Miaoxin, 60–62

Moshan Liaoran, 55–56, 60, 72n34

Mount Hiei (Jp. Hiezan), 51–52, 74, 86, 148, 218

Mount Tiantong, 36, 74, 86, 266 fig. 10.2, 267–268, 272–276

Muan Xingdao, 195

Mujaku Dōchū, 268–269

Myōan Eisai, 15, 48, 192, 207, 241

Myōzen, 48, 132n30, 219

Nanyue Huairang, 29–32, 40, 43–44n8

nenbutsu, 9–10, 36, 222

Nichiren, 112

Nirvana Sutra, 56, 125, 135n43

Nishida Kitarō, 156–157, 161n58

Nishitani Keiji, 143

Ōbaku Zen, 15, 193–195, 241–243, 249

Ōuchi Seiran, 169, 214

Platform Sutra, 60, 154–155, 183, 199–200

Pure Land, 63, 110–112, 211

Rinzai
  compared with Sōtō organization and
    operation, 24–27, 193–194, 237
  and Zen of contemplating sayings,
    23–24, 34–35, 180

robes
  elephant trunk robe, 235–237, 236
    fig. 9.2
  gold brocade robes, 239–242,
    253–254
  perspectives on material culture of,
    237–242
  relevance of Vinaya to, 16–17,
    235–238, 236 fig. 9.1, 243–247
  transmission by Sakyamuni, 238–242

Rujing
  as teacher to Dōgen, 35–38, 219–220

Ryōnen, 51–54

Saichō, 192, 196–197

Seishōji, 79 fig. 3.1

Sekiun Yūsen, 197

Shimen Linjianlu (*Shimen's Record of the Monastic Groves*), 35–36

Shinran, 110–113, 222

Shōbōgenzō (*Treasury of the True Dharma-Eye*)
  fascicles of
    "Baika," 93
    "Bukkyō," 36–38
    "Busshō," 100–102, 135n43
    "Butsudō," 36, 142
    "Daigo," 34–35, 40–41
    "Gakudōyōjinshū," 98
    "Genjōkōan," 122–127, 132n25,
      147–153
    "Hachidainingaku," 221
    "Hakujushi," 102
    "Kankin," 32–33
    "Kattō," 55
    "Keisei sanshoku," 80–81, 95–97
    "Kenbutsu," 29
    "Kūge," 93
    "Mujō seppō," 97
    "Raihaitokuzui," 46–47, 50–57,
      65–66
    "Senjō," 31–32
    "Shinjin gakudō," 29
    "Shōhōjissō," 29
    "Shōji," 126–127
    "Shukke kudoku," 46–47, 63–64,
      66–69
    "Uji," 152
    "Zanmai ō zanmai," 37–38
    "Zenki," 127–128
  Jūnikanbon Shōbōgenzō
    and comparisons with Dōgen's
      earlier writings, 64–69
    studies of, 6–7, 34–36, 81–82
    translations of, 6, 54–55, 102, 126–127

See also *Bendōwa, Mana Shōbōgenzō,*
      and *Shōbōgenzō Zuimonki* under
      Dōgen's writings
shōmyō (Japanese Buddhist chant). *See*
      kōshiki
Shōtoku Taishi, 240
Silent illumination, 23–25, 49, 77–78
Sōjiji
   architectural body of, 264, 269–272,
      270 fig. 10.4
   figural body of, 272–273, 276–281
Sōtō Zen
   and Critical Buddhism, 8
   and lineage, 173–174, 206–207
   and Rinzai institutions compared
      (*See* Rinzai)
   and rituals, 196–197, 213–214, 223–230
   See also Zen precepts; robes
Su Shi
   as cited in "Keisei sanshoku" ("Sounds
      of Valleys, Colors of Mountains"),
      80–81, 95–97 (*See also* "Keisei
      sanshoku" under *Shōbōgenzō*)
Sudden awakening, 25

*Teiho Kenzeiki (Annotated Edition of
      Kenzeiki),* 16, 214–217
Tenkei Denson, 197
Tettsū Gikai, 265–268, 266 fig. 10.2,
      272–275, 283n16
Tōfukuji, 249, 264–265
*Tokudo Wakumon (Questions about
      Ordination),* 195, 198–199
Tokugon Yōson
   *Busso kesa kō (Thoughts on the Kesa of
      the Buddhas and Ancestors),* 239
Touzi Yiqing, 176
Tsūgen Jakurei, 171, 279

Wansong Xingxiu, 97–100, 108n40
*Wudeng Huiyuan (Combined Essentials of
      the Five Flames),* 172–173
Wumenguan (Gateless Barrier), 150
Wuzhun Shifan, 72n35, 241, 249
Xuedou Chongxian, 175–177

*Xutang Heshang Yulu (Discourse Record
      of Preceptor Xutang),* 31
Xutangji (Vacant Hall Collection), 176

Yangshan Huiji, 31, 60–62
Yinyuan Longqi, 194–195
Yogacara Buddhism, 143–144
Yōkōji, 171
Yokoseki Ryōin, 169
Yuanwu Keqin, 128, 175

zazen, 10, 24–28, 35–43
Zen
   and overview of women practitioners,
      10–11, 47–51, 62–63
   and philosophy of, 142–147
Zen precepts
   Chinese and Japanese background of,
      191–193
   at Eiheiji, 201–205
   meaning of, 188–191
   at North American Sōtō temples,
      206–207
   and Ōbaku school influence on,
      193–195
   Sōtō development of, 196–197
   in Tendai, 192–193, 196–197
   as used by Dōgen, 189–193
Zenkaiki, 199
Zhaozhou, 97–104
Zhenxie Qingliao, 25